'Follow Iain Sinclair into the cloud jungles of Peru and emerge questioning all that seemed so solid and immutable. *The Gold Machine* made me angry, sad, envious of Sinclair's beautiful, evocative prose and grateful that I did not have to endure a soroche headache to gain a new understanding of colonial attitudes and the damage we have done.'   **Barry Miles**

'Sinclair's discursive, intensely literate prose knits together time and place.'
Washington Post, Best Travel Books of 2021

'*The Gold Machine* tracks a feverish descent into the darkness of Peru's colonial past, as Sinclair follows in the footsteps of his nineteenth-century forbear. Written with his customary linguistic flair, this is a vivid and revealing addition to a unique body of work.'
Merlin Coverley, author of *Psychogeography*

'Excavator, outlier, alchemist. Sinclair's formidable gaze turns backwards, forwards and touchingly inwards. A father–daughter pilgrimage to the rapids and along the bloodline: panning for salt, coffee, gold, misdeeds, consequences, presence, absence, family…and self. Disarmingly tender, generous and brimming. A book of wonder (noun and verb), from first word to last I was agog.'   **Keggie Carew, author of *Dadland***

'Like Fitzcarraldo carrying a boat over mountains to fabulous worlds, Sinclair backpacks all the known legends, skeletons and lies, to tightrope a lurching dazzling bridge between generations. His, ours and those to come. Splendid in corruption. Wealthy in shock. This is the invaders' New Testament. Jamming gold coins in our eyes for lenses, leaving nothing to pay the boatman, because after this reads you, there is no place to go. A masterpiece.'   **B. Catling, author of *The Vorrh Trilogy***

'Sentence for sentence, there is no more interesting writer at work in English.'   **John Lanchester**

THE GOLD MACHINE

Tracking the Ancestors from Highlands to Coffee Colony

IAIN SINCLAIR

ONEWORLD

A Oneworld Book

First published by Oneworld Publications in 2021
This paperback edition published 2022

Copyright © Iain Sinclair 2021

The moral right of Iain Sinclair to be identified as the Author of this work has been asserted
by him in accordance with the Copyright, Designs and Patents Act 1988

ISBN 978-0-86154-373-1
eISBN 978-0-86154-071-6

Typeset by Tetragon, London
Printed and bound in Great Britain by Clays Ltd, Elcograf S.p.A.

Illustration Credits: Huitotos at Entre Rios with Barbados Overseer and
Guamares Indians of the Huitoto Tribe in Dance Costume taken from
The Putumayo, The Devil's Paradise: Travels in the Peruvian Amazon Region and
an Account of the Atrocities Committed upon the Indians by W. E. Hardenburg
(London, 1912). Shima-Shima with Plant, courtesy of Grant Gee.

Map of the 2019 route © Erica Milwain

All other illustrations © Iain Sinclair

Oneworld Publications
10 Bloomsbury Street
London WC1B 3SR
England

For Farne and Arthur Sinclair,
their dialogue

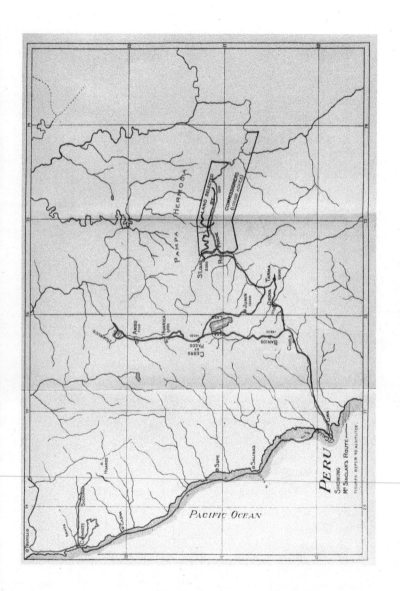

PERU

SHOWING

Mr SINCLAIR'S ROUTE

FIGURES REFER TO ALTITUDE.

PACIFIC OCEAN

CONTENTS

FURIES

PROXIMA CENTAURI

I am the Gold Machine and now I have trenched out, smeared, occupied...
   – Charles Olson, *The Maximus Poems*

After this road, what then? You've said it yourself, there'll be another one like this. What then, Peru?
   – Tim Binding, *Beneath the Trees of Eden*

He doesn't have any family, he's a writer.
   – Julio Cortázar, *Hopscotch*

GLINTS

BY THE BROWN RIVER

I woke early on a bed of broken slats in a house on stilts, across the beaten dirt from a fast-flowing river. Less a house, in truth, than a bamboo-walled cabin with a red tin roof on which rain drummed at the appointed season. Sunrise and sunset were also predictable: a bleary six a.m. glance at my watch and a six p.m. nod, when cicadas launched their irritated summons to cloud jungle vespers. Darkness dropped like a theatre curtain. The shack had been built to accommodate visitors the villagers really didn't want.

'These people are basically shy,' the anthropologist warned, 'and that can manifest as disdain. They are fearful of psychic contact. And proud to the point of arrogance.'

We come as thieves disguised with gifts.

3,162 miles from Hackney. 152 miles from London to the mining town where I grew up. 389 miles from there to Aberdeen, the city from which my grandfather travelled to South Wales. We know how far we have come, but we don't know why. Or how we can adapt to this place. Or who we are without familiar markers, the trees and stones and cracked windows that know us. That confirm our passage.

The long night, after the dogs had settled, was a wrestle under a snap-assembled mosquito net which made me feel like one of the black piglets we had seen in the animal market at Chupaca; wide eyes and pink snout pushing against the imprinting mesh of the sack, stoic before slaughter. Riverside insects were replete, otherwise engaged. In any case, I had a shirt impregnated with chemicals ninety-five per cent guaranteed to repel them. It was the five per cent, when I heard them fizzing against the television set, hung on the wall like an erased portrait of a forgotten ancestor, that kept me scrabbling to stay inside my claustrophobic coop. It would have been easier to sleep on the floor.

The bed had two widely separated functional slats and a couple of others in critical disrepair. After a brief interlude the uneasy visitor, hungry for the respite of dreams, would sink through the gap, as through the boards of a rotten swampland coffin.

Rising in the privilege of the still sensational and pulsing dark, it was more appealing to step out for a piss among the trees than to paddle across a slaughter of muddy footprints to waterless *en suite* facilities. The only detail that offended me was the suspended television set. Electricity was an invasive and potentially lethal extra, flaring, even when switched off, in arbitrary revelation like a cheap headpunch vision, then flickering in frosty static and fading away. The presence of that screen, dripping with unattached wires, was a blatant attempt to turn part of the settlement into an adventure tour Holiday Inn. Even dead screens whisper. The villagers see us as white ghosts, hollowed of meaning. And they are justified in that.

In earlier times, when a member of the extended family sickened and died, they held the house responsible, burnt it down and moved on. An empty house prepared for some wealthy alien, a faceless stranger who may never come, is a dangerous thing. The face reflected in the TV screen when you try to flatten your hair before the communal breakfast stays in the screen after you depart.

There are chopped, stripped trees left on the ground to act as benches, entitled chickens are pecking the dirt around them. I don't see any of the villagers about their business, but I know they are watching me. I amble out, not sure how to make a morning circuit of it, down the thin strip of beach. The sand is fine-grained, a mortuary grey. Fetched against a thick balsa pole, part of an uncompleted or washed-up raft, is a display of bright blue plastic bottles, silver cans, oranges, black bags, broken twigs and dead leaves. The hills on the other side are hidden in threads of fine white mist. I walk slowly as far downriver as the beach will take me, before the village submits to the jungle. Then I return, poking and sifting.

Later that morning, before we set off on our compulsory hike to the waterfall, a small delegation of elders approaches Lucho, our guide. They have witnessed my short tour with some alarm. And they have a question for the intermediary. 'Is the old man looking for gold?'

SOMETHING OUT OF SOMETHING ELSE

The jungle began in London, a set of unstable particulars less secure every time I set foot outside my door. I read so intensely around my project that reading became the project. I unscrolled duplicitous maps. Teasing fragments showed no sign of cohering. This Peruvian expedition had been an unspoken obligation most of my working life. It was now a necessity, perhaps an endgame. I spent hours arranging recovered family photographs against group portraits of killer bands of Ashaninka posed against the walls of the Coffee Colony with their antiquated weapons. Uncensored glares burnt a challenge through fading museum reproductions. Angela Carter, commenting on my fetish for postcard divination, called up 'the profane spirit of surrealism'. She knew that cards, laid out in a preordained grid, must tell a story. And that torrents of desperate words would have to be expended to complete it. 'At once they become scrutable', she wrote. 'They are images of imperialism.'

The warriors were right to be fearful, as I was, of this form of psychic contact. And capture. They were not defeated by military opportunism or the choking tentacles of capital. They were leeched of life force by cameras, by the self-serving reports of adventurers and priests, by the double game of Seventh-day Adventists promising treasure harvests on the day of final judgement. With the Victorian passion for books of adventure, summoning young men of spirit to the farthest reaches of Empire, came library shelves of coffee histories aimed at seducing neophyte planters. The map in my head, soon to be translated into real-world geography, was as much a fiction as one of those territorial advertisements drawn by some unscrupulous Franciscan missionary, hot for preferment, and escape from the barren back country of Andalucía. Priests of no family, dazed by the golden caves of the great cathedral and the satellite churches of Seville, ventured everything. They knelt, before shipping out, never to return, before glycerine madonnas touched by the Midas finger of a single transmuting ray of sunlight. The doodled map in my notebook, like the maps of those unholy fathers, was broken into bullet-point incidents: mules, mountains, rapids and rafts. And men with bows and spears.

My daughter Farne lent me a thick, ring-bound bundle of papers: *Campa Cosmology: The World of a Forest Tribe in South America* by the anthropologist Gerald Weiss. 'There is no such occurrence,' Weiss wrote, 'as a creation of something out of nothing, but only a transformation of something out of something else.'

In my cycle of haunted London dreams of a jungle village I might never reach, it was hard to separate the shaman with the drum, the *tampóro*, from the circling, swaying, rhythm-intoxicated dancers moving around the fire. Or emerging, so it seemed, right out of the flames. I couldn't see through the curtain of smoke. I was dreaming the same dream my father and grandfather had dreamed, after they died. The place where our founding ancestor waited with a sick king for balsa rafts to be constructed, so that he could take to the river.

They knew that song, the children, old men and even the monkey-trickster with the skin-tight skeleton suit. But when a very ancient, wrinkled, parchment-skinned grandmother introduced, softly, in a throat whisper, a new song, they picked it up at once. And they laughed when she plucked a dark leather pouch from the neck of her cushma and squeezed a drop or two of tobacco syrup onto to her lizardly tongue: before feigning instant intoxication, heart-seizure, and falling, poleaxed, to the ground. She was playing it and experiencing it with the same relish. And the other dancers tumbled with her, still laughing.

Scorched earth and ashes are raked into a black carpet, sliced and rolled like a freshly laid English lawn. And a rigid body, my own, eyes wide open, is laid in the yawning gash. The living ground, untouched by human hand, covers itself again, leaving no trace of the swallowed sacrifice. The swaying dancers, still drumming, melt away into the forest and the night.

That was my recurrent dream before I left Hackney. Resinous *quinilla* woodsmoke formed an active column, straight up through the windless night, before wrapping itself around the platform of the sentinel tower on which I had hidden, in order to witness the secret ceremony of my own internment. The necklaced shaman listened to the protests of the crackling wood as the flames licked and devoured.

7

'The Hollow Ones,' he pronounced, 'will be roasted like white-lipped peccaries and returned, as food for our fellow men, in the reaches of the jungle where paths fail.'

Hungry flames converted the report from the American Museum of Natural History into ash, which would, soon after dawn, be swept up, black-bagged and dumped in the river. William Faulkner talks about how ghosts always travel half a mile ahead of their own shape. My jungle dream was like that. An unreliable preview. Travel before travel. Understanding before experience. Experience before evidence. Random thefts from the library of the lost as prospectus for a journey outlined in some Book of the Dead.

The cosmology of the Campa, according to Weiss, and according to the blackened page I read in my dream, predicted and preordained my ancestor-stalking trip to Peru in the summer of 2019. A journey that would require the nudge of an impatient and better-informed daughter.

> Heartsick for his lost grandfather, Kíri decides to go downriver... A group of his relatives pursue him, intent upon killing him... They attempt to shoot him with their arrows, but only shoot each other... Kíri then advises the survivors to kill him by driving a spike down through his head and body into the ground.

I had another book, written by my Scottish great-grandfather, and published in 1895, as my source and inspiration. Arthur Sinclair travelled downriver on a balsa raft. In some way yet to be defined, I believed that Arthur was out there, in the territory, a hungry ghost unconcerned with 'closure'. Too many words, too many journeys on trains and planes, left me sick and used up. It felt as if the world I knew was about to go into quarantine. Shivering, sweating, sneezing, before this crisis arrived, I reached for the nearest Faulkner and treated myself to torrential language-clots from Yoknapatawpha County. But there was no escape from the suck of river sand and the jungle village. I had hardly begun *Absalom, Absalom!* when I found this sentence: 'And anyone could have looked once at his face and known that he would have chosen the river and even the certainty of the hemp rope, to undertaking what he undertook even if he had known that he would find gold buried and waiting for him in the very land which he had bought.'

The land my unquiet great-grandfather purchased through the act of describing it, and the months of his diminishing life he donated to this adventure with its tumultuous consequences, called me out. Before I could start where he finished, and write my way back to him, I would need to uncover some part of who and what he once was.

DIRTY SAND

Lucho Hurtado, a short powerful man of the mountains, moved swiftly and easily between worlds. He possessed all the implements required to confront potential difficulties of the trail. Patting the numerous pockets of his rough fisherman's waistcoat, he was reassured of his readiness to follow the Amazon from 'its farthest origins to the final encounter with the Atlantic Ocean'. He offered elite travellers the opportunity to 'meet locals from the cloud forest and low jungle, and to feel the way of living of the people in different ecosystems'. Lucho made Huancayo, a railway terminal, his base: a busy, dizzy, traffic-fretted, horn-blasting dust sprawl where altitude-sick travellers could earth their hammering migraines and find a tourist-appropriate hotel where they could set up an authentic round of pisco sours while the floor trembled beneath them. He would never knowingly undersell his pitch, but Lucho had solid investment in backpacker hostels and an upstairs restaurant specialising in pizza and scorched chicken variants.

After a few long days on the road, our eyes shut on blind bends and detours around landslips, Lucho brought us to his finca, which was titled from abbreviations of the names of all his children. A composite word that looked as if it had been constructed to represent something impossible in the Quechua language. The children now lived with their mother in another country on the far side of the Pacific. The small farm was somewhere to take stock, to dip in a green pool that might yet become a fish speculation, and to prepare for our descent, on foot, to the river.

The stories came, after dark, at the long table where we took our communal dinner. We had brought, against advice, a bottle of native Peruvian wine, and it did not disappoint. It was every bit as wretched, perfumed like cheap hair oil, as Lucho had warned. But there were assorted herbal beers on offer and, for the reckless among us, a mouth-numbing hit from the moonshiner's carboy with the metal tap. This festering trench water had a few inches of bloody scum on the surface. And it was just possible to see something as thick as my wrist floating, or *moving*, through it. A decapitated snake. The medicinal potion took months to ferment, dripping slowly now into china mugs, where faint pomegranate patterns had been brutally dissolved by the acid of previous infusions.

The kitchen was a gracious room with crossbeams like a native hut, but high-roofed in recycled corrugated materials and dressed with stained-glass windows rescued from failed investments, demolished hotels, bars, bordellos. The finca was a history of reconsidered projects, nothing wasted. A huge, nailpaint-loud red American fridge was free-standing in the middle of the floor, like a resprayed version of Kubrick's monolith from *2001: A Space Odyssey*. A pop art trophy scavenged from some Cola-supplied counter-insurgency base in El Salvador. The fridge was not connected and now served as a store cupboard for preserving important documents from the depredations of ants. It was surrounded by bunches of green bananas, freshly cut that morning by visitors trusted with lethal machetes. Sliced razor-thin and quickfried in deep fat, the plantains would provide a crunchy base for our fish dinner.

Lucho's village 'boy', reversed baseball cap and matching labial-pink T-shirt, took the ritual launch of the yarning session as his cue to climb on his motorbike and head home, to partner and first child. The young man had heard it all before, but Lucho was disappointed to lose him. He liked to see his drivers and field workers join us at the table.

The first of the session's tales concerned a tourist party he was about to lead over sections of the Inca Trail. Before they set out, a group of riverside Ashaninka, with whom he had previously dealings, came to Lucho's house in Huancayo, to demand a particular favour. They knew that, from time to time, he undertook diplomatic and railway business in Lima. Would he carry a sample they had procured, on their own land, for analysis? They were convinced that river sediment contained traces of gold.

He could not refuse, but Lucho was appalled. If the analysis was positive, he knew that speculators would move in. Sections of the forest would be felled, the ground chewed up, and the river clogged with spoil. But he had been entrusted with this burdensome task, it was an obligation if he wanted to sustain his mutually beneficial relationship with the Ashaninka.

The tourist troop were staying, before they headed off to the mountains, in a palm-fringed border town hotel, a place owned by the brother-in-law of the police captain and used for entertaining visiting dignitaries and minor tax officials. Trivial but annoying difficulties – rooms unprepared, detritus of all-night parties floating in the swimming pool – were sorted out by a few sharp words. Lucho's driver was on time and occupied giving his fly-suicide windscreen a wipe, while the walkers, Germans and South Africans with experience in the bush, loaded their kit. They were ready for any hazard and welcomed the thought of it. That is what they were paying for, dollars preferred.

But that scoop of native earth carrying the expectations of the tribe, the task laid on Lucho… *where was it?* Disaster. He had left the bottled sample at his bedside in the hotel. He was forced to abandon the excursionists. They were all competent, they could make camp, find water, start a fire, and wait for his return.

Lucho demanded the key to his old room. He turned the place over. Nothing. No trace. He stormed the desk: who was responsible for cleaning? Send the miscreant up at once.

A nervous boy appears, denies everything. Lucho opens his travelling bag and shows the empty slot where the sample should have been. He also shows, quite by accident, he affirms, a large Bowie knife with a serrated, bone-carving blade. The boy backs off, trembling. He runs from the room. And out of the hotel.

The police, associates of the hotel manager, arrive. Lucho's interrogation is lengthy and physically persistent. He is left in the cells to consider his fate. But the sample, the potential golden harvest, is never found. Eventually, papers sorted, he is released. And, looking on the bright side now, he does not have to bear the guilt of being, in some measure, responsible for the ruinous exploitation of the land.

THE SILENCE IN THE FOREST

My great-grandfather, guided – in his view – by a pair of duplicitous and drunken priests, was stumbling and slithering down the old Ashaninka salt route, now a future trade highway, towards an encounter with the indigenous chief who would give the command for the construction of balsa rafts to carry the invaders along the Rio Perené to impassable and unmapped rapids. The commissioned surveyors, former planters from Ceylon, were done, ready to lie down where they stood, cocked weapons resting across their laps. As is so often the way of these things, they had, at their lowest ebb, stumbled on a great secret. It was hidden in plain sight a short distance from the settlements of Metraro and Mariscal Cáceres, linked villages that would, in a few years, come to be dominated by Seventh-day Adventists, offering schools, chapels and medical centres. Charitable developments covertly sanctioned by the Peruvian Corporation of London, the insatiable predators who would establish the great coffee estates on which these villagers were obliged to labour. Giving up their old gods for golden promises.

> *But the road was a villainous rut at a gradient of about one in three, a width of about eighteen inches, and knee deep in something like liquid glue*, Arthur Sinclair wrote in his published account of the 1891 expedition. *Before we had gone five miles one-half the cavalcade had come to grief, and it was some weeks ere we saw our pack mules again; indeed, I believe some of them lie there still. We soon found out that the* padres *knew as little about the path as we did ourselves, and the upshot was we were benighted. Shortly after six o'clock we were overtaken in inky darkness, yet we plodded on, bespattered with mud, tired, bitten, and blistered by various insects. Whole boxes of matches were burned in enabling us to scramble over logs or avoid the deepest swamps. At last*

> *there was a slight opening in the forest, and the ruins of an old thatched shed were discovered, with one end of a broken beam still resting upon an upright post, sufficient to shelter us from the heavy dews. It turned out to be the tomb of some old Inca chief whose bones have lain there for over 350 years, and there, on the damp earth, we lay down beside them, just as we were. Our dinner consisted of a few sardines, which we ate, I shall not say greedily, for I felt tired and sulky, keeping a suspicious eye upon the Jesuit priests.*

The trail guides, Franciscan not Jesuit, were *not* deceiving this trio of white adventurers, hiding behind beards, dispatched by the Peruvian Corporation with a contract to survey and affirm. Sinclair's party was being processed down an ancient and haunted desire line, from the Mountain of Salt to the living, surging, serpentine river, by way of the burial place of a godlike warrior, a splinter of origin: an emanation of Father Sun. The missionary priests were initiating these pale outsiders, nudging them forward with hints and selective misinformation, through the maze of psychic energies intricately woven to protect this place and to keep it free from the curse of visionary capitalism. 1891 was a fateful year, with three major expeditions – military, engineering and commercial – hellbent on pioneering routes for exploitation of this savage and enduringly lovely Eden. The wilderness garden from which the unrighteous had been expelled. And forever excluded.

The salty residue of the sardine feast was a feeble sacrament to offer to the sodden ground on which they struggled to sleep.

> *We were told, by the way, that the bones we were handling were the bones of Atahualpa, so treacherously murdered by Pizarro.*

A fantastic fable the priests concoct to entrap the credulous colonists with their moleskin journals and Kodak cameras. But in lisping such lies and alternative histories, the unholy fathers were also demonstrating respect for tactics employed by Indians under interrogation: agree reluctantly, after sharing food and exchanging gifts, to tell strangers whatever they want to know. Then contradict yourself, offer multiple versions. And deny all knowledge of the original conversation when you meet on another day.

Atahualpa, the 'last Inca Emperor', was strangled with the infamous garrotte on 26 July 1533, before his clothes, and the strips torn from his skin, were burned. A merciful amendment to the original verdict: barbecuing at the stake. This sinister ritual was enacted many miles from Metraro. It was said that the Inca offered to fill a large room with gold, in order to ransom his life. After the mock trial, more of a preordained ceremony than a considered evaluation of guilt and innocence, an attendant friar, Vincente de Valverde, pressed his breviary into the affronted hands of the condemned man. Atahualpa was then baptised into the Catholic faith and marked with the name *Francisco* – in honour of his conqueror, the Spanish illiterate suckled by sows, the butcher of worlds: Francisco Pizarro.

Gold, more spirit than substance, was pure intoxication. So fill the wooden holds of creaking cargo fleets. Stack the mass of bloody plunder in the expectant watchtowers of Seville. Cast another heretic saint for another gilded cathedral. Bless the armies of the damned.

Túpac Amaru, hereditary Inca rebel, was beheaded in Cuzco's Plaza de Armas, forty years after the death of Atahualpa. A persistent Andean myth claimed that the buried head would soon reconstitute itself, grow another body and initiate a golden age, a second and more powerful Inca empire.

Arthur Sinclair, a Scot who was not so easily deceived, soon discovered that the place where he had slept was dedicated to a different Atahualpa, the charismatic Juan Santos, a highlander who adopted the title of the last Inca emperor when he led a very effective revolt against the Spaniards in the 1740s.

I arrived in Mariscal Cáceres with my daughter Farne and the filmmaker Grant Gee on 9 July 2019. We were determined, if it were at all possible, to persuade one of the villagers to guide us to the burial place of Juan Santos Atahualpa. The point of connection with my great-grandfather's published narrative.

The Ashaninka we had already interviewed offered so many contradictory versions of the same tale: the shrine or hole or cavern belonged with the legends of childhood. A song of the grandmothers. With truths it was forbidden to reveal. With the land. *Their* land. Juan Santos Atahualpa had emerged from some obscure generative source like a black nuclear sun; a light so brilliant that eyes hidden behind shielding hands could peel away the skin gloves protecting the brittle bones of their fingers. The great chief, the undead and unsleeping commander, was said by some to be a spectre of whiteness: Juan Santos had travelled in foreign lands far across the ocean. And walked home across the obedient waves. Before he was betrayed, buried, divided, dispersed – and resurrected as a whispered myth, the gift-delivering, sun-crowned albino Messiah of the Adventists.

We were bouncing and shuddering up the mountain road that had evolved from the original 1891 incursions of military engineers. My great-grandfather was not impressed.

> *I have in other countries travelled in tracks traced and made by elephants, and had reason to admire their gradients and marvel at the topographical knowledge displayed, but anything so perfectly idiotic as this atrocious trail I had never before been doomed to follow so far. It was a relief to leave it and cut our own way through the jungle.*

A few miles out of Santa Ana, where rainy season landslides had turned the river to a ditch of red, mud-coloured rocks, we had to cede a little of our headlong velocity to avoid jolting over a ragged man sleeping in the middle of the road like a performance art traffic-calming device. He was known. He would stagger to his feet in a few hours and make his unsteady way back to the nearest hamlet, where he would find a little food and drink, enough to sustain him for another day. He was part of the intricate clockwork of the territory.

The road had as many twists and eddies as the river. As soon as we started to climb, the cruel gradient committed itself to preparing us for Mariscal Cáceres. Tumbledown shacks made from scavenged planks owed their survival to the capitalised electoral slogans painted on their sides: (EL NEGRO) VENEGAS, EXPERIENCA y CAPACIDAD. There were graphic illustrations, like Jim Dine or Roy Lichtenstein, of a thick yellow pencil against a red background. The suggestion is: please make your mark on the ballot paper. Put your X right here. Get the representation you deserve. There is a wider world beyond the road, beyond the river. Beyond the coffee plantations.

Around a hairpin bend, beyond the point where an old woman had a stall serving some locally fermented drink, was a big blue sign with a schematic picture of a stooped pedestrian, propped up by a pilgrim's staff. He appeared to be skipping across a torrent. CAVERNA JUAN SANTOS ATAHUALPA 11.6 km. And another skeletal silhouette of a man at the mouth of a cave: CAVERNA METRARO 9.9 km. The implication being that the cave of Juan Santos Atahualpa is 1.7 km beyond the village we are approaching. But when we return, at the end of the day, the blue sign has vanished.

The old lady we left behind in the smoky twilight of the village settlement beside the Rio Perené told us, as we blinked and rubbed our eyes, that the cave – she had never been there – was once filled with weapons used in the rising against the colonists. In time, the Spaniards found and stole them. Now, dusty-mouthed and shaken, when we arrive at Mariscal Cáceres, Bertha, our former interviewee, is there ahead of us, helping to prepare the fish. She says that the body of Juan Santos was laid to rest in the cave on a bed of gold. Gold recovered from the Spaniards. And gold, when it is heaped up, multiplies. Breeds of its own volition. Juan Santos guarded it. The cave and the legend.

One of the village elders said that the shrine was just a few hundred yards from where we were sitting and talking. It would take us ten minutes to walk there. No more. When we had shared food.

After the meal, several hours in the preparation, was done and the exchanges made, the chief came to see us, a tame green parrot perched on his finger. The parrot whispered something in his patron's ear. The chief said that he would lead us to the cave. But it was surely too far to walk before light failed, so we would have to ride in our car and follow our guides on their motorbike.

The official biker was a slight, stringy man, with a cultivated bandit beard. And a baseball cap with a green leaf and an italicised slogan: *dope*. It was too easy to typecast this Netflix character as a trafficker, a coca mule who knew the best paths between the Salt Mountain and the Gran Pajonál. But the village chief, sitting behind the biker, was in charge. Neither man wore a helmet. They took us for a mazy hallucinogenic ride, twenty minutes, forty minutes, past plantations of blackened bananas, over treacle tracks fast reverting to streams. Without warning, they stopped. And beckoned us to follow.

The man in the *dope* cap used his machete to cut a bamboo walking pole for Farne. The path through the jungle was steep. We imagined the sound of a distant torrent. The chief, in his flip-flops, was moving fast. We gripped the insecure curtain of vines under the dripping rock. The cliff crumbled as we rubbed against it, trying to stay on the provisional track. When our guide was gone, we hooked ourselves to saplings, right where we were; catching our breath, but scarcely breathing, as the biker explained how the chief needed to confirm that the path to the cave of Juan Santos Atahualpa was clear and navigable. 'It's not so very far, twenty minutes more.'

Thickening sugars of excitement, not fear, are absorbed into the green luxuriance of the enveloping trees. Sap informs our sweat. Our feet itch to form roots and drink from the reddish soil. If we can no longer hear the sound of the chief pushing the branches aside, there is no reason to expect his return. This is a commonplace of the novice in the jungle. 'It is not the presence of unfriendly natives that wears one down,' Michael Taussig wrote in *Shamanism, Colonialism, and the Wild Man (A Study in Terror and Healing)*. 'It is the presence of their absence, their presence in their absence.' Place, when breath is swallowed and held, forgives the distinction between myth and documented witness. 'People buried in an underground of time in the lowland jungles are endowed with magical force to flower into the present,' Taussig claimed.

All forward momentum, towards the cave and the teasing prospect of gold, is stalled. Warm saturated air flows through us. We steady ourselves against the curtain of slippery vegetation. Martin MacInnes, in *Infinite Ground*, a novel of disappearance and diminishing volition, catches the peculiar and disabling inertia that comes with being in the right place but the wrong story. 'For the moment he didn't seem specifically located, just general in the sounds of the birds calling, water dropping, twigs breaking and the branches falling.'

It was a process of folding into the baffle of the silence. We were made aware – father, daughter, great-grandfather, on our quite distinct journeys – of a shared identity. And of the mute presence of the biker, the man in the *dope* cap, our trickster familiar. And his special relationship with the low jungle and the path; how he was permitted to pass through, only so long as he stayed on sanctioned routes, stayed within his agreed role. But now he was separated from the chief, the man who had bounded so swiftly beyond sight and sound. There was only the smothering foliage and a projected sympathy between trees, birds, stones, streams and intruders. The leathery fronds of the giant ferns were slatted blinds filtering a seductive distillation of sunlight – before, on the stroke of six o'clock, it withdraws completely. We were no longer waiting for anything or anybody. There was no conversation.

'He was the deep sounds in the forest that had no explanation, the shadow at the edge of one's vision,' Joe Jackson wrote in *The Thief at the End of the World*. He is describing the fever dream of a renegade English plant-hunter and rubber pirate, Henry Wickham. Broken in health, attended by vultures perched on the end of his cot, the planter waited patiently for the end. He was nursed by neighbours who knew that he was doomed because he whispered that he had seen the *curupira*, 'the little pale man of the forest'. An acknowledged harbinger of doom. 'The souls of those who died at the hands of the *curupira* wandered forever in the forest. Survivors left part of themselves beneath the canopy and were never the same.'

What had my great-grandfather, processed by two drunken priests down this same track, left behind? What would we leave, beyond some lame attempt to describe the magic of the forest suspension in which we found ourselves? Time is annulled. I thought, in an involuntary fugue of remembering, of trying to report, with accuracy, a golden November morning in Victoria Park. In London. The home that is fading so fast. A rising sun was dissolving the mist over the lake and working a natural miracle too ordinary to record. That place and this place, the *then* and the *now*. My identity lost somewhere between the two. The profligate autumn harvest of London plane, lime, copper beech, cherry and chestnut.

There was a man on the long avenue of the people's park, gripping a pilgrim's stave in his right hand, elegant in a long black coat, like a jaded but inappropriately predatory architect in a French film. He was walking steadily backwards. As if to confound his own mortality and win back a few precious hours. I watched his confident progress. What would happen, I wondered, when he reached the railings? He swerved slightly, made an adjustment, and passed on, before dropping out of sight. He could have been a world-tramping sadhu. Or a regular Hackney dude proud in his calculated eccentricity. The famous backwards walker. As posted on all good social networks dedicated to trivia.

Random memories do not help, even those yet to be programmed. We might never move again. The chief will not return and our biker guide is not permitted to lead us out of the jungle without him. We cannot invent the sound of the waterfall. Or the oracular echoes of the secret cave. There will be few better moments in our lives. A breath held stays held. Slowly, we give ourselves up to a pre-linguistic *where*. And to the stately dance of articulate shadows. 'The evidence of his family line and all its members,' Martin MacInnes wrote, 'stained in the leaves.' The leaves were the watchers.

The way had not been hard enough yet to offer revelation. Arthur Sinclair, out of his knowledge, on the cusp of fever and hallucination, fated to bring back a favourable report, did come out of the rainforest, after that terrible sleepless night. He rested his head on a pillow of bones, animal and human. He was released from the strangulating confusion of the blasphemous jungle. Into the visions my daughter had chosen to challenge.

> *I shall never forget that calm, bright Sunday afternoon when we looked out for the first time on the great interminable forest of the upper valleys of the Amazon. Right in front of us as we stood with our faces to the east were evergreen hills of various altitudes, all richly clad, and undulating down towards the great plains of Brazil. We were standing at a height of 4,600 feet, but, even in that clear atmosphere, could see but a comparatively short distance; still it showed better than any words can convey the extent and richness of this vast reserve, and the absurdity of the cry that the world is getting over-crowded. Why, we have only as yet been nibbling at the out-side borders, and are now trying to peep over the walls of the great garden itself…*
>
> *The faint buzzing of bees, the subdued chirping of finely feathered birds, the flutter of brilliant butterflies, are the only commotion in the air, itself the perfection of summer temperature. What a glorious spot in which to form a quiet, comfortable home! Imagine this all the year round, every month seedtime and every month harvest. What crops of vegetables and fruit might not be produced in such a climate and such a soil! Had poor old Malthus only been permitted to look upon a country like this, so rich, and yet so tenantless, his pessimistic fears of the population outgrowing the means of sustenance would have quickly vanished.*

What rapacious innocence! How persuasive the completed Sinclair report lying on the desk of the investors in Leadenhall Street in the City of London. Already the golden expectations of the forest are turning green. Blood berries, soon to be harvested by indentured Ashaninka slaves, are ripening on the high ground where the boundary fences of the Coffee Colony will be set. Overseers must be hired. And armed. Barracks with barred windows will be constructed around the enclosed patios on which the abundant coffee harvest will be raked and left to dry. And books of unreliable memory will be published only to bring forth other books.

FRETS

THE MAP ON THE DOWNSTAIRS WALL

'The past is everything. The future flows into the past, and cultivates the past, and renews the topsoil – if that's possible.'
 – Ed Dorn

It took about four and a half months to sail from Tilbury to Colombo. A drowsy and libidinous interlude for military passengers and excited emigrants, while officers, sailors, underpaid 'lascars' and harassed cooks stood watch and worked. The remission of the epic voyage became a shared dream; time for aspirant colonists to shuck off the husk of old failures and to invent new and improved biographies. On deck, at the stern rail, in the cool of the night, the travellers were dazzled by star fields they had never before admitted. Men talked over their cigars, exchanging stories, former lives mutating into new fictions. Think of Joseph Conrad's five merchant-marine voyages to Australia. As first mate on the *Torrens*, he became acquainted with John Galsworthy and E.L. Sanderson, who had been searching the South Pacific, unsuccessfully, for traces of Robert Louis Stevenson. The failure of that quest redeemed by Conrad's mesmerising conversation, the angular tilt of his chin, the maritime anecdotes.

Assigned brides, traded by exchange of business correspondence to Ceylon planters, men they scarcely knew, often from the same country, even town or village – Aberdeen, Turriff – had too many nights in which to reconsider their awful fate. Trousseau laid out between tissue sheets, protected by canvas, and scented with lavender. Dried rose petals, virgin undergarments. Silver-backed hand mirrors, ivory combs, wrapped soap, pills, potions, scents. Painstakingly copied or newly composed poems. The brides did not complete the voyage. They came ashore in the furnace of Aden, and returned home with some fresh young officer who would, after a few fretful months, be back on the sea.

Arthur Sinclair, shipping out in 1858, at the age of twenty-six, had the leisure, for the first time in his life, to write. To learn how to process events he had experienced or witnessed into prose, brisk and serviceable enough to intrigue the editors of newspapers in Aberdeen and Colombo; good men with whom he would build lifelong relationships. The favoured form was the anecdotal letter. Acceptable copy ran all the way from shipboard humour to a posthumously crafted obituary for which his long and busy life was a rehearsal. Every decade or so, my great-grandfather's letters were collected and edited as fugitive chapbooks. But in so many tight-packed double columns, so many laboriously forged sentences, running into sprawling paragraphs, Arthur said nothing whatsoever about his family, his wife and six children. Where did he meet her? And how did she respond to a career of strategic migration?

And how should I respond to the gallery of photographs hanging on the wall of a downstairs lavatory in Hackney? These strangers, the oldest of them younger than I am now, and the youngest of the boys a grandfather who died before I knew him, stare out, unmoving, trapped by the tricks of a paid professional. From time to time, while washing my hands, I take a shamed glance at these accusing ghosts. Who are they? What do they want with us?

Arthur Sinclair and his unadmitted partner, the former Miss Margaret MacGregor, shepherd their proud brood: the three sons, another Arthur, Norman, Henry (my grandfather), and the three daughters, Maggie, Catherine, Gertie. The group portrait is credited to E. Geering of Aberdeen. Geering's premises were established at 416 Union Street in 1893. Which would mean that the sturdy, confidently smiling paterfamilias had recently returned, not so much the worse for wear, from a year adventuring in Peru.

Margaret sits, hands clasped, at the centre of the composition, the still point. She has withdrawn into herself, away from the tedium of the occasion, barely acknowledging the dutiful progeny that surround her. The oldest daughter, in a white-collared version of her mother's dress, already the unmarried carer, rests a protective hand on young Norman's shoulder. Her slightly younger sister presses against the fabric of her father's dark all-weathers suit.

E. Geering,   *Aberdeen,*

Out of the tidewrack of family mementoes, postcards, books, objects, clothes, furniture, these are the images that have passed through the generations from the last years of the nineteenth century. From all the unrecorded deaths and entrances, rootless Sinclairs now share a Hackney wall with strangers, with my wife's paternal forebears on the edge of the Fens, the English flatlands. The dead ones grow younger as we age. Sometimes Anna dreams that her farming mob, loud and argumentative, are gathered in her childhood Lancashire home, questioning our summons. And waiting for us to join them in the long silence.

It is not much to go on: the two great-grandfathers, Sinclair and Grassick (father of my grandmother), in separate studio mid-shots, now hanging, survivors of our own domestic clearances, side by side.

And credited to two competing Aberdeen photographers: E. Geering and Alexander Wilkie. There is a traveller's tangled salt-and-pepper beard for Arthur. And something more considered, the opportunistic proprietor of a Californian Gold Rush hotel, full moustache and bar-bered bristle-streak depending to a dinky spade chin, for Mr Grassick. We know nothing about this man, beyond the pictorial evidence of a raised collar and a thickly knotted, plant-bespattered tie. Some vestige of a riverboat gambler's confidence and style.

Moving along the rogues' gallery of our chosen ancestors, we come to Arthur Sinclair's intimate family group: the patriarch with the same undeceived expression he displays in his individual portrait. And then: the same family, the children much younger now, with rocking-horse, attendant maids in starched aprons, babes, and an expanse of coarse grass around a large, plain house revealed in a postcard as 'Banff Castle, Banff'. The card has been sent to Miss Gertie Sinclair of The Elms, Manor Place, Cults.

'Sorry couldn't obtain p.c. of Eden House. Had a lovely holiday.'

My impression is that there was a social fall, a retrenching in more modest circumstances. Arthur had returned, a made man from Ceylon, to settle in Scotland. Padded by colonial investments. In the Banff photograph he sprawls, boots on a stool, reading a newspaper. And then it all went badly wrong. The insects took their revenge.

The final photograph, of an Edwardian couple, is a rather grave and dignified wedding portrait from Aberdeen in 1904. This one is just out of reach: my father's father and mother. I never knew either of them, they died prematurely of their various cancers. I associate these invasive and terminal conditions, on no evidence whatsoever, with the translation from Aberdeen to industrial South Wales. You come out of your established territory, occupied and worked for centuries, at a cost. There is a period of necessary adjustment before descendants, benefiting from your sacrifices, can thrive.

My grandfather Henry Sinclair, 'a medical practitioner in Glamorganshire', as the obituaries have it, inhabited the house where I grew up, and where he lived on, through inherited overcoats and images like postcards sent from beyond the grave. I handled the cold weight of the revolver he acquired at the time of the General Strike in 1926, but I did not fire it. This pocket weapon was a Webley .450, known as the 'British Bull Dog' model. It was kept, wrapped in linen, in a cigar box at my father's bedside. The design originated in 1867 and was adopted by the Irish Constabulary a year later. An ivory-handled pair were said to have been carried by George Armstrong Custer at the Battle of Little Big Horn. 'British Bull Dog' revolvers were issued to all employees of the Southern Pacific Railroad Company. My grandfather made the round of his patients, many of whom, out of work or too poor to pay, were treated for nothing, by motorbike. He would not be stopped by roving bands of strikers, with their justified grievances. He was by temperament a conservative. My grandmother, on the other hand, was a committed Liberal. There is an excited account in the local paper of a visit to the town by Herbert Gladstone, son of William (Grand Old Man of the Party). Every word of his speech, every cheer, every aside, is reported. Herbert comes, in delirious procession, to the doctor's house.

> 'At Bridgend the station was crowded with spectators, while at Tondu the residents turned out in thousands in order to catch a glimpse at the son of the Grand Old Man as he passed through. At Maesteg, however, a reception of the most triumphant character awaited him.'

The contrasting shades of political opinion of the ancestors gathered in our crop of photographs never came between them. Marriages did not turn on debate over public events. Such things were unmentionable, or they simmered quietly, mild aphrodisiacs of theoretical difference.

I registered my never-known Scottish grandfather, the one who made the move to Wales as a young medical assistant, fresh from the University of Aberdeen, only through whatever residual traces could be absorbed by running my fingers over the thin skin of photographs. Frozen moments survive to carry the burden of biography. Henry Sinclair, a young man, seated in the front row of his cricket team. Then the mature householder, neat moustache, three-piece suit, watch chain, wedding ring and pipe. He leans against the grain of pebbledash, the fogged border of net curtains: the house where I grew up, the back of it, spaces I explored. This stranger was the printed spectre of wherever I came from, caught and fixed; my grandfather's left hand, with the wedding ring, resting on the rough concrete of the windowsill. And his other hand, so gently shaped, was a perch for a large green Amazonian parrot, his special favourite. His jungle familiar. On one of my scavenging expeditions I found the big cage on a stack of coal in the garage and put it, right away, into my first film. I liked everything about that parrot portrait. I saved a place for it, as an illustration, in my early book of poems, *Muscat's Würm*.

For the last sighting – and by that time, wartime, I was in or almost in the human world – the retired doctor is an old man in a summer garden, too thin for his tailored grey suit and grey homburg. But he is moving, so he's alive, and repeating his actions every time the sprocket-driven procession of still frames is jagged through the projector. A

16mm home movie recorded on a camera retrieved from a captured U-boat. My grandfather is under sentence and at his ease, taking tea in the sunshine, attended by his daughter-in-law, my Welsh mother. His eyes are weak now and he looks uncannily like the exiled James Joyce, recuperating from another operation. He holds up a slice of seed cake and his obliging Scotch terrier jumps. And jumps. And jumps again. I refilmed the sequence, from the screen, on 8mm, to become part of a six-year 'Diary' of community life in Hackney. The image is degrading. The cake is held out. The dog jumps and falls. And jumps again. Thin bones from an enveloping sleeve, clawed grip.

But it's my grandmother's face in the wedding photograph that entices me. An expression which is not quite melancholy, but which engages so directly with the photographer. No artifice, no special plead-ing. Here is a face in which I can, if I reach for it, find some trace element of myself. The young doctor, curled moustache, high collar, wrists lost in celluloid cuffs, gazes off to the side, under control but primed for the first rustle behind the curtains, coming catastrophe. Dark weather for dark times. The woman's dress falls to the floor in icy layers of satin and lace. It is perfected, this confrontation, and it will never happen again. She does not have the long-nosed hatchet look of the other highland women. The print of Scottish storms carried away to distant lands and, sometimes, back again.

Alongside the family portraits on the lavatory wall was Arthur Sinclair's map, drawn by hand during the course of the voyage of the *Albemarle*: 'London to Ceylon, 1858'. The ink is brown like insect blood, the paper is curling and tanned. They came through the Bay of Biscay in February and around the Cape of Good Hope in May. A dotted line of progress, logged each night, reminds me of the real route sailed by the fated Donald Crowhurst. His meandering South Atlantic suicide shadowed by phantom reports of nautical miles never actually achieved. The *Albemarle* comes close to brushing against a mammary protuberance acknowledged as 'South America'. The vessel gives St Helena a wide berth in April and puts in at Tristan da Cunha. 'Total distance: 14000 miles.' On Arthur's map, Australia has somehow drifted far to the north.

And a vestigial Indian subcontinent is capped by 'Hindostan'. In Britain there are only two notable settlements: London and Banff.

When, on our return from Peru, I met a pair of previously unknown Australian cousins, I was presented with another beguiling cache of postcards and photographs. And I was touched to discover, among the ephemera, a railway ticket, 3rd Class, from Aberdeen to London (St Pancras), via Tay & Forth Bridges, Settle & Bedford. A miraculously preserved record of that momentous journey? Tilbury and out. The ocean of the world in which to drown the past.

What was left after all those archival interrogations, and what stayed with me for every mile of my attempt to track Arthur's route over the Andes and down into the cloud forest, was the enigma of that unyielding smile. The creases of amusement framing an alert and penetrating gaze. The interplay between conflicted instincts: the engaged and informed observations of the professional plantsman and the cynicism of a travel writer twisting the world to conform to his portrait of it.

With a legible hand and a swift stroke of underlining emphasis, my great-grandfather has autographed his engraved portrait. He insists on taking responsibility for a biographical version somebody else has authored. Credit must be disputed with the ever-obliging E. Geering of Aberdeen. Arthur Sinclair, recorded, is subject and object.

VISITING AGENT

'Travel is a good thing. It stimulates the imagination. Everything else is a snare and a delusion. Our own journey is entirely imaginative. Therein lies its strength.'

– L-F. Céline, *Journey to the End of the Night*

When Arthur Sinclair, who was almost certainly unaware that he shared a Christian name with the renegade poet Rimbaud, and whose writing was a sidebar to his travelling and not the imperative that propelled flight from home, came to publish, five years before his death, *The Story of His Life and Times as Told by Himself*, he got the whole matter done in thirty-four brisk pages. He recycled, as so many authors do in the diminishing light of a fading career, strategic selections from previously issued material. He cannibalised back numbers of the *Tropical Agriculturalist*. The way he promoted himself, in bold caps on the cover, was as **PLANTER AND VISITING AGENT**. A sanctioned spook, or double man, fingers in the soil.

> *In a snug, little farm-house at King Edward, Aberdeenshire, I was born one dreigh day in December, 1832.* The autobiographical sketch opens in orthodox fashion. *My earliest recollection is a ploughing match, or 'love darg', by the neighbours on the occasion of my father retiring to Turriff, an adjacent township.*

My great-grandfather was sent to school at the age of five, where he learned to knit: 'a technical education which has not as yet proved eminently useful to me'. He matriculated in carrying peat to the classroom and committing approved biblical texts to memory.

> *In my tenth year my school education virtually ended, untoward circum-*
> *stances followed… my father removing again to a bleak country district,*
> *where the school and schoolmaster belonged to a type so poor and primitive*
> *as to be quite a revelation in the village-bred boy… My parents were*
> *descended from an old Jacobite stock, at this time still rather at a discount…*
> *And here I may say ended my schooling and began my education such as*
> *it was and is.*

Arthur's father took work where he could find it as a jobbing thatcher. Whatever the family's 'untoward circumstances' in an era of agricultural 'improvements', rent increases and clearances, Arthur did not choose to expose them. Or to allow his father, mother and unnamed siblings any significant space in the late-life confession. These things happened, in a certain order, but it was always about finding land of his own, a home place with a garden, a favoured setting to be recollected in confident prose, but not actually occupied for any length of time: movement was the highest truth. The only country where Arthur could retire in 1900, when his chapbook was published, was the past.

'For sale,' wrote Rimbaud in *Illuminations*, 'homelands and migrations… perfect comfort, perfect enchantments, and the noise, the movement, the future in which they conspire.'

Internal Scottish migration, brought about by crop failure and fungal blight, was commonplace. Rhythms between subsistence and shortage defined the seasons. But, as T.M. Devine reveals in *The Scottish Clearances (A History of the Dispossessed, 1600–1900)*, tenant farmers, labourers and cottars were more fortunate in Banff, Kincardine and Aberdeen than their fellows in the Lothians and Berwickshire. There was better land and a 'more balanced agrarian situation'. The alluvial soil of the estuaries and the 'carse' lands furnished the most extensive areas of continuous arable in the whole of Scotland. There was abundant corn and pasturage.

> *I was not lazy; indeed, my little garden was already looked upon as an oasis*
> *in a wilderness of moorland farms, and a neighbouring farmer seeing my*
> *industry, gave me off a corner of a field measuring perhaps quarter of an*

> *acre, which I tackled with as much diligence as any Chinaman, getting up at 4 a.m. and working till late at night.*
>
> *The year was 1846, the summer one of the loveliest of the century. A little burn rippled past the grounds in which by way of relaxation I bathed, caught trout and culled the Nymphaea from its margin; but my special pride was a plot of potatoes: the grand old blue kidney, nowhere now to be seen. No coffee planter ever saw with greater interest his first 100-acre clearing burst into blossom.*
>
> *Early one July morning I got up to watch the flowers expanding, when I observed what seemed drops of soot upon the tender green leaves. It looked like the work of some malicious miscreant, but no footprints were there, and I felt fairly puzzled. Next morning there were still more 'soot drops', and everyday during the week added to the mystery, till at length the haulins began to blacken, and a sickening smell greeted me as I approached my precious plot. I was only 14 years of age, but I shall never forget my first great discouragement as a planter; and when a quarter of a century afterwards I saw coffee attacked with a similar blight, I could not help remembering my early sorrow and fearing how little science could do for us.*

The potato blight was not as devastating in Scotland as in Ireland, but the loss of a subsistence crop, by the early nineteenth century a major part of a native diet shifting from grains and gruel, hit hardest in Argyll and the Western Isles. There was a push towards emigration, especially (for agriculturalists) towards Canada, with the United States favoured by mechanics and big city dwellers. Banff and Aberdeenshire suffered less. Arthur's early exposure to the magic of the noble potato, those sweetly edible earth eggs, led to a lifelong affinity. But his innocent first love had mildew on her cheeks.

Having crossed the Andes in a mule train, scrambling breathlessly to 17,000 feet above sea level, there was an identity-revising, life-affirming vision of the new world.

> *A region unlike anything we have ever before seen... The clear sky above, the occasional clouds chasing each other up from the valley of the Amazon, only to be dissipated on the snowy peaks which they cannot possibly pass,*

above all the glorious sun, so welcome a benefactor here, that we can no longer marvel that it was the great object of worship by the Inca… Excellent wheat and barley are grown… This is also the home of the potato, it having been cultivated here as carefully as it now is in Europe, perhaps hundreds of years before America was discovered by Europeans. 'Papa' they are still called, being the old Inca name of the tuber; and the quality is fully equal to the best we have produced here; moreover, they have some varieties better than any of ours, one of which I hope to introduce to Scotland.

From this moment in the Peruvian journey that defined his life, and in many ways the journey for which he had always been preparing himself, Arthur began to intuit, without fully developing the conceit, that there was a connection between the challenging existence of the highland settlements in Scotland and the land occupied by indigenous people on both banks of the Rio Perené. Once that debatable proposition had been aired, coincidence would somehow manage to supply the evidence.

Looking back on his heritage, late in the day, Arthur laid claim to coming from 'discounted' Jacobite stock as a way of sentimentalising the meanness of his childhood circumstances, the lack of inherited ground, and the family's removal to harsher country. The punitive savagery of the London government's repressive measures, after the defeat of the last Jacobite uprising in 1745, and after the slaughter of the clans at Culloden field, found an echo in the inherited myths, reinforced with every telling, of the Ashaninka in Peru: the songs of loss, years of slavery following the establishment of the coffee colonies. With no exodus in prospect. No offshore oil strikes. And nothing to hope for beyond the remote prospect of finding gold. Or winning the lottery.

The Hanoverian enforcer, who inherited his role from Prince William, Duke of Cumberland, was William Anne Keppel, the second earl of Albemarle. This aristocrat's chosen tactic was total war: ground-zero devastation, with the affirmed intention of deporting, as involuntary Australasian colonists, often in chains, the remnants of a diminished highland populace. I wonder if Arthur pondered the proud name of the vessel that carried him from Tilbury to Ceylon? The *Albemarle*.

And did my great-grandfather, finessing his autobiographical summary, remember the diatribe published in *Gentleman's Magazine* in June 1739, the one quoted by T.M. Devine in *The Scottish Clearances*?

> 'In this great Extent of Country, Ignorance and Superstition greatly prevail: In some Places the Remains even of Paganism are still to be found… Inhabitants being destitute of all Means and Knowledge, and without any Schools to educate their Children, are entirely ignorant of the principles of Religion and Virtue, live in Idleness and Poverty, have no notion of Industry… are subject to the Will and Command of their Popish disaffected Chieftains…'

Patrick Sellar, henchman of the Sutherland land barons, one of the most hated and feared of the clearance agents, expressed his contempt for the smallholders and cottars he unhoused, dismissing them as ungodly primitives or 'aborigines'.

The same language came back with Victorian pirates of Empire laying out their rubber and coffee plantations on the banks of the Upper Amazon. At the climax of his survey for the Peruvian Corporation of London, Arthur Sinclair expresses his awe at the fecundity of the low jungle and his justification, as the apologists for the great Scottish landowners had it, for granting rights of exploitation only to those who had the means to carry the process through.

The young Arthur Sinclair is resourceful, hardworking, and independent of spirit: the qualities he comes to admire, or demand, in others. I think of the poet John Clare, who adopted an elective Scottish persona when it suited him, to honour his mysterious itinerant grandfather, and in sympathy with the plaid-wrapped drovers resting, watering, feeding their cattle on the long drive from the borders to the meat markets of London, where they serviced a perpetually hungry militarised regime. Highland cattle were being organised as an industrial resource, penned and fattened at the expense of survivalist clansmen outside the cash economy. Just as, much later, the Peruvian coffee planters introduced cattle to destroy the permitted gardens of their debt-encumbered labourers.

With his first earnings as a gardener, my ancestor, the future plants-man, hiked to Aberdeen and bought six volumes of James Hervey's *Reflections on a Flower-Garden* – as Clare had tramped from Helpston to Stamford, before the bookshop opened, to secure a coveted copy of James Thomson's *The Seasons*. And like Clare, Arthur paused on his return journey to investigate his purchase.

> *As I walked from Aberdeen I could not help sitting down occasionally by the wayside to dip into it.*

My great-grandfather soon discovered Oliver Goldsmith and Thomas De Quincey.

> *The beauty of the prose-poems and neatness of the humour was such as I had never before met with.*

The practical mysteries of propagation and grafting now cohabited with another less focused compulsion, the urge to write. After reading Alexander von Humboldt's *Essay on the Geography of Plants*, the volume-hungry youth conceived an ambition to follow in the author's footsteps, over the Andes to the golden lands.

> *For eighteen months I laboured here; the work was hard but interesting enough. Yet, the plants were only native trees or handy flowers from temperate latitudes, and I, longing to make the acquaintance of exotics from warmer regions, now apprenticed myself to a garden where there were good hot-houses, preparing, like many a better man, for what was to follow... Through the Balsam (Impatiens), Nepenthes plumeria and the Gloriosa superba, I was first introduced to Ceylon. I was in my element, and my special hobby and delight was in tracing every exotic I came across, to its original home, a labour which gave me much pleasur-able reading.*
>
> *In four years I had reached the top of my ambition as a gardener, and with the wide world before me began to look towards the Tropics for a more congenial field. I had already begun writing for the local press. My first*

accepted article being on 'Evergreens', a contribution which led to the life-long friendship of Mr. Wm. Alexander, Editor of the Aberdeen Free Press, *and one of the kindliest, purest-souled men I ever intimately knew.*

———

Apprenticeship completed, and the itch to be elsewhere declaring itself, Arthur came under the patronage of a wealthy proprietor with overseas estates. Sir John Cheape, who was paying a visit to Lady Elphinstone, made a detour to the garden where my great-grandfather worked, in order to ask for his advice on sending certain varieties of rhododendrons to Ceylon.

> *'Will they grow?'*
> *'Unquestionably.'*
> *'How do you know?'*
> *'I have just been reading Dr Hoffmeister's book in which he says that Rhododendrons not only grow wild at Nuwara Eliya and other upland districts, but on the very top of Adam's Peak he found a gorgeous display of blooms.'*

Cheape is impressed by the confidence of the reply, the bookish display of the young autodidact, and he decides to ship Arthur out to his estates near Kandy, in company with the rhododendrons and a letter of instruction to the manager. Sir John, an engineer and military man, a brigadier-general when the Second Anglo-Burmese War broke out, was accustomed to swift and decisive action. He had a sure eye for talent. And ambition.

The landowner with whom Cheape had been staying, Lady Elphinstone, made a significant gesture in the direction of opening up previously inaccessible highland territory, by cutting, on behalf of the Great North of Scotland Railway Company, the first ceremonial sod of a line that would run to the west, from the outskirts of Aberdeen to the town of Huntly. The plan was to forge a link, from Inverness by way of Aberdeen, with the railways of the south. Lady Elphinstone's husband, Sir James, 'marvelled at the physical strength of the navvies' cutting the track – as Arthur was later to marvel at workers 'hung over the cliffs by ropes, looking like venturesome apes', when they built the pioneer railway over the Andes. A venture that would link Lima with the permanently smoke-shrouded hub at La Oroya, a filthy smelting settlement where grazing areas were already being turned into a dust desert and mountains into scarred albino monuments.

Not quite two years after Lady Elphinstone's incisive thrust at the turf, with the faintest of bows towards her baronet husband, chairman of the Board of Railway Directors, the line opened to goods traffic. Labour was cheap in those days and there were fewer foot-dragging political considerations and no computer systems to bed in. A week later, a special passenger train made the run successfully, attended by bands, commemorative poems – 'What ho! Ye sturdy Burgers' – and hundreds of waving schoolchildren. Dressed tables were laid out for a banquet in a marquee set up in a field beside the River Bogie. A feast attended by company directors, engineers, substantial landowners and selected farmers from along the route. Sir James delighted the assembled throng with a speech promising that this modest little railway, less 'florid and ornamental' than some others, would carry passengers 'safely to the end of their journey'.

Five days later a passenger train held at Killybrewster station was hit by an engine coming from Huntly. The driver missed the danger signal and ploughed into the back of a Third Class carriage, reducing it to matchwood. Other carriages were forced from the line. There was one fatality and numerous injuries among the third-class passengers. The single reported accident in the superior carriages was to a certain Captain A. Lewis, 'a gentleman belonging to Lloyd's', who was travelling north on matters of marine insurance.

My great-grandfather, having used his time on board the *Albemarle* to establish himself as the ship's scribe, comes ashore in Colombo on 10 June 1858, and heads straight to the offices of the local newspaper, the *Observer*. Then away to the hills.

> *My destination was Rangalla, a district that stood A1 in coffee planters'*
> *estimation, and Battegalla, which was acknowledged at that time to be the*
> *finest hill estate in the island. Mr Duckworth, the fortunate proprietor,*
> *resided there and received me with great kindness. His father – one of the*
> *merchant princes of Liverpool – I had visited before leaving England…*
> *Battegalla was indeed an ideal estate, combining good soil and shelter with a*
> *glorious view of the rich lowcountry beyond, 350 acres bearing at the rate of*
> *fully 15 cwt., per acre, an ample labour supply, rising prices, and altogether*
> *the prospects were as bright as ever they were before or since in Ceylon.*

All the high moments of Arthur Sinclair's life seem to involve a
sudden sweep of landscape, an elevated view, and a splendid prospect
of new territory that, through a play on words, is translated into *career*
prospects: good fortune with yellow sunsets rippling through the pores
and veins and capillaries and conferring the Midas touch on the transported observer. Fertile ground, famous yields, capital accumulated.
And somewhere along the way, unmentioned, uncelebrated, a silent
family.

A letter from the editor of the *Observer* arrives at the hill station with
the news that Captain Collett of the *Albemarle* is stalking the waterfront
like a figure out of Conrad, 'with an armful of papers from Aberdeen',
featuring Arthur's contributions from the voyage. And now Ferguson
of the *Observer* wants to put in his own bid for the services of the
newcomer's pen. And coffee prices are climbing and climbing: golden
blends, golden days. Arthur is in demand as soil magus, visiting agent
and coming author.

> *Few outdoor occupations could be more attractive than coffee planting in*
> *the 'fifties'. Coolies were more docile than they are now, the surrounding*
> *Sinhalese less corrupted and more respectful. The busy crop season was soon*
> *over and then came ample leisure, the interesting process of pruning, the*
> *beautiful blossoming time when bumper crops were estimated, after which*
> *those so minded could readily be spared for a sporting trip to Bintenne.*
> *Monotonous as the work seemed to many, to me it was a daily delight,*
> *albeit the climate had its drawbacks.*

Ceylon remained the shining pearl, the setting to which Arthur returned, the island where two of his sons, their histories lost to me, became planters in their turn. The rainy season came on him unexpectedly, torrents poured through the weather-boarding of the bungalow and the newcomer shivered. There was no fireplace, no flannel shirt. He went down with 'a rattling case of dysentery', nature's gentle cull. The new beginning was almost the end. Arthur was carried thirty miles to Kandy by his estate workers. Dr Charsley, who inspected him that first evening, said: 'If you have any little matters to put right, any important letters to write, I would advise you to see to them now.'

The body was wasted, the dreams feverish, but the convalescence was sweet. And 'never to be forgotten'. The doctors took Arthur for drives to the Peradeniya Royal Botanic Gardens, a designated satellite of Kew. Conceived and laid out by King Wickramabahu III in 1371, as a pleasure garden for his Queen, the park was 'converted' by the British, six years after the fall of the last King of Sri Lanka, in 1821. Arthur was enchanted. Wherever he found himself on future questing travels, in other lands, he made it his business to seek out, inspect and evaluate the botanical gardens.

> *Dr Thwaites did so much to encourage and gratify my taste for plants. It was during one of these visits that I saw the first cuttings of cinchona ever introduced into Ceylon being planted in a propagating frame.*

The miracle of quinine! Cinchona is an evergreen tree or shrub native to South America; to Peru, Ecuador and Bolivia. Its bark yields the invaluable quinine, the colonist's friend. The most efficacious anti-malarial medicine then known to mankind. Episodes of state-sponsored bio-piracy delivered cinchona to Ceylon. Arthur, in his weakened state, still a little delirious, was there to witness the initial propagation. Attempts were being made by British expeditions, approved or freelance, to smuggle cinchona from the Andes to Kew. The justification, as ever, being that natives could not be trusted to harvest and exploit an important life-giving drug without outside direction. There was a Christian obligation to steal in a good cause. Indigenous people, driven by necessity and under the direction, very often, of ruthless plant-hunters, ripped out the trees with no notion of replanting what seemed to be an infinite god-given resource, the healing fruits of a lost Eden. Religious fundamentalists preached and pontificated: god's tactical plan, from the moment of the original expulsion from the garden, was to allow wild-eyed desert prophets to rediscover and reclaim the benefits renounced by Adam. Every plant, in its intricate structure, was a small reflection of the divine plan. Joe Jackson in *The Thief at the End of the World* discusses the era of cinchona's propagation in Ceylon.

> The *reality* of plant transfer was not at issue. What emerged with the 1859 cinchona theft was a new rationale. The Earth was a treasure house that had to be managed: Nature belonged to man to harvest and 'improve'. This was especially true in the tropics, where vegetable riches ran rampant but were also wasted and destroyed. By the Victorian era, when the British Empire had endowed its expansion with a moral flavour, the idea had a new urgency. Not only the conquest of nature was at stake but the course of the future... To Benjamin Kidd in his 1898 *The Control of the Tropics*, the native had no right 'to prevent the utilization of the immense natural resources which they have in charge.' This certainly applied to the profligate Andeans killing off the world's shrinking stock of quinine.

What Jackson exposes is the covert aspect of the Royal Botanic Gardens, Kew, as a 'great machine' designed to facilitate eco-piracy on behalf of Empire: a gold machine. By 1821, Kew had become an instrument of the State, with a mandate to supply the estates and gardens of the colonies and dependencies. Beyond recuperative walks opened to make strollers feel good about themselves, there was the obligation to carry out bio-pharmaceutical research and development. A new academic discipline was launched: economic botany. Plants were shipped to where they could turn the best profit, from wilderness to plantation.

Promoters of twenty-first-century Sri Lanka tourist packages, not the softest sell in the light of recent hotel bombings and interracial

atrocities, gloss the Peradeniya Botanic Gardens as a small paradise rescued from the colonial era. 'It was the British colonialist rulers (1815–
1948) who destroyed the invaluable forest cover of a thousand wooded
hills from Kandy to Badulla in the Central Highlands. Lands protected
by the gentle sway of Buddhism, which indoctrinated a respect for
all living beings. Wooded hills were converted to Ceylon Coffee and
following the devastation of "coffee rust" in 1869 to seamless hill plantations of tea. The very same British Colonist rulers established the
Peradeniya Botanic Gardens that contribute, today, towards the enlightenment of concepts of floriculture conservation, birdlife conservation,
butterfly conservation, biodiversity and sustainability.'

Arthur recovered, worked, thrived. He entered what he called the 'busiest
portion of my life'. Travelling 'over the length and breadth of the island
for the next ten years', as Visiting Agent, he was 'almost continuously
in the saddle'. For a writer, this was rich experience: long solitary rides
in all weathers, the registering of slight differences in soil conditions,
expanding taxonomies of flora and fauna. And always, over the brow,
in the next valley, a new estate, another 'character' to engage with, to
register and record. The process is Conradian, with an anticipatory dash
of Somerset Maugham. Arthur relished the company of these isolated
men, out of their homelands, many were fellow Scots. He relished eccentricity and difference. He had little time for the 'average John Bull who
bullies appus and kicks kudirakarens'. And there were plenty of these,
incompetent, put away by landed families, or left, unchecked, to chase
the coffee boom, letting rich harvests rot while they caroused, indulged
and sickened.

When Arthur returned from his convalescence, he found his associate, 'poor Mr Duckworth', in the midst of the season's crop, attempting
work for which he was thoroughly unfitted: wet coffee cherries lay five
feet deep on the barbecue. A sickening black smoke could be seen for
miles around.

There were sportsmen, big and small game hunters, dedicated drinkers, amateur poets and addicts. There were planters driven mad by the
rain and the loneliness. There were suicides and murders.

> *Mr Duckworth, though not a planter, was a gentleman of refined tastes, and managed to employ his time in a very interesting, if not very profitable manner: a musician of no mean order, he could paint passably and even dabbled in verse, would often send a messenger to call me from a distant corner of the estate to hear or see his latest effort, and if I could but suggest a word or half a note by which a line would go more smoothly, he was more pleased than if I had added another cwt per acre to the crop. 'Don't go away,' he would say, 'tiffin is coming, and what do we pay kanganis for but to look after coolies.'*

Among Arthur's closest friends was one of the eastern Wodehouse tribe, Mr Haye Wodehouse. They travelled together and exchanged letters. They agreed a joint account to subscribe to literary magazines of the day.

> *Son of Canon Wodehouse, a family of stupendous pedigree, Haye was a highly polished, scholarly aristocrat with all the advantages I most lacked, yet he was pleased to discover many affinities in our reading tastes… This of itself was an education for me which I greatly appreciated… Wodey was always dignified and leisurely, whether dressed for dinner or enjoying his matutinal pipe… He was inclined to be lazy, but always suave and kind to the meanest coolly!*

It was inevitable that Arthur would attempt something like a fiction based on his years as Visiting Agent. Aged forty-six, he chose to publish his novella in Colombo, under a pseudonym. The chapbook was entitled *How I Lost My Wattie. Or, Life in Ceylon and the Coffee-Planting Experience of an Auld Scotchman*. This is now a pretty rare item. The National Library of Scotland reports that 'no other copies have been traced in the UK'. I have Arthur's own, and it makes strange reading. The narrative is in Scottish dialect, a first-person voice improving on something close to Arthur's experiences from his arrival in Colombo. Coming ashore and 'meetin a rascal o' a Portugee on the street', the hero is led to a coffin warehouse. 'About a dizen ready-made coffins, an richt abun them hung a board: – *Conveyance for Hire*. I was the first tae tak tae my heels; and we never halted till within the Fort gate.'

Here is a reforgotten curiosity, a dialect docu-fiction, in picaresque mode; a moral fable of venturing, of love and loss, published in 1878 in Ceylon. The narrator's mother sells the farm left by her husband and passes on £1,500 to her waster son. With which he determines to 'become the laird o' a coffy estate'. And accordingly he picks out 'the maist likely bit o' wood – or *jungle*'. The facts and figures of investment and return haunt the story, along with the inevitable lurking disasters: sorry advice, government meddling and thieves on all sides.

> *My expectations o'neist year were mair than realized. I got 400 cwts. o'crap – which wis shipped tae my accoont an brocht me som £1,400 in Mincing Lane. Meanwhile, my ootlay increased at an awfu an some what unaccountable rate, sae that in makin up my bukes I got the following result: –*
>
> | | |
> |---|---:|
> | *Actual estate expenses* | *£ 850* |
> | *Agents' charge and interest* | *85* |
> | *Visiting* | *100* |
> | *Commission on rice & crop* | *170* |
> | | ___ |
> | | *£1,205* |

The novel, with its underlying anxieties, shadows Arthur's brief autobiography of 1900. The true cost of abandoning family and homeland. Surely it was time to cash in?

> *Beginning with a modest dozen estates, they gradually increased upon my hands, till at the end of my second year I had three times that number, and in a few years more the numbers rose to 100 or about one-twelfth of the island's extent of Coffee, and my duties were not merely to report on the conditions of the estates, but to direct the cultivation and estimate the crops... My remuneration was now over £2,000 per annum, equal to that of the Lord Bishop! And yet I retired at the age of 40! Some remain the year too long... There was much to induce me to stay; but the superior attractions of Aberdeenshire prevailed.*

Family gathered around him on the grass, Arthur reclines with his newspapers. He reads, and he continues to write letters, to friends in Ceylon and to the Aberdeen press. I wonder if, in the hour of his success, in the acquiring of property and the securing of investments, he thought back to the clearances and the Gaelic songs of loss. The keening highland chants in the wake of lands enclosed for the penning and fattening of cattle, before the great drives south. These folk poems were like the tribal songs chorused by the Ashaninka people in their circling dances. 'The gold that is in the calf-skin is what dispossessed the people. The gold of the red hide. And its influence is not good.'

Arthur Rimbaud, visionary poet, fugue walker and despoiler of libraries, sickening in his trading post, wrote home to his 'friends' in July 1881. 'I'm back from the interior, where I bought a considerable quantity of hides. I've a bit of a fever at present. I'm leaving again in a few days for a region totally unexplored by Europeans; and if I succeed in definitely setting out, it will be a journey of six weeks, hard and dangerous, but which could be profitable.'

Gold and hides. Journeys and dreams. The voices resonate, confirming and contradicting. Torn maps fall out of previously unopened books to tempt us. I press my nose to the old dried leather and the chipped gilt lettering of Arthur Sinclair's definitive 1895 volume. The expedition to the headwaters of the Amazon.

PASSAGE MONEY

'Every great theft demands a mastermind, and he requires the machine to help launch his schemes. In the case of cinchona and rubber, the usual genesis was reversed. The great machine came first, awaiting its machinator.'
– Joe Jackson, *The Thief at the End of the World*

He travelled to Peru by way of the Isthmus of Panama, having visited, 'in passing', the islands of Barbados and Jamaica: 'the two oldest and most valuable of our West Indian possessions'. Arthur Sinclair notes the advice of Cromwell, after the Lord Protector had already shipped out a labour force of a thousand pressganged young Irish women and girls. 'And as to the rogue and vagabond species in Scotland, we can help you at any time to a few hundred of these.' As indentured workers for the sugar plantations, the dispossessed highlanders were a cheap and plentiful resource. Cromwell was happy to be rid of them. They could sweat and pray to their alien gods as a rehearsal for coming generations of transported African slaves.

The filter through which Arthur evaluated landscape never shifted far from Aberdeen. Now, after his years on the coffee estates, he had a sharper eye for opportunity, future prospects. 'The climate and vegetation strikingly remind one of Ceylon, but alas! the abandoned hillsides testify to the greater labour difficulties of the poor planter here.'

They sail for Panama, with my great-grandfather brooding on 'the first land seen', Porto Bello in the Gulf of Darién.

> *Here, about 200 years ago, some of the very cream of our countrymen were landed and sacrificed to the contemptible jealousies of our neighbours. Terrible was the loss to so poor a country, and heroic the struggle, but it*

> *was of no avail against such fearful odds, and, now, the only really useful lesson we can learn from the disaster is, that even Scotchmen are not equal to manual labour in the tropics; and, whatever inducements selfish individuals or soulless companies may hold out, it may be accepted as a general rule that Europeans are unfitted for field labour in purely tropical temperatures. It may be all very well for overseers, who live in luxurious bungalows, and view their fields from under the shade of ample umbrellas, but it means death to the exposed pick-and-shovel man.*

Cycles of famine, economic dependence on England, a decline in shipbuilding had the lowland Scots casting envious eyes on the apparent colonial riches of their neighbours. The Bank of Scotland was established in 1695 and subscriptions were raised in Amsterdam and Hamburg for a Scottish venture; a colony, a new city to dominate the overland route between the Pacific and the Atlantic. The gleam of fools' gold sponged twenty per cent of all the money circulating in Scotland. Five ships sailed under orders 'to proceed to the Bay of Darien, and make the Isle called the Golden Island… and there make a settlement on the mainland.'

Some, perhaps the lucky ones, perished on the hellish voyage. The fleet set sail from Leith on the east coast to avoid the surveillance of English warships. Of the original settlement of 'Caledonia' nothing is left but overgrown traces of a boundary ditch. That ground, tainted by miscalculation and failure, is still virtually uninhabited. The indigenous people refused to trade. Crops withered. Malarial fevers culled the weakened and starving colonists. Promoters, staying at home in Scotland, embezzled funds. The undercapitalised project incurred the displeasure of the East India Company. After eight months the Colony was abandoned. A second expedition in 1699 was an even worse fiasco. 2,500 settlers left Scotland, a few hundred returned.

Landfall, and easy days touring plantations and strolling through botanical gardens on the West Indian islands, lulled Arthur, once again, into the dream of a new beginning; past failures were discounted, future challenges postponed. The tone of voice remains jaunty and clubbable. Humour deflects horror. There are no intimate confessions and no apologies. We have to wait for the terse summary of 1900 to be given even a glimpse of that other life, the domestic. My great-grandfather returns to his heart-place, the home in Ceylon he favoured over all others.

He makes a pilgrimage to the bungalow, the estate on which he lived and reared a family. Primrose Hill, 'though now uncultivated', was not fallen into dereliction or abandoned.

> *Hundreds of trees and flowers – escapees from the Botanical Gardens – grew there where they never grew before; the fruit trees I planted thirty years ago, jak, mango, coconut and lime, now waxing old and bearing heavily… The* Bougainvillea, *with its rose-coloured bracts, hides the crumbling ruins of the godowns, while the* Inga Saman *trees which, on the recommendation of Dr Thwaites in 1870, I transplanted from the garden now throw a grateful shade over the old bungalow, looking so inviting and with its sunny memories doubly interesting. The view from the verandah greener and richer than of yore; the old sugar estate – an abandoned common in the sixties – now a splendid sheet of luxuriant and valuable tea… Yet one cannot live upon a wealth of wild flowers or on the distant view however lovely.*

———

From the rail of the ship, as he contemplates the first sighting of the Isthmus of Panama, Arthur remembers the horror of a chapter of Scottish history he would prefer to forget. Colon, the port where he comes ashore, is 'a very wretched spot'.

> *It is only in a Spanish Republic that the existence of such a pestiferous place is possible… Fortunately, a fire has burned down and purified a large portion of the town… rendering it, for a time, less dangerous to sojourners.*

The original Spanish invaders, wary of encroachment on their silver routes, the golden highway out of Peru, resented the upstart Scottish intrusion and made it their business to sweep away even the ashes of the disappeared Colony. Ash was an enduring motif in the dance between fertile land and the sufferings of those who worked it.

'High mortality was concomitant with money and the sheen on the dollars was not from gold but blood,' Faulkner wrote in *Absalom, Absalom!* 'A little lost island in a latitude which would require ten thousand years of equatorial heritage to bear its climate, a soil manured with black blood from two hundred years of oppression and exploitation until it sprang with an incredible paradox of peaceful greenery and crimson flowers and sugar cane.'

And now for Arthur, with his losses and regrets, his hopes of turning still unvisited Peruvian land into green bounty, new plantations to compensate for the devastation of *Hemileia* in Ceylon, the act of stepping ashore is the acceptance, even in Colon, which looks and sounds like a cancer, of the curse of being trapped between worlds; between no-going-back and a future that is already mortgaged and used up. Colonists and authors and eco-warriors all know that the *exotic* is simply another set to exploit.

> *The outlook from the carriage windows is not exactly inviting. Deserted villages, palatial bungalows abandoned, ponderous machines rusting among the malarious jungle, flit past in slow succession, while at the various stations a few poor ghostly whites and hundreds of dark and hungry-looking old canal labourers scramble to make a penny out of the sympathetic passengers... There is not an acre of real cultivation; we simply pass between living walls of natural greenery... The descendants of Europeans living near the Equator seem to degenerate more rapidly and thoroughly than they do at a safe distance from the Equator.*

—————

As a former bookdealer, I had the habit of doing my detective work, before the story began to tell itself, by interrogating printed material, the more ephemeral the better. Planters exiled to Ceylon had the time on their hands to produce a stream of self-congratulatory and commemorative booklets. One of these – *Jubilee of the Planters' Association of Ceylon (1854–1904): Illustrated Souvenir of the 'Times of Ceylon'* – had a pencilled note, 'See page 32', on the flyleaf. I took the hint: 1867 and the Planters' Association is 'in a parlous state'. Dissenting noises are being heard on all sides, how Keir, Dundas & Co. are packing the committee with placemen and taking over struggling estates. The accusation is refuted by listing the leading planters of the day: 'Not one of whom had any connection with K., D. & Co.' But that list includes two familiar names: G.H.D. Elphinstone and A. Sinclair.

Elphinstone must surely have belonged to the landed family with whom Arthur's patron, Sir John Cheape, was staying when the young gardener was taken up and shipped out. And now, deep in my storage box, I discover a rather tattered buff-coloured booklet, an offprint from the *Tropical Agriculturalist* (February 1900). The booklet delivers a pen portrait, with accompanying photographs, of 'The Late Sir James D.H. Elphinstone, Bart. & Sir Graeme H.D. Elphinstone, Bart.'

Close reading reveals notes signed by 'Old Colonist'. I know this to be one of Arthur Sinclair's pseudonyms. The style, with its characteristic fondness for colourful anecdotes, clearly belongs to my great-grandfather. He tells how Elphinstone, when he decides, on a whim, to sweep a gravel path, is mistaken for one of his gardeners. With hilarious consequences. Lady Elphinstone brings news to her husband, as he patrols the lawn.

'You are the father of twins.'
'Two! That's one too many for a poor man.'

The anonymous author plays metafictional games by awarding himself various minor walk-on roles. Arthur is listed as attending a dinner celebrating the coffee enterprise, and chaired by Sir James Elphinstone, but he does not take a prominent part. The most intriguing aspect of the pamphlet is a landscape-format photograph: 'Sir James Elphinstone amongst the Planters.' Behind the shaggy bearlike group is a low shed with the steep ridged slopes of a plantation rising threateningly behind. The planters have an abundance of untamed beard to shame Shoreditch. They look like a Devil's Island crew, denied barbers, and gathered, prisoners and warders together, around their visiting commandant. The 'Old Colonist' concludes by naming those who posed for the group portrait at Kadienlena Harvest Home in January 1870.

'Arthur Sinclair,' he says, 'kept in the background.' My great-grand-father *might* be the one who positions himself at the end of the second row, where he crouches, half-hidden. The only one who is at liberty to deny that he was ever there. Arthur quotes Charles Lamb: 'All, all are gone, the old familiar faces.'

Persisting, I arrive at the proper books, leather-bound, lettered in gilt, decorative covers and spines: false glitter on a dingy shelf. There aren't many antiquarian items left. *Ceylon in 1888* by John Ferguson has a presentation inscription: 'To Arthur Sinclair, Esq (Birkhill, Dundee), the oldest & best friend made in Ceylon by the author. 1883.' Ferguson was one of the editors and publishers of the newspaper responsible for so many of Arthur's reports. His book is a promotional exercise, lavishly produced, with engravings, foldout maps and charts. Chapter XI is headed PRESENT PROSPECTS FOR CAPITALISTS IN CEYLON. 'Still a good field for investment – Its freedom from atmospheric disturbances – Shipping conveniences at new harbour of Colombo – Low freights – Cheap and unrivalled means of transport – Large tracts available for tea and other tropical culture – Openings for young men with capital – High position taken by the Ceylon planter.'

'As a body,' Ferguson writes, 'Ceylon planters are among the most intelligent, gentlemanly, and hospitable of any colonists in British dependencies. The rough work of pioneering in the early days before there were district roads, villages, supplies, doctors, or other comforts of civilization, was chiefly done by hard-headed Scots: men bivouacked in the trackless jungle with the scantiest accommodation under tropical rains lasting for weeks together, with rivers swollen to flood-level and impassable, while food supplies often ran short, as none could be got across the wide torrents.'

But the book that excited me most also helped to move Arthur's story towards the final chapter, his fateful expedition to Peru. *The Great River (Notes on the Amazon and its Tributaries and the Steamer Services)* was published in Paternoster Row, London, in 1904, a year before my great-grandfather died. The half-title has his wavering ownership signature. There are so many haunting black and white photographs and casually speculative maps that *The Great River* feels more like an alternative-world graphic novel than a PR pitch for the Amazon Steam Navigation Company. The steamers pictured, coughing smoke, stern wheels spinning, are ready to be auditioned for Werner Herzog's *Fitzcarraldo*. There are illustrations of 'Hauling Canoes through the Rapids', remote trading stations, tapirs, alligators and 'Types of Amazonian Indians'. Selective portraits of rubber plantations put a gloss on the barbarous horrors exposed in the report commissioned from the Irish diplomat Roger Casement. Photographs can be so easily suborned, edited to advantage. They mean what we need them to mean. Casement's lucid reports and his diaries from the Congo and the Amazon, actual or improved by the Secret State, must be read alongside the images he captured for criminal evidence or private pleasure. Both duties, the public and the personal, are crawling with guilt and shame.

'With his gun at hand, ready for any shot,' writes the anonymous provider of the Steam Company's promotional copy, 'the visitor can paddle for miles through this fluvial paradise, wandering through a perfect Elysium of beauty, where scarce a ripple disturbs the water, and the foliage is mirrored so clearly that it is often difficult to determine where the reality ceases and the reflection commences.'

The introduction to *The Great River* comes with a full-page pen and ink drawing suggestive of antebellum Mississippi: two dandified plantation owners, puffing on cheroots, shake on a deal, while a swaying waterfront lady, like Carmen Miranda in blackface, balances a huge platter of fruit on her head. The photographic illustrations of indigenous people are neither ethnographic nor authentic records of encounters. They are studio-contrived to expose naked, pre-adolescent breasts, male weapons and headdresses.

> The scanty population of the upper districts of the Great River is largely composed of Indians and half-castes, who have gradually been brought within the pale of civilization by communication with traders and others… It is a remarkable fact, attested by the best Amazonian authorities, that the Indians cannot withstand the heat of the climate so well as the negroes (of whom, however, there are comparatively few up the rivers) and, indeed, the Indian seems to suffer from its effects more than the White man does.

Transported Africans, formerly enslaved on the plantations of Barbados, become, by force of circumstance, themselves the enforcers, the corporals charged by rubber barons like the infamous Julio César Arana of Iquitos, or Carlos Fermín Fitzcarrald, with hunting down runaways pressed into servitude. The corporals are required to carry out tortures, whippings, amputations, brandings, burnings and drownings, when insufficient quotas of rubber are returned from the forest. The whole unnatural system has been turned on its head; victim becoming victimiser becoming victim, in the service of remote investors and a booming market. The corporals are the metal-tipped tentacles of a rhino whip hidden in the drawer of a partners' desk in the offices of the Peruvian Amazon Company, chartered and thriving in London, where the obscene oligarch Arana kept his house. And entertained compliant bankers and magnates.

Casement's camera filtered hurt. 'I'll leave my bones on that damned trip,' he says in Mario Vargas Llosa's novel *The Dream of the Celt*. Sickening, willing his coming disgrace and execution, like that other knight, Walter Raleigh, with his futile voyages in search of El Dorado, the civil servant took down the strategic confessions of the men from

Barbados – on the promise of helping them to be repatriated to the island which was never their home. The condemned cell was a necessary device in which to make a reckoning of a spoiled life.

In Vargas Llosa's novel, the plantation owner, Victor Israel, a Maltese Jew, replies to a challenge from Casement. The man tasked with producing a report into the iniquities of the rubber trade asks his reluctant informant if he has ever tried to understand the point of view of 'the people you call savages'. How do they feel when 'white or mestizo gentlemen come with rifles and revolvers and demand that they abandon their families'?

'Do you put cannibals of Amazonia on the same plane as the pioneers, entrepreneurs, and merchants who work in heroic conditions and risk our lives to transform these forests into a civilized land?' Israel replied.

A civilised wilderness remains a wilderness. And 'civilization' is rapidly and comprehensively wilded. The virus of horror – *the horror, the horror* – is shipped out with the stolen plants. Herzog's riverboat, dragged over a mutilated hill by paid Ashaninka extras, driven to this inexplicable task, becomes a tin can in the rapids, a smashed shell with bloodied technicians, paying a posthumous homage to that man of history, Carlos Fermín Fitzcarrald.

The rubber baron was buried in Iquitos General Cemetery in 1897. He died at the age of thirty-five, in company with a Bolivian business associate, when his ship the *Contamana* went down on the Urubamba. A fate that the indigenous members of the crew might have seen as a blessing, a confirmation of Fitzcarrald's messianic status. The river was accepting one of its own. In Puerto Maldonaldo you can still view the skeletal remains of the wreck, its ribs being slowly crushed by the serpentine fecundity of the jungle.

The Amazon, efficiently serviced by steamers, twin-screw vessels of good speed, fitted with electric light, was open for business. After preliminary chapters on ships and wharves and railways, *The Great River* offers a useful summary of the state of rubber cultivation, the best methods and the highest yields. 'It would thus appear that the supply of Rubber in Amazonia is practically inexhaustible, for although a few trees may perish every year through injudicious tapping, there are numberless seedlings constantly growing up in a wild state to take the place of the ancient stock.'

An upbeat introduction concludes with a paragraph recommending the services of the Royal Mail Steamers of the Booth Steamship Company Ltd., with their head-office at 30 James Street, Liverpool. There are three or four sailings a month for Pará (at the mouth of the Amazon), after coaling at Cardiff. 'The voyage occupies about fifteen days.' The young Casement, sent away from Ireland, worked as a clerk for the Elder Dempster Line, another Liverpool shipping concern. They traded between Britain and West Africa.

The Great River closes with advertisements for valves, engines, hauling-lines, Manila rope, rubber goods, railway carriages, bridges, jetties and English Royal Sanitary Ware. A page is reserved for The Booth Line. FREQUENT & RAPID SERVICE FROM LIVERPOOL TO PARA & MANAOS (RIVER AMAZON). PASSAGE MONEY, FIRST CLASS: FARES FROM ENGLAND & PARIS TO BRAZIL, FROM £21 to £30. PARTICULARS TO BE HAD ON APPLICATION.

When the Barbadian overseers, having confessed their part in the atrocities, accept Casement's plan, to smuggle them out to La Esperanza, and then on the first boat to Manáos, their interrogator confirms that he will be there to pick them up on the *Atahualpa* of the Booth Line. A nice touch, this invocation of the original Inca chief and his Andean successor with his cave of gold.

Casement fears for his life. The agents of the Peruvian Amazon Company understand the implications of the report. And the possible consequences. But what might not have been appreciated at the time was that the director of the pioneering Liverpool shipping line, a man of remarkable drive and energy who sailed on the maiden voyage to the Amazon in 1866, was Charles Booth, instigator of a monumental statistical research programme, *Life and Labour of the People in London*. Booth's colour-coded maps of previously unexplored urban terrain offered the well-intentioned classes as much of a terra incognita as the Amazonian rainforest. If the psychogeographers of the 1960s looked for the beach beneath the streets of Paris, Booth tramped the alleys and tenements of the Victorian night with an implanted fever dream of the jungle: the cries of beasts, the dirt-crusted alien hordes crammed together, waiting to be classified, patronised and made ready for improvement.

THE BEAST IN THE JUNGLE

'This horror of waking – *this* was knowledge…'
  – Henry James

Look closely at late photographs of Charles Booth. Look at what is printed on tightening skin, the mask pinching against bone resistance: family, property and good works. There is a heavy price to be paid for material success. Those maps of poverty, menu cards of London's shame, are coloured with Booth's blood and breath. Where so many of the grave beards in my story – Arthur Sinclair, Roger Casement, and the regiment of half-mad adventurers disappearing into the jungle – believe that the *great thing*, the transformative mystery, is elsewhere, across the ocean, accessed by risk, sweated miles and tamed natives, Booth knew that the condition of darkness was waiting in the city. It was a qualification of ignorance.

Later urbanists, like the Beat Generation writers and poets in wartime New York City, hustling through subterranean versions of a mechanised hell, and shipping out in the Merchant Marine, fantasised about the ultimate high: the death trip of the Amazonian vine. Yagé, ayahuasca, daime. Burroughs and Ginsberg making their pioneering junk-sex tourist expeditions through Peru, Panama, Ecuador and Chile in the late 1950s. Exchanging letters.

'The whole fucking Cosmos broke loose around me,' Ginsberg reported from Pucallpa, Peru, in 1960. 'The strongest and worst I've ever had it nearly… I hardly have the nerve to go back, afraid of some real madness, a Changed Universe permanently changed.' But what Burroughs retrieves is the confirmation that the membrane between the fiction of the jungle and the fiction of the city is wafer thin. You can put your fist right through it. When Manhattan collapses into pharmaceutical chaos in *Blade Runner: A Movie* (1979), he asserts that the city of his imagination 'has come to represent all cities'. The swarming fish from private aquariums have been dumped into the waterways of New York. 'Freshwater sharks cruise the Hudson.' Wild animals have been released from the zoo in Central Park. Pushers roam the ruined streets selling jungle vine extracts. 'Amazon pill meester? Very good price… \$500.'

The ageing Booth is trapped within the subtle light-creep of mortality in a photographic portrait. High cheekbones and frown lines like incisions for a botched facelift. Tight mouth muted in a neatly barbered beard. Waistcoat pulsing with constellations of tiny white points, a chainmail mesh under the best Irish tweed. The haunted expression is a rictus of caste. He has seen so much on his London walks, more than he could erase on the fifteen-day voyage to Pará. But the jungle he will never penetrate absorbs him. In the sudden, shrieking darkness it lets him know what is surely coming. The heavy tides of the London streets stall his progress. He is one of those urban witnesses that Rilke identifies: 'People who have been walking too long and simply stop.' It is more painful to be stopped than to be dead. Dead in life. But these compulsive tramps, mad for statistics, are worse than stopped, they are lost. After so many laborious circuits, the walk continues without the walker.

Born into a Liverpool family of corn traders in 1840, Booth took the company into the leather business, and then shipping. He opened up regular transatlantic routes to South America and down the Amazon to Iquitos. Alongside these mercantile activities, he spent much of his fortune on organising a comprehensive inquiry into the horrors of London. He was obsessed with the spectre of urban poverty, the jungle that might at any hour overwhelm us.

There is such morbid beauty in the 'Descriptive Maps of London Poverty' that illuminate the seventeen volumes of diligent statistical harvesting that comprise Charles Booth's *Life and Labour of the People of London*. The maps are strangely modern, anticipating digital captures of a self-revising topography. Painterly grids, stitched from numerous wearying journeys of research, solicit further journeys.

Reliable maps are the first requirement of the colonist. The lower depths of Victorian London, still unfathomed, were a potential resource. Religion was weaponised, the church had its armies of occupation. Booth's meticulously graded delineation of 'chronic want' converted 'vicious, semi-criminal' blots and pestilential 'dust holes' into attractive destinations for trespassers: journalists, missionaries, evangelical Christians, and lowlife novelists excited by evidence of blight; the sooty blush on the complexions of a tubercular workforce. Those canvas-backed classroom maps celebrating imperial trade routes were an inspiration. There was always somewhere to discover and to possess by force of arms. But who wants to voyage into local rumours of hunger and poverty? Who wants to peek into dark places stacked with the spectres of cruelly abandoned old age? And yet some primitive instinct draws us towards the cave of the 'lowest class' from which no light escapes, and from which it is almost impossible to ascend.

Arthur Morrison published his *Tales of Mean Streets* in 1894. 'But who knows the East End?' he wrote. 'A shocking place, where he once went with a curate; an evil plexus of slums that hide human creeping things; where filthy men and women live on penn'orths of gin... The East End is a place, says another, which is given over to the Unemployed.' Jack London shouldered his way into the territory as a muscular tourist in rag-and-bone-shop disguise, primed with notebook and camera, to make a documentary report, *The People of the Abyss*. A travel journal that behaves with all the swagger of fiction. The novels of George Gissing navigate the perimeter of ruin, the point at which a respectable clerk or jobbing author might fall through the colours of Booth's Poverty Map, from the purple of moderate comfort to the dark blue of shame. Curdled beer and butchery: the miasma of London poverty, carried on that dreaded 'wind from the east', was a singularity he was driven to explore and describe.

Taking up Booth's maps, we notice the fading of the City of London, the disappearance of Hyde Park, and the tactful erasure of the grim pan-opticon of Millbank Penitentiary. Acknowledged sites of recreation or containment are not required in this comprehensive survey. The river-side settlement, the walled City of investment, doesn't register on the

Poverty Map: *nobody lives there*. Nothing thrives except debt and credit. The products of the Amazon, of India and Ceylon – rubber, coffee, tea and cinchona – are traded in the Mincing Lane exchange. But those unmentionable activities are left as secure as the society gatherings in Julio Arana's palatial mansion.

A few paces away, through the portal of some tight alleyway, beyond the hustle and stink of a sprawling street market, colour begins: blues, purples and blacks. The immigrant quarter of Whitechapel is the authentic English jungle, a brick-built Amazonia with few exploitable resources apart from the hidden lives and habits of its voiceless tribal inhabitants. 'As there is a darkest Africa,' Booth wrote, 'is there not also a darkest England?'

It is no surprise, then, to discover that the intrepid London night-walker, in his other life as an exporter of skins and cured leather, the active director of a Liverpool shipping line, launched the first passenger service along the Amazon River. By 1900, at the height of the rubber boom, Booth's company ran fourteen ships. He was implicated in the economy of wilderness exploitation at the same time as he was casting light on the effects of this covert trade, plants and timber, on a city that was growing, hour by hour, like a proud cancer. The world's greatest port, as it knew itself, with its banks and temples and grand squares, was another exploded Iquitos, a riverside sink of shacks and shelters. And sea-coal-smoked slaves.

'I cursed every minute I gave to it,' said the exhausted Booth at the conclusion of his epic project, the most comprehensive private survey into London poverty ever undertaken. But he wanted, like Bunyan or Blake, to bring those labours to vision: 'so that the streets of Jerusalem may sing with joy'. In practical terms, Booth's persistence led, in 1908, to the introduction of a universal old age pension that would not be means tested.

Following on from the social scavenging of Henry Mayhew, Booth's largely self-initiated project was the encyclopaedic masterwork the century demanded. It refined and, to a significant degree, invented the academic discipline offered as inspiration to future generations. School Board Inspectors and police officers on the beat helped to fill the hundreds of notebooks Booth's willing volunteers brought back from the territory. One of them, George Duckworth, was Virginia Woolf's half-brother. The survey was sustained by a network of connections with the great and the good, facilitated by Booth's wife, Mary Macaulay: Beatrice Webb, Octavia Hill, Canon Samuel Barnett.

The first Poverty Map was coloured in 1888, the year of the Jack the Ripper murders. Booth himself, booted and bustling, set out from Toynbee Hall on Commercial Street to navigate the landscape in which the bodies of the mutilated victims were found. His assault troop of researchers, led and advised by native guides, those police officers and school inspectors, scribbled their documentary fictions.

> The native keeps to the back streets… You are robbed in the West India Dock Road: off goes the thief down Chasam Street, you follow and if you are close enough behind him can manage to land yourself in Chasam Place. There he suddenly disappears… The chief vices of the island are drink, gambling and betting, and thieving… Once anything is found lying about and portable not a boy would not try and remove it… There are no brothels in the island, the nearest approach is the presence of a few absent sailors wives.

Tightly packed notebook pages are dressed with local colour and moralising attitudes worthy of Seventh-day Adventists making their pitch for land to the Peruvian Corporation: with your generous help and support, we will cure the ungodly of their vices.

Deepwater docks are crowded with the militarised fleets of the East India Company, with West Indian sugar traders, and elegant tea clippers for the opium trade. Forests of masts thicker than the steeples of City churches. Minatory riverside warehouses are black cliffs scented with cinnamon and pepper, their exotic perfumes struggling to infiltrate the sulphurous gloom.

And it has never dispersed, this darkness, even under the multiple layers of future development. Pyramid towers and heritage museums will not hold back the creeping tide that threatens to overwhelm our thin veneer of civilisation. A savage otherness even afflicted a sensibility as fastidious as that of Henry James. Retreated to his Chelsea flat, 'the haunt of the sage and the seagull', the novelist suffered two strokes and became paralysed on the left side. His rooms, at No. 21 Carlyle Mansions, Cheyne Walk, were close enough to feel the traffic of the river. A friend reported that she heard James say, after he fell: 'It's the beast in the jungle, and it's sprung.'

CASEMENT'S CAMERA

'When I came back, I had become another man.'
   – Teodor von Martius, *Amazonas*

Photographs are negotiations lurid with consequence. With that blink of the shutter, image theft becomes a Faustian contract between twinned states of not-knowing; between being alive (but never quite sure of it) *and at the same time* fixed in the absolute certainty of death. Nothingness.

The film we have chosen to watch on this particular evening flows steadily on for just as long as we let it, then fades to reverie, underpinned by an urge to misremember. To improve and re-edit. So we shut off, micro-doze on the sofa, and drop into deeper regions of trance, before some unanticipated action brings us sharply out of it with the revelation that *we are seeing what we already know*. This thing has happened many times before.

Attracted by the concept of parallel voyages down the same river at different eras, I was looking once again at Ciro Guerra's *Embrace of the Serpent*. The base narrative – steady drift with staged interruptions exposing the defining dramas of Amazonian colonialism – rubber plantations, fever priests, messianic cults and ayahuasca quests – is derived, as the film's director tells us, from the travel journals of the anthropologist Theodor Koch-Grünberg (1879–1924) and the Harvard ethnobotanist Richard Evans Schultes (1915–2001). 'These diaries,' Guerra says, 'are the only known accounts of many Amazonian cultures.'

Shock waves from previously attempted river trips spill over subsequent voyagers like unnoticed viral blessings: the bad thing waits, hovering over a surface barely disturbed by the dip of paddles, without impatience. Until that moment on the rocks when, coming ashore, the boatman pauses and rests, exposing the scars on his naked back. He has recognised this location, under this configuration of stars, as a recurring point of origin.

In *Embrace of the Serpent*, Jan Bijvoet, as the fictional character derived from Koch-Grünberg, has become a Beckettian husk wrestling an insane accumulation of evidence – baskets, artefacts, specimens, tools, journals, sketchbooks – through swamps and over slithery stones. He knows that he is mad but he husbands the memories of the horrors he has suffered. They are all that is left of the person who set out. The archival cargo must be brought safely back. 'Leaving them is leaving everything.' The objects in their heavy boxes have become the only tenuous link with Germany, his dream of home. More dead than alive now, the wildly bearded actor (possessed by the unquiet fetch of the historic man) is shuddered into a simulacrum of robotic animation when his guide, Karamakate, a warrior-shaman, blows powder up his flaring nostrils.

Rattling with malarial tremors, the explorer washes a photographic plate in the river. It is a portrait, a capture of Karamakate, defacing the thin glass. These plates, Ciro Guerra said, are the only record of the existence of the people of the forest. They were the inspiration for his film: frozen stares of confrontation, outside linear time. Richard Evans Schultes, following Koch-Grünberg's traces, accumulated his own monumental photographic record with his Rolleiflex. Now, channelling this image stream, Guerra launched his film of record. Recording what never happened, twice.

The photographic plate, distorted or revealed by the force of the clear water, was the splinter in my eye. When I witnessed the actor, I also witnessed some other reluctant memory, a confrontation previously experienced and buried, or yet to happen. A child being bathed in the river, held under, drowned or baptised.

Karamakate is alarmed by the vision. 'It's me.'

'It's not you. It's an image of you.'

The indigenous guide turns the plate over, to see what is on the back. He recognises the emerging duplicate as a *chullachaqui*, a replica. Something that looks like the subject, but is hollow, empty. A shell left to wander the world without volition.

When Ashaninka villagers are confronted by an importunate stranger that person should know that it is advisable to lay out goods, weapons, cameras and gifts, for inspection. The warriors circle slowly. They choose certain items to touch and stroke. To sniff. Then they walk behind the stranger, who must not move, not a muscle. The villagers need to be sure that this unknown being has a solid back. He is not hollow. So we were advised by our guides. So it was reported in the old journals. A *chullachaqui* has no personal memory. It floats through the world like one of the undead. It is lost and abandoned in a time without time.

The only immortal spirit, which is the spirit of place, moves through many bodies, many lives. Invaders try to protect themselves with cameras, guns and sketchbooks; futile attempts to register and categorise a landscape with no need of their witness. A second Eden from which they have, according to their own superstitions, been expelled.

On his last expedition, sinking into malarial nightmares which would only conclude with his death, Koch-Grünberg travelled with the cinematographer Silvino Santos and the American physician Alexander Hamilton Rice. The material they brought back was edited into a film called *On the Trail of El Dorado*. This latest gold hunt, funded by what David Grann in *The Lost City of Z* calls Rice's 'bottomless bank account', was a comprehensive, quasi-military invasion involving teams of experts, new wireless radio systems and an 'oak-propeller hydroplane with a complete set of aerial cameras'. Whatever slumbering ghosts were left under the jungle canopy were expelled by the pioneer eye-in-the-sky surveillance sweep of Dr Rice's hydroplane.

'The expedition, despite the unfortunate death of Koch-Grünberg, was a historic achievement,' Grann concluded. The previous travelogue by Silvino Santos, *No país das Amazonas* (1922), was sponsored by J.C. Araújo, a Manaus company with substantial interests across the Amazon region. The film was blatant propaganda for river traffic and the good life of the rubber plantations. Industry was progress. Brazil accepted modernity with arms wide open like the statue of Christ the Redeemer in Rio de Janeiro.

After the episode with the photographic plate in the river, a symbolic drowning of the near-naked Karamakate, and after the refusal of a necklace offered by Jan Bijvoet (as 'Teodor von Martius'), a necklace that was never his to give, the intertwined river journeys of *Embrace of the Serpent* flow into one: revelation of the site of revelation. And power of vision by ingestion of the vine, *caapi* or ayahuasca.

'It is not possible for me to know,' wrote Koch-Grünberg, 'if the infinite jungle has started on me the process that has taken many others that have ventured into these lands, to complete and irremediable insanity… All I know is that, like all those who have shed the thick veil that blinded them, when I came back to my senses, I had become another man.'

The second traveller, Richard Evans Schultes, following Koch-Grünberg down the river, was followed, in his turn, by a character who does not feature in the Guerra film: William Seward Burroughs. Schultes graduated from Harvard a year after Burroughs, the invisible student. The future addict-author was already proposing a man who made up memories to order. 'He guarantees you'll believe they happened just that way.'

The Harvard alumni enjoyed a brief correspondence in the aftermath of a chance meeting in Bogota, where Schultes was carrying out research into the effectiveness of hallucinogenic plants. In an episode reported by Burroughs in *The Yage Letters*, Schultes is lightly disguised, to protect his professional status, as 'Doctor Schindler'. Schindler is part of a phantom programme initiated by 'a U.S. Agricultural Commission'. From as early as 1942, the questing academic was gainfully employed as field agent for the government's Rubber Development Corporation. A subsequent Guggenheim Foundation Fellowship funded practical research into Amazonian ethnobotany. These backcountry expeditions convinced Schultes to predict the coming destruction of the rainforest and the irreversible disappearance of plant species, animals and indigenous people.

Burroughs asked about yage.

'Oh yes, we have specimens here. Come along and I'll show you.' The doctor had sampled the vine. 'I got colours but no visions.'

For Burroughs the vine was the grail. He was a compulsive travel snapper. There are many captures of him wielding his camera, or with it draped around his neck on its thong, like the jaguar-tooth ornamentation worn by Teodor von Martius in the Guerra film. But there are no photographs in the original 1963 City Lights edition of *The Yage Letters*. The cover illustration of a *curandero* from the Vaupes region of Colombia is reprinted by permission of the Botanical Museum of Harvard. Was it taken by Schultes? Co-author Allen Ginsberg's ink drawing of 'The Great Being' (an eye surrounded by flying fish and plant tendrils) looks like a page from the fictional sketchbook created for von Martius in *Embrace of the Serpent*.

Schindler refutes the Burroughs suggestion that yage could prove a sacrament for telepathy. 'That's all imagination, of course.' But the spectral writer persists. Over the coming decades he refines his theory of the 'image vine': how one image placed next to any other in a twisted DNA chain, snapshots taped to the peeling wall of the latest flop, proposes a narrative. Anywhere leads to everywhere. Like the word, the image is a virus. What Burroughs brings back from his encounter with Schultes is the inside skinny on the corrupt liaison between multinational pharmaceutical giants, Ivy League colleges and the juiciest ethnobotanical research grants. As he lays out in *Blade Runner: A Movie*, numerous discoveries made in the Amazon, natural medicines more effective than anything industrially manufactured, were ignored, suppressed or subverted.

> In 1956 a contraceptive drug developed by the Amazon Indians was submitted to an American drug company for testing and eventual distribution. One dose prevents pregnancy for seven years… Here we have a precise method of population control, at a time when overpopulation is an ever more urgent problem. Drug companies rejected the drug, since it would cut their profits. They could sell a pill a day forever, so who wanted to know about a Pill that lasts for seven years?

Much of the underlying tension, never openly expressed, between Arthur Sinclair and Alexander Ross, on the survey of 1891 with which they had been jointly tasked, involved cameras. Ross, who was never credited in my great-grandfather's reminiscences of Ceylon, was a fellow planter. And perhaps a rival. The younger man was hungry for miles to cover, facts to be verified. Ross kept and protected his own journals. But it was Sinclair who came back from Peru with pictorial evidence to support his version of their adventure. He returned with the camera he had used. It was given the status of a family relic, and passed from son to grandson (two more Arthurs). Ross suffered the loss of his archive boxes in an unfortunate accident. Glass negatives were smashed. Portraits of persons and landscapes were drowned beside rare plant specimens.

In a lecture entitled 'Exploration of the Amazonian Provinces of Central Peru', read before the Philosophical Society of Glasgow on 5 April 1893, Ross explained how the expedition had successfully crossed the Chanchamayo River on a wire suspension bridge, 'wide enough for a mule to pass, but extremely shaky'. The disaster occurred on a similar bridge over the Tulumayo River.

> The muleteer stupidly allowed two of the pack mules to try and cross together, with the result that the one carrying two air-tight boxes, in which were all my papers, books, camera, and dry plates, tumbled into the river. The poor beast was swept down several hundred yards and drowned, while the boxes were got out some hours afterwards, battered out of shape, the locks intact, but the contents in a state of pulp. The camera came to pieces in my hands, as did a new roll-holder containing films, with some valuable negatives, while many of the packets of dry plates had burst, exposing their contents to the light. Hence the want of better photographs than I have to illustrate this lecture.

Lectures by returning travellers were a highly competitive form. The talk became the accepted history of a now fabulous experience. Arthur Sinclair, always prepared to perform, with or without images, journeyed to Melbourne as barker for the Peruvian Corporation. He was tasked with boosting the economic possibilities of the coffee colonies on the Perené, finding investors and enticing young men to strike out for a second chance. At the other end of the social scale, he was looking for coolies and plantation labourers.

The manager of the Peruvian Corporation lent Ross a collection of slides, so that he could demonstrate the advance of civilisation by way of the new railway over the mountains. The planter filled out his programme by cobbling together a few other photographs, 'mostly taken by myself', and assembled from the 'second journey' of investigation, the one that followed the joint exploration of the Perené. Beyond the rapids, and the desertion of the bearers, the story was all his own. Arthur had collapsed, falling from his mule, on the return journey over the Andes. He convalesced in Lima, with subsequent visits to accessible haciendas, and tours of burial mounds along the coastal regions. Time to read up on history. And write.

I was summoned to meet the last Arthur Sinclair, my father's first cousin, in his southwest London semi-detached house, shortly after my marriage to Anna, and our provisional perching in a single Hampstead room. Arthur lived with Iris, his second wife and former tennis partner, not too far from Wimbledon, where they had enjoyed some success in a doubles tournament sponsored by the *Evening Standard*. There are no photographs of the occasion and my memories now are as much of the interminable drive across town and the unlikelihood of the encounter as of our conversation and the meal we did or did not enjoy. The invitation came, I suspect, because my father, in his retirement, had reached that stage of life where he was looking back. He had begun a project of re-establishing contact with whatever remained of his Scottish family, with the unspoken subtext of accessing any information to be had about the explorer, the legendary grandfather. He had already made package trips to Sri Lanka and Peru, but not to the remote headwaters of the Upper Amazon. Something unfinished was worrying at him. The hours he worked were long. He was often called out at night. There had never been enough time to get to the bottom of the story.

Arthur's surprising telephone interruption, a shouted summons to the communal, overheard-by-all phone at the bottom of the Hampstead stairs, was also about London. He was both welcoming and testing us: would we stay, become part of the money machine, or would we weaken and move on? My relative commuted to the City, a Mincing Lane tea broker, still in the old family trade, working in the offices where he met his wife.

We must have passed the audition. We were invited, now with children in tow, to stay for a night at their retirement property on a hill overlooking the sea in Salcombe, on our way to a holiday bungalow on a Devon farm. Arthur's tennis days were done, but Iris, much younger and childless, was still active on court. She was a little nervous of the invading Sinclair horde; our troop of five had been joined, unexpectedly, by my parents. Extreme cleaning and polishing, along with questions of what the children would eat and where they would sleep, took their toll on Iris, an affectionate woman not quite sure how this great gathering of the generations was to be managed.

Anna remembers: the sea. A short walk on the next morning. The irritated waves. She remembers how, after the meal and getting the children to bed, we were sharing a convivial bath. Iris rattled at the door, announcing that she needed, urgently, to search the medicine cabinet. She was obliterated by a tumultuous migraine. And I remember the tour Arthur gave to show off possessions inherited from his namesake. It was not so much the books and papers, this time, as the objects: a brass telescope, a cigar-cutter, and a number of vintage cameras. One in particular, burnished and restored, had been carried into the Peruvian jungle.

After the substantial Salcombe property had been divided, and the collection rationalised, Arthur died. In due course, Iris moved to a manageable flat in a Hampshire retirement home. Once a year, in December, we had a long telephone chat – first Anna and then myself – with a person we liked but scarcely knew. In a room we pictured but never visited. Iris said that she couldn't look after all the things that Arthur had accumulated over the years, but she did have the explorer's camera. Her husband had said that he wanted me to have it. To pass it on, eventually, to my son, to William. And there was something else: the camera had film inside. There were images from Peru that had never been printed.

The exchange did not happen. Cards stopped coming. Iris was no longer available when we tried to call. In the end, thanks to Anna's persistence, we discovered that the old lady, fading fast, had been moved to another place, but the managers of the home were unable or unwilling to give out the address. 'For her protection,' they said. It took months, identifying ourselves to solicitors, providing papers and documentation, to track down the final address. Iris had died. Arthur's camera disappeared with her effects and mementos.

But as my great-grandfather's much-travelled camera vanished, another instrument, responsible for a catalogue of vivid and challenging images from Amazonia and the Congo, was acquired by the Kerry County Museum in Tralee. This camera became part of a display assembled to celebrate the legacy of the man put ashore on Banna Strand in 1916: the former British diplomat and civil servant Sir Roger Casement. 'If you ask,' Vargas Llosa tells us, 'you can also see the overcoat of rough wool he wore on the German U-19 submarine that brought him to Ireland.'

In the ghostly film footage of Casement at his desk, and in the snatched newspaper pictures of the fallen 'traitor' processing stiff-backed towards trial and execution, you have the lineaments of a consummate performer folded tightly in on himself before curtain call. Just another Irish sacrifice in the wake of Wilde; the inspiration for future myths of honour and betrayal. Casement's life, as we unpick it now, is all surface and disguise. There is a jousting relationship with Conrad; two investors in imperial cruelty, two calculated beards, their paths crossing in the Congo in June 1890. Conrad made a telling withdrawal from Casement's store of darkness, his handsome dealings with morality and corruption. The records he kept, the photographs and the diaries (even if they had to be forged and completed by others). The necessity of getting the story, at all costs, back to civilisation, readers still open to shock and surprise.

Conrad would finesse the impressions he gathered into the deeper truth of fiction, but he declined to involve himself in Casement's political crusades. When the moment of crisis came for this 'limpid personality with a touch of Conquistador', the arrest on the shore, the calvary of

Pentonville, the exiled Polish author, with his unyielding mask, refused to put his name to a petition for clemency.

He preferred to craft, in a letter passing the responsibility on to R.B. Cunninghame Graham, a portrait of Casement that reads like a film synopsis: 'I have seen him start off into an unspeakable wilderness swinging a crookhandled stick for all weapons, with two bull-dogs... at his heels and a Loanda boy carrying a bundle for all company. A few months afterwards it so happened that I saw him come out again, a little leaner, a little browner, with his stick, dogs, and Loanda boy, and quietly serene as though he had been for a stroll in a park.'

My great-grandfather's camera, which had acquired for me a magical status, was gone, sunk into the subterranea of provincial dealers, junkshops or costive private collectors, from which, one day, it might re-emerge, drained of its venom. Film removed, exposed, neutralised. Casement's camera was a quasi-Catholic relic, churched in a tourist museum. The captures made on the instrument that accompanied him into the forest, along with his black notebooks, his bulldogs and faithful boy, have been preserved, assessed and catalogued by the National Photographic Archive in Dublin.

What potential image vines, as Burroughs would see them, are here! What devastating consequence when any two photographs are placed side by side on a table! In making a selection from such titles – 'House at the edge of a jungle in Brazil', 'Group of tribesmen from the Putamayo performing a ritual dance in costume', 'Man and three boys, two holding rifles, in the Putamayo region', 'Man with pouch around his neck and holding spear, in the Putamayo' – the dutiful researcher is already shaping a legend of his own desires. Photographs are confessions made in public. The glazed stare of nakedly exposed victims who can never escape. The denied motion implied in a frozen frame's permanently stopped momentum. From these portraits the dark matter of the 'black' diaries can be invented. Some prints document the atrocities of colonialism. Others nominate one riverside set against all other possibilities. There are 110 items in the collection. The bones of a novel are scattered in a vitrine, open to any casual visitor with a reader's ticket.

But the photographer is also the subject of his own photographs. Every exposure is an autobiography. In his wicker chair under a tree older than Heaven, hat balanced on knee, stick at his right hand, Casement is primed to spring up and march away. But, for the moment, you could say that he is planted. He ponders that word, *plantation*. It invokes not only the savage reality of the Putamayo rubber colonies, but the migration of a disaffected or expelled tribe: the Plantation of Ulster. And the seeding of generations of blood feud and political conflict. Half a million colonists decamped, many from Scottish highlands, into the arable counties of the north. Roger Casement, as a boy, was returned to Ireland, planted with paternal relatives in County Armagh, and educated at the Diocesan School in Ballymena.

In Africa, brooding under the tree of forbidden knowledge, Casement recalls or anticipates, as darkness falls, a procession of still photographs flickering into a form of primitive cinema.

(1) A barechested youth lounging provocatively against a rough wall. In a bleached landscape of stones and cacti.

(2) The half-completed or half-destroyed buildings of a coffee plantation, barracks or slave house.

(3) The rear view of a young boy, naked, displaying his wounds, while another man, trousers rolled, seated on a log, faces the camera.

(4) A frowning man in striped workshirt. A day labourer, cradling his own or a borrowed child.

(5) A warrior with sling, spear and scrotal pouch, staring off to the right, into the shadows of the trees.

(6) Two nude warriors with thin rifles. Between them, an unweaponed boy. Behind them, a man in white shirt and hat.

(7) A shaman/warrior brandishing a clump of vegetation on a long stick.

(8) An overseer, unyielding, thumbs in thick belt.

(9) An indigenous river pilot, in borrowed nautical cap, posing at the rail, a prehistoric fish in his left hand.

The Dublin photographs recalled my excitement at finding a pack of inscrutable postcards at the time when I was beginning to feel my way into the estuarine tales of *Downriver*. The cards were described, in the first chapter, as being on display in a pub called The World's End, alongside the Thames in Tilbury. Angela Carter called the cards 'unutterably strange'. But she guessed, quite correctly, that they were the key to this novel: 'at the end of time... in a city of the near future with a hallucinatory resemblance to London'. I knew that too. And I made the connection with my great-grandfather shipping out from Tilbury to the colonies. The postcards were illustrations for a book that was still to be written, but which had already been lived.

One of the volumes the *Downriver* scavengers dig out from a terminal Tilbury Riverside junkshop is *In Tropical Lands: Recent Travels to the Sources of the Amazon, the West Indian Islands, and Ceylon* by Arthur Sinclair.

———

Now it all makes perfect no-sense. The postcards outlive the perpetrators. Stories form and reform like tributaries cursed with never finding their way back to the main stream, the great brown river. Casement's Secret State interrogators fabricating their own version of history, and assisting the condemned man towards his preordained martyrdom, persuaded him to draw a treasure map. Major Frank Hall, the MI5 operative code-named 'Q', dictated an accompanying note, confirming that the traitor's valuables were to be divided up among his interrogators. Two members of the Royal Irish Constabulary, proudly packing their 'British Bull Dog' Webleys, received £50 in gold and silver coins. But that bounty was nothing in comparison to the £10,000 Kerry County Museum paid to acquire Casement's '*Treasure Island*-style' map at auction in Cheltenham.

Drawing not only on Stevenson's frontispiece sketch of 'Skeleton Island', but also on his Congo acquaintance, Joseph Conrad, Casement doodled a map to show where he had buried gold, intended to arm Irish revolutionaries, on windswept Banna Strand. Consciously or unconsciously, he was invoking *Nostromo*.

> 'Señora, shall I tell you where the treasure is? To you alone… Shining! Incorruptible!'…
> 'No, Capataz,' she said. 'No one misses it now. Let it be lost for ever.'

GUANO

'Howard and George observe the Chinese passengers on the lower deck. The Chinese are chasing the gold rush.'
— Mark Blacklock, *Hinton*

Arthur admired the Chinese. As reliable workers on the Ceylon coffee plantations and as independent business folk in the settlements of Peru: they grafted, they thrived. Hospitality was a requirement. Chinese families cooked whatever they had for itinerant guests. These meals were appreciated and reported in Arthur's letters. My great-grandfather never missed an opportunity of comparing and contrasting Chinese and Peruvian national characters. The Chinese were industrious, uncomplaining and smart – basically, Scots Presbyterians in disguise. Peruvians (apart from potato-cultivating Andean highlanders) were slippery Catholics, or wilderness innocents who had been, misguidedly, entrusted with the keys to the primal Garden. In every town and two-mule village, Arthur noted priest-bedevilled drinkers of ungodly potions, and sallow invertebrates sprawled on benches, thirsty for a dole of shade against unearned sunshine. The inbred inheritors of Spanish colonialism, occupiers of estates, did little, existing in palatial squalor: gilded thrones with steaming pigshit on the floor. A spineless and corrupted race of music-hall captains and avaricious tax gatherers.

Years later, in Melbourne, Arthur made headlines in the local press when he intervened to prevent a rude Australian on horseback from whipping a Chinese pedestrian out of his path. Commentators were astonished. This visiting Scotsman might as well have championed an expendable Aboriginal. Or a rabid dingo.

What Arthur did not advertise – and how much he knew is unclear – were the rings of hell, lifted from Dante, of the Chincha Islands off Peru's desert coast; smouldering ridges and dank caves of seabird droppings; stinking guano beds where indentured Chinese immigrants, tied in debt peonage to eight-year contracts, slaved to supply the mainspring of the nation's wealth. And, in time, to bolster the hefty portfolio of the Peruvian Corporation of London. Profits from the guano trade underwrote silver mines and railways. 100,000 Chinese coolies suffered to forge that economic miracle. In clusters, straining, lifting, hammering, they drew shining metal lines across the map. They endured, or they ran away; only to be hunted down like convicts, and returned to whippings and torture, or another successful escape by suicide.

The earlier Andean people understood the value of the accumulated droppings of gulls and cormorants and boobies. Their use of a god-given resource was ecologically sound. They collected guano, rich in nitrogen, phosphate and potassium, as a fertiliser. For thousands of years, they improved the soil and fed their potato beds. The Incas restricted access to the islands and punished, with death, those who disturbed the nesting birds.

A balance was maintained, between resource harvesting and species protection, until 1802, when the Prussian geographer Alexander von Humboldt, visiting Callao, began investigating the exploitable properties of guano, and composing a report intended for European readers. Young Arthur Sinclair, with his garden earnings, bought a copy of von Humboldt's *Essay on the Geography of Plants* and revised his own territorial ambitions. The Andes infected his imagination.

But guano had other properties: it was a valuable ingredient in the manufacture of gunpowder. A theoretical potential for mass destruction had to be put to the test with war games and border squabbles. Empire-building ambitions wildfired out from barren rocks of compacted bird-shit. But it was the arrival of commercial whaling that triggered the chain reaction that led to the War of the Pacific (1879–1884). Whaling ships, engaging in trade with Peru, were returning with their holds half-empty. Francisco Quirós y Ampudia, a farsighted man of business, negotiated a sweetheart deal between a merchant house in Liverpool, a group of French investors, and the Peruvian government. It was agreed to make all guano beds a resource of the State.

Guano was exported in bulk to Europe. One of the potential consequences, it has been suggested, was that a containable strain of potato blight from the Andean Highlands, a contributing element to the Irish Potato Famine, was a stowaway in the whalers' hold. If imported fertiliser did indeed inflict collateral damage, there is some relevance for Arthur's history. Without question, the blight reached Scotland, nudging small farmers and cottars into abandoning their land and shipping out as colonists, planters and adventurers. The devastation of my great-grandfather's potato patch in the corner of a highland field was perhaps delivered from the country where he would make a final push towards mending his ruined fortune.

The Chincha Islands were worked to exhaustion. Such was the never satisfied malignancy of capital: it devoured its own entrails, bile and blood, dung and gristle. Rich in elements, guano's prime selling point was the blessing of rapid decay. It transformed itself, promiscuously, sculpting new combinations from its acidic properties. The bounty of the avian sewage farm was initially quarried by transported Africans – until the point was reached when profits accrued in dealings with Europe began to be exploited, for strategic reasons, as a means of offering a measure of freedom to 25,000 slaves. In their place came desperate Chinese labourers, many duped into believing that they had arrived not at a Devil's Island of lung-shredding dust but at the Californian gold mines. Some of the incomers were buried alive in landslides of guano, others fell into the ocean and drowned. They were a cheap resource and could, quite legitimately, be worked to death. Guano is a welcoming host for parasites: it harbours *Histoplasma capsulatum*, a fungus causing histoplasmosis in humans and animals. Histoplasmosis, as William Burroughs, hauling up his tangled vine of images, appreciated, is the first symptom of HIV/AIDS.

Investment is insatiable. There can never be too much. But it comes with a fabulous menu of evil indications and freeloading viruses. The War of the Pacific was madness, operatic gestures of pride leading to dire political consequences. One-sided naval engagements and Fred

Karno armies butchered with real weapons. Bolivia lost her access to the Pacific. Her ally, Peru, robbed of the birdshit bank, crashed her investments. Chile's coffers groaned, as taxes poured in from newly acquired territory. Peru defaulted on railway bonds and found herself deep in hock to foreign bankers. The government was obliged to give up vast tranches of fertile land they had never adequately mapped to the Peruvian Corporation of London. The Corporation moved smoothly from guano to railways.

The expedition on which they sent Arthur Sinclair and Alexander Ross would survey the potential for industrial-scale exploitation of the cloud forest. The original contract, in the Spanish language, lost somewhere in the voluptuary bureaucracy of Lima, was found in London, among the archives of the Corporation, held in Kew. It was copied and carried away by my daughter. Farne assembled the tragic documents in convenient files, so that they could be brought with us when we travelled to Ashaninka settlements on the banks of the Perené. It was not yet clear what possible reparation we could make.

TASMANIA

'Dissonance is produced by any landscape that enchants in the present but has been a site of violence in the past.'
   – Robert Macfarlane, *Underland*

For ten years, having returned to his homeland, 'with considerable financial interests in Ceylon', Arthur Sinclair 'extracted as much enjoyment out of life as perhaps falls to the lot of ordinary unambitious mortals'. This boasted lack of ambition is an obvious authorial feint and not to be taken seriously. But the modesty was genuine: the modesty of a man of means who will spend much of the spare time that accrues from the neurosis of constant travel, close observation and the compilation of reports, in writing about himself and his adventures. *Without giving anything away.* Without pain, or doubt, or dark-night-of-the-soul. Without family crises. 'Monotonous as the work seemed to many, to me it was a daily delight.' In Ceylon, on a remote estate, Arthur had discovered the hermit's secret: elective tedium. Invariable labour. Sleep. Then more of the same. The words mount up. The crops flourish. But he retired.

If he stayed in motion for ten years, jolted on horseback from plantation to plantation, now he would vegetate in one place for the same length of time, recovering that tentative faith in ownership his highland ancestors had lost. Did he have the store of years left to learn that you have to be born to creative indolence, to the art of living on your land values and investments? It takes generations of inbreeding to be fit for staring across a breakfast table, at rods of black rain pricking the estate, without the reflex compulsion to spring up and out. The yawn of aristocratic ennui is hard won. It smells of wet spaniel, steaming horse tweed and cold untouched kedgeree.

There are no great revelations, post-mortem, in any life. What does the published Arthur Sinclair 'In Memoriam' of 1905 have to tell about those years of rehearsed retirement? Nothing. At the final reckoning, with so much ground to cover, so many voyages, the Scottish return is a sequence of coloured postcards, census forms and changing addresses: waiting on inevitable disaster. In the photograph that accompanies the obituary tribute, Arthur is crinkled in that smile of secret knowledge while pretending to read a folded newspaper. One of his own field reports? The delight, at this achieved retirement of which he speaks, is palpable.

> A most engaging conversationalist, Mr Sinclair was never happier than when describing to his friends the rare plant life of the many distant portions of the world he had seen. He was a Fellow of the Linnean Society and a Fellow of the Royal Colonial Institute. He was a Liberal in politics.

As we have seen in the photograph on the lavatory wall, Arthur's family is strategically positioned across the grass in front of Banff Castle, an arrangement of achieved possessions: sons and daughters, nursemaid and babe, with a status almost equal to the rocking-horse. The small print in the *Observer* is a struggle. Soon there will be banner headlines. There is a dark shadow creeping across the investment horizon like those minatory 'drops of soot' on the young planter's original potato patch.

> *At the end of this time I fell amongst thieves, and as misfortunes rarely come single, the* Hemileia *must needs play havoc with securities in Ceylon at the same time, so that I began to look abroad again for investments and occupation, resulting in a trip to* Tasmania, *an adventure often talked of with friends now gone.*

Subtle plagues wait quietly for their moment, some unaccountable episode of interspecies transmission. Fungal karma: the obliteration of holdings inspired an ill-judged and ruinous search for gold. The attempt was too blatant. Wealth, as Victorian novels imply, should arrive slowly and steadily, through the generations. You don't just shovel it out of the ground, out of land occupied by others. The blind strike at Tasmania cost Arthur most of his remaining reserves, and set him up for the final punt, out by rail from Lima, then by mule to the far side of the Andes.

Accessible sources offer sparse information on the gold-prospecting venture. 'He made a trip to Australia,' admitted the memorial tribute. Arthur's own summary in his brown-paper 1900 autobiography is almost as terse.

> *My prospecting during these three years cost me over £2000, money not by any means wasted, as I gained in return a more thorough knowledge of this beautiful, if in many respects over-rated and sadly misguided island than many of the natives possess, and learned to appreciate better our own beautiful native land on which there is yet ample room.*

———

John Ferguson's account of *Ceylon in 1883* outlines the disaster that struck the coffee harvest, but he is obliged to give the episode a positive spin. 'The present financial depression and scarcity of capital in Ceylon can readily be understood when a succession of four bad seasons, involving a deficiency in the planters' harvest equal to five million pounds sterling, are taken into consideration. There have been periods of depression before.'

A classic boom and bust cycle. And an invitation for those with deep pockets to hold their nerve. 'Wild speculation' is treated as a meteorological condition. 'Financial shock' as an earth tremor. 'A London capitalist, who visited the island, said the most striking picture of woe-begone misery he saw was the typical "man who owned a coffee estate". Yet this was followed by good seasons and bounteous coffee harvests.'

Arthur pincers his open newspaper against the offshore breeze and never hazards an emotion beyond his standard enigmatic smile.

> The colonists who make fortunes in the island do not think of making it their permanent home... The 'accumulated profits' made during the

time of prosperity, which at home form a reserve fund of local wealth to enable the sufferer from present adversity to benefit by past earnings, are utterly wanting in Ceylon… Ceylon, in fact, is a sort of 'incubator' to which capitalists send their eggs to be hatched, and whence they receive from time to time an abundant brood, leaving us but the shells for our local portion.

On permanent display: the golden eggs of an asset-stripping colonial culture. Transport moored. Treasure in London vaults.

Money has been sent here to fell our forests and plant them with coffee, and it has been returned in the shape of copious harvests to the home capitalist, leaving us in some cases the bare hill-sides from whence these rich harvests were drawn.

Having critiqued the failure of European investors and profit takers to adequately engage with the island, Ferguson arrives at an unexpected conclusion. The true profit was for the humble plantation labourers, Tamils from Southern India who were 'saved from starvation' by the generosity of estate owners.

No wonder that to such a people the planting country of Ceylon, when all was prosperous, was an El Dorado, for each family could there earn from 9s. to 12s. per week, and save half to three-quarters the amount… Nor ought we to forget the Tamil Cooly Mission which is doing a good work in educating and Christianizing many amongst the coolies, mainly supported as it is by the planters.

Ferguson goes on to quote Sir Edward Creasy: 'I have seen more human misery in a single winter's day in London, than I have seen during my nine years' stay in Ceylon.'

If Ceylon was a logical destination, Tasmania was a mid-life crisis, representing the pivotal moment when Arthur decides not so much to prospect for gold as to write about it, to surf the prevailing fashions of nineteenth-century fiction. It feels as if, brooding in his chair on the grass in Scotland, dozing off, making indecipherable notes, he turns to a pile of romances. The broken world is better viewed as a novel.

I discovered, among Arthur's late-century books with their decorative covers, *The City of Gold* by W.H. Davenport Adams. A stepped Mayan temple, in gilded relief, emerges from an unyielding jungle. Here, already, are the base elements of the journey that Arthur is dreaming and which he must one day take. The intoxicated abundance of the forest – 'masses of glorious foliage… a girdle of gardens, orchards, plantations of agave, and fields of maize, so richly studded with luxuriant flowers that the whole seemed a fairy-land of bloom' – was offering access, the right invader at the right time, to the promised goal. 'To retreat was not less difficult or dangerous than to advance; and with a firm countenance and a steady step they continued their march towards the Golden City.'

Tasmania is as far as you can go without passing into the polar ocean. Robert Louis Stevenson, in the years before he transported his tubercular lungs to the leper colonies of the South Seas, was lodged with his family in a highland cottage at Braemar, Aberdeenshire, where his stepson, Lloyd Osborne, sketched the outline of an island. Myth would have this holiday vision as the germ of *Treasure Island*. Stevenson made additions and improvements, but the map he provided for the frontispiece of the first edition in 1883 was lost, either in the post or among business papers at the offices of Cassell & Co. in London. A second version had to be supplied, lacking some of the inspiration of the original: a black border more like a hole burnt in the paper. The map provoked the words that follow:

> The next morning we fell early to work, for the transportation of this great mass of gold near a mile by land to the beach.

The first Stevenson map, on a scale of three English miles, was never found. And that, Arthur came to realise, at the conclusion of all his venturing, was the best definition of treasure: an imaginary fortune that can never, and should never, be excavated. The treasure is the journey towards it.

As much as anything now, Arthur was intoxicated by the contract between island and gold. Had he read 'The Gold-Bug' by Edgar Allan Poe? 'He was of an ancient Huguenot family, and had once been wealthy; but a series of misfortunes had reduced him to want.' And, in consequence, Mr William Legrand, like my great-grandfather, is tempted to find himself a 'very singular' island. Poe's creatures dig, they discover a treasure. 'The chest had been full to the brim... There was not one particle of silver. All was gold...'

Sun gods. Gold-plated saints and madonnas. Gold fillings wrenched from the mouths of the dead.

But Arthur was no 'amateur emigrant', he was a hardened professional; so much of his life had been spent in transit; reading, talking, sending letters to newspapers. If an account of the missing Tasmanian years could be located somewhere, we would have the romance of gold: my great-grandfather's *Nostromo*. He was beginning to understand, along with the circulation of ocean currents, the base equations of capital.

Gold was the catalytic agent. The opening up of a richly yielding gold mine at Mount Morgan in Queensland in 1882 made its primary owner, William Knox D'Arcy, a very rich man. He reverse immigrated – as Arthur had done, after his modest success in Ceylon – to set himself up in the grand style in London. And like the Spaniards of old, he had his profits shipped back in the form of gold bars. But profit is restless: D'Arcy used some of his accumulated small change to acquire oil leases in Persia. 'His company, the Anglo-Persian Oil Company,' as Jim Richards explains in *Gold Rush*, 'went on to become British Petroleum – founded on Australian gold.' Colonial dividends, at the end of one century, biased towards the trading houses of the City of London, secured profitable geo-political interventions – burning wells, leaking tankers, terrorist 'outrages', disorientated whales swimming up the Thames – for the next.

Tasmania was the redacted chapter, the broken link invalidating the genetic chain that led back to essential truths about my great-grandfather. Three years after Arthur Sinclair published *In Tropical Lands*, a much more significant title came to the attention of the reading public: *The War of the Worlds* by H.G. Wells. A title that invited constant re-invention and misinterpretation. The invasion metaphors were too tempting. Wells begins: 'With infinite complacency men went to and fro over this globe about their little affairs, serene in their assurance of their empire over matter.'

The master of prophetic fiction goes on to explain, in his preamble, that we should consider this attack from Mars in the light of our own neurotic compulsion to attack, possess, and convert. The Martians, like colonists in Ceylon and Peru, considered earth dwellers as aboriginals, 'inferior animals'.

'And before we judge them too harshly we must remember what ruthless and utter destruction our own species has wrought, not only upon animals, such as the vanished bison and the dodo, but upon inferior races,' Wells writes. 'The Tasmanians, in spite of their human likeness, were entirely swept out of existence in a war of extermination waged by European immigrants, in the space of fifty years. Are we such apostles of mercy as to complain if the Martians warred in the same spirit?'

Whalers and sealers made camp on Tasmania's virgin fringes. By 1832, the year of Arthur's birth, there were around 13,000 settlers of European origin on the island. They brought with them 200,000 sheep to crop and trample on the aboriginal population's hunting grounds. The first colonists were overwhelmingly male. They engaged in wholesale abduction and rape of the women they found. The 'Black War' between natives and invaders was reckoned by Australian historians to have brought about the total elimination of the indigenous population. That war concluded in 1832.

Nothing I could find in any of Arthur's fugitive publications, or in newspaper references to his life and career, cast much light on the Tasmanian years. It felt as though two islands, Ceylon and Tasmania, were being yoked together: one as a spoiled paradise and the other as the crucible of coming darkness.

> *It is safe to say that no such calamity has befallen Scots colonists since the Darien disaster, though in the Darien scheme the amount of money*

> *involved was not a twentieth part of the amount lost by the inroads of this
> very insignificant looking parasite.*

The brave stuck it out, waiting for their luck to turn, or diversifying into tea, while others 'lost heart and retired to the Antipodes'.
A barren land less suited to genteel retirement it would be hard to
imagine.

And then, out of nowhere, or an accounts office in a Melbourne
suburbs, came an email with attachments.

Dear Iain,

*We share an ancestor! I am descended from Arthur Sinclair's second
daughter, Catherine. She moved to Australia and married George Angus.*

*You still have the family name and so must be descended from one of
her brothers. Which one?*

*Do you have any information about the family? I have some letters and
photos that I will happily share with you if you are interested. I am aware
of Arthur's book 'In Tropical Lands' – it has been described as something
of a classic, isn't that nice?*

I am attaching a few photos.

I would be very pleased to hear from you, so I am hoping you will reply!
> *Kindest regards,*
> > *Susan Voutier (Filing Clerk)*

Of course I did reply, immediately. And I began to correspond with
this recovered cousin. It appeared that Catherine, travelling with her
father, met and married a fellow Scot, and settled in Australia. Susan
Voutier's grandmother was Catherine's daughter. But ours was not a
fortunate family. Catherine had five children. Her first daughter, Jessie,
died of gastroenteritis at a few months old. Her second, Kitty, was five
when she succumbed to pneumonia on a return voyage to Scotland.
She was buried at sea. The only son, John Sinclair Angus (known as
Jack), pictured with medal and folded arms, was twenty-one when he
was killed at Gallipoli. The fatality, in the immediate aftermath of that
hideously misconceived war game, could not be confirmed. Some years

later, a search of the battlefield found a white Bible with Jack's name and address.

There were more photographs, more postcards to consider. And a grouping of Arthur and his children that I had never seen. For the first time, Arthur is not smiling. But he is accompanied by his entire tribe: now the children are young adults. Susan told me that the portrait was taken to mark their return to Scotland. Beneath the account of Arthur's funeral that she sent, along with a family tree, was the torn headline from a missing article: A RUBBER VENTURE.

Susan was persistent in her research. She combed through boxes and family files, paying particular attention to newspaper cuttings. 'I know Arthur wrote under the nom-de-plume of "Old Colonist" and I have an exercise book with a few samples.'

This was the prompt I needed. I had seen 'Old Colonist' material somewhere when I cleared the massed cupboards of my parents' house in Wales. Now I attacked the even more compacted midden of my own attic. I recovered a tranche of documents, early photocopies: a serial account (rich and detailed as the published Peruvian material) of Arthur Sinclair's gold-prospecting expedition to Tasmania.

Putting aside my copy of the Folio Society edition of *The War of the Worlds*, I was struck by the resemblance between Grahame Baker's frontispiece illustration, showing the cyclopean Martian 'Thing' emerging from the crater on Horsell Common, and the floating eye of Allen Ginsberg's ayahuasca vision reproduced in *The Yage Letters*. The poet had given his sketch a title: 'The Great Being'.

HELL'S GATES

'Some inch of Scotland in my blood.'
 – Don DeLillo, *Americana*

It was a disconcerting experience, combining recognition with novelty in equal measures, to greet Susan Voutier and her sister Catherine on our Hackney doorstep. And to take an impulsive step towards them, as if to offer an embrace, and then at the last to hesitate: a firm handshake and a froth of welcoming babble. We were not, on the Scottish side, much of an embracing family, but we shared our curiosity about a discontinued heritage. Old Arthur Sinclair was the only one to gift us with some form of written record.

The sisters, as I understood it, were leaving Australia for the second time in their entire lives. They had long plotted a 'return' to the home country. I was surprised – thinking that their methods and inclinations must be like my own – to learn that they had visited none of the addresses associated with Arthur and his family. They based themselves in Edinburgh and took the tourist excursions that best fitted their agenda. It was good to have discovered this connection, and to have physical proof of the family journey to Australia.

We liked each other and the meal progressed very well. Farne joined us and says that the stories went easily back and forth, despite the fact that our visitors were both somewhat deaf. Catherine ate slowly and carefully, a kidney condition meant that she had to avoid potassium. Neither of the sisters had children. Catherine, the medical librarian, was married. Susan lived at home. And there was a brother who was not well. Like my father, Susan didn't drink. But she made no objection to our indulgence.

They were a generous pair, these sisters, on unfamiliar ground. Susan delivered a memory stick, which I tried to download but only managed, as usual, to drop into the unfathomable well of nothingness where the Cloud dissolves. She also brought a small pink box that contained something of Arthur's that she wanted me to have. A family relic. In fact, she wasn't quite sure that it *had* belonged to Arthur. Or indeed what its history and purpose could have been. She called it a 'thumb ring'. If so, Arthur must have possessed the prehensile and opposable thumb of a particularly delicate lemur. Thumb rings were usually worn over gloves to protect the pad during archery. This item, burnished copper with a dull red stone set in a solar design, felt like the membership token of some obscure Masonic sect. There was also a handwritten note from Susan's mother, Margaret Helen Ironside Angus: '[This is] a very old ring, perhaps a "thumb ring", which must have belonged to my mother's father, Arthur Sinclair. I'm sure it must have been made in Ceylon.'

The ring sits nicely on my little finger, the facets of the red stone catching (and swallowing) London light, as I start to pick my way through Arthur's reports from Tasmania. Susan, in one of her emails, reminded me that the photographs carried by her family to Australia were 'the next best thing to having their loved ones with them'. Most of these group portraits and individual *cartes de visite* were taken by studios in Aberdeen and Orkney, but the final one, wife and six children present, a more serious affair, is credited to the Anson Brothers of Hobart, Tasmania. For the first time, Arthur is not smiling. None of them are smiling. They have been transported to the Ultima Thule among colonies and they have run low on expectation.

I began to read the ninety or so pages, in the form of letters, that Arthur composed for the *Aberdeen Free Press* and the Colombo *Observer*. He flagged the series as 'In Search of a Home in Tasmania'. Gold was not the driver, it was land. Arthur was now an established part of a northeast Scotland diaspora, restlessly relocating from colony to colony – India, Ceylon, Australia, New Zealand – looking for that one good place: 'an abundance of elbow room'. It was never about mining. The challenge was to take advantage of climate and soil, to plant healthy crops, and secure adequate shelter. The letters date from 1886. Arthur's nom de plume has shifted from 'Young Scotchman' to 'Old Colonist'.

> *Why man, an island as large as Ceylon or Ireland or 18,000,000 acres occupied as yet by a population only equal to that of Aberdeen, the granite city. And, oh, man, the glorious rivers now stocked with salmon and trout! At present my notes must be brief, for the time of dreams and sentiment is past and the time for work has arrived...*
>
> *My first impressions of Hobart were anything but disappointing: its spacious streets, handsome freestone buildings, beautiful vegetation and delightful temperature more than fulfilled anticipations.*

Is this, at last, the looked-for paradise? The family are in tow, present but barely mentioned. They must be housed.

> *To find temporary shelter for my family was my first duty. I had not very much difficulty in arranging a good hotel at two guineas per head per week for board and lodging. This accomplished, I walked out to the Botanical Gardens to see what this celebrated climate and soil can produce. And for a few hours I simply revelled amongst the numerous old European friends which seem to have found so congenial a home. Giant geraniums, brilliant verbenas and a perfect jungle of Helétrope, greet me as I enter the gate. The gardeners though civil are not very communicative.*
>
> *I could willingly spend days in these lovely gardens, but I am reminded that a more pressing if less agreeable duty awaits me, viz.,* house-hunting, *which here, as at home, I find to be the most worrying, wearying work I ever engaged in. My requirements were simple and definite enough: 'To rent with option of purchase, a good house with orchard or small farm, river frontage, &c.'*
>
> *'No need to advertise,' said agents in London, 'you'll find at once abundance of what you want.' In vain however I scanned the papers on arrival and those terrible imposters the house agents by their most exaggerated descriptions gave me many a vain journey.*
>
> *My chagrin may be imagined on finding the 'rich land' to be an exhausted and abandoned field by the side of a lagoon, without the ghost of*

Hell's Gates

a tree or shrub: here a thistle and there a sweet-briar tried to find their way through the baked *clay, but both seemed inclined to give up the struggle in despair. Years ago there evidently had been a roof of some sort, but this portion had entirely disappeared.*

And so the fruitless chase begins.

The sun was now high in the heavens, and the day proved one of the hottest of the season, the thermometer recording 100.2 in the shade… The house was deserted but in fair order… The orchard of about 2 acres was fully stocked with apples, apricots, plums and peaches, and, though quite abandoned, bearing really astonishing crops… I now sauntered on the lawn. 'This,' thought I, 'is exactly what I dreamed of and the sooner I secure it the better. With what pleasure I shall mow down these weeds! Renovate the flower-garden and see the orchard put in order! And then should some old Ceylon friend come and see me… only think of the fishing!'

Having set up his pastoral pipe dream, Arthur is immediately confronted by the politics of place.

The owner is a very wealthy man and does not care to let or sell. Though living in Victoria he is one of the largest proprietors of Tasmania, owning 93,000 acres chiefly along the principal river valleys, many of the blocks shaped fan-like so as to take in as much of the river frontage as possible. In short, Mr X is a species of land-grabber, the bane of this and every country they exist in, and the pitiable Government of this colony, while enforcing strict laws upon the poor little immigrant, wink at the squatocrat who may hold 100,000 acres and not employ a dozen men or spend £100 in the colony. But, by George, their day is coming! 6d an acre tax on all uncultivated land would work a cure. Out of 6,000,000 acres alienated, I do not believe there are really 100,000 in cultivation in this colony.

My next move was to try and secure if possible a block of virgin forest, out of which, I feared not, I would in time, carve an estate for myself. The official, however, in the Lands Department smiled when I hinted at a water

95

> *frontage: no such land seems available and yet 12,000,000 out of 18,000,000 acres are still in the hands of the Government.*

Blocked on all sides in his attempts to establish a Scottish farm or plantation at the end of the world, Arthur sets out early on a series of brooding, solitary walks.

> *The deathlike stillness all around made me feel like an intruder in some spiritual or unearthly sphere. My own footsteps were the only sounds that reached my ears for the first hour. Strange people the residents of Hobart! Like their surroundings fair enough to look upon, but apathetic and uncommunicative.*
>
> *I now start on an extended tour, or series of tours throughout this beautiful island. I have thrown aside 'Official Handbooks and Guides' and simply judge for myself as I move along… Awful Tory place this! I expected to find enlightened Liberal people; but no, they are 50 years behind! A friend, who was here the other day, was astonished at the state of matters. The present Bishop is a good man.*

Arthur plods on in a melancholy fugue, firing up his indignation at the latest betrayal by established settlers and the grand larceny – as at home – of a remote squatocracy. This was the blackest crime in my great-grandfather's report: the wilful failure to make the best of the land, and the refusal to work for all the hours of daylight, to labour and to self-improve. Desperate roads and muddy trails carry this diligent Scottish tourist to phantom estates, attempted or abandoned. He notes memorials to the failures of Empire and the vanished voyagers with their heroic legends. An ecology of profit harvesting and future ruin. He realises that he has come, hauling his family with him, to a dismal theme park of imperial crimes and misdemeanours.

Passing dead gum trees, 'gaunt skeletons extending their blackened arms from a height of 250 feet and upward', Arthur finds a eucalyptus associated with Lady Franklin: '107 feet in circumference at four feet from the ground'. Of London Huguenot ancestry, Jane Franklin was the widow of the explorer Sir John Franklin, the deluded voyager who perished in quest of the Northwest Passage. She recalled her husband attending a divine service held in the bole of one of these gigantic trees. Franklin, in earlier times, had been Lieutenant-Governor of Van Diemen's Land; while Lady Franklin and her attendant, Christiana Stewart, were the first European women to travel, on foot, overland from Hobart to Macquarie Harbour. The titled lady expressed her concern over the treatment of female convicts. The museum she established in Hobart, as a symbol of the Colony's cultural aspirations, was later employed as an apple shed.

Walking among the gum trees before trudging on to the township named after Franklin, Arthur raged.

> *The most valuable tree, however, in this part of the world is the Huon pine,* Dacrydium Franklini, *which is restricted to this island, and most abundant in this locality. An extensive trade is now carried on in this fine wood, used for boat-building, house furniture, and anything for which oak is used in England; it is very durable, and in the hands of the cabinet-maker takes on a beautiful polish. I am afraid to trust myself to express exactly what I think of the unmitigated vandalism which destroys those fine trees for the purpose of dibbling a few potatoes or scratching in a few grains of oat-seed; and yet the poor immigrant – driven back from the agricultural land – is not to blame, but no language is strong enough or gibbeting bad enough for the men who have idiotically bartered away the millions of acres of purely agricultural land in this island. The shady transactions by which these lands were alienated will not bear light, and the sooner light is brought forcibly to bear upon them the better.*

Horrified by the blinkered folly of the fruit growers, 'the hopeless state of the strawberry beds, or jungles of raps and brambles', Arthur decides to blag his way into a jam factory.

> *I observe that in most cases the cultivation of small fruits is being abandoned here, the price realised at the Jam Factory being insufficient to pay for the gathering.*
>
> *To speak plainly, it is no factory at all. Merely a receiving house, and a very dirty one. The immense quantities of small fruit smell like a pulp*

> heap, as they are pitched into large casks, and the only curing they got here
> is a bit of burning brimstone, the fumes of which are blown into the bung
> hole! In Melbourne, the mess is boiled with sundry additions and sent out
> to the world as 'Finest Tasmanian Jam'.

———

The Tasmanian relocation, a false step, draining resources and the determination to make a fresh start, was valuable in unexpected ways: the nakedness of the land exposed the machinery that exploited it. Denied ground on which to work, Arthur became more philosophical. The frustrations and obvious corruptions helped him to formulate a less predatory vision of the future. The story takes on a more contemplative and poetic resonance.

> *Wearied by house-hunting, I sauntered out to solace myself by a solitary*
> *walk. Presently, black clouds began to gather between me and the sun, and*
> *lighter ones to chase each other along the summit of the hills. I had left the*
> *main road and was walking leisurely along a somewhat rougher track in*
> *search of a museum which the guide books told me Lady Franklin erected*
> *in one of the most secluded and beautiful spots.*
>
> *Sitting, somewhat disconsolate – and maybe whistling 'Why left I my*
> *hame?' – I saw approaching a gentleman with a boy leading him, appar-*
> *ently (as indeed he turned out to be) quite blind. Glad of someone to bear*
> *me company, I spoke, and we sat together. I was much struck with the keen*
> *intelligence of this gentleman, who, notwithstanding his deprivation, seemed*
> *to know more of this country than anyone whom I had yet met, but he fairly*
> *staggered me when he began to point out some fossil shells near to where*
> *I sat – and as he went on with a minute and glowing account of the geology*
> *of the locality, I glanced below his blue spectacles, but no light was there.*

The encounter with the blind man in blue spectacles and the boy who leads him takes on an oracular aspect. Arthur's confidence in the fate that led him to this wilderness has diminished, to the point where he hungers for dark histories and prophetic revelations.

'*Yonder,*' *said the old gentleman,* '*where the river takes the second bend is Risdon, where the first consignment of English settlers pitched their tents in this colony, and a capital selection you will see they made. It was some time before they came in contact with any natives, who were naturally very timid, and probably a more innocent and harmless race never inhabited a country on this earth. Here they lived chiefly up in the Kangaroo Valley, whither you are now bound, and it was near this spot where we sit where the first most unfortunate conflict took place. A herd of kangaroo having been raised, the excited natives turned out; men, women, and children, joining the chase. On went the herd towards the river, and on went the native hunters, cheering and howling, but unarmed with spear and arrow. The English settlers hearing the noise rushed out armed, fired a volley and killed twenty, following up their "victory" by stealing some of the women and shooting down the poor men who tried to defend them. Now who in this instance were the savages?*

'*For such gallant acts the first settlers got large grants of land; indeed most of the best you see was simply gifted away by the then so-called Government, and it is to the sons of these early settlers, the present lucky owners, that our boys are supposed to touch their hats. They rarely, however, visit their lands – living abroad and holding on, no doubt in the hope that some day the Government will be obliged to buy back the land as they propose doing in Ireland. This land monopoly is the curse of Tasmania, and is the chief if not the sole cause of the present backwardness.*'

A blind prophet out of William Blake has come to Arthur in the disguise, as my great-grandfather recognises, of a fellow countryman, a native of Kerriemuir. He grasps the old gentleman's hand and they wander off, 'arm in arm', into the landscape.

'*But how came you here?*' *I ventured to enquire.*

'*Come along and I'll soon tell you all.*'

The sun was now shining brightly, and the overgrown hedges of sweet briar were scenting the air with a perfume so home-like. I glanced at the hills and the snow was gone, and everything seemed as fresh, green, and warm as a July morning in Banff.

There is no treasure to be hacked from the earth, no silver or gold. No cash crop ready for export. No forest to be cleared.

'Now, I'll show you my fortune.'

A cottage in the bush. 'As canty a wife and sweet little daughter as ever graced a Scottish home.' A milk cow, an affectionate watch-dog and a hundred head of poultry. Arthur sketches a fantasy of revised migration, channelling his yearning for home, as the chance encounter fades into sentiment. He returns to his search for Lady Franklin's museum.

———

It was found inconvenient for the general public. The temple was despoiled and the whole of the treasures collected by the accomplished lady were carried off to Hobart. Its occupation gone the building is gradually falling into decay.

Lady Franklin, it appears, was a noted pedestrian. She would strike off from here into the country, galloping over the first range of hills. Arthur asks what is to be found on the far side. None of those he challenges can help. 'I've been here forty-seven years,' said one man, 'and never went to see, and never mean to.'

'Well, I do,' I said as I walked away. Like an old war horse I smelt the jungle afar off, and, feeling my vest pocket to make sure of my little compass, I steered direct for the western shoulder of Mount Wellington.

It was while resting at the foot of a fern tree that I observed a singular looking square stone lying in the steep rocky rivulet. What seemed at a little distance to be curious carving, on closer inspection, turned out to be perfect casts of many a strange shellfish, all probably now extinct; but how on earth, or rather in water, came these fish here?

Upwards still upwards I climb. For pure unalloyed enjoyment commend me to the forest–clad mountains; but with a view to turn this to some practical account, I must now begin to take notes of the nature and depth of the soil. And while I sit on the trunk of this huge tree, looking out through

> *the gap its fall has made on the beautiful valley of the Derwent below, it strikes me as highly probable that the best of the land for fruit-growing in this country is yet untouched.*

Perhaps, after all, the good life may be realised? Arthur deviates between his vision of the island of Tasmania – no longer Van Diemen's Land – as another paradise, soured by the transgressions of remote owners, and a dry and crumbling turd squeezed from the fundament of Australia. Such potential harvests blighted by the choking soot of prisons and asylums.

My great-grandfather, in solitary contemplation, begins to appreciate that there might be another way: leave well alone.

> *A few days ago I remarked that after coming 12,000 miles I did not mean to sit down at anybody's back; but now I am disposed to change my tack, and from such a vantage as this I would gladly look down upon the small fry below. But, say the planters of Tasmania, it would take £100 per acre to make such land as this fit for fruit-growing – that is to say, take out all stones and roots; but the question remains, is it necessary to take out stones and roots? I venture to think not; but we shall see…*

What Arthur concludes, when he finds time to brood, is that a choice has soon to be made between the measured but costly interventions of the planter and the rude gamble for gold or silver. The extraction of precious metals promises richer dividends – and catastrophic consequences for the natural ecology of the island. He sees how Tasmania was drained of manpower when rumours of a gold strike came across the Bass Strait from Victoria.

> *In 1853 the gold fever broke out, and the bone and sinew of the island crossed the straits in a body numbering 34,000. More than half her able-bodied population left at this time. Hence those abandoned gardens.*

The Victorian gold rush brought an end to the 'opportunity' for 'free' passage on convict transports. Colonial proprietors feared that potential offenders, low types, poachers and urban sneak thieves, would commit some minor felony in order to get themselves shipped out in chains, fed and watered, *at no charge*. And that, making landfall, these miscreants, often Irish, would immediately escape and disappear into the gold fields. The history of both these sorry islands, Tasmania and Ireland, they insisted, had been forged in the teeth of the ingratitude of slaves and Aboriginals and convicts offered the chance of redemption.

Arthur prided himself, in his meanderings, on his good fortune in encountering, and attending to, eccentric figures met at the wayside. These were messengers of fate. The characters, if you were capable of acknowledging them, who would carry the story forward. There is an episode in Melbourne that reads like a response to Edgar Allan Poe's 'The Man of the Crowd'.

> *The whole of the inhabitants seem to be in the streets. Cities twice the size at home, with streets one-third the width, are not so crowded. And how rudely they jostle! My poor aged companion, a man over 80 summers, got sadly fagged… I forgot to introduce my aged friend, indeed I have a diffidence about it, knowing that few men in Melbourne would care or could afford to know him, and yet I look upon him as one of the greatest treasures I have found in Australia.*
>
> *Poor auld Archie Watt! Were I an accomplished storyteller, I could make every Banff man's heart bleed and many a Briton's blood boil by the simple recital of your wrongs. Born near Gamrie, early in the century, Archie was, at the age of 30, sentenced by a drunken judge, on the evidence of a lying gamekeeper, to transportation, subjected to the cruelty of official jailors and the more damnable inhumanity of the early settlers in Van Diemen's Land.*
>
> *And yet Archie has come through it all, with a faith firmly fixed above. The old man, it must be confessed, has two gods on earth: his little library of well-thumbed books and a fine old fiddle on which he interprets the lively inspirations of Marshall, Gow and Petrie, with admirable taste.*

Arthur guides Mr Watt into Melbourne's leading bookshop, where the old man breaks down at the sight of so many volumes.

> *The great bookseller himself is a busy litterateur, never producing anything*
> *very specific, yet a very industrious hack.*

This pompous individual, like so many in the trade, fancying himself more of an author than most of the pretenders taking up space on his shelves, leaves the tedium of mere business to his wife; a 'lonely maiden' he found, on one of his scavenging expeditions: 'vegetating' in Tasmania. He acquired the item at an advantageous price. And put her to work, to cover his overheads in the transaction.

Concluding his initial survey of Tasmania, Arthur decides that he must confront the shame that still resides in certain alien structures imposed on the virgin landscape.

> *Yonder palatial building on the brow of the hill – commanding a view*
> *which any rich English lord might well envy – is, we are told,* The
> Institution. *A building for a similar purpose at Launceston is pointed*
> *out as* The Depot, *and it takes some little time for a puzzled stranger to*
> *discover that these are simply* Poor-houses. *The building we have just*
> *seen contains some 700 paupers, costing the public between £8,000 and*
> *£9,000 a year. Paupers! There are no paupers in Australasia, the guide-*
> *books say. I have come a long way to find the conservative working-man,*
> *but here he is at last and I'm not enamoured.*
>
> *The marvel is that there is so little cultivation in a locality so highly*
> *favoured as this: the melancholy fact again forces itself upon us, that for 100*
> *miles on either side of this river the land has simply been frittered away, and*
> *converted into sheep-runs.*
>
> *A beautiful little oasis in this wilderness is New Norfolk. An air of*
> *substantial comfort pervades the township, with its two excellent hotels,*
> *well-supplied stores, neat churches, schools and library, to say nothing of*
> *the capacious Lunatic Asylum. For, strange to say, men and women go mad*
> *even in this perfect climate, where bare existence is a luxury.*
>
> *Still, all this is, I believe, curable in time and there must be a bright*
> *future for an island so enriched by nature and advantageously situated as*
> *Tasmania, but it will take many a long year and a very radical change of*

> *Government to accomplish this; meanwhile, it remains a delightful sana-*
> *torium for Australia and India,* and nothing more.

Exhausted by a remorseless tramping after facts, his frustrated quest to locate the right piece of ground in which to plot the next chapter of his life, Arthur drifts back to thoughts of Scotland.

> *I well remember, years ago, rambling on Holburn Head, near Thurso. It*
> *was one of those delicious mornings in July which no climate under the sun*
> *can surpass. And as I lay down at full length on the grass with the laverocks*
> *singing above me, gazing intently on the North Atlantic Sea, the smooth*
> *bosom of which heaved like the breast of one in calm sleep, I had glimpses*
> *there of something I cannot name, though sufficiently definite to mark a*
> *milestone in one's inward life. And now at the uttermost end of the earth —*
> *on the southernmost point of inhabitable land — I gaze on a similar scene*
> *with feelings of awe, wonder and delight. Who does not at times wish to*
> *retire into solitude? Who would always travel with tattling tourists? What*
> *change could be more thorough and refreshing than a solitary ramble on*
> *some secluded shore, where for the time all your worrying anxieties may*
> *be forgot?*

A nostalgic episode of reflection in nature, out of Rousseau or Thoreau, at the end of the island, at the end of the world, and presaging inevitable horror. The horizon darkens. But Arthur has realised his defining vision, an outward motion of his soul. He is not quite ready to act upon it. And it will not come again. It never does.

———

> *The waves of the great Southern Ocean seem to have crumbled and eaten*
> *away the softer portions of these shores, leaving the basaltic rocks standing*
> *like tall pillars to guard the remaining portions of land. It was into this*
> *Peninsula that Governor Arthur in 1830 attempted to drive the poor abo-*
> *rigines, by means of stretching a cordon across the whole island.*

Taking to the water, Arthur is carried into Norfolk Bay on a small steamboat crewed by two sailors. When my great-grandfather enquires about the function of the 'curious looking boxes' spaced at regular intervals along the shore, the skipper explains.

> *'Those are the remains of Sentry-boxes in which watchmen were placed to prevent the escape of convicts from Port Arthur, and on these numerous jetties you see, jutting and zig-zagging into the water, were chained bulldogs so ferocious that no one could safely go near, even to feed them. Their meat had to be placed within reach by a long fork. Sharks were introduced into these waters and fed daily upon raw meat, by which diabolical contrivance the poor prisoners were hemmed in. Yet, goaded to madness by fiendish cruelties, they often braved even the dogs and sharks.'*

Even with Arthur's confirmed taste for the picaresque, he has heard enough. But the ancient mariner persists.

> *'Did you ever hear the story of Martin Cash?'*
>
> *'I am in no humour to listen to it just now, another time please, meanwhile land me at the Neck.'*
>
> *'You need not hurry yourself. It is good moonlight.'*
>
> *An abandoned and much dilapidated stone building stands on the narrowest part of the gap around which I note some luxuriant specimens of the Cape pelargonium in full flower. The Neck is only a bank of sand, rising 10 to 15 feet above the water. On one hand the tranquil bay and, on the other, the huge waves of the Pacific lash the beach with relentless fury. I pace the distance between: only 80 yards from watermark to watermark!*
>
> *I cross over a ridge through the bush, to take a peep into the 'Devil's Blow Hole', where the waves, having forced their way through a subterraneous passage, come snorting through an ugly hole. It was one of those times and scenes in which most thinking persons have occasionally found themselves, when we are unfit for study or action, but in which the soul seems live and awake.*
>
> *I had walked farther than I had intended and, long before I reached the Neck again, I heard the whistle of my little steamer, reminding me of the*

> *approaching night. I decided – after consultation – to ask the captain to*
> *steer for Taranna, which we reached about dusk. I parted with my craft,*
> *meaning to walk home next day via Foriester's Peninsula. Meanwhile*
> *I seek the shelter of the Tasman Hotel, where I was glad to find a good*
> *log fire and plenty of the usual cheer – roast mutton and oceans of hot tea.*

———

Having digested the nightmare of *His Natural Life*, the novel of
Tasmanian convict life by Marcus Clarke, published in volume form in
1875, Arthur decides that duty calls him, 'on a dreary wet Sunday', to
explore the prison at Port Arthur. Images of the whipping-to-death and
other brutalities suffered by Kirkland, one of Clarke's characters, haunt
Arthur as he begins his melancholy tour of inspection.

> *But the fate of poor Kirkland was indeed merciful compared with many*
> *which I have myself witnessed.*
>   *In a sequestered hollow, two miles from Hobart, there stands a series*
> *of somewhat ungainly and dilapidated buildings, in one wing of which*
> *are collected the remaining dregs of the Port Arthur system of discipline, if*
> *indeed those poor drivelling maniacs can be said to still live. They num-*
> *bered 58 when I visited the place. It is a sickening sight. There stands the*
> *blethering Irishman who probably began his public career by shooting 'the*
> *blackguard who paid the rent'. And there beside him, with finely formed*
> *head but now vacant eye, is the poor Yorkshire man who had a quarrel*
> *with his brother over their father's effects, and having helped himself to a*
> *cow he thought he was entitled to, the angry brother gave him in charge; he*
> *was tried for cattle-stealing and off he was packed to Van Diemen's Land.*
> *Yonder, crouching in a corner beating the points of his palsied fingers against*
> *his toothless gums, you see all that remains of what, 50 years ago, was as*
> *stalwart a young Scotchman as ever grew on the east-coast of Buchan; his*
> *crime was killing a brace of rabbits and knocking down a gamekeeper.*
>   *A few weeks ago, there died here one of Marcus Clarke's heroes, old*
> *blind Mooney, for whom I particularly enquired, but found that all that*
> *remained was his parchment. The document on which his crimes and*

punishments are recorded. From this document, I learn that, in addition to the original sentence, Mooney was sentenced, no fewer than four times, to be hanged. But like cats with their prey, the officials of the day could not think of putting so game a fellow as Mooney out of his pain; besides, their occupation would soon have been gone if all had been hanged who were sentenced to be. The proper application of the lash became at once a work of art and a specific for all offences great and small. I read that for 'complaining of his food' Mooney gets 100 lashes; 'complaints against a constable, 150 lashes'.

'How many did he receive from first to last?' I enquired of the present obliging and humane superintendent.

'The doctor and I counted up to 2,000, when he got tired and disgusted,' he said.

Yet Mooney defied them all, positively declined to work; he swore at the Commandant, rebuked the Parson, and even looked into the face of a Governor and deliberately called the Queen's appointed a damned fool! But what the lash failed to do, the model prison and solitary confinement accomplished. The mind was successfully unhinged and the victim became a drivelling idiot. Yet, strange to say, in spite of all his torments, Mooney lived to the 'goodly' age of 78 – when, under any conceivable circumstance he must, I hope, have made a happy change.

I took ample notes of the old Port Arthur Prison Settlement as I wandered through the buildings on that dismal Sunday. The curious will readily imagine with what feelings I passed the 'barbecue', where of old the floggings took place during the week, and on which thousands were mustered on Sunday morning, to be driven to church in their irons.

I peeped into the huge kitchen with boilers and patent lifts still intact. I crept cautiously up the stairs and gazed along the great dining halls and dormitories. I summoned up courage to walk between what seemed like miles of dark cells and issued into a well-lighted hall, the walls of which were lined with neat shelves indicating what had once been the Library. The shelves are empty now, but in the corner of the hall an immense heap of books had been pitched like a cartload of rubbish. I pounced on this pile. They were well-bound copies of the English bible! Nobody was looking on. I stole one as a souvenir and walked away with it under my arm.

I now visited the Model Prison, erected some 15 years ago for 'Lifers'. It is said that no prisoners ever came out of it alive and sane.

The building in form may be said to resemble a starfish or octopus. The great dome had been elegantly fitted up as a theatre or place of entertainment for the officers and their families. The sounds of revelry, however, did not reach the poor wretches in their cells, for the building was so contrived, and the arrangements so complete, that not a sound, or whisper, ever reached their ears, save the voice of the chaplain.

I stepped into some of the now tenantless, but still dark cells, and struck a match, and looked around: there were strange hieroglyphics there, but in some cases the walls were padded like mattresses, in order to deprive the inmate of the luxury of knocking out his brains. I walked into the spacious chapel, and was struck by the effective contrivance for keeping each individual safely apart, and preventing the possibility of a man seeing his next neighbour or anything else save the parson.

Caught in a microclimate of deafening absence, Arthur seemed to anticipate the final adventure, his expedition into the Peruvian cloud forest, where the indigenous people had not yet been exterminated. Once again I recalled Michael Taussig: 'It is the presence of their absence, their presence in their absence.' These shadows would never be scraped from the walls of the cells. Arthur, conscious of Tasmania's position as the last landfall for whalers venturing in the polar sea, has his Melvillean Father Mapple moment. He feels the urge to preach to a deserted chapel.

I mounted the pulpit and in imagination addressed the empty pews. At either side of the pulpit is a lectern, or reading desk, reserved, I believe, for armed constables. The slate still lies there on which had to be noted the slightest delinquency or inattention. Yes, here stood the priest with Bible and Prayer-book, and there the constables with slates and pistols: strange surroundings in which to deliver the meaning of love! *Was it any wonder that traces of impatience were occasionally noted, and slight manifestations were frequently heard and punished, such as the simultaneous clanking of irons as the priest repeated the words: 'That it may please Thee to show mercy upon all prisoners and captives.'*

I had enough of the prison, and was glad to retrace my steps to the hotel. I went early and comfortably to bed, but soon awoke, howling to get out of a dark cell. I imagined I had been shut in by the sudden closing of a spring door! It proved a weary night, though much relieved by dipping into the bible I had found. On the fly-leaf of which I noticed a neat pencil sketch of a very innocent looking child, and on the margin was written the words 'James Egan, 6 years 8 months'. Poor Jamie had been noting down the weary months as they dragged slowly along. I wonder at his ultimate fate – possibly a decent home in the bush, more probably a Lunatic Asylum.

The iniquity of sending the scum of Great Britain to pollute this fair isle has often been animadverted upon. I confess I cannot see it. On the contrary, though wrecked by the wickedness and cruelty of local officials, it was I think a providential arrangement and truly excellent scheme for introducing labour to a new country. And if we look upon crime as a disease brought on by want and the effects of a wretched climate, what could be more merciful to the victims, what more likely to prove curative than a change to this genial atmosphere?

Meanwhile, the question is, what is this immediate locality of Port Arthur good for? Let us look at those pear trees in the paddock. There are but two, and these are much destroyed by cattle, but though now mid-winter there is still an abundant crop of luscious fruit left hanging. Can such fruit be turned to account? Can the thousands of acres of good forest land surrounding this beautiful harbour not be turned into magnificent orchards?

The London Times *recently had the following: 'Tasmania is a country which has been kept back, and even made retrograde, by cliques, jobbery, and landed monopolies, a country ruled by antique and benighted statesmen.'*

This is perfectly true: Statesmanship has gone literally to seed, for I find there is a paid Government official to every 116 of the population! Is it any wonder that an exodus has set in?

Now that the Chinese are prohibited, the European loafer has to be treated with, and he rules this country. One good thing Tasmania has done for me, it has effectively cured my democratic tendencies.

All my great-grandfather had accomplished with his painstaking survey was the confirmation that Tasmania was not the right place in which to establish a new home. His family, unmentioned since the initial dispatch, were still lodged, we are left to assume, in the same Hobart hotel. While the bearded paterfamilias trawled the island for serviceable anecdotes to enliven his disgruntled prose.

Laid out, full length, on that wild southern headland, watching the waves, Arthur was back in his native north, the fleeting moment of vision when he connected with ancestors who had ventured from Norway to Orkney. And, by myth, onward to Greenland and America. He had tasted the wafer of the thing that cannot be named. Now he would have to hazard one last Australasian push, confident in the certainty that it would fail, this march into the interior. Gold! The old chimera. A madness worse than the ravings of the model prisoners in their panopticons. The ambitious 'Young Scotchman' of Ceylon, who had become the broken 'Old Colonist' of Tasmania, would reclaim his own name, when that folly was done, for any subsequent publication.

INTO THE INTERIOR

'Money brings money. That gold business was good. Famous!'
  – Joseph Conrad, *An Outcast of the Islands*

Viable land for planting was not to be had in Tasmania, but the gold bug continued to scratch in the night. Arthur weighed the prospect of returning to Ceylon to start again with tea against the remote possibility of a mineral strike. And he became, in partnership with J.W. Norton-Smith, James Smith, W.C. Alcock, William Robert Bell and Robert Quiggin, a provisional director of the Heazlewood Silver Lead Mining Company. The Company was initially registered with a capital of £45,000, in 45,000 shares at £1 each.

> *I only wish tea was as easily floated as minerals. It's truly astonishing how a poor country like this will go in for speculating in mines, or anything in the nature of a gamble. Only yesterday morning this company was advertised, and in a few hours 30,000 shares were taken up!*
>
> *But 90 per cent of the mines mean ruin and desolation nevertheless. Agriculturally speaking this is really a poorer country than I had any conception of and I now begin to understand why it is left a desolate waste. It shows lamentable ignorance or gross cruelty to talk of sending Scottish Crofters out here! I have some of the saddest tales to tell of misguided immigrants. What would Ceylon men think of £23 per ton, to transport provisions and produce for 16 miles, which is the ruling rate from Waratah to the Heazlewood mines?*
>
> *Such a rush! In January, there was no silver mining in Tasmania, now there are a score of Companies, and shares going up 300 per cent. First shipment of 50 tons this week. Never recommend an old India hand to go*

> *to New Zealand or Australia any more. It's ruin to the majority. No rain*
> *for over 4 months on this coast; no crops, potatoes under two tons per acre;*
> *codlin moth and scale in every orchard; a few seasons like this, and but for*
> *the mining, the island would be abandoned. The scarcity and low type*
> *of labourer here is appalling. The only thing they are fit for is to petition*
> *Government to keep others away.*

Arthur is forced to acknowledge that he is implicated in the madness of a late-century cycle of boom and bust – and now, after his series of solitary rambles, those landscape epiphanies, he is prepared to go over to the dark side: mining, despoiling, speculation. He abhors the Australasian culture of compulsive gambling, betting on horseflesh and anything that moves, flies or swims: the culture of chance and magic and fate. The culture, in his terms, of waste. And suicide. And red-eyed, black-tongued disappearance into the bush. He abhors the addiction of Australian youth to cricket and other sports. He abhors the boosting of coffee (and the crash). And the boosting of gold (seducing farm labourers from New Zealand, Ireland and Scotland). The boosting of property and the vanity of pretentious structures with no occupants. He abhors all of it, up to the tipping point when he finds himself obliged to join the troop of bearded desperados heading, on a rumour, into the interior.

> *Tremendous booms in property in Melbourne just now, indeed every one*
> *owns that it is quite ridiculous, and there will be sore hearts and empty*
> *purses very soon. People are rushing from here to Melbourne, where build-*
> *ing and all sorts of speculations are going on.*
>
> *The ingenuity of man could scarcely have chosen a fitter place in which*
> *to act the devil. Every feature of the landscape seems to wear an air of feroc-*
> *ity, rigour and despair. On the one hand the perilous gates and tempestuous*
> *sea: on the other the impenetrable forests, skirted by imperious thickets.*
> *Many a harrowing tale is told of poor maddened convicts escaping into the*
> *inhospitable bush, and many a skeleton has since been found, not only of*
> *absconders, but of gangs sent in search of them. But although wicked men*
> *may be permitted to form, and for a length of time, to govern a gehenna,*
> *fortunately they cannot make it eternal.*

> *It remains for the present generation of colonists to change all that, and a few months hence I fully expect to see a population of some thousand diggers – not perhaps the most desirable members of society – still an improvement on the past. The Victorian Syndicate has already undertaken to make a tramway to Mount Zeehan, a distance of over 20 miles at a cost of £70,000, and work on the Mount will be commenced forthwith. Meanwhile, to show from what meagre unpromising beginnings we start, I send herewith a true copy of our mining manager's last report: –*
>
> *He writes under date March 15th: 'I am sending two nuggets of silver-lead. I am discharging one man on Saturday; there will then be one man beside myself. I do not think there will be any necessity to do any deep sinking, as we cannot sink without six men at least. Mr Brown from Broken Hill has paid us a visit, and I took him round to see our lodes. He examined them, and carried away specimens. It has been raining for eleven days, and is still raining. The look-out is not very cheerful with regard to provisions, which are very scarce just now, but we have one consolation – badgers are very plentiful. They are good eating, and there is a great run on them by the miners.'*

Bunkered down in a township 'as inviting at Stromness, which it much resembles', Arthur busies himself interrogating returning diggers.

> *They were showing various nuggets valued at from £3 to £10, which they said they got by simply digging up some scrub. For the first time in my life, I felt half tempted to join a party, including an old gentleman of 74, here being organized. But I thought better of this digging expectation and went out for a quiet stroll instead.*

———

The fever persisted. Arthur called his next report 'A Trip into the Interior: Mining Prospects'. The small township hotels with their log fires and transient populations of tale-tellers, conmen and drifters, resembled the shiftless gold addicts, hanging on in Mexico, in B. Traven's *The Treasure of the Sierra Madre*. 'It was really the thought of their present situation and how to alter it. Only money could alter it, and money was closely connected with gold. Thus the thought of gold gained on them until they thought of little else.'

Traven's novel opens with his character Dobbs sitting on a 'thoroughly bad' bench. A rail is missing and he cannot decide if the punishment is deserved. He knows that it is 'unjustified'. And in that instant of self-knowledge, the basic flaw in his project is revealed to him. Man's fate is *never* unjustified. It happens because it happens, because you were foolish or brave enough to make the first move. That missing rail in the bench was the broken slat on my bed in the jungle hut. The question the Ashaninka asked – 'Is the old man looking for gold?' – was the right question in the wrong place. Or the right question to the wrong old man: it was Arthur Sinclair who was tempted and fell. He agreed to join the expedition into the interior being organised by the Hon. James Smith.

'We have already got a good geologist and assayer,' Smith said. 'And we will make you the botanist of the party.'

Arthur demurs: he knows and loves his plants, and he is always running soil through his fingers, but he lacks academic credentials. He has not been assigned to gather specimens for Kew. But he accepts, and the party sets off, first by coach and then railway.

> *The whole of the land in this district, through which the railway now passes, was given away by a faithless Government to the Van Diemen's Land Company. Like most great Land companies and big landlords, they have proved but indifferent stewards. I am also willing to acknowledge, as I have learned by painful experience, that the climate and soil of Tasmania have been ignorantly overrated. Oh, for a million of the much abused Chinese! What a transformation Tasmania would show in a few years! But what's the good of speculating, while all the best of the land is locked up?*

The Van Diemen's Land Company, here challenged by Arthur, was an earlier version of the even more ravenous Peruvian Corporation of London; the guano-harvesting, railway-constructing, silver-mining company that would, in a few years, give my great-grandfather his final commission. V.D.L. Co. was founded in 1825, receiving a royal charter and a grant of 250,000 acres of land in what is now Tasmania. They imported sheep, cattle and farm labourers, before diversifying into timber and paying handsome bounties on thylacine extracted from Tasmanian tigers. This generous offer contributed to the extinction of these animals. In 2016 V.D.L. Co. was purchased, for 280 million Australian dollars, by the new global economic power, Moon Lake Investments, controlled by Lu Xianfeng. Arthur's frequently stated wish for an active Chinese presence on the island was granted.

The gold-hunting party debate Darwin's evolutionary theories, Arthur being more of an enthusiast than the others. The local newspaper announces the arrival of the prospectors in Waratah. 'The party, consisting of a gentleman and two coffee planters, started with knapsacks for the west coast this morning.' Away they trudge, in the footsteps of their guide, a veteran bushman. Arthur has a grudging admiration for the guide and calls him 'the Philosopher'.

The road leading from Waratah to Corinna is characteristic and in every way worthy of Tasmania: a bush track recently completed and already condemned. The gradient for the first two miles is about one in five, then, for a mile, almost level; here we cross the River Arthur; after this we again ascend a burst-my-gall path of 1 in 4. Just see how the Philosopher plods on! No mistake about it, these water-drinking men can walk. The villainous road is made upon what is here called the corduroy *principle, which simply consists of placing logs of wood side by side across the mud.*

There are no inhabitants, save perhaps a few adventurous and vagrant prospectors like ourselves, but there can be no doubt that there is a great future before this portion of the island, containing as it evidently does the richest deposits of both gold, silver and tin in the colony. Ample indications of both gold and silver have already been discovered, although the locality even yet has been but partially explored, owing to the impenetrable nature of the vegetation. Horizontal bush is here forming a barrier, breast-high, everywhere obstructing the traveller who would venture from the corduroy track.

> *'Good thing this horrid nuisance, like your Tasmanian devil, is peculiar to this island,' I said, as I stumbled in trying to reach a beautiful specimen of native pepper.*
>
> *'It might be worse,' said our ever-amiable Philosopher. 'It might have had thorns.'*

In Peru, when struggling with a steep climb in the foothills of the Andes, after a ride on the world's second-highest railway, we learned that you buy time to recover breath by asking dumb questions or offering anecdotes to the man who guides your party.

> *I would have preferred more leisure on this journey: the day is very hot, the shade under the noble tree-ferns is very inviting, and the undergrowth of vegetation in this horrid climate becomes most interesting; but the strides of my guide, the Philosopher, seem to increase as the sun gets higher, and the gradient becomes more abominable. Midday, however, came at last, and by a unanimous vote a halt for dinner was agreed. In a trice the billy is hung from a tripod, and a fire speedily blazing under it. In 10 minutes the tea is being handed round, or rather each man helps himself, for alas! no kindly coolly waits upon master in this benighted land. I may say that the metallic-tasting liquid universally imbibed in Tasmania is no more like tea than turpentine is like sweet milk.*
>
> *There were not many 'courses' at this dinner, for the half hour was soon up, and so was our philosophic guide, who has no taste for after dinner libations and who abominates smoking.*

Sweating, unshaven, still hungry, they push on, coming to resemble, with every passing hour, the archival photographs I have seen of the mining camps. Arthur's urbane beard would appear a barefaced challenge to the real prospectors, the desperate ones who bristle against shacks and diggings. Half savage and proud of it.

> *We have not met nor seen a living creature, and no sound greets the ear, not even a buzzing bee. It was not without a feeling of relief that I noted some little black clouds obscure the sun as we trudged along, now climbing*

over a ridge, and now rapidly descending to what proved to be the Whyte River. Here there is actually a small hut prepared at the expense of the Government for the reception of travellers. Never was the sight of four walls and a roof more welcome, for rain now fell in heavy drops. Soon the swags were thrown on a prostrate tree, while one of the party ventured to inspect the interior. It was not inviting: the earthen floor had never been swept since it had a roof above it, while a heap of suspicious looking rags disclosed the fact that the place is permanently inhabited by 'Jerusalem travellers'. 'Anything would be better than this,' we said, as with a creeping sensation we shoulder our swags and depart.

Silently now we trudged on, up one ridge and down another; the situation was getting decidedly tedious, when all of a sudden our guide turned at right angles and went scrambling into the bush. Follow him we must. At length an opening came, a plot of knife and button grass, and, beyond that, two tiny tents, to which we hurried. All sense of weariness soon forgotten in the agreeable surprise of seeing some 50 tons of rich silver ore. The Philosopher's hammer has again been at work, and to some purpose, for here is what may turn out to be the richest silver mine in Australasia, though, strange to say, the Tasmanian newspapers have not had an inkling of the fact. The old miner I have been talking to declares he could easily put out an average of two tons per day, and as this means 240 oz. of pure silver, and 70 per cent of lead, there is evidently money to be made, even if we reduce his estimated output by one-half. To me, however, I must confess, the life of a digger has few charms. Some must dig, I daresay, but compared with the life of a planter, it is a barbarous and demoralising business.

No gold then, but a strike that could carry significant consequences for Arthur and his family. But gold was still the dream, the great engine of desire. Arthur was fired by a story Percy Russell published on 13 January 1887, in *Colonies and India*. It was titled 'Tasmanian Gold'. Russell describes as 'fact' the account he gives of a certain Captain Osborne, after he lost his ship and all hands at Macquarie Harbour.

He alone was saved to tell the tale, said Arthur, *how he wandered in the inhospitable and dense bush for many days, till found all but dead and quite*

> *speechless and imbecile by a settler's child. How, in after years, glimpses*
> *of reason and speech returned, and how he ejaculated to his daughters on*
> *his death bed: – 'Macquarie Harbour, up the river – gold, gold, I saw it*
> *glitter, be sure and send for it, good girls; I'll tell your mother (in heaven)*
> *how rich you will be.'*

Finding himself in the same territory now, Arthur cannot shake off
the romance of the dead mariner's obsession.

> *I will confess that the story awakened a keen emotion in myself, and at least*
> *added considerably to the zest with which I prosecuted recent explorations,*
> *in the locality indicated, without however much success as regards gold.*
> *In some of the creeks I did come across the colour, but that was all, though*
> *I heard whispered rumours of nuggets of fabulous weight having recently been*
> *picked up. It was to silver that my attention was more immediately directed.*

The Ashaninka, living with a more flexible concept of time, recognised
that the old man – myself channelling Arthur – *was* looking for gold by
the river, fingering the sand, searching for glints in the water, in train to
becoming my own great-grandfather. Without, at that time, appreciat-
ing that the quest was open-ended, unresolved. That the quest *was* the
quest. With no material benefits. No gold for Arthur in streams with
real names on a fabulous map and only mythical journeys as inspiration.
The dying man's fever vision inflicted on his resistant daughters. No gold
and not much silver: mining was never to be Arthur's trade. His moods
rose and plunged with the boom and bust of predatory colonialism. A
company was floated to blot up the last of his reserves, to clear the way
for further adventures on the thorny path towards enlightenment. And
the tangled nest of unfinished stories he would leave to his inheritors.

———

> *In two miles we cross the Hazlewood River, named after an early pioneer*
> *who, for some reason best known to himself, spelt his name 'Heazlewood'.*
> *Crossing this very respectable stream on a rickety bridge, we proceed to*

'Long Plains', where we observe numerous indications of recent prospectors in search of the precious metal. All that is actually known is that it was near this spot that one McGinty found the famous 94 lb. nugget – probably some of poor Osborne's treasure.

Corinna is our nearest port, and we reach it dead beat, for though only 20 miles from Hazlewood, it is a rough and not very interesting road. The Corinna, as the Aborigines called it, is however a noble river, in volume of water exceeding the Derwent, and is by far the largest river in Tasmania.

This is a wild coast, little known and generally avoided; but, as there seems every probability of its becoming famous for its minerals, it was decided a trip to Macquarie Harbour might not be uninteresting, and accordingly, after resting a day, we start along a winding path, the first dozen miles being through dense forest, the remainder through comparatively open country. The first stage is to Trial Harbour, 28 miles by the path. Trial Harbour or Remina (every township in Tasmania has two names) is about as miserable a place as one would care to come across – and, recently, a bush fire having added to the horror of the surroundings, this whole township was burned down, the inhabitants only escaping with their lives by running into the sea. Temporary huts have again been built, but the charred remains of many a table and chair may be seen, strewed around. Poor as the place is, it is destined to see better days at no distant date. Yonder mountain, at a distance of only 11 miles, bleak and rugged as it looks, is believed to rest upon a foundation of silver ore, so rich and abundant that the eyes of capitalists from all parts of Australia are now turning towards it. A dozen Companies have been formed, and within the past fortnight six have been floated with capital from £30,000 to £40,000 each. While a Syndicate from Ballarat has offered to make a tramway from Mount Zeehan to Macquarie Harbour. Bravo! There is hope for Tasmania yet.

This hope was soon to be dashed, left in a burnt and smouldering landscape with a scattered population of desperate frontier starvelings running into the ocean. Shares boomed. Prospectors and investors stampeded to ruin.

> *There is not perhaps in the wide world a place of worse reputation than Macquarie Harbour. Port Arthur was a paradise, and Norfolk Island an asylum, compared with this perfect pandemonium. Here nature combined to form scenery in keeping with the terrible tragedies enacted. Overhead an angry sky and a temperature so chill and humid that animal life is with difficulty preserved. Lashed by frequent tempests, this rugged region shows but little vegetation, save in the coarsest and most massive forms; no grass for miles around sufficient to feed a goat.*

Arthur, wandering at a loss through this desert of discredited dreams, decides to compile a basic dictionary of the language of the eradicated people. Lacking original sources, he works from the notes left by a man called Jorgensen.

> *The son of a Danish watchmaker, Jorgensen first attracted attention in 1809 by making a descent on Iceland, and in the name of Great Britain taking the Governor prisoner! He confiscated all property, subjecting the inhabitants to the most unscrupulous despotism, before appointing himself Dictator, and coolly writing to England that he had another colony for them! The reply was a man-of-war which at once took the impudent fellow a prisoner to London, and ultimately gave him a free passage to Van Dieman's Land, where, being tolerably clever and very unscrupulous, he soon became a leading spirit.*

Using Jorgensen's papers, Arthur compiles an Aboriginal vocabulary of around 100 words: Dance = *Rialangana*. Dead = *Moye*. Fire = *Tonna*. Devil = *Rargeropper*.

> *I am often struck to find how few English words serve the turn of the average bushman. Travelling the other day to Emu Bay, I had opposite me in the coach a young bushman, who, although he kept talking, never during the three hours I noted him, used more than 25 words! Though not very elegant, I was struck with the extreme simplicity of the arrangement. With such intellectual surroundings who would scruple to take their family into the bush?*

———

'Kodak in hand', Arthur travels to Melbourne. He is accumulating capital only in the sense of building up material resources for stories that may never be told and books there will be no time to write. In later years, trying to summarise the lessons learned from his travels, Arthur confessed that he had 'compared Tasmanian hospitality rather disparagingly with the spontaneous entertainment we received from *hill* tribes of Peru'. The 'petty jealousies' between colonies, he found 'lamentable'. Fretful suspicions and dark rumours of gold strikes, passing back and forth between Tasmania and Victoria, reminded him of the guano skirmishes between Peru and Chile. His prophetic conclusion, before he returns to the ocean, is that the real threat to Australia will come from China. 'The systematic and cowardly cruelty to the inoffensive Chinaman must, in the nature of things, bear fruit – and if competent revolutionary leaders were to arise in China, it might fare badly with the great race of borrowers, city builders, "reconstructors", and first-prize cricketers who at present inhabit Kangaroo-land.'

After such lively exchanges of insult, Maoist visions of coming geo-politics, and the confirmation that he had no business in mining, Arthur shipped out on a dreamlike Conradian voyage; island hopping, reading, musing, and starting essays that would never be completed, until he arrived on Samoa. Where he was quite pleased to discover that cricket, 'after due deliberation', had been outlawed and 'tabooed'. He made landfall just ahead of his fellow Scot Robert Louis Stevenson. But he managed to get away from the place where the author of *Treasure Island* was 'kidnapped by death at a cruelly premature age', as Ian Thomson has it. In his *Financial Times* review of Joseph Farrell's biography of Stevenson, Thomson concludes that Samoa was where the glint of 'granite' finally broke through the wandering writer's 'old velvet-coated' Edinburgh prose.

Restless as ever, Arthur makes one last push, a five-hundred-mile journey into the Australian interior. Within eight miles of Wagga Wagga he discovers a 'model' farm of 3,600 acres. It is called *Bon Accord*, a name associated with Aberdeen: the motto of the city. Legend has it that 'Bon Accord' was used as a secret password in the fourteenth-century Wars of Scottish Independence. The established toast of Aberdeen – 'Happy to meet, sorry to part, happy to meet again – Bon Accord!' – manages to incorporate words from a Masonic poem, 'The Final Toast'.

The Wagga Wagga estate that Arthur admired '*was originally selected by the son of a prosperous biscuit baker in the Granite City – hence its name*'. *Bon Accord* was also the name chosen by Arthur's medical son, Henry, for his own house, with its porch and colonial features, on a hill in the Welsh mining town Maesteg, where he settled with his family. The house in which I grew up.

In excited research mode, notebook ready, Kodak primed, Arthur catalogued *everything* about the district: industries, soil, climate, and testimonials of local witnesses. The leading man of affairs in the area, Mr Fitzhardinge, is invited to dinner.

> *But it was otherwise ordained. The residence of Mr Fitzhardinge lay at the other side of the railway, which for 17 years he had crossed in safety. But on this fatal night, the poor man, confused by shunting operations, was knocked down and literally beheaded, his brains scattered over the line.*
>
> *Next day, instead of dining with Mr Fitzhardinge, I had to look upon his body lying on the floor, with well-formed but mangled head in a basin beside it. Business was suspended for the day, all Wagga attended the funeral.*

The Australasian adventure fades out on the unspeaking head in the basin at Arthur's feet. There are no oracular whispers, post-mortem. The interior of this harsh land has yielded none of its secrets. The family must be gathered up, once more, and a slow return, in circumstances worse than when they set out, plotted.

FEVERS

FEVERS

THE ADVOCATE

'The Advocate is stopped in the street by someone importunate.'
  – Geoffrey Hill, *The Book of Baruch by the Gnostic Justin*

The Advocate wrote on trains. Duties, commissions, and scattered family disposed him across the railways of Europe, always with tasks in hand. He was surrounded by Post-it-defaced books, Mexican magazines, and further books scrupulously annotated. He laboured, indulgently, on translations from the obscurest scribblers, and he scanned all the sources referenced by his chosen authors. In hub cities – Paris, for example – this diligent pan-European man of culture arranged his itinerary… in from Brussels, out to Strasbourg, on to Spain or Switzerland, assuaging bankers and bureaucrats, charity czars, climate-change celebrities, outliers covering the backs of oligarchs… in order to steal at least one hour to confirm his favourite oxymoron, the pre-plotted *dérive*. Passage Brady to rue d'Enghien, eyes open for the stencilled outline of the local muse: Sakin Cansiz, a senior member of PKK shot in the back of her head on 9 January 2013. A balanced walk, then, to flatter rising panic, to keep the hounds of history in their cages.

When the Advocate arrived on my Hackney doorstep, he had flown in – a necessary penance, black-masked, denying himself access to print – from Buenos Aires, for an eleven a.m. with Chancellor Osborne and Sajid Javid at No. 11, Downing Street. Coffee and biscuits. Wilted white sandwiches. And courteous misunderstandings. The co-operative future for financial services. Tactful avoidance of anti-monopoly regulations. The Advocate, as a proud Andalucían relocated from the City of Gold to the home of the European Parliament, was the soul of discretion about this other life; we tramped many miles in several capitals, discussing and debating the sprung rhythms and buried intentions of reforgotten Whitechapel poets, before he revealed any part of how his superimposed but utterly distinct careers fitted together.

The subtext, in a negotiation more fruitful and much less corrupt than the recent insanity of our opting for undiluted red-raw Trumpery over European fudge, was that poetry kept him alive. And certifiably sane. That the great poetic corpus, respectfully approached, proved how any serious man or woman should behave, and more besides. Poetry countered the pressure of derangement the Advocate masked with a politic smile and the unaffected courtesy of a civil servant hired to be quieter, wiser and more diplomatic than the diplomats he supported and advised. My own underlying motive was to tap this man for information on Peru. To use his language skills, his Mediterranean Catholic origins, his practical experience of aid missions to endangered cloud-forest settlements, to prepare us for the rapidly approaching expedition in the hoof prints of my great-grandfather's mule train.

The Advocate's strategy, he explained, was 'not to hide, but never to actively boast of attainments, as poet or lawyer or man of affairs'. The enlightened Eurocrat translated fugitive late-modernist screeds while the sickly lights of indistinguishable nocturnal cities and flatlands spilled across the train window. He said that he had witnessed, 'in shame', the tweeded metropolitan squire Nigel Farage, when, smirking, he turned his back on the parliamentary hemicycle in Strasbourg, while four saxophonists played 'Ode to Joy'. But he had also sat up through midnight hours of yellow-filtered reverie in mind-forged philosophical dialogue with Jacques Derrida.

To prepare for our Hackney encounter, by transporting himself back to remembered campfires in Peru, the Advocate – a fastidious abstainer – broached a serious Cuban cigar from a complimentary box received from a Left Bank documentarist returned from the fusion jazz nights of a cultural solidarity conference in Havana. This sacrifice, grim hedonism, left him heavy tongued, dry in the throat, out of the office for two days, but possessed once again of a considered menu of accountable facts: contacts, potential problems.

And there was magic in that title: *Advocate*. An invocation, not only of Kafka and *The Trial*, but the rigours of the Scottish legal system. Too sickly for the family trade in lighthouse construction, Robert Louis Stevenson was 'admitted advocate' in 1875. A distinction he soon debauched among the low life of Edinburgh.

I told my daughter, who was, rather reluctantly, project managing this expedition, booking train tickets and lodgings, cars, trucks, and meetings with indigenous people, that we had found our translator. The Advocate was ahead of us. He had anticipated – having confirmed his hunches with embedded diplomatic connections – the difficulties and dangers we might face. And he had absorbed, to the last comma, my great-grandfather's book *In Tropical Lands*. Now he delivered an admirably balanced legal judgment, breaking the headlong momentum of the original quest into key elements, locations and personalities.

There was the Franciscan Convent at San Luis de Shuaro, controlled by the mysterious Padre Sala, the heavily-armed monk who guided Arthur's party across rivers and along salt trails, clawing their way up muddy slopes to Metraro, and down again, slithering and swearing, to the village of King Chokery on the Perené. But the critical point, an intersection of ancient paths, the Advocate informed us, was located on the 'high Pajonal plateau' with 'an overview of the valley and the endless succession of hills stretching towards the Amazon basin'. If we achieved this paradise vision, we would be close to the burial site of the legendary Juan Santos Atahualpa.

'I do not think this can easily be done by foot.'

Meanwhile, the Advocate would correspond with Franciscan archivists at Ocopa, requesting further information on Sala's journals and papers. And he would report back, in a few days, on conditions in the Rio Perené territory. He knew that there was an 'EU-sponsored project' in place, encouraging subsistence farmers to switch from coca production to ethical coffee – and other less sensitive (and far less profitable) alternatives.

His man in Lima, recently returned from Oxapampa, advised the Advocate to use a trusted driver and to avoid, at all costs, flying directly to Jauja. There was a woman, he said, a Sino-Californian agronomist, living somewhere between the ruins of the Convent at San Luis de Shuaro and the Mountain of Salt, who could broker introductions – if we could find her. She was rumoured to disappear into the low jungle for months at a time and to act as a courier between messianic Adventist groups, *narcotraficantes* and the last remnants of dispersed Maoist guerrillas.

Any journey around or beyond the rapids at Ipoki should be broached with extreme caution. 'My friend reiterated in detail his warning about the no-go areas,' the Advocate said. 'This is an acknowledged *shadow* zone occupied by scattered coca growers from the poorest parts of the altiplano; *choris*, as the Ashaninka call them. There are outbreaks of spasmodic violence, unreported massacres and revenge raids. The Peruvian State is very much absent. Local myths represent the jungle around Satipo and the confluence with the Rio Ene as a reservation of the undead and the unburied, the hollow ones, *maninkari*. All looking for innocent meat, fresh hosts.'

I passed the Advocate's notes to Farne, who was doing the real work, making calls, combing archives, lining up inoculations and selecting flights. She was not so grievously seduced by poetic myths and fantasies of 'cultural appropriation'. She conducted Skype conversations with anthropologists and arranged interviews with indigenous people who knew and trusted only those with whom they were already in dialogue. Like me, she was impressed by the erudition, courtesy and contacts of the Advocate, but she did wonder, in the light of developments in Brussels and London, if he would be able to join us, as promised, as our translator in Peru.

'And what,' she said, 'does he mean by *shadow* area?' Apparently, Farne told me – and she was kept up to the minute with developments by her husband, who ran an ever-alert corridor of BBC news – something was afoot in Europe. There was alarmist talk about a divorce and a crank cadre mouthing off, fouling the Twittersphere with their bull-headed determination to 'make it happen'. But I couldn't take any of that seriously. I was too much absorbed in Peruvian bibliographies to have the time to indulge newsprint and shouty, purple-faced broadcasts by sloganeers.

'He seems like a lovely man, but does he always keep to his arrangements? The political parties in the European Parliament are setting their constitutive committee meetings for July 10, just when we're hoping to launch on the river. How can he get away?'

I had to admit that the Advocate, who was one hundred per cent reliable, was rarely able to arrive at the *precise* hour and place he had fixed long in advance. He disliked driving and he didn't understand public transport. He was a walker, a cyclist. And, anyway, he would be coming through London soon. He wanted to take a proper look at locations mentioned in a poem. I would discover everything I needed to know at that time. For a ludicrously overqualified bureaucrat, a person of plural cultures, this man subscribed to the weirdest theories. And he involved himself, as I knew all too well, with the writings of the strangest people.

The Eurostar slid into St Pancras like an obituary for the better life. I waited, alongside a stand-up piano that an albino child in fur mittens was punching with her elbows, to embrace my walking companion. The Advocate spun out of the peristaltic tide of bemused or taxi-rushing travellers like a heretic missionary set on divorcing himself from his unworthy flock. He was alpine hooded and smiling. A grey-blue glaze of entitlement behind rimless spectacles. He carried a black bag over his shoulder, containing books and papers, wafers of truth to protect him from scuttling disbelievers.

I led him, briskly, away from the station and into byways and less frequented squares, fenced parks and ancient passages of the preoccupied city. The Advocate was unique, in my experience, in that he kept up an unbroken monologue while noticing and commenting on all the oddities I showed him. When I stayed for a few days in Brussels, the situation was reversed. But I chose to speak only when questions of detail were required, or when I found some parallel with London, ground covered in the recent past. The Advocate had a theory I struggled to grasp, and only began, very slowly, to understand when we struck out to imprint it, like a phantom equation, on the landscape. It started, he said, with a visit by Euro parliamentarians to the Large Hadron Collider at CERN and a subsequent high-level conference of desert astronomers and space botanists in Santiago, Chile: a life-changing obsession with Quantum Entanglements.

We navigated the Belgian capital, Joseph Conrad's frosted 'sepulchral city', down a golden path already tramped, or still being tramped, by the shades of Vincent van Gogh, Rimbaud, W.G. Sebald and the Elephant Man, Joseph Merrick. We seemed to be climbing, breathlessly and at pace, away from the former brothel in which I had been lodged, now through empty public squares, bone-white in the declining winter sunshine, to broad steps that led to the offices of the Société Anonyme Belge pour le Commerce du Haut-Congo, where Conrad received his riverboat command from the managing director, Albert Thys. The Advocate pointed to the doorway at 10 rue de Namur, a former military school, with a triumphant air. As if he had been a party to the original interview, running a practised eye over the small print of the contract. Which should have been signed with a large X in blood.

Emerging on Leadenhall Street, and the cluster of guided walking groups and red-spectacled architecturalists recording the exposed lifts and pipes of the Lloyd's Building, to be sure that it was still there, I revealed to the Advocate, who was keeping shorthand minutes of our excursion, the building that had once housed the proud offices of the Peruvian Corporation of London. In 1890, Arthur Sinclair put pen to paper – my daughter found a copy of the original contract – at just the moment when Conrad was accepting his own commission to the heart of darkness.

'Is that coincidence,' I said. 'Or entanglement?'

'Close,' the Advocate replied. 'Or both at once. Or perhaps some other syndrome for which I have not yet found a name. Voiceless versions of ourselves are looped in a spiral of past events. And, by the way, the door I showed you in rue de Namur was not necessarily the *right* one. Journalists favour the address because the African International Association has its headquarters there, but scholars point to another doorway, a few yards further up the street. We will have to go back. You appreciate that memory is merely a minor function of location. We need absolute precision, in order to recollect what and when we are. True gnosis must be meticulous with the smallest alien details of facts.'

The Advocate was exactly like the 'compassionate secretary' Conrad recalls, and lightly glosses, in *Heart of Darkness*: a man 'full of desolation and sympathy'. In Mincing Lane, where coffee from the colonies was traded, with heaped samples from various estates laid across long tables, we had a startling view down the diminishing funnel of the narrow street, and across the river, to the Shard: part twilight-subverting sail, part astral pyramid. 'It was just as though I had been let into some conspiracy,' Conrad wrote.

The following morning we rose early, to follow the flow of sewage down the 'Green Way', a raised earthwork tending towards the Thames at Beckton. Whenever we paused at a relevant marker, the Advocate dissected aspects of the London poem he had translated. Sometimes he recited a few wildly rushing stanzas in performative Spanish: dry brown tones dressing these peculiar fragments, lick by lick, in unearned dignity.

Approaching the ugly Death Star of the former Olympic Stadium, a hollow cradle to be appreciated only by drones and surveillance satellites, the Advocate froze. He stuck out an arm, to touch, feel and rub knuckles against the coarse surface of a filthy concrete bunker. 'This,' he said, 'is the Oracle Shrine.'

I settled myself on one of the tank-trap obstructions while he made notes. But when I approached a window slit in this defensive pillbox, placed here in the certain expectation of invasion and never dismantled, a charm against Vikings, Nazis and other economic migrants, *I heard the bunker breathe*. The tensile net of a spider's web across the aperture, silver against the dark interior, was a frenzied blackboard demonstration. An afterimage of the squeaking of chalk.

It was unmistakable. The Advocate trembled. Urine-soaked rags, mummified dog turds and dead pigeons in rancid tabloid cerements, ritually magicked into a single entity, were groaning in their reeking prison nightmare. My companion swept the foul nest with his phone-app torchbeam. *The Oracle of Place was talking to him. And only to him.* A rough-sleeper, snoring and snorting through a broken nose, was humped on a living mattress.

Here, demonstrably, was confirmation of the Advocate's thesis: what more is an oracle than an echo chamber for our insecurities? Nothing is validated without a witness. But that witness will require a further witness to confirm his insight. And that witness… And so on. What is happening now must also be happening to another twinned particle in some remote galaxy. Some parallel shell world. *Entanglement*. You could brand it. Look how that carcinogenic spoil heap in front of the Bow Quarter, the former Bryant and May match factory, echoes the blasted topography of the smelting plant at La Oroya in Peru. Look how the scuttled vessel on the foreshore at Woolwich, waiting to be cut up for scrap, chimes with Herzog's cinema translation of the rubber baron Carlos Fermín Fitzcarrald's riverboat, wrecked in the rapids on the Urubamba.

By the time we reached what the Advocate called the 'simultaneous quantum entanglement' of Arthur Sinclair's *Peruvian Mountain of Salt* and Beckton Alp, a blunted cone of arsenic, heaped from the ruins of a bombed gasworks, and overlooking the A13, we were initiated into a split or superimposed reality: at once London and South America. The itinerants camped in overgrown landfill declivities, and among the gravestones of an ancient burial ground near the flyover, were also the people of the dust shacks on the edge of the railway out of Lima. They hawked fruit and bottles of fizzy drinks, religious toys and medallions, to a line of cars stalled at the lights and strung out for miles by never-ending construction projects.

As we squeezed through the perimeter fence intended to keep casual ramblers away from the fabulous range of contaminants layered into this failed speculation, a dry ski slope rubber-carpeted over simmering topsoil and unexploded bombs, we were stopped by a pair of intrepid New Hackney psychogeographers whose sat-nav gizmos refused to acknowledge this decommissioned dune. We pointed out the entrance to the Green Way and they trotted off, happily, in the direction of more accessible edgelands. And the catalogue of approved grand-project follies.

Tough vegetation, fattened on illegal pollutants, rioted in jungle profusion over the lower slopes. I found myself tangled in bushes of dark red berries, unpopped blood blisters reminding the Advocate of coffee cherries he had seen on the highlands of the Gran Pajonál. There were no longer any misgivings about the journey ahead of me. I swiv-elled through a 360-degree panorama, stunned by the totality of the unreal mushroom city, the irregular plantations of failed retail parks, the sewage filtration beds, the glistening black snake of the river. And the whistling necklace of perpetual traffic, road and sky.

The Advocate quoted the poet Ed Dorn, one of his manifold enthu-siasms: 'We'd all rather *be* there, than talk about it.'

What we talked about in the bar of the St Pancras Hotel, while the Advocate waited for his train, and for the arrival of Farne, who would be joining us to run through the final details of our travel plans, was cattle. Another gift for alcohol-fired entanglement. Any topic casually tweezered into the light of day, the Advocate asserted, continues to ripple across the infinite curvature of space, happening everywhere at once. Before dissolving into the futile pursuit of that radical disappoint-ment we call memory.

A couple of rounds of heavily fruited wine from the Advocate's remembered country cost us not much more than a single upgraded ticket on Eurostar. Polished glasses were delivered, like a prison sen-tence, with barely concealed contempt, and a 'complimentary' goblet of unglazed popcorn. The over-mirrored bar was impure pastiche, an attempt to revive the louche atmosphere of that Michael Andrews group painting, *Colony Room*. But now, in the yellow absinthe hour of suspended travel, the mirrors had trapped a gathering of the dead. A cohabitation of scrubbed and suited individuals with no prior con-nection or purpose, beyond the killing of time, the neurotic checking of fist-screens for unreliable updates. Rumours of imminent departure were the excuse for breaking off unwelcome encounters. Waving for bills presented on silver trays.

We should have been sitting on a sepulchre in the neighbouring churchyard. The Advocate emphasised the obvious link, discounting scale, between the socio-economic consequences of introducing cattle ranching to the Scottish Highlands and to the pampas of Argentina. Some of those Borgesian ranchers and their savage gauchos were of Scottish origin: the dispersed making good.

Eyes burning behind faintly tinted spectacles, a stray lock of hair signalling towards an elegant eyebrow, the Advocate riffed on how his native country in the south of Spain was defined, in just the way, in my early speculative poetry, I had projected lines of force across London, by migrant routes trampled by massive herds from the north. The cattle were entitled, he said, to process through estates, provincial towns and public gardens. And to invade his homeland, a former paradise of fruit, vegetables and goats.

His thesis echoed the way that a ban, endorsed and refined by smiling lowland advocates, was imposed on the importation of Irish cattle into England. This led, inevitably, to a beef boom in Scotland: smaller beasts, bigger land clearances. And burdened crocodiles of displaced Scots and Irish shipped out, to become ranchers, colonists and planters, in their own turn.

My companion pushed back his glass and reverted to his other identity. He checked an immaculate and previously unused 7th generation iPad. 'From this point on,' he said, 'we are in *perpetual* motion. Like those cattle. All together, bellowing and stamping, towards the same unforeseen and definitive resolution.'

By the time Farne arrived from Old Street, documents at the ready, it was clear that the Advocate would be with us on the expedition we were about to undertake. He was deeply implicated in the venture and the libraries of research that surrounded it. But he would be with us only in spirit. 'I will have to invent my own private version of a dream journey to Perené,' he said. 'I cannot, in conscience, step aside from what has to be done in Brussels.'

So we embraced, all three, and my correspondent slid back into the crowd from which he had emerged twenty-four hours earlier. To no one in particular, I whispered those lines from Geoffrey Hill's last testament: 'By nightfall, Advocate will supplicate in vain.'

LIMA

'Schlegel appeared to be trying to rewrite history while having his own family history rewritten into the bargain.'
— Chris Petit, *Mister Wolf*

Still a little lightheaded, but eager to engage, I am out there at first light, waiting patiently to find safe passage across the flow of Avenida del Ejército. I have to access that promised view of the Pacific Ocean. To confirm what was only a twilight fantasy in the window of our cab, after so many dislocated hours in the air. And already, fifty yards from our comfortable Miraflores hotel, the foetal figure curled beneath the counter of a shuttered fast-food operation is challenging the limited permissions of casual tourism. Perhaps he is waiting on his hour to wash dishes? Or reserving this cold stone shelf for one more day alive in the city? The smell of basted chicken saturates a dirty white shirt. The residue of cigarettes he cannot afford. Much of my remembered self, after that transatlantic flight, remains in transit.

Cockroach taxis on the hustle, beaten-up cars, and vans with yawning rear doors: they cruise the tired line of humans waiting for workers' buses. They are touting for anyone ready to part with a few coins for a shared ride. I experience a sudden frisson of unearned fellowship with these characters of the morning: the entitled of this broad avenue and the hidden ones who have reserved niches in the doorways and friendly shadows of tributary streets. But, as soon as I reach the palm trees and smart apartment blocks of Malecón de la Marina, I am back with the universal procession of infolded joggers in uniform black. With the head-clamped cyclists of Hackney. The elbow-pumping aristos of towpath and esplanade, their stylish vests imprinted with slogans boasting of marathons completed. And the conspicuous charities of bankers and brokers. The academic affiliations, actual and elective. The more comfortable your material circumstances, the earlier you have to be available to claim a space in the neighbourhood park. With rolled up mats, for exercise not prayer, or exercise as prayer. With personal trainer, boxing pads, bondage devices to hang from trees. And elegant but lethally effective sound systems. They are all here too, the entitled ones. At the other end of the earth. Of course they are. Moving and talking. Business and society. Life is with them always. The landscape requires them.

But there is already a noticeable difference. There is physical distance between the chilled and the unchilled, the cool of the coffee drinkers and the rage of the coffee producers. The unchilled ranters and headbutters and grievance shouters of my home territory cohabit with occupiers and producers. They pass freely, if unseen, among and alongside the cyclists and preoccupied fathers jogging their infants to nursery. In Miraflores, the workers are separated from the fortunate ones. Lima is pure hierarchy. Convenient labourers, Indians and displaced peasants, are let in, uniformed, to smooth the pavements for the runners, to water the gardens. But the invisibles stay invisible. And silent.

'All this in a forty-minute stroll before breakfast?' Arthur Sinclair said. 'You read so much into things so soon?' His voice, which I had never previously heard, carried the Scottish countryman's derision for the shiftless Cockney. Actual Cockneys took me for an Australian or a New Zealander, a struck-off doctor or bent detective. In my dotage, they called me 'Boss'.

'You travelled the world,' I fired back, 'but you never, truly, had a place to call your own. The home business was nostalgia, melancholy reminiscences for what you never had.'

'I had the sea,' Arthur said. 'Turn round. Look on it. And tremble.'

The motto of our hotel – SEIZE YOUR DAY – is also the creed of this fortunate district. Make it happen. You are the elect. Far, far below, beyond crumbling cliffs of emerald green, the green of plastic football pitches under lights, are the frown lines of successive breakers, wrinkling and smoothing out. They froth and stain. And beyond these minor agitations, one fact still too large to comprehend: the Ocean.

There are too many visible barriers to risk a swim. I am not quite ready for that baptism in novelty. There is too much water. And it is protected by a silver strip of headlong commuter traffic along the Circuito de Playas. An obstacle course, with zigzag climbs, waiting for Grand Prix status. And then a long sweep of peppery sand, like crushed glass. The cliffs, netted for their own protection, and naked of vegetation, oversee clumps of mixed forest, palm trees with light poles. The scene is lost in a fug of exhaust fumes and sea fret. Red dust blows in from the perpetually destroyed and renewed squatter camps that shadow the railway and stretch back to the hills.

Not enjoying my great-grandfather's leisurely advance, by sea, Caribbean landfall and isthmus railway, I am disorientated by a marine park dedicated to mathematicians and archaeologists. There are tactful references to the established tourist mysteries of the land: Nazca lines and spirit figures laid out as flowerbeds. This is a high-maintenance zone serviced by masked Andean labourers. Water is an indicator of privilege: swivelling fountains playing on immaculate grass, jets pissing over clipped hedges into an enclosure occupied by personal trainers and their clients. With spaces under the trees reserved for passing philosophers.

I liked all this enough to swivel on my heels and head straight back to the hotel, to meet Farne for breakfast. I wanted now to be advancing on her terms, more than my own. Her reading of the Peruvian exercise was challengingly direct. I didn't relish playing the part of a clumsy translator, between the writerly defence systems Arthur had erected and my daughter's determination to make him declare himself; to recognise the consequences of his selectively reported actions. I had my own tricks for navigating cities known and unknown. I could always find time to notice MOVISTAR, a blue telephone pad hooked to a fence and padlocked against theft. I appreciated this object's relationship to the portrait of Frida Kahlo, eyes tightly closed, exhaling a bleeding red heart over a Douanier Rousseau jungle. But these are just snapshots. Kahlo's mimetic trance is positioned directly above an unoccupied blue rectangle of tarmac reserved for electrified disability scooters.

Arthur Sinclair, in his turn, was determined to open the account of a Peruvian journey by declaring his alienation.

And now, when in the capital, I am afraid I shall disappoint you, for I am not fond of cities; my heart longs always for the quiet country beyond. A simple man, my tastes lie among the simple people on the mountains, or in culling the common weeds by the wayside. I cannot, therefore, enter here into any detailed description of Lima, which at one time, we are told, was considered the gem of South America, and though now somewhat sullied, is still beautiful; picturesquely situated, with a climate almost perfect, the sun rarely scorching, and the rains never bedraggling the inhabitants.

BREAKFAST

'Don't go there!'
  – Francis Ford Coppola
  (advice to James Gray, director of *The Lost City of Z*)

The beautiful Farne, who, at certain times, can look so disconcertingly like my wife, like Anna, is not famous for her good humour on rising. She likes to ease in slowly to the new day. And I respect that. I have my own eccentric routines. But it was a while since I had breakfasted with my daughter. I can live dangerously from time to time and I looked forward to renewing the experience.

It was another life when our three children, separately and in competition, stormed the kitchen, clicking on the heating system and the shouty television, to provide a cushion of barbarous yelps to complement their disgruntled crunching. They remember every one of our crimes and misdemeanours, things done and undone. Especially mine. And those indictments stand unchallenged. The role of the parent is to become a willing scapegoat. It is always our fault, even as we recall the wrongs visited upon us. We are more forgiving of grandparents, the indulged old ones on the cusp of fading away altogether. Those teenage strops and hormonal furies are never entirely forgotten, but they are forgiven, because those too, every last one of them, must be laid at the door of the preoccupied father. When Anna ripped the phone from its jack after Farne declined to come off our solitary landline, two hours into some vital late-night chatter, my wife blamed herself. She is pleased that she caught my warning eye before she reached the critical point of throwing our oldest daughter out of the house. But Farne was born to independence and would be leaving anyway, to travel her own path, away from our ignorant interference. She would walk Upper Street in Islington until she found work in a bookshop, and saved enough money, with a second job at the printers who produced my small-press books, to fly out at eighteen, and on her own, to join an adventure tour in Peru. That country, she said, was a 'lifelong' obsession.

This was the pulse of it and the reflected pleasure: to see Farne, with her coffee and juice, showered and rested, hair tied back, smooth and prepared, enjoying a full scrambled egg and trimmings plate, without having to contemplate the hairy roots and skeletal fish, slow cooked over dirt and smoke, waiting for her in the jungle.

There were two items, side by side, on the breakfast table: *In Tropical Lands* by Farne's great-great-grandfather and her own, carefully composed statement of pursuit.

> My motivation is to make contact with the tribes. They are the part of the story that always fascinated me. I want to try and hear some of the history from their point of view. They believe that modern times began when the Peruvian Corporation arrived. Their understanding of the world is based around the river they live on. The only general directional terms for the surface of the earth are *katonko* (upriver) and *kirinka* (downriver). They also believe that somewhere in the sky is the river of eternal youth, *Hananerite*, probably inspired by the Milky Way. This is where the good spirits bathe to regain their youth and maintain their immortality. So I think the journey is a meditation on mortality. More personally, it's a way to connect with my grandfather, my memories of him from when I was seven and stayed with my grandparents in Wales, for a month, to recover from an operation: the strange shrunken heads in the garden room, maybe that was when I first heard of Arthur. And finally of course the journey is a way to connect with my father, and to connect my story with his.

This notion, of Farne picking up stories of Arthur from my father, while she convalesced after an emergency appendix operation, was factored from my own recall. From our recent conversations. Farne's initial memory was that when she announced that she would be going to Peru, I produced the original 1895 edition of Arthur's book and presented it to her. The gift was double-edged, a family curse being handed on. My daughter's close reading and subsequent research brought that element into the light.

She came to Lima for the first time exactly one hundred years after Arthur's unimpressed countryman's brief visitation.

'It felt,' Farne said, 'like landing on another planet. I remember stars so bright that it was like someone had turned up the voltage. Then I remember walking slowly at altitude and feeling the struggle for every breath. I remember the weight of jungle rain on my head. In London drizzle today, I drum my fingertips on my own children's heads and tell them that this is *nothing*, they should feel the rain in the Amazon forest. My adventure in 1991 was a well-worn path, what must it have felt like to arrive in 1891?'

Our first child did so well to carry the name we landed on her through school and university. It was that era. Baptisms of plants and seasons and holy islands. I decided, just a few weeks before she was born, that we had to jump in a borrowed van and head north to Lindisfarne. Poor Anna had to be helped up a slippery ladder, before she could roll onto the harbour wall, after a trip in a pitching boat to the Farne Islands, where colonies of gulls swooped and dived, affronted by our unseasonal invasion. Something had pulled us to the rocks of the northeast.

While Anna rested, in the late afternoon, on a bench in the grounds of Lindisfarne Priory, I rambled the ruins in a cloud of unknowing, beckoned onwards by an entirely orthodox hallucination, a brown hooded figure, all hood and no face, always disappearing around the next abutment, the next stone column, under a rainbow arch, and on through the broken ribs of a church armed against seaborne invaders. We confronted each other for an instant. Then he was gone. But the manifested print of this remote thing, in its absent heat, was confirmed. As pagans, we tried to get Farne christened in the Priory church: no go. Luckily our first child was not a boy. I don't think either of us could have lived with 'Cuthbert'.

'I have dreamt of making this trip to my Peru my whole life,' Farne wrote. *My* Peru! As if that also was part of the Lindisfarne hallucination, of my state of mind, travelling north: a reaching towards Arthur and his natal territory. But *In Tropical Lands* raised obvious problems for my daughter: our projected itinerary had to question the activities of the Peruvian Corporation and the history of the Perené Colony. Peru reneged on their overdue bonds, the State was in hock to the City of London. Michael Grace negotiated the so-called 'Grace Contract' in 1889, cancelling all debts in exchange for British ownership of the railways for sixty-six years. An associated land deal offered up 2,000,000 hectares to the intrepid colonisers. Arthur Sinclair, along with fellow planter Alexander Ross and P.D.G. Clark, the man from the botanical gardens in Ceylon, was hired to survey this underexplored and barely mapped ground with a view to future exploitation. *In Tropical Lands*, published in Edinburgh, London and Ceylon, was the colourful story of that expedition.

Farne's primary aim was to contact the Ashaninka, even perhaps the last workers from the Coffee Colony, and to hear the timbre of their voices. She explains, in her document of intention, that my motivation will be 'looking for the ghosts of my family and putting them to rest'. That's not quite it. Nothing so noble. I want to find Arthur, out beyond the rapids, alive as all the other wandering spirits in that territory, caught in the floes of a plural time that existed centuries before he made his first contact with the tribal people and persuaded them to cut balsa logs for rafts and take to the river. 'The Ashaninka believe,' Farne concludes, 'that the dead continue to exist alongside the living, often in a malevolent way.'

Grant Gee, the independent filmmaker who was slipstreaming our expedition for a parallel but quite distinct project of his own, said that he was going to try to get down to the Miraflores shoreline. Water was the hinge of his documentary fiction. His protected camera would dip under the sediment-clouded Thames, or the murky English Channel, and emerge in the rolling surf of the Pacific, or the swift clear currents of the Perené. Farne might have fancied an early dip too, but she needed to push on with her checklist of Lima possibilities. As a professional production manager, comfortable with choppering crews into the Arctic or finding some devious method of making payments in the collapsed economy of Argentina, she had our adventure comprehensively pre-plotted and costed. Swimming, especially open-water swimming, was her release from the pressures of work and family. As a child she had been brave to the point of recklessness. When we took a rowing boat from Turk's Boatyard in Cookham, in the direction of Marlow, aiming for a shallow beach on which to picnic, the infant Farne went straight over the side. And down. 'I'd seen you do it. I thought I could swim.' I grabbed her hair as she bobbed to the surface. Later, when she *could* swim, and strongly, she followed me into wild late-season Welsh waters, into deep gravel pits and Dartmoor rivers. But today the first tentative entry on her Lima agenda was a walk to the South American Explorers Club, an interesting-sounding venue for which she had accessed an unconfirmed address.

This tramp proved a nice metaphor for much of what followed. Time was connected to the piques of the weather. Like the dust haze that covered the city, movement occurred in a soft-focus buffer zone between the heightened subjectivity of the pedestrian and the absolute refusal of this invaded film set to oblige our 'seize your day' intentions. The 'comfortable twenty minutes' offered by the hotel receptionist became a very long hour of traffic-dodging and shade-chasing. The given address of the Club was a locked gate and a muted house with shuttered windows. The property behaved like an abandoned embassy in a country where diplomatic relations had been precipitately withdrawn. Further enquiries at the Brazilian/Peruvian Cultural Institute, on the corner of the suburban avenue, only carried us back to another lifeless building. The Explorers Club was a Borgesian test. A test we failed, spectacularly, until we understood that the only thing to be explored was our own incompetence. The Club had long gone (exploration now rebranded as Adventure Tourism) – although, as we learned later, the franchise was once operated by Lucho Hurtado, the Huancayo man Farne found to act as translator and to guide us through the cloud forest.

Without admitting it, I nurtured the fantasy of a London club out of Conan Doyle or Jules Verne, where my great-grandfather would still be sitting, deep in conversation with Peruvian geographers, who would, very courteously, be telling him – 'honoured sir' – to alter his plans at once and to work his way, more decorously, up the coast, towards burial mounds and other cultural sites, much easier of access. He might acquire, as indeed he did, the Moche pots and other excavated artefacts that took Farne's attention when she stayed in her grandfather's house in Wales.

I tried to picture the Edinburgh medical man Arthur Conan Doyle perusing a pristine copy of *In Tropical Lands*, as background research for Professor Challenger's adventure in *The Lost World*, especially one chapter, 'Tomorrow we Disappear into the Unknown'.

> Lord John had found himself some years before in that no-man's-land which is formed by the half-defined frontiers between Peru, Brazil, and Colombia. In this great district the wild rubber tree flourishes, and has become, as in the Congo, a curse to the natives which can only be compared to their forced labour under the Spaniards upon the old silver mines of Darien. A handful of villainous half-breeds dominated the country, armed such Indians as would support them, and turned the rest into slaves, terrorizing them with the most inhuman tortures in order to force them to gather the india-rubber, which was then floated down the river to Para.

And I remembered that *The Lost World* was the book my father had given me, without explanation, immediately before my departure for an English boarding school. In just the way that I had presented *In Tropical Lands* to Farne. Books were better than speech.

Libraries cling. Undead volumes are persistent. Grave goods should always be returned to the designated dark. Which is why, after my father's death, I passed all the excavated Peruvian objects on and kept only the books and photographs. Arthur, who returned, after the jungle, to take a more leisurely account of the capital – 'Lima, beautiful Lima!' – weakened. He rambled. He took in the sights. Like us, he was soon made aware of grand but futile colonial buildings thrown up against the land's determination to return to desert.

> *In this otherwise perfect climate, we live in a perpetual halo of dust... By twelve o'clock each day the wind blows the fine particles into every corner and crevice, and to travel abroad at mid-day is to eat your way through the thick clouds of drifting dust, with ears and nostrils stopped up. Nothing looks tidy in the house, and outside nothing looks fresh – the foliage and flowers being always more or less begrimed.*

BONES

'All distances here are measured in clichés.'
  – Stephen Minta, *Aguirre*

To identify some trace of Arthur's passage through Lima, at the beginning and the end of his Peruvian survey, we decide to take a cab to Plaza Mayor to inspect the bones of the city's founder, Francisco Pizarro. Where my great-grandfather made careful pen and ink sketches of heavily ornamented facades, and photographed grand squares emptied of human traffic, before inspecting the totemic skeleton of the conquistador, Grant Gee searched for the right gizmos to activate his disorientated phone. If I captured an image of the same bones, lodged in their glass coffin in the Cathedral, would some radioactive isotope of memory play back from Arthur's 1891 Kodak violation, in which the fleshless Pizarro is presented as a standing figure with hungry black eye sockets?

Our driver has no notion of where to find Plaza Mayor, his vehicle is too clean. We discovered by experience that the more battered a taxi-for-hire the better. Ditto for the jockeys. Feral auto-wrecks operate in competitive packs, making wild, improvisatory spins and sudden foot-down surges through dangerous streets they have never before attempted. The hanged plastic saint swings wildly as we corner or take off from some unexpected or ignored speed bump. The hotel-summoned driver is new to the game, servicing the least profitable tourists, and successfully stalling us on one of the ugliest inner-city motorways, where we are affronted by giant Cola hoardings that screen a series of cancelled and provisional hotels, in the process of being elbowed aside by the mirrored vanities of flourishing narco banks: William Gibson fossils of a vanishing future. The motionless line of smoke-wheezing vehicles is worked by frowning men and women from the mountains and the camps, peddling sugar drinks, fruit, newspapers and religious statuary.

Squealing away, at last, from this elasticated city's motor hell, our cab eased into narrow streets splendid with golden nameplates, disdainful colonial architecture, and well-armed indigenous police waving their batons. We were permitted to advance no further towards the Cathedral. We disembarked and submitted ourselves, with the flux of the crowd, to the general surge on a line of yellow metal barriers guarded by masked and black-capped paramilitaries. Access to Plaza Mayor was denied. For now, yes. For hours, certainly. Perhaps for days. Forever. There would be ample time for Grant to sort out his phone, before we broke for lunch, while we studied our maps and revised plans. Holding true to Arthur's prejudices, we identified a Peruvian-Chinese restaurant, with custard-yellow walls, red lanterns, and smooth businessmen of many races in dark suits: QIU CHOYTAC. Arthur's photocopied portrait with beard and enigmatic smile looked happy to be lying among the plates on the table. He had us where he wanted us. Tomorrow we would be on the train.

Now Arthur's voice, his incantations from published reports, read and re-read, whispered in my ear, like the remote echo of an instructing authority, unheard by others, manipulating secret service personnel, and presidential bodyguards in paranoid thrillers.

My great-grandfather noticed that in Peru, 'as in Australia', the 'capable, patient and faithful' Chinese had to 'cope with unreasoning prejudice and implacable hatred'. Whenever possible, Arthur enjoyed Chinese hospitality.

> *I have entered his house, studied his domestic life, and can testify that his genius for cookery relieves the wife of much drudgery… Is it any wonder a woman soon comes to adore such a husband? Compare her lot with that of many a wife tied to a clumsy Scotsman or an uncouth Colonial, and wonder may well cease.*

Arthur sponsored the notion that 'the man who produces most and consumes least is the true aristocrat.' And therefore: the Chinese were 'the coming aristocracy of both Peru and Australia'.

Our platters were heaped with prawns in yellow rice, supplemented by a good selection of hot sauces, along with compulsory litres of poisonously sweet Inca Cola. But the real hit of this interlude was the dynamism of the interference patterns swimming so rapidly across a giant TV screen that hung in place of the usual fish tank or generic landscape in plastic relief. Unlike England, where news is 'balanced', mediated, padded with journalist-fronted reportage and interview exchanges between competing egos, this relentless flow was immediate and raw. It presented us, in ways it would take weeks to achieve by walking the streets, with a graphic psycho-portrait of a nation in chaos. The morning's crime capers unfolded as we watched, predatory cameras were part of the action: DELINCUENTES ROBARON 10 MIL SOLES DE AGENICIA BANCARIA. Motorbike raiders, armed police. Delirious footage sound-dressed with levels of Copa América knockout hysteria, rising to a scream of appreciation as the cops go in for the kill. Camera phones, random surveillance captures, gunshots, bodies: it is all happening as we chew and sup. History here is jumping: protests, bands, processions, the poor from the shanties carrying out spontaneous bank robberies as political theatre. Sequences cut abruptly from smudged monochrome to lurid colour. Maoist cadres invoke Atahualpa, the armed redeemer. Presidents fake their own deaths.

To punctuate this all-action movie, they offer calming inserts from an ongoing political soap opera exploiting looped shots of a humbled walk between car and courthouse, as a series of disgraced former ministers, and the inconvenient children of presidents, prevaricate and plea-bargain and achieve infinitely postponed legal resolution.

Lucho, when eventually we meet him, after our train ride over the Andes, explains that even the presidents who are supposed to have committed suicide enjoy comfortable afterlives. They have been spirited away to villas in Brazil or Colombia. Other high officials, major drug dealers imprisoned forever in remote, single-use jungle prisons, are running their empires as they always did.

On screen, the same soberly dressed woman, today, tomorrow, next week, walks the same few yards of street and corridor, pressed by security and cameras, in an eternal Bardo of not-proven injustice.

———

As suddenly as the black-pyjama paramilitaries in their baseball caps had appeared, they vanish, along with the yellow barriers. There is nothing *visible* to stop us entering the deserted Plaza Mayor. We can purchase a ten soles ticket, allowing us to search the echoing vastness of the Basilica Cathedral for the bones of Pizarro. Keggie Carew, author of the prize-winning *Dadland* memoir, told me that she had taken shelter from tear gas in this church: 'Something to do with Shining Path.' She was left, sprawled on the floor, gasping for breath. Eyes streaming. And in just the right state of mind to appreciate the overwhelming heritage of fixed history perfuming the incense, the candles of remembrance, and the theatrical relics.

Before we left the restaurant, I asked one of the waiters if he knew why the Plaza had been closed. 'The police, they were concerned about another protest. Gay and lesbian rights.'

The Basilica Cathedral is a revision of a revision, an anthology of clashing but complementary styles. We drift through this elevated exhibition of gilded martyrs and sallow, waxy Christs with sacrificial crowns made from golden sunburst arrows. Sorrowful women offer practised gestures of obedience to the mounds of gold and silver heaped around madonnas in dim caves and side chapels. Arthur declared this version of Catholicism a good religion for the ladies of Lima. 'The priests are not greatly respected by the husbands and fathers,' he said. 'They do not admit them to their tables. They leave their wives at the church door.'

The heraldic aspect of the disputed bones of Pizarro, arranged in shallow vitrines and scarlet treasure chests and marble monuments, under epic paintings of the conquest, still works its stage-managed magic. Mortality – the mortality of the witnesses – confronts itself in all these polished surfaces. Voices, coming from no identifiable source, reach the chapel-museum where Francisco Pizarro's tomb is displayed.

Arthur Sinclair filed his own report:

> *Here I was shown the remains of the 'Gran Conquistador', a fit relic for this holy of holies. Pizarro, the pitiless tool of priestcraft and the conqueror*

for covetous Spain, had, like the last Napoleon, one redeeming trait in his character, viz., a taste for architecture, of which this cathedral is an example...

During my stay in Lima a question arose and was earnestly discussed with reference to the identity of the mummy preserved in the vaults of the cathedral, whether it really was the mortal remains of Pizarro, or whether it had been surreptitiously bartered by some sacrilegious thief. One theory was that during the War of Independence the royalists secretly carried off the treasured remains to Spain and left a mummy of similar bulk in its place, and this story was favoured by Americans whom I met in Lima... The matter now assumed great importance, and a committee of anthropologists was appointed to critically examine the mummy and report to the ecclesiastical and municipal authorities...

It was on the 26th June, 1891, the 350th anniversary of Pizarro's violent and bloody death, that the coffin was opened amidst the almost breathless but intense anxiety of the populace... On removing the lid the body was found almost in its entirety and completely mummified, still partially covered by rags of silk... and the remains of a finely embroidered linen shirt. The body was quite desiccated, and of a dingy white colour. On close examination it was found that certain portions were amissing, viz., the fingers, toes, and certain other parts, having been cut off and removed. From the appearance, the committee were satisfied that these mutilations had taken place immediately after death... These atrocities had probably been committed by an exasperated populace on the corpse as it lay where it fell, atrocities which can scarcely surprise us when we look back upon the life of cruelty, avarice, treachery, and rapine, which had thus been summarily closed...

The report of the committee of anthropologists was published with commendable promptitude on Saturday, 27th June, 1891, and occupied four columns in El Comercio *newspaper of that date. The conclusion come to was that the identity of the body was absolutely established, not only by general indications, but by evidence of wounds on the neck and elsewhere, which, after lying three and a half centuries, the mummified corpse clearly disclosed. The conformation of the cranium has a very marked resemblance to that of the typical criminal of to-day. The lower jaw protrudes*

> *abnormally, a certain sign of a brutal man. The chief peculiarity, however, is the knee joints, which are so unusually large as to look like a deformity. The total length of the mummy is fully six feet.*
>
> *After having been carefully scrutinised, the precious relic was handed over to the care of the Metropolitan Chapter, who placed it in the Chapel of the Kings in the Cathedral of Lima, where the curious may now see all that is mortal of Pizarro resting on a couch of crimson velvet, the whole being enclosed in a marble tomb with glass sides.*

Which was where we now stood, hoping to glimpse the lunar reflection of Arthur's bearded and beaming face in the shine of the damaged cranium. This was not the skull disinterred in 1891 but another, dug from a box in a musty crypt in 1977. I said nothing, but I held to the irrational belief that, from the casting of these pathetic bones, the measuring of distances and angles, a 'direction of travel' would surely declare itself, to set us on the right path.

Allen Ginsberg, a young man in dedicated pursuit of his muse, and the answer to the riddle of the absolute, came here in 1960: seven years before I met him in London. And seven years before his fame had become a snare and an encumbrance, with nuisances like myself dogging his footsteps for interviews, for oracular pronouncements he was in no state to deliver. But deliver them he did. The Beat poet was weary of describing his auditory William Blake visitation in Harlem, the one that confirmed his lifelong task, his vocation, but describe it he must, bringing something fresh each time. He said nothing whatsoever about the equally significant revelations, under ayahuasca, in the Peruvian jungle.

The poet checked into the Mercado Mayorista, on this square, and then struck out to find a Chinese restaurant, where he enjoyed 'a good bite' of badly fried shrimps. 'I must look crazy to the waiters,' he wrote in his travel journal. 'Strange wildhair debonair selfassured prophet – in Chink restaurant of the World-Night… scribbling the final definition of God.'

I investigated these blatant coincidences of cultural tourism only after my return to England. But the deep voice of Ginsberg, its rhythms and beard-stroking reflexes familiar from many hours at an editing console, trying to synch speech to movement of lips, was easier to track than the written words of my great-grandfather. The posthumous Arthur existed as a set of fading photographs, unreliable maps, and the stories left behind to provoke this future journey. Like all the other visitors to Plaza Mayor, Ginsberg commented on 'dry bones, mummies, shells, & empty thankless skulls with holes for eyes and empty space where a brain once palpitated and thought and schemed more Cathedrals.' He was astonished by the reality of these things: 'once they were real as me.' In the confusing network of streets beyond Plaza Mayor, the 'Indians' experience death every day and 'take cancer for breakfast'. They understand, better than any of the intruders, that they are fated. The tourist poet, like Kerouac before him, a master of cultural appropriation, is determined to share and exploit that achieved condition they gloss as 'lostness'.

With a single day in Lima, it felt right to stick as close to Arthur's narrative as was possible, and to read the country in the way that he always did, by taking himself off to the nearest botanical gardens. It appeared from our very basic map that we could walk from Plaza Mayor to the Jardín Botánico by way of 'Chinatown'. Spanish colonial cities of the conquest give proper attention to watering early, to tending plants with affectionate care, to enclosing and guarding their shady oasis gardens. Here was relief from the heat: sites of leisured conversation, private thoughts and illicit assignations. The degree of civilisation in any nation could be measured, Arthur reckoned, by the quality of its botanical gardens. And the state of its zoos.

> *One of the first objects of attraction to me is always the botanical gardens, but an enquiry for these elicited only a shrug of the shoulders from a Limeno, and at length a confession that the gardens were not what they once were, in fact, that they were abandoned. The Chilians, alas! had been there, tethered their horses amidst the choicest flower beds, cut down the noblest trees for firewood, and carried away the rarest shrubs to Valparaiso. Not content with this the vandals also appropriated the statues and seats, stole the lions, shot the elephant, and, sad to say, these terrible Chilians walked*

> *away with several hundred of the fairest Limeñas, the flowers of many a*
> *decent family…*
>
> *Altogether the Chilians, notwithstanding the fact that they took a few*
> *souvenirs of their visit, behaved tolerably well during the time they were in*
> *possession of Lima. Ask any shopkeeper, and he points to plate glass mirrors*
> *with several bullet holes; nevertheless he says, 'I wish they were back again!*
> *Trade was never better than then, and what the Chilian bought he paid*
> *for, which is more than I can say of my own countrymen.'*

The more we channelled the 'lostness' of the Beats, the faster we walked, and the more the unknown streets became a culturally diverse replay of the most picturesque parts of Hackney and Whitechapel, with added vim: piping musicians, handcarts carrying away the remains of markets, narrow shops, bead curtains, bar counters, deals being cooked, cash-money pocketed, accounts settled. Stinks of fish, fruit and flesh. Human and animal shit congealed and steaming. Impossible bundles effortlessly shouldered. Sacks dumped.

Progress slows as we weave and swerve and drudge onwards, unconvinced that Arthur's botanical gardens can still be located in this quarter. Until, at last, flagging badly, we are reassured by the tease of scrofulous palm trees reaching over a spiked fence. The surrounding adobe walls are crumbling into red-brown dust. The main gates are closed and patrolled by a uniformed female custodian who is under strict instruction to let *nobody* into the grounds without full accreditation. We persist, telling Arthur's story, producing the book with his portrait, to no effect. 'Impossible.' Out of the question without written and stamped permission from the director. This is now an institute for serious research and experimentation.

Even in post-war neglect, Arthur found inspiration in the gardens. He compiled a lengthy list of 'rare and valuable' plants. Grubby, footsore, chafing with our various burdens, we claimed to have travelled from Europe specifically to pay our respects to these gardens. We could not afford to fail. We were as urgent as Klaus Kinski, in filthy white suit, coming off the Amazon in *Fitzcarraldo*, and *demanding* to be given access to the opera house. He has to be let in, otherwise the film will fold. Herzog's metaphors and conceits will collapse. But fail we did, falling at the first hurdle. We were left, poking our cameras through the decorative ironwork, trying to carry away some documentary record of what appeared, superficially, to be dull and neglected ground.

Back at the hotel, there was a package for Farne from Lucho, welcoming her to Peru and supplying a promotional map for our railway trip, next morning, over the Cordillera. There was also, more alarmingly, a letter for me. I don't know how he found out where we were staying, but the Advocate had his sources. The further he was from our expedition, in a strictly geographical sense, the more pressing the intimations of our self-appointed spiritual mentor.

'The modern virus of elegant parasitism penetrates Peru through the open door of its Europeanized capital,' his letter, diplomatically franked in Guadalajara, began.

> It is surely more than 18 months that I have the feeling of living in a slow-motion disaster. First Lehman, then Greece, then Charlie-Hébdo, Greece again, Paris again, Brussels, now Albion. I have been travelling, as you are at this time, and I can tell you: Lima is over. The bankers have returned to their burrows and the bureaucrats carry papers and suitcases. I am right now in Mexico. But the IMF meeting I am forced to attend looks more like a shirt manufacturers' convention: everybody knows what the other is going to say and there is no appetite for alternative garments. I spent 11 hours in Buenos Aires of which 180 minutes was in a taxi. There was a troubling sense of making a return, but, in truth, there was no return but a seamless delivery into a parallel district of Brussels.
>
> On the Lima–Mexico flight I sat next to a woman who happens to be an honorary consul in Sonora. I mentioned Lowry, but his name did not ring a bell. I was happy to have a few hours to return to English poetry of the years before Thatcher. And this is why I am writing to catch you now, before you strike off for the interior. Do you remember a book you published back in 1973, in an edition of a few hundred copies?

With the letter, as if in confirmation of the Advocate's notion of a brief return to a site of unfinished mourning as the involuntary translation into a 'parallel' topography, he enclosed a photograph of what I took to be the notorious Palais de Justice in Brussels, while still under construction. It was nothing of the sort. I don't know how I had missed it on our tour. Under the admitted influence of Joseph Poelaert, who played Albert Speer to the grand follies of Leopold II, a Peruvian architect of Polish descent, Bruno Paprowsky, was commissioned to create a prestigious courthouse for the Avenida Paseo de la República in Lima: a diminished duplicate of the Brussels Palais, lacking only the magnitude of the original dome, that swollen boil. The Peruvian Supreme Court, conscious of this loss of status, put in an immediate request to the Belgian authorities, to provide plans from which a suitable dome could be concluded.

I had to wait until I was back in Hackney to follow up on the Advocate's other hint or warning. In a rarely visited chapbook of poetry from 1973, I found these lines: 'LIMA was one message. Maps drawn, graves robbed, collapse on the Andes.' I guess that Arthur's story must have obsessed me for the length of Farne's life, nagging away until she decided to bring this journey to fruition.

Among the preliminaries for the silver-stamped and blue-covered book, I was caught by the photograph of a young baby, being cradled by me, in my scruffy jacket and period moustache, somewhere in woodland. This was Farne. The Peruvian quest started in that moment. In Epping Forest or Welsh duneland. She's asleep and I'm watching a shot I have set up being taken by my wife.

SOROCHE

'My own experience… was fainting and violent vomiting. There is no real preventative, and no two may suffer alike. Travellers are usually warned in Lima to beware of taking alcohol: its effects are often fatal during suffering from *soroche*; and in the face of such warning I hesitate to give my own experience, which was that a moderate use of stimulants was decidedly palliative.'

– Arthur Sinclair, *In Tropical Lands*

I was diligent about the breathing exercises that Lucho prescribed as the most effective and cheapest antidote to the inevitable mountain sickness (or soroche) we would face on the second-highest train ride in the world. Our guide, who was due to meet us at the station in Huancayo, had a briskly pedagogic tone in his communications. His way or suffer the consequences. Farne took on the instructions that suited her and ignored the rest. We had our own quests, to be defined in the undertaking of them, while Lucho, drawing on years of experience in 'finding out how all these different people lived, what their customs were and what crafts and products they created', had a very firm preconception of the adventures his faithful band of elite tourists *should* undergo, in order to conform to his vision of the good life as good business. Good for all. Indigenous people, aliens and canny providers: an ecology of active awareness.

Take one deep breath, fill your lungs, hold it as long as you can, then let the breath slowly out. It was as crude as that. I sat on a bench in St Leonards-on-Sea, indulging in the play of light over the English Channel, before drawing in a decent capture of ozone, burger fizzle and sour seagull derision. Then I dragged myself up seven flights of steps in the concrete hulk shaped like a cruise liner. The medicine was repeated two or three times, every day I spent at the seaside.

The other trick was much easier, coca tea. Steady infusions of maté, either in teabag form, before first light in the hotel, or with brimming cups of floating green leaves later in the day. Arthur was certainly a fan: 'One of the most precious plants of Peru. A bush about 3 feet high, the leaves of which seem to sustain the natives for days without any other food, enabling them to undergo fatigue.'

Lucho had advised that we should arrive at the station by six a.m., several hours before our train was due to depart. I perched with my tea on a weird, semi-circular, aquamarine sofa, like a Dalí pastiche, in which Mae West's plump scarlet lips had been frozen and tightened into a heroin rictus. On the wall behind me were sculptures of bombed roses, their petals assembled from the detritus of a breakers' yard. The supposedly energy-donating coca beverage had a narcoleptic effect, leaving me pleasantly detached from what lay ahead. And more in tune with the alternate-world versions proposed by my great-grandfather and Allen Ginsberg.

'Alone in hotel across the street from Presidential palace,' Ginsberg wrote in his journal. 'Pizarro's bones, I glimpsed in a glass coffin one block away, 500 years before me here.'

In subdued reverie, the American poet drifts out in search of something undefined, 'a dark street full of beggars'. His feet hurt and he feels like a sickly spy, an outsider afraid to raise his eyes from the pavement. Those pavements, wide and inevitable, between the square with the Cathedral and the Presidential Palace, was where we walked, immediately after inspecting Pizarro's bones. Farne felt that we should take the measure of the station, the Ferrocarril Central, before we turned up, next morning, to catch the train.

This was the former Estacion Desamparados. Ginsberg and Arthur Sinclair passed through, poet and planter, both surveyors, after their own fashion, of a dark future predicted by this proud temple to the new way, the railway built in part by Chinese labour. There was an imposing Egypto-classical facade, with baroque trimmings, like an Amazonian bank or opera house. But there was also, as we discovered before the sun rose next morning, a dead zone at the back; a dangerous, dog-stalked, dirt shack wasteland, where cab drivers would confess their bewilderment and punch haplessly at their sat-navs. Or where cars and trucks, head-to-toe, would make fidgety nocturnal exchanges.

Farne told us that this building – we passed, unchallenged, into a marbled entrance hall – had once been the headquarters and the office suites of the Peruvian Corporation of London. And that made perfect sense: managers, with their imported oversize desks and furniture, could look from their balconies, down the line, and glory in gleaming silver ladders of futurity running towards territory yet to be exploited. From the start the railway was politics. Would it service the industrial horror at La Oroya? Would it ship out refrigerated containers, the abundant but perishable fruits of the cloud forest? Or would, as was almost certainly going to be the case, the new railway yield to the power of the road interests, the unions and the controllers?

The Andean train now ran once-a-month excursions, Lima to Huancayo and back, as a tourist experience. The grand railway project, in which the Peruvian Corporation was involved, began in January 1870, with a labour force of 10,000, made up of Peruvian, Chilean and Chinese workers, living hard and breaking their way through the most resistant terrain.

Still absorbed with the Peruvian author's Roger Casement fiction, I was interested to see that the gracious, light-filled, pillared spaces of the old ticket hall had been converted into a tribute exhibition for Mario Vargas Llosa, the failed presidential candidate who had spent many years living in London: Casa de la Literatura Peruana. Curated photographs and labelled relics of the novelist took their place alongside the bronze bust of Enrique (Henry) Meiggs, the railway's American backer and impresario. And the employer of the visionary Polish engineer Ernest Malinowski (1818–1899). 'Where a mule can walk, there I can lay my tracks,' he boasted.

We wandered outside, to absorb the atmosphere of the deserted platform, its columns and flagstones, before taking a quick circuit of an exhibition of anarchist posters and defiantly smudged single-sheet publications. I decided that this was a good spot in which to hide the first of my photocopies of Arthur Sinclair's smiling Aberdeen portrait. His pale grey ghost would track us as we tracked him across the territory. The bearded Scot seemed to fit very well with this documentation of sanctioned subversion.

In the yellow twilight, making our way back to the Cathedral, we gave space to a longhaired Jesus figure in tattered robes and leather sandals, leaning on his staff, and blessing potential pilgrims, as he processed, milk-eyed and unseeing, between station and public square. He was obviously a familiar of this set, ignored or tolerated by the black-pyjama paramilitaries, who were still lined up between the great studded doors of the church and the barrier of transparent thermoplastic shields stamped POLICIA.

Before dawn, in the sodium penumbra of low-lit public buildings, we are back at the Cathedral. Our cab has been stopped by police with leashed dogs and heavy weaponry. They are primed for a sneak return by the regiment of gay activists. We are forced to drag our bulging bags and camera equipment to the locked gates of the station. Lucho had advised us to be there in good time to cover the train's irregular and opportunistic hour of departure. But we are quite alone, squatting with our luggage, in a dead city patrolled by armed police and the never-ceasing Jesus figure, who is blessing the unrisen, and wearing out a narrow strip of avenue between Plaza Mayor and the unlit station with its decorative iron gates.

Time stalls, pleasantly. After an unregistered interval, costumed figures carrying musical instruments are allowed inside. And then, smiling broadly, a man in the bright red jacket of a holiday camp trustee holds up a sign: WELCOME TO PERU Ms. FARNE SINCLAIR. With grave formality, he shakes our hands. And presents us with our individual promotional maps. It will not be long now, he promises, before we are let through to the platform.

Under the clock of Estacion Desamparados, Ginsberg met the 'old poet', Martin Adan. 'My shade was visiting Lima / and your ghost was dying in Lima.' The smell of death was on the pavement, before he took the mountain train, in search of his own visions. 'Almost without thinking, I left Lima this morning at dawn – packed rucksack & walked across street from Hotel at 6:30 AM to take train to Oroya, headed for jungle Pucallpa.'

Lucho, who would be waiting for us at the end of this long day, has worked hard to talk up the experience of the train ride. He doesn't believe in letting his punters simmer quietly in contemplation of the unravelling landscape. He wants travel to be active: bullet points of necessary historical fact, plus folk dances and cellophane food, nicely timed to combat the threat of soroche.

> Through its journey, the train traverses six climatic zones, sixty-eight bridges, seventy-one tunnels and nine zigzags. The train travels at a speed climbing twenty-seven feet per minute. The train reaches its highest point at Galera Tunnel, 4,751 metres (15,583 feet), just past the highest passenger train station at Ticlio.

Our luggage is removed. Other travellers appear, mainly excursionist Peruvians and Latin Americans. Musicians strike up and the dancers, stamping to get warm, shake it. The lead female teases the iPhone-thrusting crowd with the libidinous provocations of a rubber snake. And then, at last, in our 'Turistico' class compartment, with its pale blue headrests accurately matching rectangular blue windows in the curved roof, we are away. Native nurses in starched white uniforms and facemasks are not yet required.

Settling back, taking the measure of the train to which we have committed ourselves, I hear Arthur's voice. Our other guide.

> *By rail to Chicla, 87 miles, thence on mule-back. This railway, it will be remembered, is, without any exception, the highest in the world, and the engineering the most audacious. 'We know of no difficulties,' the consulting engineer said to me; 'we would hang the rails from balloons if necessary'.*

———

Shuddering with convulsive tremors almost like the throes of child-birth, the train edges backwards out of the station. We take our places on an open observation deck, beyond the pisco bar, and choke on red dust. The movement of our comfortable transport, a Jules Verne sub-marine on silver wheels, creates its own sirocco through the resistant city: a procession of truck garages, wrecking yards, pharmacies and breeze-block low-builds the same colour as the impacted dirt on which they stand. Most of the railside structures are roofless and provisional. Groups of migrant workers down from the hills, from the shacks and camps, wait patiently at crossings for pick-ups offering a day's poorly paid casual labour. Improvised dwellings, with plastic sheets keeping out the restless desert, are parasitical on the tracks. Everything is abraded in dust. Cinder heaps blowing back to the mountains. And unstable mountains, poxed by vertiginous settlements and accessed by rickety ladders, sliding inexorably towards the city.

Skeletal trees are the grey of death. The faces of the people are carved by grit. Early traffic is deranged. The scene, in the travelling shot from our raised platform, looks like earthquake recovery. Walls have been whitewashed to carry slogans and block-capital messages that have to be read backwards. A new business, based on bucket and sponge, has opened alongside the common burial ground: CAR WASH. When the train slows by a Centro Medico, optimistic fruit-sellers hold up balls of compacted orange dust. The crumbling leaves are dust. Dogs shake themselves compulsively. They roll and rub and lie in the dust. The people of the railway must have as many words for dust as Greenlanders have for snow.

Our train is not only reversing towards the mountains, it is rewind-ing the film of time: Arthur Sinclair and his fellow planter and witness, Alexander Ross, have nothing to add. 'On the 7th July, 1891, after the completion of preparations for our journey to the interior, we set out from Lima by the Central Railway of Peru,' said Ross, always so punc-tilious about salient facts, in his 1892 talk to the Royal Geographical Society. 'This route is well known and need not be again described.' As a Scot, he drew words carefully from a deep purse.

Ginsberg, brooding on experiences still ahead, notices 'mountains of capitalist garbage', but thirsts to move on through the 'transcendental and sublime' to the 'unintelligible – which is our real task'. Nothing outside his train window is deemed worthy of note until they reach a town of industrial horror. 'Dirty but full of Indians... I drank Cocoa & had Siroche [*sic*] headache.'

Haunted and hollow-cheeked, unwavering in his commitment to the task, Grant Gee keeps on shooting, rocking with the rhythm of the observation car. This journey, as we climb steadily without moving from our seats, is much more than the film of itself. Those facts of rock and process that the Victorian planters held in reserve are still legible and overwhelming. Across the aisle are an English family, the only other Europeans signed up for this experience. The father is returning to country he once knew, having worked as a geologist for one of the mining corporations. He points out features to wife and daughter, who prefer to arm-wrestle, unwrap sandwiches and burrow deep in blockbuster novels.

After another colourful swirl of intervention by the dance troop, and some tactical shunting, the train rolls forward. I resume my seat and obey Lucho in drawing down, and holding, a deep breath. The strange aspect was that I felt no pressure to let this breath go, to exhale: *ever again*. I could have remained in a suspended state, as the ash and clinker mountains folded in on us, and the parasitical road became a twisted thong, threatened by rock falls, while it crept through resistant thrusts and gullies.

After the reluctant release of the indrawn breath of Lima suburbs, a large cup of splashy coca-leaf tea as the train struggles with the gradient. At San Bartolomé, 4,593 feet above sea level, the engine goes on a turntable, and we clamber down, already like voyagers testing sea legs.

The complicated procedures for getting the train through impossible twists and tunnels are described by the feisty American traveller Harry L. Foster in *The Adventures of a Tropical Tramp*, an account published in 1922.

> The train is continually backing part way up the mountain, then running forward again, until after half an hour of steady riding one looks down at the same spot he saw several hundred feet higher. Occasionally for variety, one ascends a long *quebrada*, circles around, and comes back on the other side. It seems to the passenger as though the train were

merely cutting geometric figures up and down the hillside, yet, it is always ascending, always getting a little closer to its objective.

The present station is now a revenant, bereft of facilities. I walk the platform with Farne and buy a substantial slice of museum-quality apple pie. This transaction is made to honour what Lucho Hurtado has already, as background information, told us about his heritage and upbringing. He spent his childhood in Huancayo, but his mother's family were from the mountains. He visited them and worked in the fields, tending to the livestock. They traded with the trains, carrying produce on board at one stop, and selling what they could, before disembarking and walking back to their starting point. One highlight as a very young man, Lucho reported, was a fleeting appearance on one of the BBC's early *Great Railway Journeys*. The train meant so much to this man that he invested fifteen years in promoting our ride with his company, Incas del Peru.

On the move again, and leaning over the side of the observation car to get the money shot as we snaked through a tricky passage of overhanging vegetation, I discovered the origin of the term 'branch line'. A cruel sapling whipped across my face, cutting through the cheek and exposing the wound, before blood flow could be staunched by a poultice of volcanic dust. The rocks are geologically autumnal. They are beginning to take on a ferrous tone, with lovely streaks of copper and red. Attendants hand out sugary sweets like communion wafers.

Arthur and his party disembark at Matucana, at 7,588 feet, to acclimatise. A sensible decision we cannot replicate, without waiting a month for the next train.

We resolved to stop for two days in order to get accustomed to the rarefied air. But we were not idle. Procuring mules, we proceeded to ascend the surrounding mountains… The hills rise at an angle of from 45 degrees to 75 degrees, and the so-called roads are really a terror to think of. In the distance the mountains of Peru, or the Andes, look as bleak and barren as Aden… but such is not the case. I have not yet seen an acre upon which the botanist might not revel, and but for the fact that I had to watch with constant dread the feet of my mule, I have never spent a more intensely interesting afternoon than I did during this memorable ride.

———

Air thins, mountain lakes and cloud-reflecting craters appear and disappear: a land without herds or humans. The only possibilities for future life are based around the spine of the railway. At Chicla, Arthur's ride concluded and the implications of his contracted survey started to scratch at his habitual good humour.

A dreary enough spot… Horses and mules from the low country frequently drop down dead here from failure of the heart's action.

Leaving Chicla, the real tug of war begins; the crest of the Cordilleras has to be encountered and crossed. A wretched road, made worse by the debris from the railway, which, for the first fifteen miles, we saw being constructed still far above us, the navvies hung over the cliffs by ropes, looking like venturesome apes. Higher and still higher goes this extraordinary zig-zagging railway, boring into the bowels of the mountain and emerging again at least a dozen times before it takes its final plunge for the eastern side of the Andes. Meanwhile, we continue our scramble to the top of the ridge, 17,000 feet above sea level. I have no desire to magnify the difficulties and dangers of this tedious ride. The great question is – What do we see when we get there? This I cannot well magnify…

Viewing this plateau from here, we have spread out before us a region unlike anything we have ever before seen, far above the rest of the world… it looks down with calm, if cold, indifference, sharing none of its alarms, and seldom indeed disturbed by the insane political broils of the lower regions… And all this bleak but most interesting country has to be traversed before beginning our descent into the promised land beyond, the real basin of the great Amazon, for which we are now bound, a region which even the Inca in the plenitude of his power never subdued, and, we are assured, no living Peruvian has ever penetrated.

———

We decant, very slowly, from the train at Ticlio, braved to sample the rarefied air. And feeling with outstretched arms like patients in a strange dark room. Or really, in my case, measuring the unbridgeable distance that separates us from the paragraph I have just read in my great-grand-father's book. As yet, despite the coca tea and the dutiful attempts to put ourselves in precisely the places they describe, the stubborn ancestors have not acknowledged our pursuit. We are failed resurrectionists. And we haven't encountered our first mule.

This was the highest station in the world, before the Chinese, who are still in evidence, and taking covert control of mining operations, constructed the pan-Himalayan line through Tibet. We stagger. Our boots are lead. Farne confessed that rising from her seat might have been a bad mistake. She was beginning to cultivate the worst headache of her life. Every yard risked on this ground is an underwater adventure. Those tremendous crags are temptingly close, but far beyond our present capacity. Harry Foster tells us that the 'looming form' beyond the station was christened Mount Meiggs, after the man who built the railway.

'Here,' the adventurer writes, 'the *soroche*, or mountain sickness, became general among the passengers. The women brought out smelling salts and sniffed vigorously; while the men called for *pisco*, the native grape-brandy of Peru.'

A line of covered railway cars on rusting wheels reminds me of the dying Welsh mining towns of my youth. ZONA DE ALMACENAMIENTO TEMPORAL DE MATERIALES. Men in orange overalls and hard hats, arms folded, watch our tragic traverse. I manage one ponderous circuit of the shuttered station and return to my compartment. And my essential travelling library. The mother and daughter across the aisle, having hoovered through sandwiches and crisps, are locked on the same page of their twinned blockbusters.

Alexander Ross informed his London audience that the settlement of La Oroya, situated at an altitude of 12,250 feet, would be 'completed in a few months'. The present village, shelter of herdsmen and farmers, was 'destined to become an important place, as point of junction for several feeding lines of projected railway'.

Sinking into an involuntary cycle of micro-sleeps and vivid dreams, as the train advances across the darkling plain, I barely notice Farne putting down her microphone to dose herself against a soroche migraine. Or Grant, red-eyed and ash-dusted, returning from the observation car, to take a thirsty slug of liquid medication, to relieve his splitting head, after long hours of grim concentration on landscape particulars.

The black sheds and smoking chimneys of La Oroya confirm a nagging sense of non-specific dread. Our tourist train, almost ashamed of its free pass through this post-apocalyptic validation of the ugly spirit of invasive capitalism, picks up speed. Profits taken from the smelting of waste have to be shipped out and laundered. The dirt from mounds of bank notes, portraits of dead presidents, returns as filthy snow, hanging in a choking pall over company gardens and improved workers' barracks with shared taps.

At which point the experience of transit tips towards science fiction: our carriage unpressurised, our surroundings lost. Other passengers scatter or slump, head on knees, or trainers up on the headrest of the seat in front. They are serviced by emergency nurses in surgical masks, wheeling oxygen cylinders. A reeling crowd from the 'Clasico' section begins to pour through, chased by clowns. Ridiculous numbers are massing on the open deck. It's like the famous cruise-liner cabin scene when the Marx Brothers are invaded in *A Night at the Opera*. After twenty minutes, you can't believe that they are still coming, the previously invisible travellers from the 'wrong' end of the train. If we hit the next bend at this speed, we are coming off the tracks. The cheaper carriages must be completely deserted, with every human onboard, drunk or soroche-sick, rammed between the emptied pisco bar and the coming dark, and primed to experience the ultimate folk-dance spectacular in a blizzard of iPhone candles. The clapping, shrieking, stomping, spinning, bell-skirted, non-authentic routine is accompanied by a manic white-face clown twisting Ginsberg's worst ayahuasca nightmares out of pink balloons.

Before night foreclosed this madness, I was encouraged to notice signs of remembered life returning: scorched yellows in the fields, solitary herdsmen, even a few resilient plants among the rocks.

———

The train stops, but nothing else does: Huancayo, the terminal station at Junín in the Central Highlands. We are so comprehensively out of synch, now, that we struggle to recognise our own bags among the mounds flung on the rapidly emptying platform. And we have to admit that we are relieved, in this creeping exhaustion and confusion, to be putting ourselves in the safe hands of Lucho, the local operator who has promised to meet us.

He isn't there and he doesn't come.

In the pulsing frenzy of the station gates, with revving motor-bikes, cabs on the tout, barking dogs, and refugees scattering in every direction, despite the stern baton gestures of a single overwhelmed policewoman, and the arguing smells of a convincing otherness, we are lost. Confounded. Frozen where we stand. Undone. It is our own fault, obviously. We have arrived more than an hour ahead of schedule. Farne's whiteout headache is blinding and Grant is in a very distant place, benefitting from his medicinal stash.

Huancayo is Lucho's town and the Trans-Andean train is one of his inspirations. It must be something serious. He is otherwise engaged tonight, dealing with a crisis at one of his restaurants or hostels. So we take a cab, and hoot, window down, into the derangement of competitive traffic, to Hotel Turismo.

'Siroche [sic] headache oxygen lack is similar to headache from Ether,' Ginsberg reported, when he got off his train. A friend lent him an apartment in which the dreams of terrible solitude came.

As always, the hotel receptionist was disbelieving of our demand for three separate rooms. But we required our own space in which the various activities – image-rendering, downloading, podcasting, and book scouring – could immediately commence.

Heroically, pale as death, Farne descends with me to the bar, at the end of a wobbly corridor dressed with strobing reproductions from Van Gogh: night cafés in Arles, screaming yellow houses, liverish portraits, and cobbled psychedelic streets where faceless pedestrians are beginning to slide out of the frame. With Lucho's advice, I managed to avoid the effects of altitude sickness, only to arrive at a hotel experiencing waves of earth tremors. Bottles and glasses did not rattle behind the bar and other customers carried on their ordinary conversations, while I knuckled the edge of my chair and felt the floor shuddering beneath me. *Where was the earthquake? And why were they ignoring it?* It took both hands to get the coffee cup to my mouth. And then our misplaced guide burst in, ordering us not to apologise for the train's early arrival. 'Good, good. Great. Let's get this thing moving. We start again new, a blank page.'

Farne is fading fast, as Lucho, a confident man with long silver mane and strong mountain face, launches his monologue: his life and ventures, calamities brought on by fate. And the *vital* experiences he has lined up for us, starting tomorrow. *Early.* Animal markets. Archaeological ruins. Hill climbs. Convents. He barely has time to accept a coffee. I notice the English family from the train hovering, books in hand, at the entrance to the bar, then backing rapidly away.

With Lucho's hotel tape of anecdotes, delivered like parables, providing the backing track for the long climb upstairs, hanging on to the banisters, I had the sudden urge to confirm how much of his monologue was factual and how much was legend. I picked on our guide's reference to his appearance in that film from BBC Manchester, *Great Railway Journeys of the World*, broadcast in 1980. The particular episode, 'Three Miles High', was presented by the *Punch* humorist Miles Kington, a dapper Anglo-Scottish traveller, from a cadet branch of the landed gentry. Kington is detached by class and education, but amused and alert, properly kempt in unyielding lightweight suit, a quiet grey with considered tie. The look, improved at altitude, by boulevardier's casual scarf. In fact, Kington is the Oxbridge epitome of kempt.

> The only thing I knew about South America, when I arrived in Peru, was to be on the lookout for revolutions.

When the train from Lima halted in Huancayo, so Lucho said, he was on the platform. And in the film. A talking cameo.

I knocked on Grant's door. He should be able to call up this phantom from the past on YouTube or some such. The documentarist was scanning hours of raw footage from the great railway journey of our own. I think he was pleased with what he'd got. And happier still to be inside, in a room that only shivered, but did not shake. He took a break, and obligingly tapped up the material I requested.

> The sun is going down, and so are we, through a valley of maize and eucalyptus trees.

Grant's digital footage, dancers, drinkers, clown, on one screen, was mute. With attractive golden hour, sun-splintered film, offering a more romantic rendering of the same stretch of track, on the laptop.

HUANCAYO: close-up of the station sign. Indigenous people jumping down to the platform from a train with a regular timetable, servicing the community. Along with Kington and supporting crew.

And here, at once, is the young Lucho Hurtado. This was a train that he needed to meet, this was his moment. He accosts the suave and uncreased journalist. He wears a thick plaid shirt and a flat black cap. He is competitively touting for one of the twelve 'almost good' Huancayo hotels. He does not smile or ingratiate himself. He pushes through the natives, not looking up directly at Kington. Or at the camera. He makes his pitch. He suggests a visit to the office. Kington patronises, with effortless charm, clearly tired after the daylong mountain ride. But Lucho is not done: he sweeps in again, offering to reserve a seat on the bus. And is rebuffed.

I get Grant to run this brief incident over and over. The empire-building insouciance of the Anglo-Scot who will be moving on, next morning, with more exotic lands to conquer and describe. And the unblinking Aztec gravitas of the Huancayo man, for whom pitching and touting and parading facts is a serious vocation. Lucho is both the man who was not there when we needed him and the man, in the past, who goes on, and on, making his rejected hotel pitch. Here already was the drama we would have to conjugate, in order to complete our journey. Without blood, sweat and tears.

CONVENTO DE SANTA ROSA DE OCOPA

'Peer into the darkness, shivering, and shivering drink the darkness up.'
 – Martin Thom, *CLOUD, a coffee cantata*

From the innocent cropping of high pasture, largely undisturbed, to a swift and stunned transit, still nibbling anxiously on green strings of good roughage, stiff and upright in the back of a truck, or lying down, bondaged, in boot of family car, to public inspection and swift sure blade, to naked post-mortem exposure on a metal grille through which thick blood runs free, shaggy pelt separated from the purest, whitest flesh, to clover-spiced barbecue smoke: mountain sheep are brought to market. Corydale and Merino. Beautiful animals inured to their fate. The stone and dust acreage of organised chaos at Chupaca is the first location on Lucho's adventure tour agenda: animal market, mountain ruins, farmhouse lunch, convent. 'Come on, let's go, vamos.' Today Peru must face Uruguay, in a tactical battle against perceived aerial threat, in order to go through to the semi-finals of the Copa América. Will it be possible to follow the match as we drive?

Although I'm concerned about leaving her alone at the hotel, I'm quite relieved that Farne is not with us. The unavoidable reality of so many doomed beasts – llamas, piebald hogs, horses, mules, net sacks crammed with piglets – offered, exchanged, traded, admired and slaughtered, gathered up in one place by farmers with high-sided trucks and improvised stalls, would not be the most effective antidote to a skull-splitting soroche hangover.

Nobody appeared at the breakfast table. Grant was working on downloading, on re-establishing family connections and sampling online *Guardian* traffic from the world we have left behind. Farne, when I knocked on her door, was sick. Pale. Barely able to stagger across the room. And clearly in no state to appreciate Lucho's crash course in the excesses of local colour. I arranged for some breakfast to be sent up. And told our impatient cicerone, who, this time, arrived on the button, rubbing his hands and pacing, that we would have to be back by three o'clock at the latest. And that the Franciscan Convent of the Missionaries at Ocopa was the one site we really *had* to visit. The Convent was an essential part of our story, holding maps and documentation relevant to Padre Gabriel Sala, the man who guided my great-grandfather to the banks of the Perené.

'Of course, yes. Come on, let's go.'

A battered car and a young Huancayo driver are waiting. Lucho meets and greets a man he says he was at school with, the owner of this and several other hotels, and away we go, foot to the deck, through tight streets packed with morning drifters, on the horn.

'So what was the biggest danger of the trip?' Anna asked, when she met us at Heathrow, on our return.

'The driving,' we replied, in unison.

Today is the Festival of San Pedro. The Seventh-day Adventist Fernando Stahl abhorred these festivals, which he saw as the devil's work. Priest-inspired orgies of drunken licence. Cocaine indulgence by highlanders led astray in the worship of their saints and idols. Blasphemous rites ruining health and the capacity to deliver an honest day's labour. Debauchery with dirty shirts.

Under low white clouds, the place of meeting and exchange for small farmers is crowded with men and animals. It is unhurried and lacking that shrill edge common to the old markets of London's East End. The farmers are inky haired, short and strong, many favouring jeans and baseball caps. The women, with their traditional layers of skirt over tight leggings, their woollen cardigans, and striped helmets, take care of business, while the men stand in groups, talking quietly, or checking their phones. It feels as if the highlanders have been deputed to take their animals on a saint's day outing, an excursion, during which they will be given the best seats in the car.

And, yes, the lambs are silent. Under a blue ceiling. In the company of the still breathing dead. Their brothers and sisters.

The market sky is always the same. Always truer than any representation of it. The particular quality of blue, picked up from the tailgates of trucks marking the edge of the permitted zone, and the denser blue of distant hills, is fed into the eyes of men and animals. Condemned creatures experience none of that bowel-loosening panic, the ripple of herd hysteria, of enclosed sheds: the mechanised hygienic slaughter of industrial farming. Chupaca beasts are saintly in acceptance. Llamas wait patiently in their family group: two brown ones, grounded, are rubbing their long necks against the standing white dominant, who turns to stare, unblinking, at Grant's camera of fate. This is a much healthier exchange than the shame of a city zoo, where we process so awkwardly in celebration of our separateness from the imprisoned species.

Where squealing piglets are just food in a bag, makeweights, mature pigs are solitary and phlegmatic, tethered by the rear hoof or slumped, legs retracted, black pillows of flesh on the sharp-stoned ground. The mules stand apart. They must find new masters, new burdens. But they will not be eaten. Except by bats and other natural predators. Unless they die on the trail. Unsold sheep come together to establish a temporary flock.

Although this colourful detour, arranged by Lucho, was never part of my premeditated vision of the Peru quest, something biblical in the relationship between men and animals took possession of me. Months later, under viral lockdown, our younger daughter, Maddie, kept us in touch with the grandchildren we couldn't visit by sending nightly film reports to Anna's phone. One of these, beyond sentiment, stopped my heart. The latest grandchild, Sami, the one born when Maddie and her troop were living with us for a few months, had begun to walk. The family are staying on a farm. The interested infant totters towards a pen of sheep. They bleat. He backs off, alarmed. Then, perhaps encouraged by his mother, he turns the corner of the L-shaped fence. And suddenly everything is new. He comes with confidence to the sheep, once more, but from another angle. They are silent. He baas. They respond. He baas again. *It works.*

But what affects me, now, is not the charm of this cameo and the brave revision of the child. The little scene, and the knowledge of who is filming it, in living colour, takes me back to a monochrome episode that I barely remember, and only as a witnessed film. The first home movie. I am the same age as Sami, more securely wrapped, tottering with the same footsteps towards the same animals, rough-pelted mountain invaders of a golf course. As caught on 16mm by my father. In watching, several times, the performance by our youngest grandchild, I was carried back to the emotion and excitement of my initial confrontation with these strange animals. I felt the heaviness of the ground, the tough spears of grass, the smoke in the wind. *This was and is a present tense.* And not what I had previously 'known', if at all, as a bleached fragment of archival film. Now lost. And probably beyond repair.

The fiesta spills around and over the slaughter field. Bands in matching funeral suits and dark glasses, with uniform red ties, tootle on their brazen horns. They have been hired at a substantial fee from another town. The procession resurrects, or exorcises, the devious spectres of colonialism. There are capering slaves and slave drivers with cracking whips. There are blackface leather masks with fleecy white beards attached, stick-on wool eyebrows and big straw hats. There are pranksters. There are twins. They dart among the crowd, to tease or challenge or rob. At the head of the troop is a conquistador, landowner, coffee plantation boss: a white man in sheep mask. He wears black pantaloons decorated with flowers and martyred saints. The celebrants halt at the church. This, we are told, is a propitious day for weddings. For carrying banners and Catholic effigies, released from their niches, to voyage in draped boats. The holy ones of the missionary monks are followed through the streets by mountain people in their finest clothes.

Lucho chivvies us away from the open ground with the animals. Tributaries around the market are reminiscent of Brick Lane in the 1970s: once you move from the established pitches, most of the action is on the floor. In the dirt. Unpoliced. Our guide inspects a fat and glistening hog, limbless, its head intact. There are stacked pyramids of guinea pigs on offer, varnished and flattened snacks. To be licked like salty toffee apples, before the bones crunch. Grant is drawn to the Andean women selling plastic bags of coca leaves, along with the alkaline substances required to extract the essence, when leaves are balled in your cheek. Coca chewing is an acquired skill. The supplementary aids can be ash of quinoa or burnt limestone.

My great-grandfather, impressed by the endurance of the men carrying his luggage over ground where he fought for breath, saw the economic potential of a coca-leaf economy. He experimented and made a favourable report, but the moguls of the Peruvian Corporation of London stuck with another addictive product, coffee.

> *Coca… is a plant not unlike the Chinese tea, though scarcely so sturdy in habit, growing to a height of from four to five feet, with bright green leaves and white blossoms, followed by reddish berries. The leaves are plucked when well matured, dried in the sun, and simply packed in bundles for use or export… Of the sustaining power of coca there can be no possible doubt; the Chunchos seem not only to exist, but to thrive, upon this stimulant,*

often travelling for days with very little, if anything else, to sustain them.
Unquestionably it is much superior and less liable to abuse than the tobacco,
betel, or opium of other nations. The Chuncho is never seen without his
wallet containing a stock of dried leaves, a pot of prepared lime, or the ashes
of the quinoa plant, and he makes a halt about once an hour to replenish his
capacious mouth. The flavour is bitter and somewhat nauseating at first,
but the taste is soon acquired, and, if not exactly palatable, the benefit under
fatiguing journeys is very palpable. Cold tea is nowhere, and the best of wines
worthless in comparison with this pure unfermented heaven-sent reviver.

Anticipating the potential struggle, in our present disorientated and
short-breathed condition, on the steep climb Lucho promised, before
a required inspection of the ruins of Pre-Columbian storage buildings,
Grant made enquiries about the purchase of a stash of coca leaves. Our
impatient guide stepped in and took control, joshing with the vendors,
clinching the sale, and whipping the leaves into his own pouch. Along
with a couple of spare guinea pigs, beaten as thin as vampire bats or
roadkill under an articulated lorry. We never saw the leaves again.

———

This is a fortunate country of neat fields and working farms, thriving outside the politics of the larger co-operatives and the sprawling Spanish estates. We climb, a little stiffly, from the car. And on, at Lucho's instruction, to a yellow-dusted hill of sharp unyielding stones. We must investigate the Huari remains of Arwaturo. But the most pressing task is to invent a foolish question, every twenty yards or so, in order to give us time to find some breath. Lucho demonstrated the best recovery position. 'Bend forward at ninety degrees, hold the breath, *hold it*, now slowly release and up again.'

With the inherited experience of his highland childhood, his powerful build, mature curve of belly, long silver hair, Lucho reminded me of Carlos Castaneda's Yaqui Indian mentor. And of the illustrations of this teasing shaman on the cover of those paperbacks that passed around in the Sixties, promoting the cult of cactus-gobbling initiation. Castaneda borrowed assiduously from the best sources and crafted a fiction of himself as a seeker mired in persistent idiocy. The anthropologist had a preternatural gift for saying the wrong thing and accepting all the humiliations heaped upon him. Lucho, I recognised, as I struggled up the track in his footsteps, was the don Juan of adventure tourism; a prescriptive *brujo* of the Inca Trail, the cloud forest, and the medicinal plants along the ridge on the summit of this hill. If any weed deserved a brief lecture, then it was worthy of our notice. If not, our instructor brushed it aside. Picking up a granite shard, Lucho demonstrated its cutting edge by slashing into the species of prickly pear cactus that offers a spurt of royal red cochineal. He explained that this natural dye is a useful product of female insects.

The *colcas*, or storage vaults, constructed from walls of fitted stone, command a notable view across the fertile valley. There are no other visitors. The ruins are guarded by a pack of feral dogs and a muttering madman. Lucho knows this person of old and is eager to avoid further entanglements. And a solicited toll. He says that he despairs of the habits of tourists, the ordinary ones who have not signed up for his instruction. Snorting, he takes himself off to gather up Inca Cola cans and blue plastic bags. Meanwhile, Grant squats on his haunches to stare long and hard at landscape he is not quite ready to film.

For a few minutes I had the ruins to myself. As at Lindisfarne Priory, so many years ago, I became conscious of a figure staying ahead, sliding behind the next wall, and disappearing into a cool stone chamber where I would find nothing but dust, before my eyes adjusted to historic darkness. Something lived between this reservoir of shadows and the harsh late-morning sunlight. A spectre I thought I recognised: my fellow speculator in virtual translation and cosmic conspiracy, the Advocate from Brussels. Cowled in wind-deflecting anorak, and gesturing emphatically in animated discussion with that other phantom of these ancient ruins, the sanctioned beggar, the Advocate was ahead of us once again. Or such was my oxygen-deprived hallucination. It seemed to be the task of this summoned entity, the international diplomat, to balance Lucho's pragmatism with a wilder poetic of place. Disbelieving, I closed in on the barking chaos, rattling a few pesos in my hand. The madman of the ruins, holding back his dogs, snatched at them. But the other one, who reminded me so much of the Advocate, was away down the easier steps to the car park. Steps for which a purchased ticket was required to make an ascent. The retreat was free. Lucho was waiting with his blue bag of collected refuse.

We come off road to visit a farm belonging of one of Lucho's contacts. Lunch is a significant matter in Peru, but I'm eager to push on, so that we can get back to the hotel in Huancayo, to check on Farne. But Lucho reveals that the Franciscan Convent at Santa Rosa de Ocopa takes its own leisurely lunch break, with ample time for a monkish siesta, and does not open its doors to the public until four p.m. Which gives us a few hours to relax and explore the farm. While we keep up with a nationally important event, the game against Uruguay.

Buildings that once belonged to an old priest, a relative of the farmer, are now a commune. Some of the barns and outhouses have tumbled down, others are being restored. There is an ancient man, grandfather or pensioned retainer, sitting on a stool in the garden, attended by a tiny, interested girl, four or five years old. The man is delighted by Grant's height, his difference.

'You speak Spanish, sir?'

'A little. Very little. A few words.'

'You speak Spanish?'

The conversation is looped. And repeated every time Grant passes through the garden to the car. The little girl is vastly amused. The old man also laughs and nods.

'You speak Spanish, sir?'

We have to learn that nothing happening is a special blessing, a blessing that is hard to achieve. Or endure. Grant stalks back and forth, to the car and the camera kit. And the musty outhouses. But he has to pass the old man on his chair.

'Do you speak Spanish, sir?'

It's a vision to watch Lucho, so active a presence, forever racing to the next location, checking on his phone, working the bubbling pots and busy women of the farmhouse kitchen.

'Give us that special bottle. And we'll take your garlic trout. It's good? Very good! Great. Let's go.'

He's in and out of the bar, sniffing the cactus drink, licking a spoon, joking with the women. Arranging to have the TV set positioned *just so* for the big game. We have hours to spare.

In an empty dining room, at a long table under faded posters of B-feature buckskin cowboy stars, Mexicans, Germans and hopeful young Jews, out from Brooklyn, playing Apache warriors, we drink and wait. The trout is pregnant with butter and crushed garlic and spilling off the plate.

Lucho and his farmer friends are appreciative of Peru's unsubtle but effective defence, based around a supremely organised roster of professional fouls. Suarez and Cavani are neutralised. Peru pluck at shirts, rake tendons and make their ankle taps only in the safe areas of the pitch. And always with a polite offer to help the aggrieved and gesticulating victim back to his feet. There are no goals. The commentator relishes the names of certain players: *Ad-vín-cula, Advíncula, Ad-vín-cul-aaaah*. The climaxing roll of rs in *Carrillo, Carrrrrrrillo*. The goalkeeper, Gallese, is the standout showman. We watch until halftime. And the bottles are emptied.

We park under the trees. The car radio babbles from the game in progress. Where nothing happens at fever pitch. Our driver gets out to ease his nerves with a smoke. We buy tickets for entrance to the Convent, where we are obliged to tuck ourselves on the tail of a group of elderly devotees heading off down red tile corridors for a preordained circuit, led by a qualified nun. Lucho makes cursory translations from her Spanish. He has his own agenda and promises to fix a meeting with the artist commissioned to depict the history of the Franciscan mission as an epic mural, a graphic novel of painful encounters, ambushes, martyrdom and vine-inspired visions.

There are still no goals. And the game is drifting towards extra time and a penalty shoot-out. Lucho says we'll hear the noise if Peru win: a universal honking of horns and pealing of bells. It will be a big night for the restaurant in Huancayo, spicy pizzas all round.

This imposing convent building, with its twin towers and preserved chapel from the period of the original foundation, its great library, museum and archives, reminded me of the Lima station from which we had departed, so many lives ago. Santa Rosa de Ocopa was the training ground and launching point for the exploration and subjugation of the interior, river and jungle, by a procession of militarised and driven priests: the bounty-hunting, map-making, soul-laundering special forces of Christ the Conqueror.

The walls of the corridors and cloisters were animated by the agonies and ecstasies of Francisco, tempted by devious women, walked over by soldier monks. Our nun had plenty to say about the paintings and the saintly man who inspired them. Lucho stopped translating and let us fall back to carry out our own inspection of the images and artefacts in the Convent's museum.

Padre Gabriel Sala, my great-grandfather's guide (and nemesis) for the ultimate push, was everywhere. His career was programmed and upwardly mobile. He captured numerous orphans for the faith, and rose to be head of the order at Ocopa. *But Arthur never once mentioned his name.*

The actions of this priest, from first moment to his ultimate disappearance, disgusted him. Sala's indulgences were too much for a highland Scot hard-schooled by Protestant fundamentalists. But Alexander Ross, who could be relied on to deliver awkward facts Arthur chose to improve or avoid, was careful to identify the man who took them into the jungle.

> Before dark we reached the convent… where we had been expected, and were now made welcome by the superior and his Franciscan brothers. Heavy rain detained us here three days, but at last, accompanied by Padre Sala, chief of the mission, and Padre Carlos, from the Ucayali, we set out upon our wanderings in the wilds, having first despatched our cargo mules.

Gabriel Sala (1852–1898) has a prominent jaw and a bristling black hoop of hair around a shaven bulb of skull. He glares into the shadows, spurning the camera's rude interrogation. He seems to have been squeezed, by some force from above, into the wrinkled folds of a dirty dressing gown. We can compare and contrast numerous photographs of record with the pop-coloured cartoon mural painted by Lucho's acquaintance. Sala, it is evident, was not only an intrepid explorer and child-hunter, but also a valued ecclesiastical historian and skilled cartographer. And he was armed against all eventualities.

'He must be an Indian,' Lucho said. 'The man has that look, not from the Perené, more like the Ucayali.'

But the Advocate's researches tracked the priest back to Spain. Through his trail-breaking expeditions, Sala had taken on the pigmentation of the country. His maps were large-scale miracles of documentation, embellished with drawings of rafts, villages he had visited and, most striking to us, the frontier Convent at San Luis de Shuaro, where he met my great-grandfather and Alexander Ross. And led them, as Ross implies, with biblical emphasis, into their forty days of wilderness.

That low white building of San Luis, more like a fort than a church, travelled through time. Red door, green door. Window apertures mean as arrow slits. This is where Arthur, conscious that he was at the limits of the known world, parked his mules.

Sala's *Mapa de las Misiones de Ocopa* lists the journeys undertaken. The 1891 expedition is the last entry.

In his published account, Arthur tries to stifle prejudice. Tries and fails. Now his version is being challenged by the priest, as well as by his fellow surveyors: Ross who will deliver public lectures to the great and good, and Clark, the agent of the State, who says nothing.

> *We had letters of introduction to the chief priest there, and after resting a day in the house of a hospitable Frenchman, eagerly pushed onwards. The trip was now getting decidedly interesting; the scenery and vegetation improved as we proceeded, while the prospects of meeting real Franciscan monks was by no means distasteful; for although I have no great leaning towards the Spanish priesthood, still I honestly tried to go forward unprejudiced, thinking only of the monks of old, and the good they did in their day. But this convent was a revelation to us. We had never seen anything quite so filthy and suspicious looking before, and would have gladly escaped within an hour...*

———

The nun gestured her party onwards and I stayed in the museum, inspecting and photographing every reference to Sala. His undeviating will to power burnt through the curdling iconography of religious sentiment. How the fortunate Ashaninka on the banks of the Perené welcomed the man on the balsa raft with his upraised cross of exorcism and his tame monkey! How the early invaders lifted their eyes to heaven as countless arrows from the forest treated them as target practice! How the Franciscan with the cattle-drover's hat patted his faithful and criminally burdened mule! But the most sinister capture of all was a framed photograph that might have been taken by Roger Casement: a frozen group of indigenous children, cropped, monkishly robed, and paraded in front of a devotional painting of the bedizened Virgin. Under an arch of dying roses. Orphans of the jungle packed in a tight wedge around the anchor of the justified Sala. Pagan innocents brought to book.

Alongside this revelation was a colourful sequence like a church-approved children's comic from the 1950s. A smiling schoolroom friar with his pot of hallucinogenic plants is compiling dictionaries of indigenous languages. *Diccionario Ashaninka* comes with heavy covers in a shade of aquamarine.

The Advocate told me that the Convent library held all of Sala's recovered writings. It was an important resource. The published selections, however, were as determined in omitting Arthur as Arthur had been in his refusal to allow the Franciscan guide to be named.

This shady room of books, with its sanded boards and vitrines, was illuminated by beams of blue and green and pink from a stained-glass window. The books swallowed light. All the catalogues of monkish scholarship and capture. The taxonomies of birds and beasts and rescued heathen souls. In 1893 Sala wrote an extensive account of child sorcery among the Ashaninka.

'Father Sala is the nodal point,' the Advocate stressed, when we walked across London. 'Everything goes through him. He is part of all the expeditions promoted by the Peruvian State or by private interests such as the Peruvian Corporation.'

The Brussels poet-diplomat's voice was so much present in the occupied silence of the Convent library that, once again, I persuaded myself that he was actually here. With us or ahead of us. Surely the Advocate was that man in the dark suit in discussion with our nun and several of the Convent bureaucrats? We needed his informed intelligence. His determination to find answers to questions we were barely qualified to formulate.

When Lucho returned with news of the achieved o–o draw, the figure I mistook for the Advocate vanished down the tiled corridor. No car horns sounded, no bells rang out, when Peru scored the winning goal in the penalty shoot-out. Gallese was a hero. But national pride was somewhat tempered by anticipation of a battle still to be won, the semi-final against the traditional enemy, Chile. Like a replay of the fateful War of the Pacific.

The drive back to town, evening cows on the road, was part of the necessary fabric of the golden hour. Fields and trees shivered and withdrew from the jaunty and inconsequential radio interlude.

Farne had recovered. She was outside in the town square until the bands struck up. And now the hotel is under siege from manic children's entertainers, a second invasion of the clowns. The receptionist has a letter for me, along with, quite unusually, the right key to my room. It is the Advocate of course. Farne had provided him with our travel plans, when we met in the St Pancras bar, and somehow the poet found a way to accompany us, on every stage of our journey towards the wilderness.

But there had been a recent collapse or petit mal seizure. 'I stayed in bed the whole day and tried to communicate with your party, precisely as you arrived at Ocopa. The archivists at the convent do not reply to my queries about Sala. So I made an immense effort of will. I attempted a ritual of teleportation. I had been reading an uncategorisable book by Reza Negarestani. He speaks about the global oil economy and petroleum as "a terrestrial replacement of the onanistic self-indulgence of the Sun or solar capitalism". I think he might be on to something.'

'Solar capitalism', for the Advocate, was the key phrase. He wanted me to be aware of it. *And aware of it now, before we entered the cloud jungle.* The thesis also applied to the criminal exploitation of the Amazonian forest, the unsatisfied hunger for green gold.

'I must know: was *your* day special?' he wrote. 'I woke with such a dizzy head. It was not blood pressure, mine is very low. It was a bad case of elective soroche: at ground level in a flat country, after a day spent crossing the Rhine, twice, on my bicycle.'

What struck me, in the stroll I had made that morning, before breakfast, around Huancayo, was the complete absence of postcards. I would have to find some other way to let the Advocate know that we were still faithful to his dream, still on track. His own condition, brain-boiled and raked with premonitions, set us up nicely for the next day's drive to La Oroya, one of the world's most polluted negative attractions. But I now understood why his subterranean friends, those countercultural Belgian architects and medical poets, called him 'Spilliaert'. It was not that the Advocate physically resembled the Ostend painter Léon Spilliaert (1881–1946), with his dandified marine ennui, and the fabulous waves of hair trumped and airfixed from the nakedest of skulls. It was the absence of sleep, the bruised rings that Spilliaert copyrighted like the twin lenses of dark glasses deeply imprinted over hollow eye sockets. It was the moral responsibility for the consequences of words, in a country built on blood and colonial exploitation: white casinos, palaces of injustice and operatic hotels heaped on a foundation of bones. Like Spilliaert, the Advocate was nocturnal, insomniac. A scholar of the small hours trapped in his library. Or wandering the city on hurried centrifugal circuits, like a character from Poe. But there was no monastic retreat for my diligent friend, no window on the sea. He never failed in his duty. He supplied a network of correspondents with relevant quotations or predictions from favoured sources, such as the sacred scrolls of the Mayans. 'Their bones were ground up. They were broken into pieces. Their faces were ground up because they proved to be incapable of understanding before the face of their mother and the face of their father, Heart of the Sky.'

LA OROYA

'The man from the depths, from the abyss, "de profundis", that is the miner. The other with the faraway look, almost daydreaming, almost a sleepwalker…'

   – Vincent van Gogh, letter to his brother, 1880

La Oroya is hell. Old hell like the crusading denunciations of Zola and Dickens. Like the stooped and burdened charcoal beasts, the miners of Van Gogh's Borinage. Colour has been bleached from the set. Acid bites through thin air. Lead clogs the blood. The river is poisoned. But the thread of settlement fouling the valley, huddling around the smelting plant, is still there, still active: unlike the heritage mineshafts and winding gear of my Welsh childhood. The town is occupied by willing casualties, fighting to preserve what they have, a life of sorts, and an income threatened by well-meaning outsiders bent on exposing corporate iniquities. And closing the project down. La Oroya is a poster for blight. It feels, at first sight, as if it has been permitted to remain, a scab on the road we have chosen, between Huancayo and Arthur's botanical oasis at Tarma, only as a location for climate-change documentaries. La Oroya is the hell we need for our story, a homeopathic dose of horror before driving rapidly away.

We set out early. Lucho had a cab waiting – 'Come on, vamos, let's go' – to take us to the bus station at Huancayo, the renegade pitch where business is done, a training hub for hustlers. He found the right man for the day's job, no seatbelts and plenty of holy medallions, along with a small white bear. Lucho's hometown had been a necessary detour. It was the terminal of the railway still under construction when Arthur launched his expedition. Now, at La Oroya, we would reconnect with the published outline of my great-grandfather's journey. Mining was already in operation in 1891, but the spur to development came with the arrival from Lima of the Ferrocarril Central Andino tracks in 1893. The full orchestration of ecological doom was not sounded until the first copper smelter was built in 1922, followed by the lead smelter in 1928. La Oroya was then the contrary of the fabled Swedenborgian Gold Machine: it was the Death Machine, bringer of plague and pestilence. Destroyer of worlds. The new township was under the control of the American Cerro de Pasco Corporation.

Arthur and his companions did not linger at La Oroya on their way to the Salt Mountain and the Perené. There was nothing to report. But they did visit the established mining hub of Cerro de Pasco on their return journey to Lima.

> *We at length reached the famous silver city of Cerro de Pasco, the highest inhabited town in the world, and one of the oldest, richest, and most renowned silver-mining centres in South America. What Broken Hill is to Australia, and Zeehan promised to be to Tasmania, Cerro de Pasco has for centuries been to Peru. The township, which contains about 9,000 inhabitants, is situated on the eastern slope of the Andes, amidst surroundings as filthy and forbidding as it is possible for any place to occupy. We threaded our way through the disreputable-looking crowd to what they were pleased to call Hotel del Universo. We had already seen and experienced some rather comfortless quarters during our travels, but anything so unutterably filthy as these premises we had never come across. The passages reminded us of a neglected poultry run in wet weather, but when we entered the bedroom we could only stand speechless with dismay, wishing ourselves back in the wilds of Perené. To sleep there was impossible, but we had a good coal fire and spent the night in sitting over it as best we could.*

The next day Arthur presented his credentials to the Sub-Prefect, in a room furnished with 'rich Brussels carpet' and heavy mirrors. Outside, slush burns to dust, before the next downpour. Mules fail. Blind kittens survive for only a few hours after birth. Some try to scratch their way up a wall, before falling to the ground. But the labour, the digging and gouging, never stops.

> *The silver-mining industry, as at present carried on here, consists in work-ing up the tailings left by the old Spanish miners… The prevailing rock is conglomerate, the silver occurring in the native state, also as mixed with pyrites and oxides, forming what are known as* pacos *and* colorados. *A large quantity of mercury is used in treating the ore, so wastefully indeed that two pounds of mercury are lost for every pound of silver extracted. Fortunately, there are mines of quicksilver within easy distance. During the last 250 years the yield of these mines has been valued at something like £83,000,000, but before they can again be worked on anything like an adequate scale an extensive system of drainage will be absolutely necessary. With this, and the extension of the rail from Oroya, Cerro de Pasco might still rival in riches all the Broken Hills and Zeehans in the world.*

Reading Arthur's account I couldn't help thinking of Conrad's *Nostromo*, published one year before my great-grandfather's death. I had already played with serendipitous interconnections of the golden age of colonialism flowing between Conrad, Arthur Sinclair and Roger Casement, in a strange obsessive novel called *Dining on Stones*. *Nostromo* could be sketching the psychological profile of Cerro de Pasco and La Oroya: that irrational hunger for mineral wealth, for mines and planta-tions at the expense of the indigenous people.

'Mrs Gould knew the history of the San Tomé mine,' Conrad wrote. 'Worked in the early days mostly by means of lashes on the backs of slaves, its yield had been paid for in its own weight of human bones. Whole tribes of Indians had perished in the exploitation… An English company obtained the right to work it, and found so rich a vein that neither the exactions of successive governments, nor the periodical raids of recruiting officers upon the population of paid miners they had created, could discourage their perseverance.'

With the revived San Tomé mine come the investors, the profit takers. The visiting dignitaries. The squalid reporters. Comes a secular fiesta to celebrate the arrival of the railway.

'My husband wanted the railway,' Mrs Gould said to Sir John in the general murmur of resumed conversation. 'All this brings nearer the sort of future we desire for the country, which has waited for it in sorrow long enough, God knows.'

The wife of the British Consul at Cerro de Pasco entertains Arthur and his companions. Always at her husband's side, the good lady helped to maintain a civilised British presence in this remote township. She was pleased to report that her health was adequate to the task, but that she had not yet resolved to leave the house. And, indeed, had no desire to do so, until 'kind fate might open up a way for her return to England'. Cerro de Pasco, hemmed in by pits and slag heaps, mine workings and their running scars, laboured to bring some burnish to the gold fever of the predatory Spaniards.

> *At Chiquirin, where we saw primitive-looking gold-seekers at work on the banks of the river, the returns are said to be very good considering the absence of modern appliances and technical knowledge, a moderate application of which could not fail to yield very rich returns. Besides the Huallaga, the auriferous rivers are said to be the Chanchamayo, Tulumayo, Pangoa, Pucartamba, and Ogabamba. The gold these waters bring down seems to come from the veins of quartz that cross the slate and crystalline formation which chiefly constitutes the Cordilleras ... It is very evident, however, that mining, like everything else in Peru, is in a bad way at present, and the cause is equally palpable, viz.,* bad administration.*
>
> *Few men know the country and people better than the British Consul, and, like a straightforward Englishman, he does not hesitate to express his contempt for the insidious knavery which goes on in Lima, and has no very exalted notion of the Hispano-Peruvian in general. For the Cholo, or mountain Indian, there seems more hope if he could only be kept from rum. It is curious to hear that amongst the more intelligent of those highlanders there is still a lingering hope that their country will some day be restored to them through the intervention of England. It will be remembered that Raleigh thought there was an old prophecy, 'That from Inglaterra those Ingas should be againe in time to come delivered from the servitude of the said conquerors.'*

The spoiling of La Oroya was a theme that Grant wanted to secure for his film. He had been researching Doe Run Peru, a subsidiary, and later an affiliate, of the Renco Group. They acquired the La Oroya smelter, for approximately 247 million US dollars, in 1993. They also picked up the Cobriza copper mine for 7.5 million. And they made a number of rather vague promises to the government's Environmental Program. Promises that were manageably ill-defined and subject to financial adjustment. Deadlines were missed and rephrased as 'standard business practice in complicated times'. Sulphur dioxide emissions reached record levels in August 2008. Levels for lead and cadmium exceeded Peruvian standards, always elastic, and resulted in respiratory ailments, malnutrition and weight loss among children, along with numerous gastrointestinal issues. The Peruvian health ministry, MINSA, found that 99.9% of the children of La Oroya under the age of seven had blood lead levels far above safety limits.

We tracked the Rio Mantaro until Lucho called a halt, so that we could climb the railway embankment and look back down the line we had ridden to Huancayo. Panting, we pick our way over a suspect bridge. The next bridge, down the valley, was said to have been blown up by Shining Path, in the days of the Maoist insurrection. Our guide, with some impatience, rattled off a sketchy history of the revolutionaries who competed, all too effectively, for influence over hard-pressed peasant communities of the mountains: adventure tourism or Marxist–Leninist resistance, there was always a heavy toll on the indigenous 'benefactors'. El Sendero Luminoso, a movement founded by an urban philosophy professor, Abimael Guzmán, in 1969, achieved its maximum visibility in the 1980s. Small independent guerrilla groups, supplied with AKM rifles and Heckler & Koch machine guns, and often commanded by women, were prominent in the highlands of the Ayacucho region. They were reputed to act with extreme brutality. After Guzmán and his immediate successors had been captured or killed by counter-terror paramilitaries, surviving bands retreated into the forests of rumour, into mythologised territory beyond the last cascades. They formed alliances with drug cultivators and exploited their hidden paths. They disappeared among the wandering spirits of tribal ancestors who had been misled by the messianic promptings of alien prophets.

Lucho visited prisons to interview many political detainees from Shining Path. They denied any part in the destruction of the bridge. Here was another corporate fix with convenient (already defeated) scapegoats. If a sufficiently plausible accusation can be formulated, it must be true. Everybody is satisfied. Up in the mountains, on the Inca Trail with one of his adventure tours, Lucho had been challenged several times by armed guerrillas. He talked his way out of some very awkward situations.

'There is one rule. Don't say anything in Spanish.'

'Why is that?'

'Because you will say something wrong. On my first encounter with Shining Path, they told me to translate. I made a big mistake. I told my people what the "terrorists" wanted. Totally wrong. "Tourist" sounds like "terrorist". So this guy pointed a gun at me. "You said terrorist. You should have said *compañero*." So never try to say something in Spanish.

'There was a strong guy with me, Austrian, trained. And a Dutchman with one eye. *He* was really funny, a character. He said, "I'm South African and I'm Dutch, and so is my grandfather. He also had one eye. We always lose one eye in our family. That's how you recognise us. My grandfather had a farm. Those guys, they're so lazy. They always turn their backs on you and say that they're resting. My father had a glass eye. He would take it out when he was driving, because he might lose it. With the Africans, to control them, he left his eye on a post and told them it would be watching, all day. Then he went off and spied on them with his binoculars. When he collected them, he put his eye back in and said that he knew they had been taking long rests with their shirts off."

'The stories those guys told... They didn't care about guerrillas. They knew what to do with them. It was a little adventure, a good one. And we're still alive.'

The car and its passengers are washed in the vampire green of the sunshade visor. This sickly glow is the only colour in the landscape. Cloud masses are scummed and slow, solidified crematorium smoke heavy with particulates. Lucho points out the scatter of ruins along what should have been a fertile riverbank. The mountain shepherds struggled for a few years with the microclimate of criminal pollution, poisoned grasses and sick animals, and then they moved away. The roofless dwellings could have come from any era, remote or recent. A naked geometry of abdication from which passing strangers are invited to improvise an explanation.

There is a visible line beyond which there is no vegetation. Hills are congealed slag heaps, rust stains giving way to chemically induced glaciation: an albino condition lived with to the point where it is accepted, even enjoyed, as a badge of endurance against all odds. For the outsider, shocked and concerned for an hour, the horrors of the company town are seductive. Even to the point at which a general theory of everything is revealed, a cubist analysis: broken blocks of sheds and shacks embedded in grey and sepia rock. To the image thief, siphoning comfortable indignation, the picture is the story.

The chimney, tall, black and tapering, is the nail around which La Oroya defines itself, workers and process. The smelter sits proud at the centre of the town, a heating system with unfortunate side effects. This is not Chernobyl. This is a vision from the multiverse: you get the fallout of catastrophe *while the thing, the Death Machine, is still operative, still in the game*. The crisis has been achieved, but domestic life, suitably amended and adapted, carries on. La Oroya does weird things with time, but it cannot conjure up a vision of Arthur and his mule train, nor permit communication with a teleported Advocate. We have never been so isolated, so alone.

I have to step from the car to photograph a monster scorpion painted on the back of a parked truck, with the chimney and the smelter in the background. Grant sets up his tripod, to confirm what he already knows. He has to work faster than he would like. But he plans to come back. His presentation bifurcates between the dark alchemy of industrial squalor and the potential visions, yet to come, of the jungle vine. Our parallel stories will never quite touch or fuse. Meanwhile, Lucho, taking position against the devastated hills – quizzical eyebrows raised, mane of silver hair – has the larger investment in territory. He understands the betrayal of the bureaucrats and he acknowledges its necessity. The world must roll on. It is all we have. 'Vamos, let's go.'

There have been so many lies. 'Lead will only harm you if you are already suffering from malnutrition,' say the commissioned medical investigators. To human ghosts fighting for breath in crowded clinics. 'Sulphur dioxide will not affect your health.'

My father, and his father before him (Arthur's son), spent their adult lives working as general practitioners in a mining community. At 30,000 inhabitants, La Oroya has roughly the same population as Maesteg, the river-hugging valley town in which I grew up. I heard something, on a daily basis, of the physical cost of a thriving economy, pits, steelworks, tin plate. I knew the compromises of medical boards and the grudging respect men had for the harsh existence that drew them from poverty. I knew it and knew nothing. I went down there into the darkness, tasted the choking heat, saw the blind ponies in their stalls, felt the cramp of the coal face and took a few lumps of prime anthracite home, wrapped in newspaper. I was a visitor on sufferance, working for his exams.

As we drove the length of this Peruvian town, I saw Wales. Social housing for the workers came in bleak barracks. With tactical plantings and a few communal taps. Football pitches had been provided. And topiary animals, llamas and sheep, carved from hedges, to replace the vanished flocks. There were even models of the smelter, the chimney and the labourers: the town was becoming a museum of memory, before memory was actually required. Our drive rekindled my delight in geographies on the cusp of extinction. Unacknowledged places where the relics of industry combine with dirty streams and not quite redundant railways. Filthy ponds on landfill sites occupied by frogs, dragonflies and malformed fish thrown out with the domestic waste.

La Oroya was not somewhere road trippers stopped to eat. But we found a place with numbered tables right on the street. Soup, in a deep bowl, with noodles and potato slices and a grey hack of chicken, defying the implements provided, revived me. Farne, having ordered, wasn't ready to put a fork in anything. Lucho, ever the professional scavenger, asked for a carton. He would heat up these scraps for his evening meal, turning his room into a jungle camp. That is, if he did not present the remnants of our feast to the llama herders he promised to locate, when we agreed to drive over the mountain track on our way to Tarma.

I drank my cup of coca tea slowly. And remembered the Italian cafés, as centres of social interaction for youths who had not yet managed to get away, who might never get away, in dim and damp Welsh mining towns. Ice cream, coffee, cake, calendar views of Sorrento, curated by a former prisoner of war from the camp in Bridgend. Someone who had taken a fancy to the place. Or one of the women. And then summoned the rest of his relatives.

This was a company town built along the river it had ruined, splashes of blue and a few pink roofs among uniform mercury greys and silvers. There were igloo shrines to mark road deaths and vases bereft of flowers. And one of the world's tallest chimneys. Day and night, the smelter, taking in waste from all over the continent, translates unwanted detritus into death. The placenta of the unborn of La Oroya is ripe with lead and other contaminates. The clouds are a sullen death duvet. Headaches. Cancers. Blisters.

Climbing prices for Peruvian metal exports boost the backcountry economy. The people cannot afford good health. They support the machinery that is killing them. From the worst concentrates comes gold. The metallurgists of Doe Run Peru evolved methods for separating and recovering precious metals as a by-product of the smelting process. From the ovens of the refinery flow antimony, arsenic, cadmium, indium, selenium, tellurium and sulphuric acid. I am no chemist. I don't know what selenium is, but I read that it has 'an electrical resistance that varies under the influence of light'.

Some of the miners, having been cut loose, casualties of a free-market economy, now scratch a living by peddling dusty oranges and green bananas at the roadside. They have burrowed into the blasted hillside. Their shacks and shelters are accessed by a fantastic Piranesi system of interconnected ladders.

Again, as in Wales, there was that sudden release, the landscape epiphany when we climbed into the mountains and bumped over the pitted dirt of the back road to Tarma. Lucho identified remote specks that might or might not have been llama herders. The black smoke, he said, was coming from fires set to burn off the surface covering of tough winter grass, in order to make sweeter growths for the lambing flocks. The ear-popping shift to the Brecon Beacons, a favourite outing of my child-hood years, depended on passing through the chain of mining towns, railway lines, spoil heaps and colliery winding gear, the infinite terraces of Treorchy, Treherbert and Hirwaun. Here, above La Oroya, the shift from the human desolation of the industrial gulag to the inhuman iso-lation of the mountains was absolute.

Arthur, on his mule, making slow and steady progress, enjoyed a closer inspection of the llamas.

> *It is a beautiful and interesting sight to see a flock of laden llamas marching with measured steps across these high table-lands, and up and down prec-ipices where mules would be helpless. The arriero, as a rule, is very kind to his llamas, and when one succumbs from fatigue he will lie down beside it, embrace the animal, and make use of the most coaxing and endearing expressions. Nevertheless, the route is strewn with the bones of dead llamas, and every journey to the coast is made at the sacrifice of many lives. For children of the higher Cordilleras, the heat and weight of air in the lowlands frequently proves fatal.*

The best guess, Lucho reported, was that those distant figures were women and our offer of gifts, stewed soup and airport trinkets, would have to be tactfully made. Perhaps the approach was better left to another day. 'Just experience the experience. You will never feel the same again.' The here of the *here*after. The more of never*more*. And the terrible now of unearned k*now*ledge.

> *Semi-abandoned as most of the great plateau is, it is depressing and wearying work travelling across it.*

That was Arthur's conclusion, not mine. Our vehicle teleports us too quickly from blight to a wide horizon with nothing to deflect the wind. And then, as we descend towards a fertile valley, the view ahead is cancelled by a sensational concrete plant. Vast and alien as an abandoned lunar base. The dystopian vision with its launch-pad towers, cylinders and fuel tanks has us scrabbling to achieve the optimum position from which to make an adequate photographic record. Around the imposed city of interlinked blocks and funnels are spread the pathetic shacks of the workers. Bunkhouses and administration bungalows are serviced by churned, red dirt roads and electric fences. Who needs so much concrete? And how far does it have to travel to be of use?

The mountain road doubles back on itself, but I can't ask for the car to be halted yet again, so that I can try to catch the silenic curtain of a metastasised forest, dressing the space between the valley floor and the concrete castle on the summit. This silvered Edgar Allan Poe plantation whistles and clanks like the rigging of a frozen ship. The slender trees are both dead and alive. They are the harbingers of a coming state of reversed entropy.

Farne has chosen well. The Hacienda Santa María was once a noted Spanish estate, where a 'last supper' was celebrated before the male members of the noble family took opposing sides in civil conflict, the war between Spain and the Hispano-Peruvians, for the spoils of conquest. Tarma is a town of gardens. We are among dogs and parrots, cats, soft-padding indigenous attendants, aristocratic chickens, trickling streams and lush plantings, groves of eucalyptus.

Alexander Ross described the arrival of the 1891 expedition.

> The road descends by gradients of great steepness, and by a track of exceeding roughness into a long and narrow valley, in which there is the merest thread of cultivation. This widens lower down, till again we are among the terraced, cultivated hill sides, and rich flat fields of the populous wayside villages of the Peruvian Indian highlanders. Tarma, 18 miles from Oroya, is situated, at 9,800 feet altitude, in a basin among towering hills, which are everywhere terraced, and cultivated. It seems

to want only the telegraph, the railway, and improved postal communication, to become one of the largest and most thriving towns in Peru.
It possesses a dry, bracing, and salubrious climate, in which sufferers
from pulmonary complaints derive marked benefit.

After this self-serving bow from Ross to the progressive interests of
the Peruvian Corporation, it is striking to note how Arthur, without
saying much – he reserved his energies for satire – makes it clear that
Tarma was a very special oasis. He could breathe, at last, and rest for a
few days, while continuing to sleep, to the annoyance of his companions, with a light burning through the hours of darkness.

Evenings were cold. There were no curtains in my room. I stuck a
photocopy of Arthur's Aberdeen portrait across the window. That smile
was now explained: my great-grandfather was back among gardens,
with plants to identify. And a sturdy table, when he sat outside with
his coffee, on which to take up his pen and improve his journal. The
scented mornings of Tarma tempted the hardy Scot into making a rare
personal confession: fear of the dark and the things that darkness hid.
There was a dispute with Ross over a door that the fastidious planter
insisted should be left wide open. The previously disguised neuroses
of the two commissioned surveyors were in open conflict. Alexander
Ross, prey to unmanning claustrophobia, needed healthy ventilation
to neutralise his suspicion of the seething dirt of improperly scrubbed
and scoured bedchambers. Arthur, at fifty-nine, was considered to be
on the cusp of old age, and his entry to the unknowable forest called
up the suppressed terrors of a narrow highland childhood. The black
inside black, the choking blanket of those never forgotten winter nights.

TARMA

'The past is full of becoming.'
  – Samson Kambalu

It was after a testing uphill walk through the back streets of San Pedro de Cajas, at the heels of Lucho, and being obliged to duck our heads under colourful Clint Eastwood ponchos, to endure thigh butts from supercilious llamas, that the crisis came: the Mexican stand-off between the determination of our guide to show us the right kind of good time, ticking every cliché of adventure tourism, and Farne's implacable resolution to pursue our enquiry into the historic crimes and misdemeanours of her great-great-grandfather. And into whatever the indigenous people of the cloud forest now thought about such events, as they had been laid out in the retrospective fiction that was *In Tropical Lands*. Even as I snapped away at the llamas and at my London daughter in her round Andean hat, while she was being nuzzled by dowager sheep, I came to appreciate the role Lucho had taken on himself as trickster-shaman of the mountains. This hustling man was pushing us to react and to find our own way of forging resistance. Resistance we would need to survive.

Tarma was a respite of hidden gardens, lilies, sparkling water, parrots, chickens, cats and sleepy attendants half-roused from dreams of an older time. We needed the same unrecorded interval that Arthur allowed himself, after coming across the Cordilleras on a mule. *It was when he didn't write that I knew all was well*. He was sitting outside, he was evaluating the horticulture. There was nothing to report to the Corporation, nothing to exploit. He smiled the smile of the Aberdeen portrait, the one I had pressed to my curtainless window, to make it appear that the Victorian traveller was looking in on me from outside, from the hills and the trees. He wanted, and Farne wanted, and I wanted, a pause. A table in the garden. Coffee. Conversation. A recording. A summary of our so-far-so-good audio diary, for the podcast my daughter projected.

It had been cold in the night and Farne wrapped herself in all the authentic layers of llama wool she had purchased as family gifts from the village weaving shed. My bones rattled under a single blanket and I stumbled out, on the hour, like a mountain climber from his tent, for an old man's piss. Arthur knew these nights.

> *The mercilessly cold wind blew right in my face; I shivered and covered my head with the blankets. Presently the old four-poster began to rock me in a way I had not been accustomed to for over half a century. I might have imagined that I was only dreaming of childhood, but a simultaneous howling convinced me of the fact that we had experienced a smart shock of earthquake. It soon passed over, however, and all was again quiet, save for the groaning of the poor restless mules, seeking in vain for food or smarting from irritating sores. Poor, starved, over-burdened mules! I shall never quite shake off the qualms of conscience I carry through life on account of these too hurried rides.*

Arthur was coming back, after the river and the rapids, over the Andes, at the limits of his endurance, sulky about being rushed by Alexander Ross, in a futile record-attempting push. In my own night of fitful Tarma sleep, with brief interconnected sequences of cyclic dreams, I acknowledged the mythical status this place held for my great-grandfather: a district capital in limbo, between colonising regimes. And the supposed depository of the captured bones of the mountain redeemer, Juan Santos Atahualpa. Men in mule masks talked to me about endurance in a language too pure for my understanding. Flies crusted the raw wounds of passage, their venomous tongues flicking and rasping. The special quality here was stasis, the pause before the pause, permission to slow down, to contemplate the difficulties ahead. And this thesis, unspoken over a breakfast of fruit and coffee essence, was shared with Farne, but ran quite contrary to Lucho's compulsion to arrange, instruct, and exhaust the potential of every hour in every day.

'Come on, let's go, vamos.'

The young driver is already leaning against his car, watching the green parrot among the pink flowers.

Before we hit the road to the hills – Inca Highway, tapestry weavers at their looms, blue-suited marching bands, street food, caves – Farne insists that we take time in Tarma, an interlude at the main square in front of the twin-towered Cathedral. She needs, at this stage, to sort out the finances. Lucho, dispenser of per diems to his team of drivers, is amenable to a quick bank visit. All the shaded benches are occupied. The Cathedral is cool. While I make a slow tour of inspection, my daughter gets out her calculator and papers, spreading them over a pew, to take care of business.

In this 'City of Flowers', Santa Ana de la Ribera de Tarma, with its sleepy shops, shade-hugging citizens, bakers, barbers, motor scooters, I feel great sympathy for Farne's gift of making her own space, wherever she happens to be. And empathy also with Arthur's renewed spirits, lifting above the morning haze, as he lets the pressure go, and stops judging the land and the people against his lost paradise of Ceylon. He came down into the fertile valley, with his mule, parsing the music of a mountain stream.

> *Here a watercourse carries grateful moisture to the Alfalfa fields below. The banks of this little watercourse are a delightful study. I can scarcely express the pleasure I had in recognising so many old familiar friends. The trees were chiefly alder and buddleia… Here also are veritable bourtree bushes; there a line of the beautiful Peruvian willow named after the illustrious Humboldt. Nor can we pass without recognition the sweet little flowers that clothe the margin of the rippling stream. The yellow calceolaria, ever ready to assert its nativity, blended with the blue salvia and ageratums, various vincas, passion flowers, solanum, and thunbergias, all so familiar and all so much at home here, gave a peculiar charm to this morning's ride.*

He does not unpack his camera. He opens his sketchbook and takes the time to record, in ink drawings, this sudden abundance of exotic plants and flowers. The sketches, intended to catalogue flora, become portraits of a state of mind. But the photographs, delivered by what Mark Twain called 'the incorruptible kodak', are very different. Mechanical images, carried home from the territory, are always, as Twain says, 'the only witnesses that cannot be bribed'.

We had been herded and we played along. It was a marvel to see, taste and smell these things, but it was unearned. We had not put in the required miles on foot or with companionable mules. The village bands in their electric-blue suits drummed into our blood. The Inca Highway was a yellow gunpowder trail into a past we could never restore. The cloudless sky was a purer blue than the day of creation. Packs of Inca Cola, under plastic wraps, were the colour of urine samples drawn from camels. Huge plates cracked under a ballast of roots, meat bricks and six kinds of potato, in colour and texture ranging from coal to salt-crusted pebble. San Pedro de Carjas, *en fête*, pulsed in the unforgiving midday heat. The stern faces of the ink-haired Andean people accepted the preordained riot of fiesta as a solemn and necessary duty.

Arthur, coming from his northern darkness, was suspicious of the way the church had infiltrated and suborned village celebrations.

> *The padre, we are told, not unfrequently joins his flock in their drunken orgies; indeed, the so-called Church festivals seem to have degenerated into blasphemous ribaldry, enough to make one shudder. It is the boast of the proud Spaniard that he has at least given the Peruvians a language and a religion. The language may be all right, but we cannot congratulate them upon their religion, and who will dare to say that it would not have been better for them had they still been speaking quichua, and reverently saluting the glorious rising sun as they wended their way to work in their well-tilled fields as in the olden time when industry formed part of their religion.*

Before, head-torches in place, we entered the limestone cave Gruta de Huagapo, slithering on wet rock, scrambling up ladders, we were required to pay a modest tithe to experience the twin pools at Cachipozo. This was an episode from which there was no recovery, until we gathered around the dinner table, under the mural of a seventeenth-century hunting scene, back at the hacienda. The descent to the pools, more like dirty footbaths or a sewage filtration system, was a sordid pilgrimage. There were manufactured myths and a Jungian misdirection that the pools represented 'masculine and feminine elements'. The day we arrived, July 1st, was the time of a much-needed ritual cleansing for the site, before newly married couples would drive out to offer lifelong commitment to their brave union. They call it 'The Fountain of Heaven'.

Royal huntsmen moved silently through the haunted forest of the improbable wallpaper, accompanied at a distance by side-saddle ladies, and all of them washed by a chalk-green fever moon. Aristocratic rituals continue, in repeated sequences, ahead of the revolutions that must surely sweep them away. In the drowsy dining room of the Tarma hacienda, we are waited on by other established rituals of service: a decorous evening meal, grouped at a long table. After Farne and Lucho have gone over their plans for the jungle, with costings and potential revisions, and after we have eaten a little more than our fill, pushed back our plates, and found some substitute position for hands no longer permitted to engage with cigars or roll-ups, our guide is persuaded to set the scene for what lies ahead with stories of his encounters with Shining Path.

'At the end of the season, we went to places I never take people. I thought, okay, I will offer these guys something interesting. There is an area of the jungle I visit, the Tambo River, and then on to La Bomba and Urubamba. There is a little possibility of meeting people, wading through at the heads of those rivers. And on again, finally, to Madre de Dios.

'These guys looked at the map. They saw the adventure. They were thinking about it. We went to the market for the logistics, the fishing gear, the knives, everything. You've seen my little backpack? The hooks, the pills. Little pots for every eventuality.

'We went to Satipo. The road was in the process of being built. We just start walking. When we reach Puerto Ocopa, I was thinking, okay, tomorrow we are going to take the boat down the river. So I go to the monastery and ask the priest if he will give us lodging for the night.

We had a nice meal with a nun. A table like this one, where we are now. The priest was talking. He said he'd heard there were strangers by the beach, *colonos*.

'The next day, when I was going to hire the boat, people were looking a little bit strange, avoiding me. Somebody came and asked if my name was Lucho. I said, "Do you have a boat?" "No, I want to talk with you." Okay. We go inside. "You and your friends must follow me." Then he pulled out a gun. And some other people came in from behind me. They were Shining Path.

'Then we were walking, walking, by part of the airport, close to the river. I remembered what the people around there had told me. "Shining Path always kill the ones they take away. They shoot them and put the bodies in the river."

'This is not going to be a good ending. The main guy was starting to shout. "Are you all Americans?" He was blaming me for bringing spies from the media. "You are Americans." I said: "Look, I go around with the Ashaninka. I have a lot of friends around here."

'I said: "I have my backpack in the monastery with the padre. You can see we have nothing to hide. I go down the river with the natives. I give them knives, things to make craft. I come here with many groups. Every time I pass, I can give you one hundred dollars per person."

'He changed his attitude. He said: "You have so many things. Why don't you leave your cameras at home?"

'I said: "I can leave you one of my knives. It's no problem. A really good chopping knife."

'He said: "Okay. Give me a hundred dollars per person. Where is the money?"

'I had my money scattered in many places, different pockets. There were five hundred dollars. I gave them four hundred. And said that now we had a deal for the next time.

'We were coming back to the place where I wanted to get our boat. One of the young guys with me, he was from Canada, said: "Lucho, if we have paid one hundred dollars each, why don't we continue?" Stupid man. What if we meet more from Shining Path? We don't have any receipts.

'When we arrive at the bridge where there is a checkpoint for the army, the special unit who fight Shining Path, they take us all inside. They already know that something has happened, but we are still alive. They keep asking these questions. Then they let us go and we walk over the bridge into town. You can feel the whole town watching, like we were ghosts coming back from the dead. I go to the little village where I have my juices, my fruit salads.

'I say to a woman I know, Ele: "Can you give me some fruit salads for my friends?"

'Her tears were streaming down. She touches my hand. She says: "Is it you, Lucho? They say that they killed you." And I tell her that I will never die.

'So we buy some beers and then we go to the hotel. We are drinking. Suddenly the blackout comes. We are getting a little bit tipsy and these guys have recalled the story of the men with guns two hundred times. And the Dutchman comes to me and he says: "When we were walking with that man who had the gun, I was the last in line. He was in front of me. So I made sure I passed you. You bastard, Lucho, you wanted me to be killed first!"

'I thought I might go out to find a couple more beers. It was dark now. But the door is chained. This is strange. The hotel is empty. What if Shining Path have dynamited the place and we are not going to make it through to the next morning? We use bed sheets, tied together, and we climb down. And we start to walk. No lights. No candles, nothing. We walk out of town to the house of my friend Velisa's father, Manuel. It takes about two hours.

'Manuel looks at me. "It is good." He is very quiet, he's a quiet person. "They told me that they had killed you." They gave us nice drinks and we tell our stories. The Ashaninka are good for telling stories. We spend the night there with them. The next day we go down the hill, across the river, and back to the same bridge where the police caught us and interrogated us.

'That was my last time, for twenty years. Until now. I never went back to that town. I came out with my life, for a hundred dollars. Some of the Ashaninka were with Shining Path. The guerrillas needed them.

Because they did not know the jungle very well. They were people from the mountains.

'I had a friend who was kidnapped and taken into the forest. She escaped. Her father was carrying her on his shoulders. There was no food. They had to eat leaves, roots and dirt. But her father told her he would get them out. This man is still alive, he's one of my best guides. Now he has tuberculosis. The daughter joined the army. The father is hunted by Shining Path because he managed to free those people.

'It's a tough story. But sometimes, when we get into the masato, we feel good to be alive. And we just laugh. We didn't finish the adventure, but we still have the memories. Maybe I will tell these stories sometime, put them all together. I am like my mother, she got Alzheimer's. The stories get mixed up but they are nice stories. Sometimes a bit crazy.'

'Thank you, Lucho,' I said. 'We are happy to walk behind you when we go down to the river, but we don't want to do anything interesting enough to feature in any of your stories.'

LA MERCED

'I was simply moving on, while the others, perhaps, were going somewhere.'

    – Joseph Conrad, *Victory*

I almost expected, as had been arranged before successive crises, political and viral, hit Europe, requiring his advice and attention, to find the Advocate waiting patiently for us at the hotel in La Merced. He would be at the bar, notebook open, a small stack of importunate volumes at his elbow, making those fastidious journal entries, in a private language more like chemical formulae than literature. But there was no bar, no Advocate either. I missed the intensity of excited and informed discourse he brought to our project, the unshaken conviction that this was still an active exercise.

We were dropped, luggage heaped around us, at the desk, waiting for someone to appear from a private office to ask if we *really* wanted separate rooms. And to shake his (or her) head over inadequate passports and pre-booked documentation.

In the pink and perfumed afternoon lull, drugged on exotic plants and the petrol-funk of cruising tuk-tuks, we found our palm-screened roadside oasis both deserted and inconveniently occupied.

'Your rooms will be magnificently prepared. Perhaps an hour, two hours. It is very pleasant beside the pool.'

As a frontier town, twinned with San Ramón, La Merced was the final barrier before the jungle and the Ashaninka. The Chanchamayo airstrip at San Ramón housed small planes that could be chartered for urgent business with the interior. In the confused aftermath of the Pacific War, the area had been colonised by Italian immigrants. But their push into the Chanchamayo Valley met with strong resistance from the indigenous people, who were only driven back towards the Rio Perené when the Peruvian government sent in the army and established a fortified barracks. There had been a bloody battle and a siege around the time when Arthur's party arrived in 1891.

Putting on time by the side of the pool, with wavering reflections of umbrellas and sun loungers, and intelligent shadows creeping across low, thickly forested hills, and flinching a little from the floating beer bottles and black thongs of last night's party, we flicked through our reference books. It was a pity that my great-grandfather's botanical illustrations were ink drawings. There was nothing to help us identify showy slashes of cardinal red among the Jagger tongues of thirsty leaf. Were they lobster claws, ostrich plume or heliconia?

Next day, Grant, whose tall, rather severe outline, more than ever now that of an island hermit, a beachcomber out of Conrad, obliged to drag his camera equipment, like an unbreakable vow, everywhere he went, set out to walk between the two settlements, La Merced and San Ramón: to prove their difference, and to place himself, before we moved yet again. And this time to territory where maps, even if we possessed them, would be useless. Trudging under the hammer of the meridian sun and trying to accumulate images without drawing attention to himself was a challenge. Beyond the token strip of convenience hotels, all the buildings, domestic or commercial, were unfinished, barely even started. The upper floors were open to the birds and stars.

My room was ready first. I was the senior citizen, most in need of a siesta. The bed was smoothed over, but indented and warm. I was just in time to catch a large man in uniform hitching his gun belt as he made, rather unsteadily, for the backstairs. The shower didn't operate and there was no plug for tap or basin. Lucho, as he rounded us up for the minibus ride to town, surmised that it was an obligation for the hotel owner, with his political ambitions, to allow the chief of police and the mayor, both relatives, to host corporate hospitality sessions, and to provide a night's board and company, when requested, for visiting dignitaries and potential investors. Occasional tourists were a barely tolerated smokescreen.

———

When we left Tarma, with its gardens of drooping white and yellow funeral lilies and scarlet geraniums, for a white-knuckle ride down the steep gorge to La Merced, Arthur was back with us. His unquiet voice was so persistent that Farne declared that we must pay our respects to Acombamba, 'a decaying hamlet' that had taken her great-great-grandfather's indulgent fancy.

> *We halted for breakfast at Acombamba, only six miles from Tarma, from which we had been rather late in starting. Acombamba is beautifully situated… with about 1,500 rather seedy-looking inhabitants, where not long ago there had been more than double that number… Every second house is in ruins, and what had doubtless once been trimly kept gardens, are now scenes of desolation. Not without its interest, however, and as one curious in such matters, I accomplished the feat of scrambling through the straggling fence, and I dare confess explored the wild spot with more real pleasure than I would look upon well-clipped bushes. Beneath a jungle of red roses were violets scenting the morning air, and many exotics as far from home as myself, including the gaudy geranium, southernwood, and costmary. How they came there is a question we leave to others.*
>
> *Women squat under the trees, industriously weaving, on the most primitive of looms, the cloth of which their husbands' ponchos and trousers are made, while their lords, such as they are, may be seen loafing in crowds around the drinking bars on the Plaza.*

Nobody was weaving under trees or congregating in the Plaza, when, well breakfasted, we hit town, but it felt good to whisper that name – *Acombamba, Acom-bam-ba, Ac-om-bam-ba* – as an invocation to Arthur's passage through the territory. His relief at dropping down from the mountains, and enjoying a trespass in a wild garden, was palpable. The contemporary Plaza, scrubbed and shady, was at the heart of a model township of white walls and terracotta roofs.

Various dead and deposed presidents were taking credit for the china blue sky, the flowerbeds, public benches and plashing fountain. One substantially bewhiskered and medal-draped statue was a bloodless realisation of the portrait of the three-times president Andrés Avelino

Cáceres, with which Arthur elected to conclude the Peruvian section of his book. A general in the Peruvian army in the War of the Pacific, Cáceres, son of a landowner, was a *mestizo*. When Lima fell, he escaped to Jauja and hid away in the wilderness of the highlands we had just crossed. For his effectiveness in mobilising a scattered peasant resistance he was known as *Brujo de los Andes*, the Magician of the Mountains. And it was a Cáceres administration that had to deal with the debt catastrophe that followed the war. He was the man who signed the punitive Grace Contract, in October 1888, conceding control of the railways, the valuable guano concession, and much unexploited land to London bankers and investors. In effect: to the Peruvian Corporation, the sponsors of Arthur's survey.

Lucho was in good spirits too. We will be heading, before too many days, to his cloud jungle farm. 'Come on, let's go.' We hurtle on and down, admiring the numerous crushed-metal installations on the banks of the river, far below. There is a pretty, freshly painted shrine at every hairpin turn. Paying tribute to mudslides and collisions.

We recognise an established ecology of the road. First come the motorised police, who never position themselves far from a good restaurant or drive-through bordello. To advance, you need the right paperwork, stamps proving that payment has already been made. Only sanctioned taxis are permitted to leave town. But then, as the road surface deteriorates, a desperate troop of old folk and very young barefoot children, with sticks, shovels, rudimentary brooms, appear from nowhere to fill potholes and drag boulders, at the last moment, from the path of overloaded lorries. These are the unofficial, unregistered and unpaid facilitators. It is up to travellers to throw them the odd coin. Where damage is most severe, and risk critical, you will find them. Their presence forewarns of blind bends and improvised detours around tunnels that have already collapsed.

'Though not unaccustomed to dangerous bridle tracks in tropical mountain ranges,' Alexander Ross told his audience at the Philosophical Society of Glasgow, 'we felt by no means comfortable as our mules picked their way along the very edge of some beetling precipice, or tried to pass, at some dangerous point, a drove of donkeys laden with small barrels or kegs of rum, which they were conveying to the towns or mines... The present road gradually descends to about 4,000 feet, and, emerging from a narrow gorge through fields of sugar-cane, reaches the Chanchamayo Valley.'

Fruit, easily cultivated by small farmers, has no real value. It is not economically viable to ship it to Huancayo or Lima. As we approach the fertile valley, makeshift stalls and screened shelters have been set up, turning the busy road into a straggling market. Lucho decides that we should stop to sample the native produce. A woman with a machete expertly decapitates a pair of coconuts and provides us with straws, so that we can stand and suck the oversweet milk. Pink plastic catheters drilled into hairy bovine testicles. Passion fruit are cracked and shelled like picnic eggs. The air is kinder now, the colours louder and more confident. We are soon in La Merced.

All was going smoothly at the San Ramón restaurant overlooking the Rio Chanchamayo, until, plates cleared and glasses filled, Lucho made his demand. When we get back to the hotel, he said, I must hand over my 'notes', so that he can iron out my inevitable misinterpretations. He will check my 'facts', before it is too late. Unfortunately, it is already too late to improve my great-grandfather's testimony – which, despite its veneer of colonialist confidence, has a potentially useful catalogue of the flora of the country. And his photographs of the indigenous people, they are not without interest. The book was a period piece, but not beyond saving. And it was a rare account, our guide conceded, of the landscape around the Perené at a period before any of the invaders kept written records.

I told Lucho that nobody, myself included, could read my handwriting. But I would be grateful if he had the time to sit down with me, in the evening, and put me right with the names of the places we had visited and the people we had met.

Farne, hair tied back, smartly presented in sleeveless black, set off by a silver necklace, is happy to have secured a modest plate of chips with a few chunks of white fish. She is still in contact with that other world, her family. Her husband, who works in the newsroom for the BBC, and has come through 'alien territory' protocols and SAS training weekends, and even camped with his mates on the edge of Epping Forest, supplied her with a tracking device, so that, wherever she went, over the Salt Mountain, in high or low jungle, on raft or fruit lorry, he would be able to follow her progress on the map. And to point it out for their children. It is always good, he reckoned, to be able to zero in on the precise point of disappearance.

Standing beside Lucho, I walked my fingers over a large-scale map painted on the wall of the restaurant. No chart I had examined, before we left England, or again in Lima and Huancayo, made sense. Fictions were crafted to favour competing prejudices: Franciscans, Jesuits, land-hungry adventurers and marauding armies. The maps in the publications of Arthur Sinclair and Alexander Ross, for example, might have been of different countries. Ross employs cloudy swirls to represent the mountains. The two elements given most prominence are 'Railways' and 'Mr Ross's Routes'. La Oroya, Tarma, Acombamba, La Merced: the dotted line is clear, until it achieves San Luis de Shuaro, when it seems to merge with the river system, before concluding at a zone of no obvious significance, some distance before the Perené meets the Rio Tambo, the Urubamba and the Ucayali. Arthur's foldout map, tipped in alongside the first page of his book, is much less detailed. He leaves plenty of blank space in which to project future developments. A sinister black box has been fenced around the Perené: 'Land Selected by Commissioners (1, 120, 000 Acres).' 'Mr Sinclar's [*sic*] Route' is a wriggling red tapeworm. There are no roads or railways.

The restaurant mural makes it appear that highway planning and convenient airstrips have finally conquered the wild places, and the people who have lived in them for generations. The actual river, below the balcony, surges over rocks, drowning our chatter. Lucho tells me that Chanchamayo means 'walking quickly and irregularly, in confusion, never satisfied with one perch, like a bird hopping, on and on, stone to stone, until it stands still and is washed away.'

—

Lucho was all movement. He wanted to counter the decadent anomie of the hotel and the pool, and our inclination towards lounging, reading, swimming leisurely lengths, and surrendering to the drama of the surroundings in which we found ourselves. Without stirring a muscle, we were serviced by native ghosts flitting between the trees, carrying clean sheets and towels at unlikely hours, and vanishing before demands could be made for food or drink.

As aspirant tourists under Lucho's protection, we must experience what has already been experienced and approved by so many others. Without protest, we were rounded up and prodded into a minibus occupied by women; factory workers and cleaners returning home, burdened from market. They were not much offended by Lucho's banter. Which, with good grace and tired eyes, they countered or ignored. The river restaurant was our destination and our promised treat.

On our return, after wrestling our bags to our rooms, it was time for a serious tuk-tuk jaunt, bouncing and bumping over a dirt track to the El Tirol waterfall. The park reservation would close before the sun went down. Our hurried walk was a rehearsal for what lay ahead. Farne, who carried her precious rucksack, money and electronic devices with her at all times, lagged further and further behind, but she kept going. She would not, of course, allow me to shoulder the burden. When we reached the pool, reddish brown and shallow, and violently agitated by the force of the waterfall, she was the first one changed, striking out, and ducking under.

At six p.m., precisely, as Lucho has predicted, the cicadas begin their warning chorus. We were lucky to find one last tuk-tuk, into which to climb, with Lucho outside, hanging grimly on the back.

The day is not quite done. There is a compulsory stroll through San Ramón before Lucho can retire, justified, to his room. We are led through a square where a market has been, to a noted coffee stall, rumoured to offer the best ice cream in town. Here, indeed, is the surviving evidence of the Italian immigration of 1884. The more industrious of the incomers settled and thrived. Painted panels around the market square promote legends of those distant wars and conquests. I photograph a blue porthole framing a sepia print of the river and the hills beyond San Ramón in 1891. I thought I could make out a diminishing mule train snaking out of town.

Drawing Lucho's scorn, we had to admit that we were too tired to embark on a wider circuit of the town's undoubted attractions. We snagged another tuk-tuk that ran out of fuel, in the tropical darkness, somewhere on the way back to La Merced. Farne, with a producer's eye for a good sequence, told Grant that in her recent researches she had identified a group of Italians who still meet, in post-colonial ruins on the edge of San Ramón, to dance the Tarantella. This is future gold. I can almost hear the gears turning as the filmmaker files that one away, for future use. It fascinates him, this hint that Dionysiac rites survive, along with ice cream and superior coffee. The original dance moves were devised, in southern Italy, as an antidote to the bite of the wolf spider. Frenzied movement, the hysterical condition known as 'tarantism', aspires to a tribal exorcism. Couples or solitary initiates could last for days: a wild courtship of Eros and Thanatos. Faster and faster, the convulsive dancers race against the drum. Immigrants from Apulia sweat out cultural poisons and leave the rounded marks of their heels on sanctified ground.

Evening meals don't happen. Bottles of beer are secured with leftover ham and cheese sandwiches. The hotel feels deserted, but the television screen never goes dark. Brazil are playing Argentina and there is the first goal I've seen in open play. The drama, mute and distant, plays out against the panoramic night and a soundtrack of berries or nuts dropping in the swimming pool.

Early to bed, I crash at once into the pit of sleep. I imagine flakes of curled distemper paint falling slowly from the low ceiling, to cover me in a glittering golden shroud. Was this the hotel where Lucho lost the sample of river sediment that he should have carried to Lima for his Ashaninka friends? The waking dream curdles into a memory of the Palais de Justice in Brussels, a sleepwalker's mesmerised tour I made while waiting to meet the Advocate for a day's tramp. In a gloomy corridor I'm sure I could never find again, I came on an ugly molten thing on a black marble pedestal. Here, caged in the pomposity of the building's fantastic architecture, was the apocalyptic beast that supports the pregnant dome, the law courts, and the padded leather doors. This creature, more than a lion, less than a bear, is eyeless and immoveable. Unappeased. In its claws are the skulls of sacrificial victims. Around its base are wound the heavy chains of slavery. Behind the crouching immanent form is a dirty window and the indifferent spread of a wealthy graveyard city.

FURIES

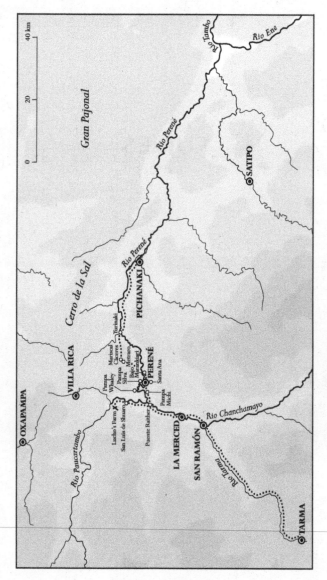

Map of the ground covered by the voyagers in 2019

SAN LUIS DE SHUARO

'This is the back of beyond,' whispered Manuela.

'No,' said Alonso. 'It's further.'

– Nicholas Shakespeare, *The Vision of Elena Silves*

Looking at the gaudy, freshly resprayed figure up on his plinth, a Disneyland stylite, I knew that this was where the real story must begin. The two ambitious journeys, 1891 and 2019, Arthur Sinclair and Farne Sinclair, were now indelibly fused. The small Convent, a missionary satellite of Santa Rosa de Ocopa, where Arthur sheltered before striking off into the rainforest, was gone, but I recognised the shape of the wall where it once stood from the drawing by Padre Sala in the museum at Ocopa. Halted at an insignificant roadside settlement, a village abandoned to a century-old siesta, I felt the pulse of a rising tide of excitement. In our truck, windows down, in a place where, for the first time, Lucho had no predigested information to impart, we were drawn back into the accounts left by the rival surveyors Sinclair and Ross.

Arthur was saddle-sore, feeling his age, exhausted by the daily mule dance, and the duty laid on him by the Peruvian Corporation, as well as his own compulsion to both experience and record. *That record I now knew was written and published as a challenge to Farne and myself, the unborn and unimagined invigilators.* Arthur was cynical from years of shuttling across the globe, dealing with corrupt officialdom, lazy appointees, remittance men. He nailed the local climate of strategic half-truths and mendacity in a phrase now applied, almost in admiration, to the political classes.

> *The worst weakness of the Hispano-Peruvian race is their utter inability
> to tell truthfully the little they do know... The common people are born
> and bred to it, but their lies are clumsy, palpable, and comparatively
> harmless. With the priests and privileged classes, however, it becomes a
> studied art. 'We must dissimulate,' said the chief priest of the convent,
> and I will give him the credit for consistency in this; for during the three
> weeks I had the opportunity of studying this great economist of truth,
> I never once knew him utter a word that could be relied upon. And yet
> we must own to the weakness of being over and over again misled by
> the arch-deceivers. Forgetful of all warnings we went on trusting that
> by some accident they might prove truthful to us. Such were the guides
> with which we entered the great Trans-Andean forest after crossing the
> Paucartambo river.*

Arthur's three weeks at the mercy of his missionary tracker were
obviously painful. Economists of the truth, subtle dissimulators trained
in Jesuitical diplomacy, the priests offended his Calvinist upbringing.
The Scottish surveyors had letters of introduction supplied by the
Peruvian authorities. But the laws of hospitality meant that the mule
party could not escape as they intended 'within an hour'. Implored
'not to insult the reverend fathers', they were forced to erect their tents
within the protection of the Convent walls.

My great-grandfather does not name the chief priest or his accom-
plices, the men they rely on to take them over the Salt Mountain to the
river. Men with their own covert agenda. False guides who would, in
the end, have to share responsibility for the hectares of Ashaninka territory enclosed for the benefit of the Peruvian Corporation of London.
To name is to honour. And something about this cowshed of a frontier
convent, holy fortress or charitable prison, alarmed Arthur. Something
offensive to his Scottish morality was present in San Luis de Shuaro.
Its precise nature was better left undeclared. Even the terminology
Arthur employs for this place is ugly. 'Chuncho' is a pejorative term,
common in colonial times, for the people of the rainforest: savages,
innocents, others. Wandering fugitives from Eden, cursed root pickers.
Cannibals.

We were introduced to a number of Chunchos. Miserable specimens they were, and more familiar than pleasant, who had left their country for their country's good. Just as a herd of elephants in Ceylon occasionally expel the incorrigible rogues, so the Chunchos, it seems, have their outcasts, male and female, who make a parley-ground of this Convent – fit converts to this specious mockery.

Something felt wrong, so wrong that Arthur begrudged a single night spent under the padre's roof. He would rather bunk down with the mules. I was reminded of the group photograph framed in Ocopa. Captured children of the forest, sad and grave. Tonsured converts swallowed in flapping habits. Arthur's chief priest sits among them, so many tadpole heads sheltered under a white madonna.

There our suspicions would have run aground, but Alexander Ross, with his passion for verifiable facts, names names. The priest is the celebrated mapmaker and child-catcher Father Gabriel Sala. The man who founded this frontier convent in 1888. And his associate, recently arrived from the Ucayali, is Padre Carlos.

'An empty room was assigned to us,' Ross wrote in his parallel but divergent account, 'in which to lay our camp beds and other effects, while an attempt to put up our own tent, more in the way of practice than anything else, was met by a hint that it would give offence, the Fathers wishing us to accept, while there, such hospitality as they could offer.'

The vagrant gathering of removed or captured forest dwellers Arthur describes is transformed by Ross into a school of fortunate and disciplined children. A choir of the rescued giving thanks.

Besides the usual buildings and offices of a religious house, there is a school-room, in which some Indian children are taught. In the chapel, service was held morning and evening, when it was a pleasure to us to listen to the responses and sweet singing by these children of the forest, led, while also accompanying on the harmonium, by the good Padre himself.

Heavy rain detained us here for three days, but at last, accompanied by Padre Sala, chief of the mission, and Padre Carlos from the Ucayali, we set out upon our wanderings in the wilds, having sent the pack mules on ahead. It had been arranged that we were to follow the track then being opened towards the River Pichis, but it proved so difficult for our laden mules that we soon got ahead of them. However, we kept on, with the idea that our guides were taking us to the residence of a Campas Indian chief on the banks of the River Perené.

———

What the Advocate, my conscience in this venture, communicated by impassioned emails and letters left at various staging posts, was that Padre Sala made it his business to collect and impound 'child sorcerers'. Where Ross, through a filter of Victorian sentiment, heard the purity of unbroken voices lifted from the abyss of primitivism, and readied for a life of obedient industry, Sinclair saw an enclosed compound of chaotic and coercive idiocy.

My Brussels friend was convinced that there must be an account of the Sinclair expedition in the archives at Ocopa. 'It is now clear,' he wrote, 'that Padre Sala was approached by the Peruvian Corporation's agent (an established lobbyist), as the best – or only – guide to the unexplored territory.'

If Arthur's published version is to be believed, San Luis was a holding pen for 'outcasts', for indentured runaways, criminals, and the broken legions of the diseased and mentally disturbed. The Advocate challenged a published scholar, one of his many Peruvian sources: 'Was the San Luis *convento* known as a safe haven for accused children or adult sorcerers whose magic had failed? Child abduction, as your book shows, was common currency.'

'The first references to child sorcery among the Ashaninka,' the Advocate reported, 'date from around 1880. In 1893 Father Gabriel Sala composed an extensive account of these beliefs and practices.'

And then Father Monclar, a noted child-catcher and head of a mission school, talked of his desire to rescue these innocents from barbarism by 'sterilizing the seeds of eternal life that we with such love have deposited in their tender hearts'.

I was nudged by the Advocate towards a paper written by one of his correspondents, Fernando Santos-Granero of the Smithsonian Tropical Research Institute. The paper was entitled 'Saint Christopher in the Amazon: Child Sorcery, Colonialism, and Violence among the Southern Arawak'. The thesis floats the suggestion that the scapegoating, torture and sacrifice of children, most frequently girls, those with the weakest family connections, had no part in the culture of the Ashaninka before colonial times.

Weighing the evidence now, we have to acknowledge: *we are the virus*. Outsiders, reckless for green gold, bring death. Cycles of devastating epidemics, gifted by priests, the military, and land-hungry speculators, reassigned Saint Christopher, a familiar on superstitious medallions, as a 'plague saint'. His role, carrying the holy child on broad shoulders across a torrent, shifted from protector and healer to malfated bringer of curses.

After an outbreak of smallpox along the Upper Ucayali in 1885, people of the area were primed for persistent whispers, three years later, about 'the arrival of a divine messenger, described as a white man dressed in indigenous attire... the messiah who was said to speak Ashaninka and to proclaim that Father Sun had sent him with a message, that the errant tribes should live like civilized men, forming villages, each with its own church.'

The military organised six expeditions to clear the ground of tribal nuisance and to prepare the way for new waves of colonists, Peruvian, Andean and alien. With the colonists came their deadly companions: measles, chickenpox, influenza, yellow fever and malaria. The Ashaninka of the Perené started to believe that the Franciscans were responsible. The arrival of the shaven heads coincided with crop failures and dwindling supplies of fish and game. The monks were doctrinally opposed to the forest and its natural magic. They were plague conduits, their black books released devils. With frontier outposts now established in the rainforest, like the forts of the Seventh Cavalry in the American West, armed monks were being charged with guiding the missionaries of global capitalism – botanists, land surveyors and mapmakers – over secret trails towards sources of pre-Christian power. The

1891 expedition, led by Arthur Sinclair and Alexander Ross, was indeed a fatal encounter. Half a million hectares of land would subsequently be enclosed and devoted to plantations competing in the production of high-quality coffee for export to Antwerp and other European ports.

My conclusion, drawn from Santos-Granero's paper, is that the persecution of possessed, groomed and suborned children, scapegoats for every lost or stolen object, every outbreak of sickness, only began in the post-colonial period. And continued, as has been well documented, along the banks of the Perené, into the 1950s. The older notion, the primal myth of a giant cannibalistic father and an evil son, a child who is an adult in disguise, older perhaps than the bloated, surfeited father, was amended by the pressure of the times. If children were witches, tamed by the eating of human flesh, seduced by the power to maim or kill, they must be neutralised by cruelty: beaten, confined in holes, laid out on smoking platforms, half-drowned, tied naked to trees hungry to swallow them, or smeared with honey and left to armies of ants. Scapegoat innocents would dig up the earth with broken fingernails and reveal the power objects they had buried. Their abused bodies would be burnt and left to the river. Legions of orphan children were simply abandoned or sold as servants and slaves to white colonists and *mestizo* traders. They were so much broken currency.

But the special children have been touched in their dreams by other haunted beings, witches or birds, insects, hybrid creatures offering fragments of bone, wounding thorns and palm leaves. Their persecutors know that they must obliterate the stalking shadow as well as the substance. Shadows never die with their mortal twins. Malignancy must be countered, in order to prevent the arts of witchcraft being passed on to other sleeping children in cold convent dormitories. It was often easier to sell the bewitched victim on. Undesirable children were traded for desirable goods. The first accounts of child sorcery, Santos-Granero claims, 'appeared in a context of accelerated change characterized by military defeat, territorial despoliation, technological impoverishment, epidemics, social disruption, and demographic decline'. In other words, the aftermath of the establishment of the Perené plantations by the Peruvian Corporation of London.

The founding myth of the intertwined and conflicted relationship between monster father and haunted pseudo-child is revised, in the post-colonial period, to a cycle of eternal conflict between grandfather and grandson: the child who refuses to become an adult. A futile heretic who angers his ancestor with 'endless questioning' and attempts to challenge the fix of history by remaking the old man's visionary journeys. Finally, Santos-Granero reveals, the disobliging grandson is held responsible for the actions of those who came before him. 'He is depicted as being so evil that he does not even hesitate to transform his cousins into animals, first vicariously, through his father, and later on directly, using his own powers.' That is to say, he bears false witness. He writes about them. About forbidden things. He recomposes, edits, makes new. Betrays.

Arthur was wrong. There is no ambiguity about the status of the man he refused to name. My great-grandfather's Sala remains a cipher, a faceless caricature, a drunk and a dissembler. He is a thief and a trickster, all the way through the horrors of the rainforest, right up to the night of his abrupt disappearance. But church records – and Sala's copious journals, in contradiction to Arthur's lively sketches – confirm the significance of this exiled Spaniard, the missionary priest. He was truly a pathfinder, an opener of trails and maker of maps.

1891 was the critical year: the land concession to the Peruvian Corporation was signed, and there were three groundbreaking expeditions focused on completing a rudely functioning road between Perené and Pichis. The economic imperative was to find a way to transport coffee from remote plantations to the world markets. To the tables of the brokers and speculators in Mincing Lane. It had already been demonstrated, in the 1860s, that the Pichis was navigable. That river was the gateway to the Ucayali and the Amazon. To Antwerp, London and Liverpool.

The first expedition, in June 1891, was led by an engineer called Joaquín Capelo, who claimed to have constructed a two-metre-wide road, over ninety-three kilometres long, between San Luis de Shuaro and the nearest established port. Sala, the dark shadow, was on hand. This route was so bad, so treacherous, that Arthur was forced to scramble back to the path of the salt pilgrims, uphill to Metraro. A subsequent report stated that: 'The expedition was assisted by Father Gabriel Sala, director of the Convent of San Luis de Shuaro, who provided it with tools, documents and various sketches.' The unfinished highway was declared open in November 1891, as a temporary measure, while the planters waited for 'the definitive road and projected railway to Ucayali'. When the Geographical Society of Lima investigated the status of Capelo's project, they concluded that it did not merit being called 'a bridlepath'.

The Sinclair/Ross mule train, guided by Sala, the indispensable fixer for state and private interests, made their journey through the territory in July and August. By October, it was the turn of the army, an expedition under the command of Colonel Ernesto La Combe. The colonel was accompanied by a man called Carranza, who left a description of an encounter with the supposed relics of Juan Santos Atahualpa. Sala made it his business to stumble, as if by accident, on this legendary shrine. A site of tremendous potency to the Ashaninka of the Pereñé. And so we have the three classic elements of 'opening up' virgin land for exploitation: engineers, surveyors reporting to remote investors, and a military force to provide security.

Through all these incursions, Sala, the short dark priest with the unblinking stare, enacts a role that none of those who write about him ever succeeds in bringing into focus. He is a Franciscan missionary, yes, and a church politician moving ever upwards, to become abbot at Santa Rosa de Ocopa. His vision of the indigenous people can come to an accommodation with the requirements of the coffee planters: the natives are primitives, mired in original sin. 'And what,' Sala said, 'should we do with beings such as these? What is done the world over? They do not want to live as men, but as animals. One treats them like animals and puts a bullet in them when they unjustly oppose the lives and well-being of the rest of us.'

Is he simply parroting what the commissioners want to hear, a theological justification for their piracy? And why does he always (mis)guide terminally weary incomers towards the shrine of the Andean resistant Juan Santos Atahualpa?

Michael F. Brown and Eduardo Fernández, in *War of Shadows (The Struggle for Utopia in the Peruvian Amazon)*, tell us how an expedition undertaken in 1891 claimed to have located the Inca's sepulchre in Metraro, where the natives 'celebrate feasts in homage to the memory of the valiant leader and each year place a new tunic on the grave'. They are quoting from a book published in 1973 by Mario Castro Arenas. Brown and Fernández go on to explain how the Peruvian government 'placed its hopes of establishing a vigorous agricultural colony along the Perené in the hands of English venture capitalists'. Coffee was now fetching a high price on the world markets. By 1893 enclosures were actively enforced, with indigenous people who declined debt peonage being expelled into the more remote areas of the Perené basin – where they could still be tracked down and hunted by Gabriel Sala, the tireless, unforgiving and excessively well-armed pathfinder.

The mission commander at San Luis de Shuaro, Arthur's nemesis, remains an enigma. His lower lip protrudes in a scornful pout: a suckler of bitter lemons. In portrait photographs, cherry-stone eyes are circled with black rings, the great task makes no allowance for sleep. Within three years of the publication of my great-grandfather's book, the priest is dead. He was the unyielding sword of god. His sketch of the San Luis Convent, displayed at Ocopa, presents a cottage Alamo, with white walls and slits for defensive lines of fire. At night the jungle screamed. Sala approved.

We heard from others we questioned on our travels that Arthur's guide was a bounty hunter, rewarded by his superiors with so much per head for every child penned in San Luis. Every innocent soul res-cued from its animal familiar. Sala disappeared into the rainforest for months at a time, buckled in ordnance: crossed ammunition belts, brace of pistols, rifle, machete. He impressed the tribal people of the river by fishing with dynamite. You can think of him as Robert Mitchum (without the cigar) in Ralph Nelson's eccentric oater *The Wrath of God*. A biretta bandit. An assassin. The founder of a new religion suited to this godless land. He will rescue orphan children from their fate, purchase others, and give shelter to a community of outcasts. But only if they unconditionally accept his Spanish god and his cruel system of justice.

Sala was against the jungle and he was of the jungle. As the promotional strapline says on the cover of the DVD of the machine-gun-toting Mitchum's drama of Mexican revolution: 'He's not exactly what the Lord had in mind.'

And there he is, waiting: Gabriel Sala in Airfix colours, mounted on his 2019 plinth, with back turned resolutely to the contemporary church and the section of wall I recognise from his Ocopa sketch.

Lucho climbs down from the truck and walks away, fists in waistcoat pockets. He is lost for a story to tell. He has no immediate purchase on this place. But I am cheered by the same degree that Arthur was confounded and thrown back on himself by the sudden loss of the turbulent Franciscan. The statue's hands are enormous. The right one seems to be reaching for the reins of a phantom mule or keeping off an importunate child sorcerer. The left one balances the big book like a wobbly tray of business-class dinner. The cuttlefish-black tonsure has thickened, miraculously: seaweed draped on a limestone pebble. The hoop of beard, never evident in previous portraits, is Gregory Peck in *Moby Dick*, the full Ahab. Now I look again, the empty hand is reaching for a lightning-struck harpoon. Sala is ready to cast off, in his pulpit prow, lantern head lost among palm fronds.

An excited cry breaks our reverie. Lucho has recovered his *amour-propre* and reclaimed the narrative. He has located an eighty-eight-year-old lady, living directly opposite the church, a witness to every important event from the physical collapse of the Convent in an earthquake to the territorial predations of the Peruvian Corporation. And she is prepared to give Farne an interview for her podcast, and to allow Grant to film her packed wall of memories: maps, drawings, photographs and fading newspaper cuttings. She knew Lucho's father, don Pedro. And his local reputation. Her name is Maria Genoveva Leon Perez.

MARIA GENOVEVA LEON PEREZ

'Being too many people, uselessly.'
  – Denise Riley

The day of our drive to San Luis de Shuaro began early with slow lengths of the La Merced pool, free of the evidence of recent parties. It was a ritual gesture of farewell to partake in such indulgence, a painless chlorine dip to launder the sins of tourism, while drifting out into the scented morning. The close-forested hills. And the shallow rectangle of ruffled water filled with sky.

Lucho, the pockets of his poacher's waistcoat bulging with soaps, medicines, knives, pouches of leftovers, offered his interpretation of the television news: the same trials, the same footage, the same postponed verdicts. The only other breakfasters were armed police, working systematically along the counter of fruits, clearing sugary cereals, stashing bread rolls. On the flat screen, motorbike raiders were foiled, yet again, in handheld travelling shots, punctuated with jump cuts. The newscaster went up a few registers when he came to the real story of the day: in depth interviews with Peruvian fans getting ready early for the Copa América semi-final against their traditional rivals, Chile.

Primed and polished, his silver mane hotel-glossy and swept back, Lucho is happy. He is heading home. He can indulge our desire to inspect whatever remains of the Convent at San Luis de Shuaro. After consultation with the Advocate, we have a wish list of key sites related to Arthur Sinclair's expedition: the Convent of Padre Sala is the first of them. Then the Salt Mountain. The shrine of Juan Santos Atahualpa at Metraro. The camp of King Chokery on the Perené, near Yurinaki. The principal coffee plantation, Pampa Whaley. And, best of all, the rapids: the whirlpool of ancestors, somewhere beyond Pichanaki.

The good humour of our guide does not last, for himself or for anyone, when confronted by the formidable inertia of the banking system. These bland premises, found everywhere, arriving with the wagons of settlers in the remotest desert outpost, are filled with captured light, but somehow airless and too hot. The smartly presented desk-squatters are yawning, obliging, but ultimately useless. Decisions are taken elsewhere. Lucho needs a thousand dollars of the budget from Farne. He also wants to shift cash between accounts in various countries. His wife and five children are in New Zealand. But he doesn't believe in charity or pampering. No handouts that have not been earned. Lucho's own start in Huancayo was harsh and it made him. He took to the streets, more or less disowned by his family. And all, as he instructs us, for the best.

He slams his card into a cash machine and it drops straight through. He curses and rants, storms the desk.

Bank time is dead time. I am happy to wait in an Italian café in San Ramón, across from the shade of the plaza. The pictorial evidence of late-nineteenth-century immigration is all around in a display of archival photographs. The shift from our colourful present – banks, shoe cleaners and a total absence of postcards – to the validated grey of a curated past sits very nicely with the morning's coffee assignment, the glass of iced water, the jug of orange juice. If there are vanished colonists in the rainforest, they are smudges of white against enveloping vegetation. There are rifles with long barrels. Big hats. Machetes. Boots. They are going somewhere and the moment was worth recording. Prints of San Ramón show the plaza as it once was, not much more than a basic church, a thatched hut and a few wandering animals. Mules, carrying farmers into town, are on the wide street where the Italian café is now found. There is a mountain halt dated '1890'. You can see how the road we took through the gorge must have looked to Arthur, but you see it drained of colour, the perfume of plants and the sound of the river. Later came the squadrons of

Italian aviators in jodhpurs and helmets. If the past is not framed and displayed, it leaks through our fingers. Around a vast television screen, in which I am reflected as I lift my camera, a series of portraits have been arranged: head and shoulders, indigenous people. The portraits are all in colour. In fact, looking closer, I see that they are coffee-bar paintings. Probably for sale.

The market has the stink of spilled blood: lightless hutches, slaughter sheds. A companionable reek, hungry to infiltrate cloth and pore, pomades hair and varnishes complexions with grease of fish, fowl, horn and hide. A microclimate that is renewed with every morning of trade. Engaged, within the action of barter, sampling, sniffing and poking, Lucho recovers his good spirits. The business here is real, unchanged in generations. The smell welcomes us. It creeps further out into alleys and plazas as the sun climbs.

Lucho has summoned the 'boy' from his farm. The keeper of a great blue-and-white beast of a truck that Lucho calls 'the horse'. The emblematic silver animal stands proud on the bonnet. The young man doesn't speak, but he has a beautiful way of registering, as he frowns over his polishing, how he owes his allegiance to the vehicle as much as to its owner. We, the paying guests, will take it in turns to sprawl among the supplies and the loose planks on the open flatbed. There is food for tonight's meal and beer for the Chile game.

Hanging on, in rushing air, we follow the glint of the Chanchamayo River. The landscape is sure of itself and teasingly calm. Splashes of scarlet among cultivated green and yellow strips. Arthur speaks of 'resting a day in the house of a hospitable Frenchman', before pushing on to the Convent. That passage always reminds me of the episode in Francis Ford Coppola's *Apocalypse Now Redux*, the version restoring forty-nine minutes removed from the director's original cut – with, most pertinently, a strange narcotic interlude when Captain Willard and the crew, heading upriver to exterminate the brute, Kurtz, with extreme prejudice, come ashore at a rubber plantation. And there time stops. In a repeatedly revised, overloaded narrative, there are suggestions that the cataleptic colonial house is nothing more than a posthumous dream for all concerned: the tasked assassination party, burdened with aspects of *Heart of Darkness*, and their hosts, rubber planters transplanted from the backstory of Vietnam (French Indo-China) to the Philippines. Everything is smoky and fluttering and too seductively lit by Vittorio Storaro. It never happened, even within the suspended disbelief of cinema time.

Now we want to engage with Arthur's report, while acknowledging the burden of other parallel episodes, fictional and documentary: Conrad's incantatory and fated Congo voyage, Coppola's chemically-wrecked post-Vietnam unwinding, as it was initially fired by the example of Werner Herzog and *Aguirre, Wrath of God*. Later, Herzog was accommodated in one of Coppola's spare properties, while he incubated his subsequent Amazonian odyssey, the transformation of an historic rubber baron into *Fitzcarraldo*. Blocked and suffering in San Francisco, the German director paid a recuperative visit to the rock bastion of San Quentin, and was soothed, as he notes in his journal, before the mooted expedition to the rainforest, by the 'linden-green' walls of the gas chamber.

As headlong travellers, we were soothed, in our turn, by a halt at the contemporary French house and a morning walk through the branching paths of the botanical gardens. There had been a plan to stay here, after finishing at San Luis de Shuaro, and spending a couple of nights at Lucho's farm. But that whim was too literal. Much better to move the story on, closer to the Salt Mountain and the trail Arthur endured, under the guidance of Padre Sala. You can't go back.

I read aloud the relevant passage from *In Tropical Lands* for the podcast Farne is recording. And we stroll among the hanging, cardinal-red lobster-claws, the drooping orchids, the scarlets and purples of the bromeliads, and the pools of giant water lilies, where we stop to watch the antics of turtles. Stilted wooden cabins, available to tourists, are unoccupied. But the gardens have been laid out to attract visitors. The trees are labelled and explained. The owner is experimenting with plants useful in medicine. He is ninety years old and living in Lima. Making our way back to the truck, I meet a gardener, a boy in a T-shirt with a picture of

London, Big Ben and Westminster Bridge. I try to tell him that we have come from there. And he chants: 'Paris St Germain! Paris St Germain!'

The fortunate encounter with Maria Genoveva Leon Perez is another echo of the 1891 expedition. Alexander Ross described how, on this stretch of their journey, the surveyors enjoyed a lunch cooked at 'the residence of a thriving Chinaman… by his Indian wife… This man, who had been twenty years in Peru, stated that he never had a wish to, nor ever would, return to his native land.' Maria is a widow now, but the relationship with her husband, another Chinese and indigenous connection, had been long and happy.

The instantaneous bonding with Farne was obvious. It wasn't just that my daughter was a young woman. There was a quick smile and a nod of recognition. As if the old lady had been waiting many years for this arrival. Maria searched out the photographs she wanted to show and then addressed herself, directly, to Farne and her microphone. Lucho summarised, where he thought it appropriate, from the old lady's softly spoken Spanish.

'This Convent,' said Maria, 'was founded by Padre Sala. In November 1947, there was a big earthquake shaking all Junín, and this was one of the first churches to fall down. Later on, it was rebuilt. Even people from La Merced would come here for services. People made friends with the "chunchos", as they called them. Our people from the other side of the river. This is a pioneer town.'

We asked if there was any local memory of the British people coming through here in 1891, with their mules, three years after the Convent was founded.

'No, but I remember what happened on the other side with the coffee plantation. It was part of the lives of all the people in San Luis. The plantation was a place we were not permitted to go. It was something like a restricted area. There was a health centre, a school, and merchandise. It was very well organised. The company, in the old times, came from England and America. They wanted to make it exclusive. They didn't want to open it up to village people. The health centre and the school were only for workers and their families.'

Maria was descended, she told Farne, from a Chinese man. He used to take tobacco leaves, treat them by rubbing, and make them fit to smoke. He would go to the coffee plantation at Pampa Whaley and sell it there. The Chinese man married a woman from Huánuco, a very different culture. Padre Sala conducted the ceremony.

We asked, again, about strangers coming to the Convent.

'When German people arrived, on the way to Oxapampa, they stayed at the Convent.'

I wanted to understand about the children Arthur described as being brought to San Luis from the jungle. Was there a record of the later life of these children, after they left the Convent school?

'I am the oldest of the community,' Maria said. But it was not clear if she meant that she had been one of those children.

'There was a moment of yellow fever,' the old lady remembered. 'Many people died. The priests decided to leave.'

'This is an interesting moment,' Lucho pronounced. 'I didn't plan it. But this lady is a good friend of my father. She knows my father. Don Pedro is a character in these areas, everybody knows him. A cousin of this lady worked with the coffee on a farm, not so far from my farm. Amazing luck! Maria is in charge of the church. You see how everything opens? You are so lucky.'

The walls of the modest room are mirrors of the cloudless sky. A Mediterranean blue is crusted with odd strokes of paint left over from some wooden door or shed. There is one brilliant yellow strip and a section of cloth with stars and shells and fish.

'*Shuaro* is a fish,' Maria said. 'A fish made of water. One of our saints.' Ashaninka settlements, it appears, are not given the names of saints. But other places, settled places like San Luis, were formed and named by priests.

Maria's weathered skin is a tissue of fine gold highlights. She is a playful woman, tongue between lips. She keeps her bright eyes on Farne. Before we go across the road, to inspect the church, she shows us a grid of family photographs: children and grandchildren, church gatherings, weddings. Young adults, the hope for the future, in formal gowns to receive their rolled certificates. A branching tree of future ancestors and unforgotten babes swimming towards the light.

Rebecca Solnit, in *A Book of Migrations*, says that 'a hundred and fifty years seems to be about the farthest reach of living memory, the length of time encompassed by an old person who as a child encountered a survivor of some long-ago drama.'

This hospitable old lady, met by chance on our journey into the past, gives the impression of being unsurprised by the invasion of her house by strangers with microphones and cameras. If she knows about don Pedro, and speaks of Padre Sala as one of his flock, doesn't she, by implication, become a witness to Arthur's mule train, setting out towards the Mountain of Salt? She is ageless and agile. The communal memory she represents is of the enclosure of land by the Peruvian Corporation of London. She lives with the presence of the absence of Sala's Convent. And the absence in the presence of the church for which she is the designated keeper of the key.

The church is a block building, cream set off by a pink grid, and accessed through a studded metal door in a darker red. Maria, with straw hat and rolled parasol, follows Farne. And is followed, in her turn, by a shaggy mongrel dog. The creaking lock has been waiting patiently for this giant key. The revealed interior reminds me of a Welsh chapel: hard pews, yellowing walls, plain table as altar, with a few verses from the gospels revealed in an open book. But the church has Catholic elements too: blooding in the windows, columns of light through the open door, and a deliriously ornate shrine. Weaponed angels protect a heavy silver frame, intricately worked with creeping plants. A gold-nappied, gold-crowned infant Jesus reclines beneath a painting of the crucifixion. As always, in the humblest settlements, money has been found for objects of pious display.

It is only when we emerge, out of a back door, into an enclosed garden, that we appreciate we are now on the ground that once supported Padre Sala's Convent. There are traceable outlines of lost buildings in the scrubby grass. There are fruit trees that survive from an uprooted orchard. We try, perhaps too hard, to identify what Ross called 'the usual buildings and offices of a religious house': the school, the kitchens and stables and the room with the camp beds where the two surveyors slept, in evident disharmony, brooding on the next day's competitive journal entries.

I found a rusted machete stuck firmly in the ground and a metal stand for votive candles. When Farne posed for a commemorative snapshot against the old wall of the chapel, I noticed faint white letters painted under the shuttered window: F.S.

'So they knew you were coming,' I said. 'Your initials, Farne Sinclair.'

'Father Sala!' Lucho snorted.

But there was no 'Father' Sala. In this place the gunslinger priest was always 'Padre'. Father of multitudes.

We swing over the tailboard to remount Lucho's gleaming blue-and-silver 'horse', for the bumpy ride to the cloud jungle farm. Our guide is happy to be returning to a place of his own, the farm he inherited from his father. There is a tangled tale of political favours to be told at the right time, over dinner perhaps, or during a hike to another waterfall.

We rumble across a plank bridge over the Paucartambo that looks as if it would struggle to support the weight of a burdened mule. The rainforest is all around us now. In the last town before we leave the road, the river is fast-flowing but polluted, with mounds of casual rubbish strewn along the banks. Shacks on stilts drop contributions of daily waste. Some of the local ladies, in short sarongs, are bathing from a muddy beach, doing their laundry and washing lustrous black hair. A toothless man-child greets me with violent enthusiasm, confused but happy to recognise an old friend. In the same fashion, and with the same light in the eyes, as Maria recognising Farne. My forgotten acquaintance from some past life runs beside the truck, right through the town, waving and calling. I watch him gesturing and shaking his head, before we pull away. He is saddened to see us depart. For another hundred years.

Farne has her own room. Lucho sleeps in established officer's quarters, behind a set of self-rigged curtains. Grant chooses his bed, in the darkest corner of the open deck. While I opt for a netted slot, close to daylight, on the first floor of the farm building.

Attended by the young village man in the wellington boots and reversed baseball cap, trained helper and guardian of the property, Lucho prepares the night's football feast. The television hangs high among the stout beams of a kitchen improvised from scavenged elements of many other enterprises, hotels and bars and churches.

Welcome bowls of soup reflect the same ecologically pure philosophy, by making use of many other recycled meals. There is beer and, with no prejudice, dubious Chilean wine. The screen flickers, burns out, settles: Peru score three goals. Lucho nods in satisfaction. The helper takes off his cap. There is a mad charge towards the corner flag by the Chile goalkeeper, Gabriel Arias. Peru's Carrillo – *'Car-illl-oooo!'* – gets to the ball before him and crosses for Yoshimar Yotún to nonchalantly bring it under control on his chest and volley into the unguarded net. I have no gift for the rapid auctioneer riffs of expert commentators, or the mumbling of former players, but I speak fluent football in taxis. All over the world.

When it was done, and the television shrouded in silence, we talked about what we had learned in San Luis de Shuaro. I asked Lucho about the practice of 'adopting' indigenous children, handing them over to the Convent. He told us about a priest he had known, a man who was still alive, and about the age of Arthur when he came to Peru. The missionary father provided shelter for many orphans, suspected witches, and others who had simply been given away, so that they could enjoy a better life, being adequately fed, housed, educated. The knowledge that this man engaged in sexual relations with children, male and female, was understood, and tacitly accepted as part of the contract of exchange. In all other ways, here was a cultivated and devout man who cared for his converts. Perhaps too much.

But the priest crossed an unstated line. He involved himself with some of the younger married women. Taboos were broken. The men of the tribe came to him in the night. He was castrated. This happened thirty years ago. Before Lucho knew him. Chastened, the father continued in his ministry and was, in general, well liked.

LUCHO'S FARM

'We are in a Mist. *We* are now in that state – We feel the "burden of the Mystery"… the beautiful quickness of the weather.'
   – J.H. Prynne (Letter to Charles Olson)

The story of how Lucho's father, a man from the city, from Huancayo, acquired the finca and the land around it, and how Lucho shared that responsibility for a time and then inherited everything, had not yet been told. It would have to be saved, with other hints, and teasing references to Shining Path, to bad politics, and to the adventures of an ambitious outsider among indigenous people, for the evening session. Saved until after the meal, and after the beer, when Grant planned to set up his camera, to rig the lighting, and to hold Lucho to a promised in-depth, film-specific interview.

We woke to wonder, it's true: the wonder of difference. The fine spiders' web of mosquito netting around my plank bed imposed a mesh filter of monochrome over the insistent colours of morning. We were like those trapped Macedonian squaddies in Stanley Spencer's 1929 painting, *Reveille*; wriggling upright, as if *they* had become the insects in the night, while mosquitoes swarmed and buzzed above their heads. And the men who were already dressed and ready for the day watched their struggles in amused contempt.

'I wanted a mixture of real and spiritual fact,' Spencer said. 'The underlying intention is a great feeling of peace and happiness.' The artist was evacuated to England in 1918, another malaria case. The fear of malaria, in earlier accounts I read, of travels in this Chanchamayo area, was frequently deployed as a racist subterfuge: white men, Europeans braving a distant land, endured the hallucinatory fevers as a badge of honour. Life and death dramas were reported as an inevitable staging post in a colonialist's progress. But the blood infections of indigenous people were presented as a racial flaw; an incestuous, degenerate strain. The American Harry Foster, for example, in his 1922 account, *The Adventures of a Tropical Tramp*, describes the 'Chuncho Indians', and others he meets, as he hacks a path towards the Ucayali, as enfeebled, pus-coloured, drooping with malaria: a symptom of their failure to man up to the challenges of the rainforest and the river. As if it were a perverse native choice, to hang on to a place unfit for human habitation.

When Foster visits the Perené Coffee Colony, he reports that a Chuncho 'savage' told him that his people knew, long before the white man, that the bite of the mosquito was the cause of malaria. They even identified the particular mosquito that carried the infection. 'That is why we painted our arms and faces,' the adventurer is told. 'The mosquito cannot bite through the paint.'

After a brief and fierce downpour, rainwater is running from the tin roof, to cascade through a bamboo chute, a foot from my bed. It pisses in a steady, melodious arc, into the green square of a meditation pool that Lucho once hoped to turn to advantage, by breeding trout. For now, visitors to the farm are free to swim. Or float. Watching the procession of clouds, indistinguishable from the press of white mist scarfing densely forested hills.

After the cold trickle of the communal shower, the deep pool is a delight; dissolving, layer by layer, the heat and dust and confusion of the journey. Lucho's farm is the first *here* in which we have found ourselves, the first place that is operational as intended, and not playing a part in the neurotic migrations of strangers. Lucho has a vision of development, exploiting natural abundance, and finding some way of making it pay. Chickens scrabble. The helper, Gilberto, arrives on his bike, and starts breakfast preparations in the kitchen.

Last night I joined Grant in attempting hosepipe laundry in a stone basin. The shirts on the line are now a little damper than they were yesterday. In a day or two, they will be rags. Lucho has identified the trumpeting birds occupying the nearest group of trees, feeling the need to assert their ownership against our rude intrusion: the pair that Grant is trying to record. I wondered if these show-offs performed unwitnessed when the farm was in its unoccupied state. Or do they require an audience, whooped from sleep and hungry for local colour? The birdcalls chime beautifully with the cessation of the sudden shower and the plashy potential of a deep square of gin-green water. The village name for these yellow-tailed braggarts, crashing from branch to branch, making a display of their loud visibility is *paucar*. Their call is a perfectly intervalled *who-what-where, who-what-where. Whoop-ya. Whoop-ya. Woo-ya.* The ornithological name for the tree-squatters is Oropendola. The intervals between whoops are somewhere between ten and thirteen seconds, Lucho says. The birds synchronise the chorus, their long Tiller Girl tails swishing like gold-sprayed pendulums. These are the feathered sirens at the border of the mist-shrouded land of the Gold Machine.

Before we can enjoy our breakfast at the refectory table, we have to harvest the produce. Farne has never been notably domestic in her instincts, and independent (or bloody-minded) enough, in her days in the family house, to pick and choose the duty tasks she was willing to undertake. She was also a night person, settling to work when the city was stilled, and never eager to leap from her bed to engage with the first light of a new day. But now, in the garden at the back of the farm, there she was, wielding a slim bamboo pole, topped with a little net, like a billiard cue caught in the pocket, to shake and catch oranges from the tree. She filled a blue plastic washing-up bowl with the forty it took to squeeze and press a pitcher of juice. And then, task fulfilled, she joined Grant and myself, for a short expedition, led by Gilberto, to the banana plantation.

The trail is damp. Gilberto's pink reversed cap matches his T-shirt. He clears the way with a sharp-edged but crusted machete. The ribbed leaves of the banana trees have been chewed and holed by insects: everybody feeds, everybody is food. The thesis is so simple. Coming from outside, far outside, ocean, city, mountains, it is too easy to become enmeshed in the sensorium of fecundity: that it *might* be possible, without bringing much to the party, to settle here in Thoreau retreat, living off whatever can be dug up within a half-mile of your hut. Other temperaments, such as Lucho's, quickened by experience, see the ground as a resource, to be turned, when intelligently worked, to profit. The trees are heavy with great green claws of bananas, hanging out, pointing *up*, begging to be cropped. But there is no economic way to get them to market. And every other person living here has access to the same natural larder.

One strike, as Gilberto demonstrates, slashes through the slender stalk of the tree. We are invited to follow his example, preferably without hacking into our own thighs. We load bunches onto our shoulders and head back. Gilberto breaks away from the trail to select, dig out, and shake the earth from a yucca sapling: the menu is complete. And very soon we are biting into the edible contour lines of the territory that surrounds us, between hills and river.

I relished the process of razoring small green bananas, or plantains, into a sizzling pan of deep fat, so much that I headed straight to the open stalls of Ridley Road Market in Dalston on my return to London. The results were unconvincing: the bananas were too old, too far removed from the moment on the tree, and my pan of fat didn't spit and sing with the same conviction. At Lucho's table the plantain crisps balanced the archaeological gravitas of the yucca root, the staple of every rainforest meal. With peppers and a few strips of butchered farm animals, we accumulated the energy required for our instructional and compulsory march to the waterfall.

This time we reached the banana plantation by way of a road trenched out by the forestry company who came to an understanding with the great dealmaker, Lucho's father, don Pedro. 'Everybody wins,' said Lucho. 'When an opportunity presents itself, grab it by the balls.' The villagers got the collateral benefit, stacked trucks rumbling through, day and night, promising local trade, even employment. Young men like Gilberto could save their earnings and buy a motorbike. With a bike, they would catch a willing partner. Soon there would be a child. Gilberto was a proud father. 'Problems come with the second,' Lucho said. 'Then these boys feel trapped. They take off for San Ramón, even Huancayo. It's hard to get them to stick, to see how the farm will develop.'

When the strangers from the city, don Pedro and his son, with their Andean heritage, arrived in the cloud jungle, those who were already there refused to believe that they would prosper. It had happened before. Some outsider with peculiar ideas took a property, played with it for a few months, and went away. Whenever Lucho departed on one of his adventure tours, the villagers helped themselves to his precious tools and equipment. 'Who needs more than one machete? That's how these people think. They are testing you. Are you *serious*? We will soon send them back to Huancayo.'

Things disappear in the night. Chickens vanish. Workers taken on to help may last a few weeks, and then they have had enough. 'But Gilberto is a good boy.' Don Pedro knows these people, he drinks with them. They laugh together. 'We are still here. We are not going anywhere. We have brought them this new road.'

The serious adventure tourists, Germans and South Africans, Dutch paramilitaries, *climb* the waterfall. Wet rock to wet rock, under the torrent, as a loosener, before the jungle or the Inca Highway. We will merely acknowledge its hydrographical potency, its role as the concluding proof in a journey of contrived moral teachings. Lucho, our stern, trickster *brujo*, is a master of this form: the pedagogic walk. Questions are not invited or welcomed. We must witness, absorb, and carry away the facts of the forest: botanical, socio-political and anthropological. Lucho has devoured the source books and he will, when a copy can be sent from New Zealand, evaluate the published account of Arthur Sinclair. He will invigilate that antiquarian cataloguing of flora and fauna. He will forgive – and correct – some of the mistakes and indulge literary aspirations.

The richest gleanings of the forest trail, splitting away from the road used by the woodcutters, cannot be photographed. The magic is as self-contained as it is delicate. Sudden movement on dripping greenery can be withdrawn in the blink of an eye. The fluttering, open-winged display of the Blue Morpho butterfly folds away into a single inky line, before I can begin to get that vision into focus. The crime was so much worse when Casement sent back a butterfly from the Putumayo, to be put on display, a dead thing, on the ground floor of the Natural History Museum in Dublin. The huge Amazonian butterfly, stabbed with a pin through the heart, is carded as being 'collected' by Sir Roger Casement, circa 1911.

Lucho stares up at the canopy of the forest, but it is too late. The monkeys have gone, driven uphill, into the darkness, by hunters and loggers for whom unenclosed nature is an exploitable resource. Our guide points, with his clean machete, across the river towards the slopes of spindly trees on the far side. Dense plantations emerging from the pall of morning mist.

'Chinese,' Lucho says. 'Ugly, invasive things. Those trees have changed the landscape.' And changed the meaning of what is out there to be read. Now there is a single white cloud, an inverted Mayan pyramid, spiked on the sharp peak of the mountain range.

Every plant, as Lucho demonstrates, has its medicinal qualities. He makes a brisk surgical incision, like a rubber tapper, in a tree that oozes a natural antiseptic. He applies the gunk to a damaged leg, which was once, before this remedy, bug-bitten and massively swollen. He could have lost it. We will notice, he says, when we visit the people of the Perené, that many of them lack fingers. Their ancestors learned the trick from Padre Sala, but they never quite mastered the knack of letting go of a lighted stick of dynamite, at the optimum moment, when they were fishing.

'Like everything else,' Lucho explained, 'it is a matter of technique and practice. For the best result, you must hold on until *just* before detonation. One beat too long and it costs you a hand.'

Before the path forked, our guide struck out with his machete, to split an ant ball and display the intricate and industrious workings. We were dutifully impressed by the tensile strength of the delicate spiders' web in which the brown ball was suspended.

Don Pedro, we were told, had a dispute with the occupiers of a rival finca, the Santa Clara. He insisted on taking a trail which could become treacherous after heavy rains. Landslides from the higher slopes were common. There came the day when Lucho's father, against his wise son's advice, followed our present route alongside his favourite donkey. The beast was swaying dangerously under huge sacks of coffee beans. 'It was madness. My father was as stubborn as his animal.'

Darkness fell. Don Pedro did not return. Lucho prepared and ate a solitary evening meal. Late into the night, while he waited at the kitchen table, there were animal sounds, something butting or scratching against the door. Lucho stayed in his chair. The old man crawled, on all fours, into the pool of dusty light from the oil lamp. He was battered, bruised, bleeding. Trousers in rags.

The donkey, prodded and switched, to pick a way around the rubble of a recent landslide, missed its footing and plunged down the near vertical slope, taking don Pedro along with him. The master was now the burden, complicating a smooth descent. Lucho's father clung to the precious coffee sacks like a shipwrecked mariner. Donkey, coffee and farmer tumbled in a cartwheel of arbitrary genetic exchanges.

After a decent interval, establishing that he was still alive, don Pedro felt for broken bones and open wounds. He needed to confirm which parts were donkey, which man, and which coffee. In just a few hours, that starless night, the tough old farmer recovered. He hauled himself, foot by agonising foot, back to the trail. The donkey had reneged on the partnership. He was dead. There was no gainsaying it. But the coffee sacks might yet be recovered – if he acted fast, before the neighbours got wind of the fortuitous wreck.

'Jungle plants healed don Pedro,' Lucho said. 'Nothing could resurrect the poor donkey. But my coffee bushes are ripening well. You will taste a cup of my own blend before you go back to England. You might find an outlet there?'

For months ahead of our expedition, Farne was in communication with the anthropologist Elena Mihas. Mihas made regular visits to Ashaninka settlements along the Perené. The people with whom she formed a relationship, the ones she recorded on a regular basis, were on a list my daughter carried with her. If Arthur Sinclair laid down the route map we would follow, Mihas was the conscience of the coming Perené exchanges. She had a term for the method of teaching employed by Lucho: 'illocutionary force'. Every anecdote has a lesson. Every plant illustrates a code of conduct.

'The Upper Perené ritual formula *afuu* (be it),' Mihas tells us, 'has the illocutionary force of a command aimed at transforming one lifeform into another.' This was Lucho's established dogma: to inspire by showing, to command by example, and to release tension through some site-specific anecdote. The absent don Pedro was the necessary hero of these parables.

The cycle of legendary tales about the old farmer have been nurtured, and improved in the retelling. They are dear to Lucho. After our evening meal of catfish, peppers, plantain and boiled rice, and while Grant is occupied arranging the required pools of darkness for his interview, Lucho recalled a period when the finca was firmly in the hands of his father. And when he, as the practical and driven partner, was spending more time on the property, with opportunist schemes for planting, fish farming, and bringing villagers along as a cadre of trained and willing workers.

In the days of the guerrillas, Sendero Luminoso, when Maoist raiding parties were competing for the attention of the local people, don Pedro was canny. He improved the provisional architecture of his assorted cabins and barns by rigging a drawbridge between the main house and the satellite construction with his locked bedroom. He would trick those thieves and killers. His doors were not only locked, they were nailed. The old man liked to balance his way, tightrope fashion, just drunk enough and waving a warning machete, across wobbling unsecured planks, before climbing in through a window. All went well, until the night the plank snapped. There were screams, more broken bones. Had he been shot?

Don Pedro had been arrested before, on a trek through the jungle. His native companions were carrying guns, hunting knives, and dynamite for the fishing. They were taken for the very thing that they were trying to protect themselves against. The military worked them over, with no particular enthusiasm, then threw them in gaol, where they were held until the old man's political connections could be contacted.

Before Grant began on the interview he needed for his film, we asked Lucho a few questions of our own. Farne wanted to know how old don Pedro was now.

'He is eighty-nine. They call him "don" as a mark of respect. It's not only because of his age. I remember – I think it was around 1968 – my father was here with us. It was close to Christmas, freezing cold. And these natives came to the house. They were talking with don Pedro. They brought money – because he left them a lot of product, things grown on the farm. They had made whatever they could and they wanted to share those bits of money with my father. He was almost in tears. He *almost* felt that he should abandon the place and leave it to them. But it's a complicated story.'

We wanted to go back over what had happened on our own journey. And to clarify aspects of what would lie ahead, if we succeeded in following the episodes outlined in Arthur's account. We talked about the village of the Ashaninka called 'King Chokery', on the other side of the Perené. I mentioned that the King's wives fed him on what was perceived, by Arthur, to be a great delicacy: white maggots. They restored him to health.

'This is not for health!' Lucho said. 'We *normally* eat wasps and maggots. They are a staple, like rice. Good protein. There are different kinds of worms and other parasites that are good to eat. And there is always yucca. If the plantation is blessed with parasites, we call them old friends. We collect them, cook and eat them. No problem.'

For Lucho's benefit, I read aloud from Arthur's account of the benefits of chewing the coca leaf.

'Yeah yeah yeah. He sees these people chewing, he wants to try. He has described it really well, how you must use limestone or ashes with quinoa. You activate the cocaine, mix it with gastric juices in the stomach. It gives a lot of energy. It is very good for old people, Alzheimer's or other sickness. Not many people in the Andes go senile. They keep working. You remember the old Chinese woman in San Luis de Shuaro? She was totally *there* with her brain. She has everything because she's a chewer. But chewing the leaves is a totally different situation from narco dealers and that stuff.'

It was Lucho's belief that after the era of the European colonists, the Peruvian Republic did not make a good start, because they didn't rescue the 'lost knowledge' of the indigenous people.

'Just imagine! The medicine! The natives have so many plants. There is so much talk about ecology. You could get rid of plastic. There are wrappings from leaves in the jungle. But we didn't learn properly. We went the wrong way. We want everything that is artificial. We are only returning to nature now that we have almost destroyed it.'

'How did you come to the farm?' Farne asked.

'Well, my father was manager of certain lands, shared with other people. There were two hundred acres for each of them. The others made excuses, they were doctors. There was malaria, yellow fever. We are talking about the 1960s. My father's friends knew that the Trans-Amazonia Highway was going to be completed. My father appointed a man called Manuel. He could speak good Spanish. He got the other natives to come around. He was basically the one who hooks people in. The natives made a deal with my father to clear the land, so that he could start a plantation. Those natives would come and go as they wanted, even to our house in Huancayo.

'But there was an uprising, Guillermo Lobatón Milla. A branch of Che Guevara, what he was doing in Bolivia. They were putting trouble into the jungle. The person in charge was Lobatón. He was held in good respect by the natives. This was something the government did not like. So they put in a base for special police. Highly trained people to destroy the guerrillas. After my father had been arrested by them in the jungle, he went back to Huancayo and abandoned this piece of land, but he kept the natives working.

'The other people involved with him were ready to give up. One had died, the doctor, and the other had sold his clinic and didn't want to be part of the deal. He went to a senator in Lima, made some money. People who had invaded the land didn't have any papers. A lawyer, who was somehow involved, said: "Pedro, I have a piece of land you can have, if you get me the money." Don Pedro had the money. He came here with the lawyer. He fell in love with the place. It was almost the same as the estate he had before. This one didn't have a road. But my father felt it in his guts. He decided to make the deal.

'I never have trouble with the natives. I know the natives. I have the contacts. After two years clearing the ground, there was a deal with the lumber company. They wanted the wood and we wanted the farm. They put a road through, and continued on, because they were searching for the right wood. For twenty years, they exploited the area, trucks coming and going. The road was very, very bad. We travel on top of the wood trucks. Trucks loaded with logs, with chains around them. That was the only way to move around.

'In the last years, don Pedro got into trouble. A bit of debt with the bank. The bank wanted to take the farm. My father fell for a bit of drinking. There was a moment of hyperinflation in the country. Dollars were up in the clouds. Money in Peru is worth nothing. The bank was going to take the farm. I was twenty-five, just married and trying to save. I had something like two hundred dollars. Two thousand dollars was *huge* money. I paid the bank, to get the farm free of debt. But the same bank that was charging my father went bankrupt. From that time, it was my right to be here on the farm. I was young. I started the restaurant in Huancayo. My father was happy, he stayed here. I came to the old house with travellers.

'We didn't have water in the house. We didn't have electricity. But these were different kind of travellers. They go for showers to the waterfall. They use candles in the night. We get up very early for adventures. We climb the waterfall or go on trails through the jungle.

'I decide that I want to be in charge at the farm. Don Pedro was a little bit better. My brothers and sisters were upset. They thought they had rights over the farm. I told them that to have rights you have to work. "Tell me, what have you planted?"

'I have done a lot of planting. I have paid the debts. In Peru, laws say that each child is allowed a share, even if they are outside the marriage. My father, in 2000, could be giving part of the farm, when my mother was still alive, to another lady who was not the official wife. I told him that I needed to get a couple of papers done. It was a lucky moment, without that paper I didn't have a thing. My brothers and sisters would want a piece. I don't sell anything. I am a person who gets attached to things. You look around this kitchen, everything comes from somewhere else. Those windows belonged to the hostel I kept for backpackers. Other bits come from my hotels. This is my history. You tell me, how can I sell my history?

'Nothing can happen until you understand the system here. I might have a bad idea, invite someone from the court, a judge. He likes the place, he can make me disappear. He pays bribes. He pays a girl down the road to accuse me of rape. The law offers no protection. My way of working with the local people is to be very open. I have learned a very simple rule: if you have enemies in your house, it is better to move out. I am working hard to sort all the papers, gather all the information, make things clear. I am going to make this an internationally protected *legal* area. We don't want any problems with the natives. Now do you understand?'

CERRO DE LA SAL

'The curse of facts and the blessing of illusions, the bitterness of our
wisdom and the deceptive consolation of our folly.'
   – Joseph Conrad

On the verandah, alongside the screaming red, phone-booth-sized
Coca-Cola machine, and staring with trepidation at hills we had travelled so far to experience, we had some friendly debate around the question of salt as a motive for travel. With no keys as yet for our rooms, we
stood in the frame of the open door and confronted the implications of
this timeless view. Farne's version, 'mountain of salt', carried the suggestion of its near homonym, *fountain* of salt: a magical outpouring from
one particular point in the green forest, a gushing salt spring. And a
secret known only to privileged guides and initiated chiefs. The location
was a significant commercial and spiritual value. Controlling salt was
controlling trade: the potatoes and woven products of the highlands,
the weapons and bright trinkets of outsiders. For feathers and pottery
paid in tribute to the local cacique. Salt was needed for the preservation
of meat and fish. It was an essential ingredient for sustaining life itself.

There was a tradition of salt pilgrimage for the Ashaninka of the
low jungle in the months of July, August and September. Before the
rainy season. A toll was paid when permission was granted for crossing
alien territory. But taxes imposed by the Spanish, and later by armed
representatives of the Peruvian Corporation of London, were fiercely
resisted. There were uprisings by groups of Campa from the eastern
Andean foothills in the winter of 1897: farms and estates of English
settlers were burnt, and colonisers massacred when they tried to demand
goods or services in exchange for access to the salt quarry.

Our own guide, Lucho, the *brujo* of adventure tourism, had delivered us to the place where we needed to be, the start of the trail on which Arthur, led by Padre Sala, entered the rainforest. Lucho had chosen his room, before we arranged, in the fiercest heat of the day, to hike towards the source of the salt bounty. He announced, before disappearing into the house, that he would carry us, early next day, to our preordained encounter at the Ashaninka village, Pampa Michi.

'Crossing the Paucartambo, about two miles from the Convent, we entered the dense forest, and struggled along a track almost impassable from its narrowness, deep mud, and absence in many parts of any sort of gradient,' said Alexander Ross.

We were on what was left of that trail. My sensation, confirmed by the solid mirage of this hill, which reminded me, in its anvil shape, of Golden Cap in Dorset, was of a portal opening to provoke wilder speculations. I remembered those months, living with that quintessential English vision through the iced-over window of the farm bedroom where I scribbled in gloves, coat and woollen hat. I was fired with new theories about London and the hidden patterns of its architectural forms, churches, mounds and 'prehistoric' circles. And the ways in which we were persuaded to move between them.

In my verandah discussion with Farne, I used the term 'salt mountain', in the conviction that the entire massif, this impenetrably wooded and blunted pyramid, was *all* salt. Because I could feel, already, before we stepped one yard into the breath-stealing afternoon temperatures, a surge of physical transformation; blood calling to salt, salt to calcium, bone to water. Dizzying, disturbing, and seductive. But first we had to find the gardener, the solitary caretaker of this deserted hacienda, and without a word in common, persuade him to lead us to the fountain or seam or quarry of salt.

We were both right, it appears. Or that is what we understood, through signs and bits of phrases, as we set out. The hill was a salt sculpture, like a Highways Agency mound heaped against winter, for a road that had not yet been built. But it contained a specific wound, in a quarry near the summit. There was an exposed vein, where as many as five hundred labourers, using iron axes and sharpened stones, had hacked out blocks of salt to be carried in baskets down to the Paucartambo River. And on, by heavily loaded balsa rafts, to the jungle settlements. The rafts voyaged in flotillas of up to twenty vessels lashed together.

The Ashaninka, who permitted us to stay for a few nights in their village beside the Perené, existed, in topographical terms, 'below the salt'. They were obliged to make annual pilgrimages that became ritual journeys keeping ancient traditions alive: rock salt tasted better and was more portable, in its convenient blocks, than brine salt. The derogatory English phrase came from a period when rock salt was beginning to be mined in Cheshire. Elaborate containers like those for holy relics were carefully positioned on tables. Only those of high rank had access to the precious condiment.

Before Lucho departed, in a whirlwind of dust, he told us that the gardener, the silent Armando, was the man to conduct us over the salt mountain. But it was early afternoon, siesta. We stepped outside the somnolent resthouse to explore the well-tended grounds. After several unrewarded circuits of the property, Armando manifests. He is inky haired, dressed in a green T-shirt that fades into the tonal range of the coarse grass, the palm fronds and the hill. The gardener lives and sleeps in inherited wellington boots. The honed machete is an extension of his arm. He is amused and alarmed when we ask to be taken on the salt road, bootless and without weapons. The madness of strangers! But if the hacienda is ever to attract visitors, he must accept such ludicrous challenges.

Effortlessly opening his stride, he is away. In the drumming tropical heat, we limp in his wake, losing heavy droplets of precious sticky salt with every step taken. The baked mud and the cutting stones of the uphill trail are visibly steaming. The cool jungle presses on both sides. We will have to break into a panting jog, if we are to catch the spectres of Arthur, Ross, Padre Sala and the mule train.

Without warning, but at a well-judged moment when we are about to be confirmed in our folly, and ready to scratch a path towards any pool of shade, Armando plunges away to the left. He says nothing, but we hear him hack and slash. Slithering, falling, hanging on to thorns and vines, attached and unattached, we follow. Through the densest, most clinging of thickets, through a thatch of spearing stalks, to a hidden salt pond: a frosted glaucoma eye in a festering swamp clearing. Much of the salt shines in conviction of its status: it cannot be chopped into neatly portable blocks and carried away in woven baskets. This salt pan is untraded ground. It is telling us that we are still on the right track. But not here, not now. Not ever.

Armando indicates again, by gesture and slow Spanish, that if we are serious about making this expedition, up the salt trail and beyond, we must acquire wellington boots and machetes. And some common language would be useful too. Meanwhile, this afternoon, we can find our own way home.

Red-brown mud queers the rim of the salt lake. There are channels, like fractal river systems seen from space, licked out by animals. Grant falls to his knees. He is mesmerised by the potential of the set to which he has been led. He sets up his tripod, but it is too late: he has forgotten how to shoot film. Pulsing salt crystals blow focus and eat exposure. Grant lies down in a swoon of obeisance. He has been pressured by the reading of him as a Conradian figure: as Kaspar Almayer at the end of that first novel, *Almayer's Folly*. House burnt down by his own hand, the ruined colonial trader shares his final hutch with a Chinese squatter who fires up his opium pipe.

> His back against the wall, his legs stretched stiffly out, his arms hanging by his side. His expressionless face, his eyes open wide with immobile pupils, and the rigidity of his pose, made him look like an immense man-doll broken and flung there out of the way.

The black-sprayed figure of the filmmaker, stretched at full length, chasing his elongated shadow across the dirty white creek, was also in thrall to an undeclared quest. Grant travelled with us as a fictional projection, while making his own fiction, drawing on whatever he found useful in our narrative. He was in active pursuit of something else entirely. And here, for the first time, since the tragic landscape of

La Oroya, smoke snaking in a vertical column from the tall chimney, he had found it. And it him.

Farne was a presence in Grant's film. She was interviewed under instruction that she should behave as if she were playing a role that might, or might not, be jettisoned when the edit was done. I was never glimpsed. Never heard. Left at home. Disqualified by age, sex, race, and previous meta-literary conceits, I was replaced by a veteran actor, marooned in a concrete cruise ship, in a Sussex seaside town under quarantine. He scrolled through old films, old albums, and the mustiest books. He was not permitted to speak.

If I *had* made the journey – and I was no longer sure of that – *Almayer's Folly* would have been the book I chose to carry with me on the flight to Lima. It was published in the same year, 1895, as Arthur's first hardback production, after a number of slim chapbooks and pamphlets of recycled journalism. Conrad started his composition in London, between voyages, in idleness. He carried the manuscript of the work-in-progress with him on his travels: to France, Poland, Belgium and the Congo. On a cruise of the *Torrens*, he pitched the project to Galsworthy. And again, as serving first mate, he tried it on W.H. Jacques, during the long voyage to Australia in 1892. The engine of the story is always a futile dream of gold. Did Conrad ever coincide, in maritime languor, with Arthur? The stiff-backed merchant seaman with the fine ear for the rhythms of speech – how a tale should be told and who was doing the telling – and the crusty Scottish planter, the bearded man who took such pride in shaping those remembered taffrail conversations between strangers. The anecdotes, the anathemas. The profits and loses of Calvinist fate.

> Almayer's thoughts were often busy with gold; gold he had failed to secure; gold the others had secured – dishonestly, of course – or gold he meant to secure yet, through his own honest exertions.

The haunted trader, painfully mismarried, housed in a decaying ruin with a daughter he does not understand, rarely thinks of his own father: 'a subordinate official employed in the Botanical Gardens'. He thinks instead of gold, but not in terms of mines or buried coins, but as an agent of material and spiritual transformation. He broods on whatever lies on the far side of mere possession. He spends his allocated bounty of words. He drains the hoard.

Nina, the fictional daughter of the 'real' person, a Dutch Eurasian called William Charles Olmeijer, who was chosen to become Almayer, is not persuaded.

Expedition! Gold! What did she care for all that?

Harsh light strobed on the white pond. This was the best sequence Grant never shot. The camera was in position, but it was not activated. Salt was a spiteful reverie. And when the Conradian documentarist pulled himself upright and left the salt pond, to follow us back to the hacienda, his shadow stayed behind, imprinted.

With every last guilder in his possession, and in confident expectation of the 'great changes' sure to follow the establishment of the British Borneo Company on the island, Almayer builds his trading post. But he is deceived. His beloved daughter is flown, but not forgotten. He breaks into his locked and abandoned office, sets fire to his papers, and burns the house down. He takes to opium and dies. Goodbye. Done. Almayer departs for the better place with one final benediction: he has learned, with his dying breath, how to forget. But the scribe of his fate is not so kind: Conrad's second novel, *An Outcast of the Islands*, winds the clock back, restoring his tragic victim to youth and folly. A life to be re-endured before it has happened.

That first 1895 novel, published to modest critical acclaim, initiates a new career for the Polish mariner. Arthur's book, of the same year, is a self-composed obituary. The old planter is settling scores and reaching towards the fictions he will never write. *In Tropical Lands* concludes, in Conradian fashion, with a chapter called 'Typical Failures'. It celebrates the ninety per cent of colonial hopefuls who are broken by the system and the climate. 'It is the evil we carry with us that usually proves more formidable than anything indigenous to the isle… the prospect of getting home again is, to the average planter, the most pleasing of all.'

The story Arthur tells of the Scottish farm boy Davie Hacket is one of unrealised expectations, illusory success, unwise connections, and a return to vagrancy and the asylum: 'a separate paddock, with a keeper all to himself'. The innocent highland youth has become 'the most repulsive-looking wreck I had ever beheld'.

We made an early start from Lucho's farm, on the day of our journey to Cerro de la Sal. We were going to walk down to the river, calling in at the village school on our way. It was our guide's intention that we should offer a short presentation, telling the story of Arthur's expedition and showing the children some of the photographs he had taken. Unfortunately, the only teacher in the establishment decided that she had other business. She decamped. Ten pupils, from knee-high to ten years old, were scattered far and wide; chasing chickens, licking stones and paddling in mud. Lucho took immediate charge and rounded them up.

Wagging a pedagogic finger, our guide outlined the historic events that brought us to their school. Then he gave out his first challenge: 'Who can run home and bring back a good *sharp* machete?' Away they went like scorch marks in the animal air. One moment they were at our shins in a silent, serious-eyed throng, then – *whoosh!* – gone. There was such dignity in their headlong scramble. The winner, a stern buzz-cut child of about eight years old, going on forty, received his promised reward: a key ring from Heathrow with bright red double-decker bus and hanged London bobby. The diminutive champion demonstrated his prowess with the blade, by clearing the grass at the edge of the school's grey concrete recreation square. Tiny tots, not much taller than the machetes they dragged behind them, joined the communal labours. Like cadet Maoists.

Next Lucho had them race the length of the field, prizes to be awarded to winners. No nonsense here about the glory of taking part. Naked Darwinism: no key rings or multicolour pens for losers. I was impressed by the instantaneous acceptance of the order, the way all of them waited, so still, for the starting whistle. But I broke the warriors' code by insisting that one of the pens be saved for a sprite of a four-year-old girl, utterly bemused by the sudden swirl of activity. She stood, transfixed, on her allocated spot, spinning in circles, as the others raced towards their prizes. When the affair was done, the children clustered around Grant, like seasoned football commentators, to watch the replay on the screen of his camera.

They had the pens but no paper. I dug out one of the portraits of Arthur and told them that they could colour it in or write their own stories on top of it. Lucho was horrified. He snatched the page back. He rolled it up and presented it to an attending mother, ordering her to give it to the teacher on her return from town, as part of an important historical display for the classroom.

With their tourist trophies safely hidden, the children returned to their games and duties, while we made for the river.

The crossing of the Paucartambo was a significant marker for both surveyors, my great-grandfather and Alexander Ross. On the far bank they would attempt trails still in the process of being adapted into the primitive roads that would, all too soon, open up the territory for commerce. Mules and cameras would be lost on rickety bridges. Ross described the perverse double nature of the river: 'here rushing on, a boiling whirling torrent, there a calm stream, flowing on its way to meet the Chanchamayo we had left behind.'

Our transit was attempted in an open cage, suspended on wires. It was evident that nothing had changed since the days of the 1920s adventurer Harry Foster.

> The cage… was a small platform, swung on cables, and operated by another cable which wound upon a small windlass at the other side of the river. I made the first half of the journey successfully, for the cables sagged in the centre, and the first half was downhill. But in the centre, the cage stopped, for the second half was uphill, and the *cholo* on the farther bank was already tired from turning the windlass. Wherefore he left me in the centre while he sat down to smoke a cigarette and think about it.

The cages were an inherited family franchise. The waters below were emphatically white-capped. Foster thought about jumping overboard, to swim for shore. He looked down and reconsidered. When he did make landfall, he was in another country: 'The Perené colony consisted of some six big estates, owned by the Peruvian Corporation, a British concern which also operates the principal railroads in Peru, collects the guano along the coast, and runs various other enterprises.'

Lucho's truck, gifting us with a cool breeze in our faces, while we jolted over ridges and potholes, and ducked overhanging branches, deposited us at an isolated hacienda facing the salt mountain. The grounds of this former plantation were groomed, watered and in bloom. Paint was fresh and the boards of the verandah had recently been swept. The red Cola kiosk was brutally polished, but nothing was plugged in. The site was like an abandoned recreation area for generously funded but unoccupied counter-insurgent paramilitaries.

Farne was in good spirits; not having eaten or drunk anything of consequence in days, she insisted on a coffee stop, at a stall run by an Italian in Puente Raither. He also supplied a slice of banana cake which a procession of flies treated like their private mountain of salt. Lucho took a full lunch, alone, in a riverside dive. It was too early for the rest of us. I renewed my acquaintance with the simple-minded man who had singled me out on our previous visit, and who was waiting, mid-road, to pick up his aborted monologue. Laughing prematurely, he listened for the reply I was not qualified to give.

Eventually, after abandoning the truck to make a preliminary tour of the salt mountain estate, we discovered a person hanging from the window of a satellite bungalow. She was trying, she said, to make telephone connection with an office in Lima. That was where bookings were validated. When the first improvised attempt failed, she sent the man we subsequently knew as 'Armando' out on the roof. It was siesta in the capital. But we were welcome to find a chair and wait on the verandah.

I sat with Farne, while we discussed pilgrim trails. We felt very close to the path that Arthur must have taken. Within the frame of what could be viewed from the verandah, we convinced ourselves that we were in the right story. This was indeed a good place in which to prepare for the past to happen. We trusted, like Aboriginal people watching patiently for the return of a comet, that whatever had been foretold in dance, or scratched on stone, would come again.

A figure emerged from the darkened interior, a kitchen zone occupied by the busy women of an unseen family. Festive in a rose-flowered blue top, she was indulgent to the notion of unlanguaged strangers coming to sleep in this house. She offered a huge bunch of keys, and left us to it. The keeper had no notion of which key belonged to which room.

I spent an interesting half-hour working through the various combinations. The room I finally accessed was clean and bare. The one thing I managed to establish was that the handwritten numbers on the tickets bore no relation to the numbers on the doors.

Farne was sitting calmly with her accounts. She said that Lucho had emerged, brisk as ever, to announce that he was going to town in search of fish, a necessary gift to carry with us to the Ashaninka village. There would be a celebratory meal of welcome. He would not be back for hours. It was likely that he'd be away all night.

The evening meal was served in an over-endowed dining room made glamorous by oil-lamp shadows. My companions were fastidious in the spurning of green salad. I took the tomato slices and arranged them around a perfect white pyramid of sticky rice, in which extracts of recent chicken were buried. Like a culinary treasure hunt.

Later, sprawling on the verandah, while mosquitoes surged and fused around a single, dim bulb, we yarned and yawned; coming around, as always at the end of a session, to the topic of gold. I tried to recall the haphazard strike, when the poet Charles Olson travelled from New England to California, in pursuit of a hot topic worthy of academic funding. He identified the degradation of the alchemical quest in the working of a hydraulic dredge used by a Canadian syndicate in the gold fields around Sacramento. They were taking out a million dollars a year and spoiling the earth, while offering no gesture of reparation to offset the damage they left behind. Corporate greed was a facilitator of new deserts.

Gary Snyder, when I visited him in his forest retreat in the foothills of the Sierra Nevada, confirmed the story. He told me that the livid scars of gold-mining operations were all around. And that was why he was able to acquire, in partnership with Allen Ginsberg, the property he named *Kitkitdizze*. A self-sufficient Buddhist community, with generators, vehicles and tools, reduced at the time of my arrival, to one unyielding individual.

Olson discovered a cache of original documents in the Bancroft Library at Berkeley. He burrowed into Gold Rush files, 'seeking out', as his biographer Tom Clark reports, 'the facts of the infamous cannibalism episode culminating the ill-fated 1846 Sierra crossing of the Donner Party'. Always, for this poet, facts. The projectiles of scholarship. 'Eyewitness accounts… straight from the mouths of the survivors.' Olson persisted, he came on the land lease deposited by Sutter and George Marshall after the discovery of gold at their sawmill.

The poet took his story to John Huston in Hollywood. Before he attempted a treatment, he went back to the terrain. 'Even as he looked on,' Clark wrote, 'the great dredges still pounded away without mercy at a landscape already soiled for generations to come. The sheer scale of this industrial rapacity against the earth staggered him, further complicating the total meaning of the gold story.'

Years later, in winter retreat in Gloucester, Massachusetts, after an abortive encounter with fellow anchorite Jack Kerouac, Olson acknowledged that he was losing it. 'The alchemy of creation was escaping him.' The navigation charts on the wall had faded to white. 'Most of all he feared the loss of his essential powers,' Clark said, 'the precious "Gold-making machine" in which his poetry was fused.'

Farne was preoccupied, thinking about Padre Sala. She wondered about the later lives of the orphans and lost children 'rescued' from the forest. Grant had been reading a book by a contemporary prospector who spent his life chasing, finding and denying the fever for gold. This man had some success in Arthur's old Australian territories, before risking what he called 'El Inferno Verde' in Latin America.

One evening, in his hammock, spinning tales as we were now, he heard about the abduction of a young indigenous girl, kidnapped from her village and forced to work in a gold mining camp, as cook and incidental sex slave. But her captors, eight *garimpeiros*, were undone by the forest, their motive power drained: the will to continue for another day sucked out by invasive root systems. They took up their spades and hacked at the trees. They slashed the insinuating vines that smothered their hut. There was no natural illumination under the choking vegetal canopy.

In the end, they fought for possession of the girl. Fought to the death. One by one, they were slaughtered. The bodies and pieces of body left where they lay, to be swallowed and absorbed by the indifferent rainforest. The last two men struck simultaneous, skull-crushing blows. Predators devoured them. There was nothing left. Not an eyeball or a shred of rubber sandal. The girl somehow made her way back, starving and emaciated, to the village. But the bonds of kinship were broken and she was suspect, a prime candidate for the attentions of the next child-harvester in priestly robes.

PAMPA MICHI

'Of course he could go upriver. Of course he could meet remote
communities. He was welcome to join them, so long as he paid.'
  – Martin MacInnes, *Infinite Ground*

Savages! Beautiful savages! The ones beyond civilisation!

Hungry for authentic wilderness, we patronise with hollow admiration. We are among savages now: our own reflections in the driving
mirrors of safe cars. Knowing ourselves a little better with every mile
travelled, we also know the savage pull of indifference. We flatter vanity
with the list of crimes, historic and contemporary, of which we are
guilty. Crimes not merely of 'inappropriate' language, of attitudes
appropriate to certain periods, of comfortable moral justifications, by
way of religion and education, but of thefts, brutalities, and piracy by
pen and broken treaty: crimes of *being here at all*. Of pecking at closed
wounds. Of tourism. That above all. Of offering the indigenous people
no choice but to exploit our credulity. Strength is savagery. Wealth is
savagery. False smiles are cruel. Our benevolence comes with cocked
weapons. And with horses.

We have left Lucho's rough-country silver horse truck behind on his
farm, there are too many of us now in the raiding party. We travel in
town cars. With hired drivers.

*...Abuelos como le esclavizaban en el tiempo de Perúvian... Bueno, cuando
aquí llegaron ya el Michelle donde que nosh an insultado, donde que nosh an dicho
este chuncho salvaje no sabien trabajar o son ociosos, vagos. Donde quieres que, le
dicen ahora mi psisano como no sabían hablar el Español mi Inglés.*

On our return to England, Grant arranged to have the Ashaninka
interviews, their curses on colonists, transcribed – along with Lucho's

Spanish translations, and his terse English summaries, which were not really English at all, as Joseph Conrad would have understood it (by way of fluid French and birthright Polish).

The tall, black-clad, margin-stalking documentarist, both watcher and participant, feels obliged to interject, to defend the use of the term *chuncho*, which has come through this laborious process from the Ashaninka original. And from, well before that, Arthur Sinclair and Alexander Ross and the hired surveyors of territory.

'*Chuncho*,' Grant glosses, 'is an alternative name of the Ashaninka tribe. A Spanish version of the Quechua word *ch'unchu*, which means "forest dwellers". Although it is not inherently a negative word in Quechua, it has come to be used meaning "savage" or "uncivilized" in Peruvian Spanish, and is considered offensive by many Ashaninka people.'

Of course Grant is quoting from approved explainers, language police. It is a minefield.

Chuncho. The word is ubiquitous.

Arthur Sinclair: *It was a relief to leave this atrocious trail and cut our own way through the jungle, or follow occasionally the paths of the Chunchos who come hither for salt. The Cerro de la Sal, or mountain of salt, lies a few miles to the west, providentially placed here for the benefit of the poor natives who come from many hundreds of miles around. The supply is said to be practically inexhaustible, and as to its savour and purity I can well vouch.*

Alexander Ross: 'Our pace was not more than a mile an hour, but shortly after dark we came out upon a small pajonal, or grassy glade. Here, under a roof which seemed about to fall, but which the Chunchos, or savage Indians, keep always thatched, and, but for broken supports, in good condition, we found the tomb of him who called himself Atahualpa.'

'Chuncho' and 'forest dweller' and 'savage' are interchangeable terms as the Scottish planters shape their narratives and file their accounts, improving the day for later presentation to bankers and backers, to packed lecture halls and liberal newspapers.

Puzzling over remote interview transcripts, housebound in Hackney, and trapped in quarantine, I binged on Amazon-ordered DVDs, ploddingly or recklessly derived from the novels of Conrad. Partly, this was a form of cargo-culting. But there was also a fetish for contact with anything called 'Amazon'. As if the traded bounty in its slim pictorial case had actually been scooped from the great river.

Close to one hundred Conrad films and television dramas – to say nothing of lost projects like the Orson Welles *Heart of Darkness* and Pinter's screenplay for *Victory* – have been produced. Almost all, if they even attempted to unlock the mystery of the original composition, failed. I thought of a moment from one of the more highly regarded translations, Carol Reed's *Outcast of the Islands*, from 1951.

Reed took his crew on location to Sri Lanka (Arthur's Ceylon) and not Malaysia. Ralph Richardson, as Tom Lingard (Rajah Laut, King of the Sea), builds a house of cards, in order to entertain the comfortably pudgy English daughter of the upriver trader, Almayer. Almayer is played by Robert Morley. And the girl, Nina, by his own biological daughter. Convenient casting brushes aside the fact that Almayer is of Dutch derivation and his wife a 'savage' Malay pirate 'rescued' by Lingard. In the film the episode with the playing cards is just a bit of actorly business for Richardson.

In the dog days of a shrinking colonial empire, we are being treated to a generous dollop of eastern exoticism. One lot of traders, the mercantile Dutch, can stand for plantation Englishmen. And Anglo-Malay daughters can be powder-white and Surrey shrill, so that they can highlight the terrible flaw of the third man in this affair, Trevor Howard's Willems. Willems is a white man who has gone rogue, on the other side of the river, with a dusky native girl. A pure savage. 'She was like a wild beast.'

In this, Conrad's second novel, Almayer's daughter, trapped in her state of not quite belonging to either of her parents' races, boasts: 'I am a white child… and the white men are my brothers. Father says so.' She demands a house of cards, built by Captain Lingard. Her 'grandfather'.

As the old sailor begins his task with a 'dirty double pack', he tells the exacting child about the gold fields, her future, his dreams.

I know what I am talking about... Been in California in forty-nine...
Not that I made much... then in Victoria in the early days... I know all
about it... Trust me... Now, delight of my heart, we shall put a third
house on the top of these two... keep very quiet... As I was saying, you
got only to stoop and gather handfuls of gold... dust... there. Now
here we are. Three houses on top of one another. Grand!

And down it all comes, on a breath. Blown from the table. Pipe
dreams of the gold machine swept away. Fade out.

To receive funding, minimal but necessary, Grant was committed to
paying lip service to the strict avoidance of 'cultural appropriation'.
Those who policed public money, by impossible forms and polite box-
tick interrogation, had to ensure that voices were heard from both sides
of any expedition to sites of ancient (and present) abuse. History was
a tangled root ball, less susceptible to overthrow than a slaver's statue.
My own belief, quite reprehensible, was that any proposal that won
approval in these self-lacerating days must have some inherent flaw. Go
back, start again, and fail better: enjoy the liberty of the disenfranchised.
Uncommissioned. Unviewed.

We had reached the point in our journey where Farne's special
interests would begin to erase the red line marked on the map by her
great-great-grandfather. My daughter drew much of her inspiration
from regular Skype traffic with Elena Mihas, a postdoctoral associate
in anthropological linguistics at James Cook University in Queensland,
Australia. At Pampa Michi, Farne hoped to interview one of the main
sources for a substantial Mihas publication, *Upper Perené Arawak Narratives
of History, Landscape, & Ritual*. Without my daughter's research into the
archives of the Peruvian Corporation and her determination to seek
out the indigenous people who had already established relationships
with Mihas, we would have been lost in the fatalism of a Conradian
romance. Farne's diligence made this thing possible. *Now*. I would have
nursed the fantasy of a Peruvian expedition for a few more years, then
let it go. My daughter, informed by and in total sympathy with Mihas,
took over the ethical guidance of our journey.

It was understood by the Ashaninka that no distinction should be made between mythology and chronological records. 'Real history' could only be manifested through the discourses of the Indians themselves. To Mihas, as to other interested outsiders, they said: '*Piñaavaite añaaniki!* Speak our language!'

The anthropologist took special care with her appropriations of privileged information. Those who had been interviewed, or other accredited 'fellow men', would supervise translations, Ashaninka to Spanish. And the results would be vetted and approved by family members. Mihas said that the Ashéninka Perené participants she interviewed, Upper Perené Arawaks, disliked 'the use of the diacritic in writing, especially in the term *Ashaninka*'. In this book, I have followed her advice. History, the anthropologist's fieldwork confirms, is smoke. At first you do not notice it. Soon you are choking and the village has disappeared. There is no division between river and sky.

Lucho did return to the Cerro de la Sal hacienda with a bundle of reeking fish. In two newly collected San Ramón cars. We were ready and waiting, bags packed, cameras stowed. We watched the cloud of dust on the road and the parking of the cars in the shade of the palms. And how Lucho gave his instructions, at wound-down windows, to the young drivers. The previously unknown family group he had brought back with him stretched and took the air. Only the young girl followed as he walked towards us. 'Come on, vamos, let's go.'

Our guide has been staying with a friend, an Ashaninka woman from further downriver. Her name is Velisa. Velisa Nicolas Chuviante. She will be invaluable, he says, in helping with translations – and, more importantly, as a person who can vouch for us, act as a go-between. The child, Camila, is her daughter. The old lady, a singer, laughing at us, is her mother. They will stay where we stay, in the village by the Perené. Lucho has known Velisa, in Huancayo, since she was thirteen.

Light rain, a 'female' downpour, as Lucho terms it, is damping the dust as we pass through Puente Raither. Farne secures her last coffee from the Italian. We buy plastic rain capes, but they are not used. They never are. They would be useless in a male deluge.

———

Out of the still-shuddering San Ramón cars and into the dance. Our driver's holy medallion is a swinging pendulum or votive offering against the infection of primitivism. And we are now part of the regular tourist transport permitted (and encouraged) by the local chief. In they come, dazed and confused, the minibus loads and the hired cars, with eyes spinning from the Trans-Amazonian Highway. These respectful cultural appropriators, with or without phrase books and cameras, have been made aware, well before they are snatched up and processed into the circle of swaying dancers, that this liberated colonial plantation, is in danger of becoming another off-road attraction: a sand-smooth car park surrounded by huts in which real people live. The perimeter fence throbs to the siren song of industrially processed rubber on hot tarmac. Percussive smacks and rattles from native dirt, pitted and flattened by convoys of refrigerated trucks.

The car radio shrieks, its cacophony of tinny voices asserting a remote connection with the world we have left behind. Lounging drivers smoke and readjust branded baseball caps. They might be *mestizo* or Indian, boys from town or village. But they don't dance. The reverie of the salt mountain is swiftly annulled by twin strokes of cochineal face paint across the cheeks. Juice of red berries from achiote bushes, before a lightning costume change. Our grungy travel kit is hidden under enveloping orange cushmas, dyed cotton sheets with a hole for the head. The whole bogusly authentic outfit topped off with haloes of ill-fitting straw headgear. We are inducted into the zombified shuffle of the dancers. Into the chugging, chanting, prison-yard vortex of our inadequately recompensed Ashaninka hosts.

Tribal actors have been challenged with being themselves, and more than themselves, heroic representatives of a threatened culture. They are cued to climb from their benches to greet and process the latest delivery of time-travellers who have invested in a theme-park précis of the traditional ways of the high jungle and the brown river. Joyless but obedient credit-card vultures grasp proffered Ashaninka hands; every tourist is paired with a member of the opposite sex. The new dancers reel like post-operative convalescents trying to make it across the floor to the bathroom, after a sleepless night on some strange hard bed. They stamp, to the beat of a skin drum, forcing blood and life back into feet that are not yet properly attached. They are wary of the provocations of a monkey-man trickster in black bodysuit and a crown of parrot feathers. His white skull face is the gearshift knob from our hire car brought to life. Monkey-man waves a thick phallic wand and twangs his bond-market braces, a cocky lord of misrule.

We have come at last to the first fruits of my great-grandfather's survey, the Upper Perené reservation of Pampa Michi. Who Michi was nobody is quite sure: a forgotten manager, one of the *colonos* called Michael? The other surviving Perené Colony settlements, Pampa Silva and Pampa Whaley, are also named after dead functionaries. What is established, in the version we hear from some of those who laboured on the plantation, is that all three bosses were killed by indigenous people. And not, as we surmised, in uprisings, late invocations of the spirit of Juan Santos Atahualpa, nor in acts of justified revenge for the loss of land: the bosses were speared in range wars, jealous inter-estate squabbles.

Pampa Whaley was reckoned to have the best situation, it was the dominant stockade. Plantation caciques manipulated barely repressed rivalries in order to pursue their own private vendettas. An Ashaninka group portrait from *In the Amazon*, a self-serving account published in 1932 by Fernando Stahl, the Seventh-day Adventist missionary, features a sullen group cradling chin-high bows and antiquated rifles. Stahl glosses: 'A band of murderers.' Photographs from the archives of the Smithsonian Institution show armed war bands. Armed, naturally enough, through barter with smiling invaders. Women and children squat at the feet of grave warriors with pudding-basin haircuts. Stahl had not yet struck his duplicitous deal with the overlords of the Peruvian Corporation. Adventists would be allowed to establish missions and schools, nucleated settlements, colonies within the Colony, on the understanding that they would 'tame' intractable natives, by persuading them to give up masato binges and polygamy, and submit themselves to a hardworking (and totally alien)

Protestant ethic. They would become company dependents. Or, as they saw it, slaves.

Stahl was fortunate that his advocacy of a cult based on the imminence of the Second Coming sat so neatly within the myths of the Upper Perené: consoling fables of a messianic redeemer. There were legends of a 'White Indian', a redresser of wrongs, and bearer of gifts, emerging in a golden aurora from the flames of the setting sun. The Ashaninka called their long-awaited saviours *amachénga* or *amachénka*. These were ever-present but invisible. They were the Hidden Ones.

In *War of Shadows (The Struggle for Utopia in the Peruvian Amazon)* by Michael F. Brown and Eduardo Fernández, it is said that a 'white chuncho', a reincarnation of Juan Santos Atahualpa, appeared in 1888. He was carrying 'a carbine of the latest model and bandoliers of cartridges like necklaces'. This was Carlos Fermín Fitzcarrald, a brutal and precipitate rubber baron, and the inspiration for Werner Herzog's very different, linen-suited Klaus Kinski in *Fitzcarraldo*. Stahl was a later emanation, superimposing his own myths on those of the tribal people. And successfully colonising the riverside settlements we were visiting. Tourism was a necessary faith, replacing animistic systems of worship and the drunken fiestas encouraged by the Franciscans. All along the river road, breakaway sects set up their own dances, their own tin-roof churches and stalls of trinkets. This was a highly competitive market economy: without the traditional raids and kidnapping.

Sitting on a communal bench in the long house at Pampa Michi, and waiting, apprehensively, for the arrival of a brimming gourd of pink masato, a skull-cup filled with what seemed to be dental-hygiene mouthwash, I remembered Herzog's creed, as reported by Bruce Chatwin: 'Walking is a virtue, tourism is deadly sin.' This unforgiving Bavarian dogma, repeated over many mesmeric interviews, lectures and presentations, had become a little threadbare: another form of cultural tourism. Almost a slogan for selling fetishised rucksacks, hiking boots and moleskin notebooks. The ones that have to be filled with the minuscule Herzog confessions that delighted Claudia Cardinale and alarmed the paranoid Kinski on the shoot of *Fitzcarraldo*. Herzog said that he expected his books to outlive his films. But there are many nice contradictions in play: the anathematiser of mass tourism is himself in perpetual flight between wilderness locations. Desperate for deserts where nobody goes.

Shooting *Nomad: In the Footsteps of Bruce Chatwin* on commission for BBC Arts, Herzog must have flinched from the mass invasion of Patagonia that slipstreamed the enduring success of Chatwin's first book. In a promotional photograph for that project, the German director is positioned beside Chatwin's leather rucksack, the gift of a dying man. In May 2018, a group of forty-eight filmmakers were invited to join Herzog at a workshop where they would 'submerge into the density and mystery of the Peruvian Amazonian jungle'. Mobility guaranteed: 'exclusively in motorboat'.

Jungle tourism caters for all tastes, as I was well aware. The wild places are now dense with spiritual seekers, who may or may not have been inspired by William Burroughs. They are prepped and packaged for ayahuasca séances with an accredited shaman. 'The jungle represents fever dreams,' Herzog glosses. Among the stories culled from his Patagonian walks and travels, Chatwin tells us that 'the worst Indian hunters were apparently not the Spanish, or the Italians or the Slavs (who account for most of the population of Patagonia) but the Scotch – fortified… with a sense of moral rectitude that they were sparing them the indignities of civilization.'

Lucho had warned us about the masato ceremony: it was unavoidable, a social obligation. We must wet the beak and make a show of rinsing, but we were not obliged to gulp and swallow. Traditional masato is a fermentation of yucca roots, chewed many times by the community of women and spat into the hollowed trough of a canoe. Now it seems they produce masato-lite by a mechanical process, without the intervention of native saliva. And the gossip and bonding conversations that always accompanied the lengthy ritual.

We swilled, Grant rinsed, and Lucho polished off whatever was left in the gourd with a satisfied belch.

The woman who led me around the circling dance on our arrival held out her hand. Each member of our party was shepherded, still road drunk and masato heady, to a particular stall of native crafts: bracelets, necklaces, bright green miniature parrots. Farne opted for a bracelet made from coffee beans. I chose a parrot whistle. Later we were told that these goods were mass produced elsewhere and delivered wholesale to all the river settlements.

It was Lucho's companion, Velisa, travelling with her mother and young daughter, who rescued the mission. This was the critical moment. We wanted, in some way, to answer for crimes that were never crimes. Not then. Crimes that could only be policed in retrospect. But there was no statute of limitations for the men who reported on the beauties of this virgin land.

Farne refused to be marched off on another choreographed tramp of instruction. She was determined to interview the headman (or business manager) of Pampa Michi. Fredi Miguel Ucayali had already delivered his impassioned diatribe on the iniquities of the Peruvian Corporation for Elena Mihas. The anthropologist composed a portrait of the man my daughter wanted to record. The chief was a witness, through the remembered stories of his grandfathers, to the malfeasance of an era many years before he was born. In his verbatim recovery of the sacred chant, Fredi endured and re-experienced the original pain.

The settlement chief dropped out of college, but still landed a position as an elementary schoolteacher in bilingual rural schools. Fredi was involved with the politics of place and he ran for office. 'During the early phase of the language project, the chief's deep-seated distrust of outsiders prevented him from establishing a working relationship with the language consultant team associated with a *gringa* (white woman),' Mihas reported. 'Eventually Fredi relented.' The chief saw his role as that of a strategist whose task it was to determine 'the socio-economic orientation of his community in the market economy'. Fredi led negotiations with travel agencies, in order to ensure a 'regular flow of tourists from Lima, who buy native crafts and bring money to the village'. His hobby was collecting framed portraits of himself to hang on the walls of his house. His set-piece performance was a restaging of his grandfather's story about the conquest of the Upper Perené at the end of the nineteenth century. This is what Farne was eager to record.

But it is no easy matter. The old prejudice against a *gringa* is still present, but disguised as an inconvenient head cold. Fredi has produced the shivers and sniffles that are a convincing response to viral messengers from the other world. Our role is to join the dance, gag down masato and spend some small change on lifeless trinkets. The established routine is to follow a guide down to the river, while he supplies the names of certain trees and demonstrates how the villagers manage their crops, and how they used to fish. Farne is not having it. Quietly, insistently, she asks for an audience with the chief.

Fetched from the compound of framed portraits, Fredi is unimpressed. The daily routines of tourism are beneath him. Visibly grumpy, in T-shirt and jeans, he is dismissive of our request. He doesn't want to talk. But then Velisa, an Ashaninka from the Tambo River, took our part. She brokered a deal: fees were discussed, so much for the twenty-minute version, and serious money for an open-ended pulpit denunciation. We paid and Fredi disappeared. To return, miraculously recovered, in cushma, with necklaces of status, red feathers, face paint. The chief was attended by the trickster in the one-piece, skin-tight black outfit. The sickly Dominic Cummings of village politics was transformed into a Lear of righteous indignation.

Fredi's sermon, a dithyrambic progression of atrocities, emphasised by fist on table, visibly moved Velisa. Tears coursed down her cheeks as she listened, seeming to hear these things, legends of origin, for the first time. The performance, entitled 'How the Whites Threw Us Out', was one of rehearsed spontaneity; something recovered, phrase by breathless phrase, and kept alive.

> Then hardly few days had passed, when those who would throw us out arrived, called by the whites "English", from the Peruvian Corporation. They arrived and surprised us in the middle of the night. They finished us. They made us flee. That's why we reside here, in this village that was built here. Because there were many of them, they completely threw us out. That's why we all fled, all those who had fear of them. That's why I live here in this native community of Pampa Michi.

People who had drawn their existence from the land could either retreat deeper into the jungle or escape, as many did, on rafts, downriver into unknown and unsympathetic territory. Those who remained were coerced into working on the Perené Colony. They were beaten and maltreated by the 'corporals' who acted as overseers. Cattle were turned loose to destroy the small areas where they were permitted to plant their own crops.

'We worked until seven in the evening,' Fredi said, 'but they cheated us. They paid with soap and clothes.' He speaks in Spanish and Lucho translates. Then the chief chants in Ashaninka.

'They arrived here. Before that time it was not like this community. We lived where we wanted. They found us, they insulted us. Our brothers were silent. They said that these savages were lazy, they didn't know how to work. When the natives threatened them with their arrows, they took our countrywomen. They took my grandparents, my great-grandparents. Our people ate the grass, *piri-piri*, or they drank it in tea, and they were strong. They fought, they escaped. The colonists chased them like savages, until they crossed the Perené River and reached the lands of the Peruvian Corporation.

'Our brothers returned. My grandparents and my great-grandparents had defeated the colonists. We can tell our children, our grandchildren. I am proud that I have native blood. What still hurts is what happened to my grandparents, my great-grandparents. They walked all over them. They died in these lands.

'I want a tourist centre, a civic centre, a hall for intercultural acts. Just as we were stepped on by these colonisers, there has to be a reward. We are the first native community near the town. We are forgotten brothers.

'This information is given so that the world will know. I want you to support me, my community, the civic centre. I want a centre with two floors, three floors. The truth about us must be known.'

He speaks in Spanish again.

'What will become of our children, our grandchildren? Our animals are disappearing. The child will not see with his own eyes, only in books. The trees are being cut down. Even the original trees that existed before any of the people. We want those ones.'

We heard and recorded Fredi's presentation. His heart-song. Velisa wept. Camila, laughing, scampered around. The old lady sat on the bench with her pouch of tobacco syrup. But my irrational belief was unshaken: *Arthur's apologia was published incomplete.* By the laws of this land, if I travelled in my great-grandfather's footsteps to the right location, rock or river or deadly cascade, I would make contact with my ancestor. He would talk to me. Those fancies had not been swept aside by the forensic research undertaken by my daughter in the archives of the Peruvian Corporation, or through her transactions with Elena Mihas. But the geo-political implications of the Sinclair/Ross expedition were becoming much clearer. Beyond the rigours of mountain and jungle, the maps and the books and lecture texts brought back, their commissioned task was to make the persuasive pitch for a major land grab. But was that all?

Arthur was well qualified to catalogue the flowers and fruits of this fertile Eden, while failing to recognise that the people living on it were an extension of the land.

> *Poor Chuncho! the time seems to be approaching when, in vulgar parlance, you must take a back seat; but it must be acknowledged you have had a long lease of those magnificent lands, and done very little with them… The world, indeed, has been made neither better nor richer by your existence, and now the space you occupy – or rather wander in – to so little purpose, is required, and the wealth of vegetation too long allowed to run to waste, must be turned to some useful account.*

Hard words for Farne to read. Hard sentiments for me to process. A conclusion that was impossible to exorcise without tracking the story back to Arthur Sinclair's own harsh beginnings in the aftermath of the Highland Clearances.

> *In short, this beautiful valley of the Perené has now become the property of a British Corporation, the concession having been duly ratified by the Peruvian Government, and arrangements are in progress for establishing a planting colony upon a scale never before attempted in Peru.*

It was only, months after my return to England, when reading a proof copy of *Inheritance: The Lost History of Mary Davies* by Leo Hollis, that I understood that Arthur was simply echoing a proposition outlined by the seventeenth-century philosopher John Locke. Locke was one of those authorities sampled piecemeal, in his leisure hours, by the young gardener. The stern English philosopher gifted moral authority to the predations of colonists.

'The natives were hunter-gatherers, who moved across the land and hunted on it, but they never settled, nor ploughed the soil,' Hollis writes. 'They could not, therefore, be the legal stewards. In contrast, the property owner ended their migrations, set up a house, tilled and sowed. They made the land productive rather than just harvesting Nature's bounty. This work justified the privileges of landlord-ship. The *Fundamental Constitutions* became one of the original texts of the British Empire, based on the notion of improvement of the land as a definition of property rights: the world was thus enclosed.'

BAJO MARANKIARI

'...but sooner or later there is a Reckoning – a "Judgment" that is to say a moment which consciousness will alter forever – to what? And how to prepare for that "Death"?'

– Allen Ginsberg, *South American Journals*

There are crossed flags of a new and provisional identity on the tribal watchtower. Flags are always bad news. But the spindly double-decker tower at Bajo Marankiari, with its thatched roof and angled ladders, is an attractive structure. Like a samurai war tower borrowed from the Kurosawa version of *King Lear*. A construct more elegant and true to tradition than any of the tin-roof tourist huts, up on stilts, in this straggling settlement between road and river. Alongside the tower is a pyramid of gathered wood, trees stripped and prepared to make a shelter for fire. The interior of this fire house, which should have remained bare, for overnight human habitation, has been stuffed with kindling. Here is a funeral pyre waiting on the return of the hunters, a furnace for communal roasting and celebration. Or for sacrifice.

The tower no longer scans the landscape for intruders. Unloved visitors are accepted as a necessary evil. They have a role to play. Once, family goods and personal belongings were burnt with the dead. The river people were migrants who could not afford to be dragged down with the weight of memory, the duty of honouring mere things. Jungle shelters, of no great significance, were simply abandoned when it was time to move on. They were left to be reabsorbed by the forest. Now they are leased to adventure tourists.

In early afternoon, the village is deserted. But we are still watched.

Paprika earth, reddish brown, has a few struggling plants and enough weeds to hold the interest of free-range chickens. The forest waits, patiently, hard against the last line of human habitation. Its time will come again. The Perené, wide and fast-flowing, stays a few yards from the door of my allotted hut. Lucho has already moved his belongings, and his adopted family – Velisa, her mother, Camila – into another hut. The huts come with narrow hard beds, a thin mattress resting on broken slats. The electricity doesn't work. But there is a television set hanging from the sweating wall.

Food is the first act. We are going across the river, onto a long sandbar whose dirty edge is decorated with a scatter of plastic bottles, black bags, and chunks of blackened wood from previous feasts. The boat, protected against the glare by a blue awning, is painted emerald green, but the green has flaked at the waterline, revealing an older layer beneath; a blue that matches the awning. The name of the craft, in block letters, is unreadable. From another time and another place. The river pilot, a warrior of steady, scornful gaze, is the only male from the village on this voyage. And, having brought us over, against and through perverse and dangerous currents, guiding the craft like a hollowed log, he does not step ashore. The beach is a reserved zone. A desert island of women gathering up wood, teasing it to catch fire and burn, arranging a metal grille across the biggest logs. When the yucca roots, wrapped in leaves, start to char, the ferryman, hands on hips, condescends to join the party. There is a young child, a girl, mute at his side.

We learn later, from Lucho, that the pilot is called Fidel Punchari: Shima-Shima (Fish-Fish) is his nickname. He is reputed to be a shaman. I never once saw him blink. Nothing deflects his horizon-scanning remoteness. He will neither acknowledge our intrusion nor engage with the indigenous women at the fire. Fidel's cushma and his red achiote stripes are permanent features, and not a heritage gesture, in playing a particular role for tourists.

The ritual of food preparation is laborious. That is the point. There must be no urgency beyond the business in hand, which is both established and amenable to improvisation. Hours in old currency, the currency of a world we have left behind on the road, are valueless. This is the time of the river. And we must adjust to it. The meal, this sandy feast, fixes our disparate group to one place – while the river, timeless and disinterested, rushes on. There is no single delegated cook. A barefoot woman in a blue cushma, with a big scarlet bow flopping from her jet-black hair, like one of the flamingo flowers we have seen on paths around Lucho's farm, has charge of the fire. She prods the embers with a beachcombed stick. An older woman, in orange, arms folded, offers advice. Velisa's mother has found a convenient mat of washed-up palm leaves, and scavenged a green paddle as a fan. Watching the progress of the meal, she mutters constantly, amused and scornful as, yet again, the fire dies and flares. Yellow plantains scorch, yucca is engorged and obscene. Secret meats have been stitched into secure leaf parcels. Lucho has a pink plastic jug of masato that he keeps to himself and a log on which to sit. He is a happy man. His job has been done. He has led us across the river.

Sentient clouds have closed off distance. The low hills are a framing device to emphasise the width and power of the Perené. The jungle waits, hungrily, behind the shingle strip at the edge of the beach. Velisa stands off, hands clasped. It is not her duty to intervene, without invitation. These are the hills Arthur navigated, before he came down to the camp of King Chokery.

> *Right below we could see the River Perené wending its way to swell the mighty Amazon, and our object now was to get down to this tributary. Unfortunately, we had lingered rather too long over this view, and it was four o'clock ere we felt inclined to move.*

We are all here now: intruders, their guide, Ashaninka. And the persistent ghosts of our various ancestors. We are gathered like the opening act of some *Tempest* play; self-wrecked and hugging the rags of past lives, cut off one from the other. We are trapped in moody suspension, forgetting how to breathe. The beach party has so much room in which to experience solitude. We are too superstitious to take the first step in an untried direction. But we will not admit our failure to 'remember a time before we came unto this cell'. There is an old Scottish term for this state of dulled reverie: *donsie*. Tired and travel sick, without headache and fever, but sick of being sick, distempered, divorced from nature. *Donsie* is everything Arthur denounced in the inhabitants he encountered along his way: Spanish-Peruvians, priests, chunchos. He found virtue only in the Chinese with their shrewd domesticity. And in plants.

'I'm no apprentice when it comes to remembering,' Kerouac said. But there is no ground for remembering on the sandbar. Or any guarantee that our picnic area will be above water the next day. The photographs of the indigenous people in Arthur's book are as vivid as the women in their colours poking at the spirit of the fire. They talk to the wisps of escaped smoke blowing back towards the moored boat.

Grant's camera is as close as we come to a clock. He allows aspects of the forgotten world to leak into this river scene by rapidly scrolling for news. He walks as far away from the hub of firewatchers as the sand island permits. He paces out the distance required for a good clean shot: if he can bring himself to set it up. A shot that will not intrude on the behaviour of the tribal people. But which will, in some mysterious way, reveal the story beneath the story.

A boy who might well have caught the attention of Roger Casement, another traveller who employed his camera as a device for masking his deeper interests, strikes off into the full force of the river. He leaves the far shore, Bajo Marankiari, and heads towards us, describing a wide curve. First, he must feint at going upstream, before letting himself be caught by the current and carried away. He does not waste an ounce of energy. He is swept along but he never offers an ugly stroke against the way the river flows.

This episode, barely noticed by the group around the fire, might indeed make a useful sequence when it comes to editing Grant's film. It has that 'slow cinema' quality directors love. The sensitive ones will let the whole thing play out in real time. Journeymen will treat the drama as wallpaper for an intrusive and unnecessary cutting-room voice. Or gasps of inarticulate celebrity wonder: 'Wow! Amazing! Look at *that*!' Does the swimmer know what he's doing? Of course he does. In the unreality of these waiting hours, an Ashaninka meal of welcome on a grey sandbar, I'm not convinced that anyone would move a muscle or raise a shout if the boy went under and was drowned. He was far enough out to be taken for a section of log or a bag of refuse displayed by the river for a moment before disappearing.

Half a mile downstream, where the sand gave up, the swimmer waded ashore. Farne was using her iPhone like a cosmetic mirror, showing a portrait she had taken to the silent but dignified young girl who looked so much like King Chokery's Queen, as captured by Arthur Sinclair. The girl's companion, a little boy with a close-shaven head and chubby arms emerging from a brown cushma, is much more excited. He reaches out for the person trapped in the screen of the alien device. His other hand is gripping a precious treasure, an untasted morsel of soft pink fruit.

Farne's progress through the topography of the Upper Perené has been tracked by Toby, back in London. She has managed to talk to her husband, most days, when reception permits. On the beach, contact comes and goes with the moody patterns of cloud. She is young enough, like Grant, to be of an age when blank time has to be mortgaged to the authority of digital devices. The nagging fear that wherever you are, you are not *really* there, or less there than the interior visions stored in the slender rectangle: *which is everything in this world, changing and revising as you watch*. And as you are watched by remote spooks and salespersons. Very soon, if it is not already here, the dark mirror will have swallowed your entire future. Everything is preordained, womb to grave. The irrational urges that dumped us on the sand island can be foretold. Stories write themselves. The watchers know the purchasers for every beer can, every biscuit packet draped along the banks of the river.

It could be the smell of the cooking, the imminence of the communal meal, but I ask Farne if she can call Anna. We are deep into the afternoon now and I calculate that it must be around breakfast time in Sedbergh. Anna is staying with her sister in Cumbria. At the point where the Ashaninka swimmer has to swing his arms in order to scramble the last yards to shore, I have a brief conversation with my wife, whose recent phone-camera is wildly surveying the angles of the ceiling.

'What! What? Who is this?'

'Iain.'

'Iain who?'

'Your husband.'

'My god. What's *happened*?'

If she let the door swing open on the bright northern morning, Anna would hear the famed 'madrigal' of another river, Basil Bunting's Rawthey from *Briggflatts*. With those mingled sounds from the two rivers, we had never been so far apart in more than fifty years of married life. Arthur is closer at hand, somewhere on the thickly forested ridge of hills less formidable, so it appeared, than the slopes above Sedbergh. But in all his Peruvian travels, in all the difficulties endured and overcome, my great-grandfather does not allude to wife and children. The point of reference is always Ceylon, an island, a manageable estate, a cultivated garden. When, task completed, Arthur returns home, there is no home. All that is left is a book recalling his adventures.

> *We had a very stormy passage. The January winds blew their worst as we approached the English Channel… The troubles of a tropical traveller do not, however, end by his being pitched into the middle of a cruel English winter. We may sing of our 'Merry England', while sweltering in the torrid zone, but a taste of London fog, a puff of Edinburgh wind, or a peep at the cold, grey granite of Aberdeen soon dispels the illusion, and confirms the truth of that saying that, after all, 'the Scotsman is never so much at home as when abroad'; and so I felt as I once more booked my passage by the familiar P. and O.*

Food was served, in portions generous enough to sustain hibernation, on plates decorated with blown pink roses. I feared for the porcelain, if we attempted to lift crockery burdened with such a weight of yucca, such steroidal chicken lumps on dark green leaves. Farne couldn't eat, but she made a nice show of picking. The women watched. Camila laughed. Everything was noticed, but nothing was said. When we were done, our shaman-pilot, standing upright, leaning forward, splendid in ceremonial cushma and necklace of jaguar teeth, took us back across the river.

The heaped pyre had now reached the first platform of the watchtower. Farne wanted to track down another of the Elena Mihas interviewees, an old lady called Bertha Rodríguez de Caleb. It was already dark when we set out and most of the villagers had retired to their huts to prepare for the evening's festivities. We have some rather vague instructions as to the dwelling where Bertha, an octogenarian, might be found. Such advice is often given as a trial of the enquirer's motives and sense of purpose. There will be false leads, just enough to deter those who are vulgarly curious. The testers don't know Farne.

Beyond the village that tourists see, there is no light. We have to concentrate on the placement of every step. There are outlying shacks with all sorts of improvised electrical arrangements and trailing wires. I suspect that this is where the workaday reality of Bajo Marankiari is to be found. There is a meagre candle glow, perhaps a television set, in the shack with the corrugated-iron roof, the one where Bertha is reputed to live.

We are lucky to have Velisa with us. The old lady, who turns out to be the mother of the village chief, Osbaldo Rosas, is reluctant to speak. She has nothing to tell us, she says. She does not *own* the stories we want to hear. She stands in the slit of the illuminated doorway, thin and frail in a long grey cardigan, bare legs chilled in the damp evening air. Her son has ambitions to take the settlement forward. He supervised construction of the huts in which we are staying, down by the river. He has a website now and he actively solicits tourists and the income they will bring.

A fire is started on the dirt of the open yard, a few bare branches and some soft white ash. Velisa squats beside Bertha, talking softly. With a protective hand on the old lady's shoulder, she is ready to translate. And to mediate. From somewhere, Lucho's companion has acquired a bunch of power plants, their roots stick from the cloth she has wrapped around her shoulder. Young Camila, head lolling in the gloom of prophetic smoke, falls asleep, supported by a log. The fire is important, Bertha indicates. It was once a thing to be worshipped. Farne extends the microphone.

'They called the god Yompiri. And they worshipped him because he gave them food. They praised their god and drank on his account. What they also worshipped was fire. My father told me that fire was our god. We would bring sticks and put them on a big fire. When they burned they would make a sound like *trek trek trek*. This was a sign that we were going to see something. That's when we would invite all the communities to pray to their gods on the following day. Then they would all come. These things were in the past until came the one from the United States, the messenger. He brought the book. He called all our fellow men from downriver. And they gathered here.'

Our guide, who was translating from Velisa's translation of Bertha's softly spoken words, said: 'That is what the lady is saying.' Velisa asked about the stone they had worshipped. And Lucho, for our benefit, paraphrased the reply.

'She says that after the god of fire came the god of stone. The grandparents and great-grandparents would sit and pray in a group. They were not allowed to talk, to fart. They had to pray in silence. If they farted it was because they did not believe. Nobody should spit, nobody should interrupt, nothing. The stone was their god. When the preacher came, he found them all gathered. He told them, "Stone and fire do not listen to you. Listen to me, here is the Bible." He said, "I am your god, now you have god, now you will follow me." And they believed him. All, all, many of them. They built a church and they prayed there.'

'That is what the lady believes,' Lucho repeated.

The density of smoke was more than could be explained by a few spindly branches giving up their heat. The smoke seemed to be coming from Bertha's nostrils. It had already put the young one, Velisa's daughter, into a state of suspended animation. It made us dizzy without stinging the eyes. Ominous shades came and went, like phantom projections from early cinema moving across the gauzy hangings that divided the yard from the living space under the corrugated sheet.

'The one who brought the Word, a white person, one of your fellow men, was called Pastor Fernando Stahl,' Lucho translated.

'Now I am asking the old lady why they called the pastor's village Metraro. She answers that she does not know, but many, many people came there. They would gather in a particular house. That is why they call it Metraro. Metraro is a place of meeting for Ashaninkas from all areas.'

The difficulty, as Bertha explained, was the lack of a pure water source. Her fellow men had to come down to the river. The Peruvian Corporation would not allow them to clear their land, in order to plant beans, yucca, plantains. The incomers brought cattle and let them trample the gardens and eat the beans.

The fellow men could not settle in downriver lands. The ways of the people were strange. They were not accustomed to these ways. They returned to Bajo Marankiari. They learned never to take goods or clothes from the settlers. The incomers brought sickness. The fellow men were forced to abandon their Iron House, a secret place in the forest where they lived away from women and where they fabricated tools. Now they worked for the company. They planted coffee. They worked like slaves, without reward. This was the civilisation the incomers brought, the Bible and debt peonage.

'There was one shaman. They say he fell asleep and saw that in this place there was the Master of Snakes, with the Master of Jaguars and the Master of Evil Spirits. The shaman said: "We will kill them." Many shamans came, they gathered together, drank tobacco syrup and fell asleep. That's why we live in peace, because shamans came and killed the snakes. Now we don't see them, all is well.'

In the smoke-thickened dusk, among women, we listened to how Bertha talked to Velisa, her soft voice whispering into the heart of the fire. The old lady is seeking, in the flickering shadows, the recitation that is part of her identity.

It was awkward to intrude into the choral exchanges of the two women, but I muttered my request to Farne. And she asked Velisa. And

Velisa asked Bertha. We had heard about the gods of fire and stone, before the coming of the Seventh-day Adventists who now dominated the settlement at Mariscal Cáceres. We had heard about pilgrimages to the Salt Mountain and pilgrimages to the cave where the bones of the pretender, Juan Santos Atahualpa (also known as Apinka), were laid. Would Bertha now tell us more about this man and her own experiences of visiting the sacred site?

Bertha said that her grandmother had seen Apinka when he was carried to a cave near Kishitariki, which is now known as Mariscal Cáceres.

'He was buried there, together with a mass of gold, which looked like bars of soap.'

The Ashaninka laid their champion on a bed of gold. They brought more and more bars until the cave was half-filled. Over the gold they put the skin of a cow and then the body of Atahualpa. Bertha's grand-mother showed her where the cave was to be found, but now the old lady does not remember. When the coffee plantation was made, only the owners understood where the grave was hidden.

'We do not know if the gold is still in the cave, or if it has been taken by those who were looking for it,' Bertha said.

'By Spaniards?'

'Perhaps.'

'By others who came later?'

'It is possible. They took away the weapons that had been left with the gold in the cave.'

The brother of Juan Santos, the one called Marinkama, is rumoured to have been buried close by, in the same hills.

'Wherever this smoke rises, that is where Marinkama is to be found. It is the smoke of the Iron House, where machetes and cooking pots were forged. So it was until the old way was lost. When outsiders came, they took away the gold. It disappeared. We don't know where Apinka's gold is. This was what we believed until outsiders and whites came. They ended it all. My grandmother told me about it, she lived in Apinka's presence when she was a child. She was in his service. When she was a young woman, she saw him die. Here it ends. I am more than eighty years old. My birthday is on the twenty-fourth of August. I have six children. Three girls and three boys.'

That night, by the watchtower, it was a very different and much wilder dance. And it did not simply conclude our first day in the riverside settlement of Bajo Marankiari, it ended all measurement by days. The blazing pyre roared and spat. We made a meal of fish soup and plantains down by the river. Then the drumming and the dancing began. The villagers circled the fire, faster and faster, chanting, and joining in with the chorus of songs they knew. Figures from the darkened huts flowed into the snaking circuit for a time, and then moved away, but the torrent of sound never lessened. We were part of it. And then we stood aside, on our own or in pairs, as we watched. Before we were gathered and brought back.

At some point, Bertha's son, the chief of the village, delivered a lengthy oration, perhaps for our benefit. It was outside the spirit of the fire dance, more like a party political broadcast. The discourse did not come, as with Fredi Miguel Ucayali, from anger at past betrayals, from the stories we had heard, but from an optimistic vision of the future. The new way, beside the road, in the hospitality industry.

After several hours, the ferocity of the fire relenting, individual figures stood out from the vortex of the dancers. Shima-Shima, river pilot and shaman, arms folded, directed the ceremony. The grave child Farne had photographed on the sandbar stayed at his side. Velisa's mother was swaying like an ecstasy clubber. Coming from further downriver, this party-loving veteran knew different songs. The Ashaninka of Bajo Marankiari welcomed her. They took up her chants and made them their own. When all her songs had been exhausted and honoured with laughter, the old lady took a pull from the pouch of tobacco syrup she wore around her neck, before offering a hit to the other women. They managed a few more staggering steps in the whorl of reeling figures, before falling to the ground in a pantomimed faint. To clapping and general applause.

Resinous smoke made a helix around what was left of the burning wood, a glowing pyramid with a golden candle at its heart. The smoke formed a reversed triangle against the night sky, the canopy of stars. Dancers slumped, following the old lady's example, settling to sleep around the dying embers.

On our return to England, Grant contacted Lucho to ask for a translation of the words of the endless chant. By that time, the village was cut off, isolated by police roadblocks. But the answer, on an unsteady Skype call, came back. Grant hummed and the two Ashaninka women picked it up. 'Kamarampi, Kamarampi...' Lucho improvised. 'Ayahuasca / Ayahuasca / I feel drunk / I see things / I see a jaguar / I see a snake / I see a salamander / Ayahuasca / Ayahuasca...'

THE WATERFALL

'Ma journée est faite; je quitte l'Europe… J'aurai de l'or: je serai oisif et brutal.'
  – Arthur Rimbaud, 'Mauvais sang'

The Advocate was telling me about the consequences of not having succeeded in quitting Europe in our company, while attempting to pursue his alchemical studies and trying, all at once, to fulfil his burdensome professional duties: poetic gold dust in an open hand, scattered to the winds of change. 'Insomnia has receded,' he said. 'I sleep less and dream more.'

But I no longer needed emails and letters. The Advocate walked in my sleep. By staying where he was, honouring his tasks, this man threw a long shadow. In those restless early morning shallows, under the dripping walls, on my broken bed, fighting to kick free of the tangle of mosquito mesh, I dreamed that I was exploring a narrow strip of sand, and coming to the point where I could look across the river and identify the place where my great-grandfather, the other Arthur, lost hours, days, weeks, at the camp of King Chokery. While waiting for the chief to respond to the ministrations of his trickster-shaman.

> *The palace was simply a thatched roof supported by a few jungle trees, and on a raised bench in the centre of the only apartment lay His Majesty, groaning. Our chief priest cautiously approached, unbuckled his flask, a sort of bladder he always carried well primed with rum – the only spiritual matter he dealt in. The tube attached to this he placed in the royal mouth, into which he injected a liberal supply of the spirit, which for the moment had the desired effect. The King, lifting his head, indicated that we might be permitted to lie down on the earthen floor at his feet, and there we lay, supperless and saturated with perspiration, till next morning. I arose,*

I need scarcely say, but little refreshed. But then the surroundings were so intensely interesting that I soon forgot my aching limbs as I gazed upon the marvellously beautiful vegetation. We were within a hundred yards of the river Perené, and after a bath in its clear tepid water I felt fit to tackle the manioc roots upon which we breakfasted.

As I walked the length of the beach, before the women started charring the yucca for our breakfast, I dreamed I was walking by a river. I dreamed the words that failed to summon an event that was happening before or after it had actually occurred.

There are chopped stripped trees left on the ground to act as benches, exotic chickens are pecking at the dirt around them. I don't notice any of the villagers going about their business, but I know they are watching me. The sand is fine-grained, a mortuary grey. The hills on the far side of the river are hidden in cloud.

I thought about my great-grandfather's namesake, the famous Arthur, Rimbaud, and the way he was done with vision and the furnace of language – lodging for a time alongside a Swedenborgian church in London and reading works by the mystic – in four short years of the most intense concentration and willed derangement. Then he travelled, to escape the pursuit of furies who demanded payment in blood and pages. For my ancestor the writing was a modest adjunct to his chosen career, a leisurely remaking and improving of colourful exploits, those endless voyages. From libraries and borrowed or stolen volumes, from restless, driven walks, Charleville, Paris, Brussels, Douai, from buried childhood tales of Verne adventures, from anticipations of Africa, the poet prefigured everything, the karma of piratical empires. In 'Mauvais sang' from *Une Saison en Enfer*, Rimbaud solicits (and denies) a personal history: 'If only I had forebears… What was I in the last century… My day is done; I'm leaving Europe. The sea air will burn my lungs; godforsaken climates will char my skin. I'll swim, trudge the grass underfoot; I'll hunt… *I shall have gold: I shall be slothful and brutal*… The whites are landing… The farce goes on! I could weep at my gullibility.' From such a glittering stream it is always possible to sift and extract whatever oracular pronouncements you require.

Nobody to be seen in the village or across the river in the unedited and plural past. But they are watching. Shima-Shima sees everything, before it happens. The villagers question Lucho. 'Is the old man looking for gold?' Speckles in the sediment are trash. There are no living fish to flash through the murky shallows.

Our plates are loaded. Another yucca feast. Yucca, plantain, catfish bones. No coffee, that devilish sacrament of the cities. Farne can't eat or drink. In my fatherly role, I'm concerned. We have a walk this morning to another waterfall, guided by Shima-Shima, the medicine man. Farne is feeling trapped by the pressure of what she has to organise, with every new action demanding soles not dollars, as Lucho originally suggested. She hasn't taken on fuel, her head is aching and the waves of this discomfort are felt by all. She is missing her therapeutic swims at Ironmonger Row. But she will shoulder her full pack and make the walk. Then, somehow, on our return, broker another set of interviews with contacts of Elena Mihas brought in from elsewhere. And all this on the evening when Lucho and most of the villagers want to settle around a TV screen for the final of the Copa América, Peru away to the home favourites, Brazil.

Grant, meanwhile, half-stripped, is sticking head and shoulders – and, more importantly, his camera – under the surface of the Perené, where everything is sullen and shifting, and lifeless. He could be panning for gold, but the villagers don't worry about him. He is not suspect, not dangerously old. And he could be fishing. It is the way I poke about, take snapshots, and make notes. Then stop and stare at nothing. I am a scarecrow in the rags of previous invaders who came with gifts and empty promises. Some of the villagers recognise, no doubt, that aura of possession, *shiretsi*: a dead person's unsatisfied spirit. Is that what I solicit? Or what I am projecting?

'Come on, come on. Let's go.'

The waking mood, as we trudge, in crocodile, along the shoulder of the busy highway, is melancholy. Sour at the edges. The damp laundry of the white clouds has not yet lifted from the forest. Things improve as soon as Shima-Shima takes us, without offering a single word, to the track through the jungle. Within minutes, so it seems, the

Trans-Amazonian road no longer exists. It has not yet been built. And the trees are reporting our intrusion. Without our guide we would be lost beyond recall; vegetation would shadow us, erasing our footprints, and eradicating all traces of our mischief.

My great-grandfather's language skills were rudimentary – like Rimbaud's early attempts at English – but he spoke fluent forest. He was alert to every shift in the grammar of growth.

Never had I seen such a variety of plants. It is one of the characteristics of tropical vegetation that plants of the same family are less sociable, as it were, than in cooler regions of the world... In the upper tributaries of the Amazon, the variety is almost incredible, for scarcely two plants of the same family can be seen growing side by side. Diversity is the rule, nature delighting both in variety and contrast...

There cannot be said to be any cultivation here, but we can see by the well-beaten footpaths leading to them that certain plants are more highly prized than others, and coca (erythroxylon) is one of the chief favourites. Around little patches of this plant the jungle is occasionally cleared away, and the coca leaves are carefully harvested.

The chief food of the Chuncho when at home is, however, the yucca (jatroba manihot)... which also obtains a certain amount of care and protection, in this case almost amounting to semi-cultivation. The plant may be freely grown from cuttings the thickness of one's finger, stuck obliquely into the ground. In about nine months the roots, the only edible part, are fit for use. They look like huge kidney potatoes, or roots of the dahlia, and taste when boiled something between a waxy potato and a stringy yam. Roasted they are better. Still, one wearies even of roasted yucca; for weeks I had no other solid food, morning, noon, nor night, and, though duly thankful for these mercies, I have no craving for another course of yuccas. Fish is the favourite accompaniment, though they do not despise a slice of wild turkey when obtainable, which is but seldom. Black monkey and white maggots are delicacies set before the king.

The shaman's face is blooded with a thick red achiote band, but he has left the necklace of ceremonial jaguars' teeth, worn for crossing the river, at home in his hut. The cushma for this expedition is more like a burlap sack, with a blue T-shirt underneath. A stout pair of hiking sandals on his feet. Shoulder bag for plants found along the way and a raised machete. Shima-Shima leads us, but he remains a man apart. The jungle expedition is an obligation of tourism, a new heresy to which he owes no particular allegiance.

The women, working together on the next meal, have been left in the village. Bertha Rodríguez de Caleb, the chief's mother, now in tribal costume, face painted, has joined them. Stalls have been set out with the tired geegaws first seen at Pampa Michi. Lucho's friend Velisa has joined the others. The children run about, waiting for one of the incomers to try a bamboo hammock. Or they stand, empty-eyed, dignified in their resignation. There is an easy system of adoption, whereby families, living deeper in the jungle, who cannot afford to support a child, will give it up to a better-placed couple, or even a single man of status in need of a servant. Or into the care and schooling of Adventist missionaries.

Shima-Shima climbs on a smooth rock to salute, with his raised machete, the continuing force of the waterfall: as Grant, bareheaded, bows to the muddy, bespattered pool with his gold-prospecting camera. This is a more modest cascade than the ones we have visited before, a sudden fall from a fissure in the rocks.

On our return from the waterfall, Lucho identifies and bags a plant that he fancies trying at the farm. Shima-Shima darts over a patch of pink and grey stones, like rubble sculpted at the whim of the stream. He has found an ally plant, a thin reed stem with a crown of leaves. Arthur Sinclair would have been enchanted by our guide. He would certainly have questioned him about the specifics of this plant. Was this the legendary ayahuasca (or *kamarampi*), 'vine of the soul': the inspiration for a new invasion?

As Mike Jay wrote in *Mescaline (A Global History of the First Psychedelic)*: 'Shamans and healers are increasingly visible, too, in the jungle retreats of the booming ayahuasca tourist scene around Amazonian towns.' Mini-break visions are available without the tedious and time-consuming odysseys of Burroughs and Ginsberg. Shamans, authentic or opportunistic, are a valuable resource. 'Even the strangest of their medicines might be worth its weight in gold.' But first the credit-card hallucinators have to overcome projectile vomiting and a shaming loss of sphincter control, spasms, convulsions, overwhelming visions produced to order 'in symbiosis with the western commercial market'.

Ginsberg was ready and willing to pay the price. He tapped into the pioneering yagé expeditions of William Burroughs and the ayahuasca monograph written by Richard Evans Schultes. 'Soul vine of Death Vine is a conscious poison,' Ginsberg said. 'The veil lifted and I saw, rolling thru a strange black chaotic dimension, a vast serpent, an endless Dragon, huge as dream – ocean liners – rolling thru dream oceans... lost in time so far back, impossible to see.'

The conjuring of Ginsberg's ocean liners sparked Grant's interest. His film, as I understood from what little I knew about it, evolved from my 2004 novel, *Dining on Stones*, in which a broken-down writer, exploiting a travel journal published by his great-grandfather, squats in an East Sussex concrete block built to look like a cruise ship. Endgame hallucinations, fed by dump-bin DVDs and home movies, play out over the grey fact of the English Channel. 'A vision,' as Ginsberg said, 'of some Golden Age Dimension, of permanently goldlike corporeal golden Olympiads.'

Quietly, intentions conveyed by body language, the tall angular Grant cultivates the short powerful Shima-Shima. In some drowsy lull, siesta or early evening, the filmmaker will be invited to visit the sha-man's dwelling and to witness the growth of a cultivated jungle vine. I have a sense that this episode, the vegetative séance, could be a way out of the narrative cul-de-sac of the film. Grant realises that he has left his spectacles at Lucho's farm. His waterfall footage may be a little fuzzier, closer to the visionary cinema of film poets like Stan Brakhage. 'First we must deal with the light *of* Nature, then with Nature of Light.' Brakhage liked to quote Blake: '*with*, not *through*, the eye.' Lucho declined to make any special arrangement to collect and return the spectacles. Collateral damage. 'Come on, let's go.'

Returning to the village on a riverside track, Shima-Shima pauses to wade out and dip the shallows. He wants to demonstrate how the Ashaninka fished before Padre Sala introduced them to dynamite. He will catch our lunch with his quick hands. He knows the best spots. He catches nothing. And moves on, without a ripple, upstream. The fish do not respond. The fish are not there. The river has been poisoned by the spillage of material progress, the short-term ruthlessness of industrial farmers and foresters.

After stepping back from the Perené and following a path made from sharp pebbles, we come to the bean fields. But beans are never served to incomers. Over a lunch of blackened yucca, which she does not eat, Farne negotiates with Lucho for translation duties. Can she persuade Gregorio Santos Pérez, another of the Elena Mihas contacts, to give an interview in the late afternoon? Lucho is not happy about this. The villagers will gather to watch the final of the Copa América on a big TV screen in a hut that also serves, some of the time, as a refreshment halt with severely limited stock. For beer, you have to tramp back to the highway from which Lucho has just returned with a six-pack to get him through the game.

It was important to Farne, despite the inevitable post-prandial energy slump, to sit down with the man who was one of the most significant associates of Mihas. Gregorio, who lived in Santa Ana, had grown up in Bajo Marankiari. He had been schooled by Adventist missionaries and he now worked as a peripatetic teacher. It was his ambition to have the Ashéninka Perené language recognised by the Peruvian State.

Grant set up his camera in an open hut, the longest in the village, the one used for meetings and ceremonies. A tentative and filtered light streamed through the pale thatch of the roof. But there was nothing to film. Lucho had stalked off, swinging his six-pack with obvious intent. And Gregorio's motorcycle had not yet arrived. We waited in the lazy boneless slump of a lost afternoon.

We saw the dust rising from the road before Gregorio, all business, skidded in. Fredi Miguel Ucayali, the village chief at Pampa Michi, had dressed to deliver his performance, a denunciation of the invading whites and the brutal enclosures of the Peruvian Corporation. Bertha Rodríguez de Caleb, in her long cardigan, in the smoke, guarding secrets, had channelled the voice in the fire. Bertha's son made the pitch for a new politics of tourism. But Gregorio was lost to us in the shredded Babel of translation, paraphrase and combat fatigue. Lucho was at his most terse and dismissive. He told Farne that she was asking the wrong questions. It was not going well. And I knew from the teacher's football shirt – CLUB ALIANZA 1901 – that he would be as impatient as the rest to get to a screen before the big game.

On an earlier and more propitious occasion, Gregorio talked to Mihas about 'the bone spirit of the old times'. The one who existed when traditional people lived in this village. The spirit called out from deep in the forest when fellow men went hunting for partridge. If males hear the voice of that spirit they cannot escape, women can. The spirit chooses to copulate only with men. The spirit looks like a monkey. It bends men right over. And it enters them.

Gregorio offered instruction in how to be a good fisherman – by the use of the plant called *sábalo*. Pounded yucca was set on the hook. Fish were caught, but not eaten. Sections of fish, rubbed with hot pepper, were placed on the arm. Fiery meat had to be held in the mouth until the saliva stopped coming. There are many established rituals to learn. But these customs have been lost.

The techniques introduced by Padre Sala survive. Unlike the fish. Arthur, launched on his raft voyage, was appalled.

> *Merrily our rafts glide down the river. Here and there we have a few yards of rocky rapids, requiring careful navigation, but beyond an occasional ducking nothing of importance happens to us. Natives, armed with bows and arrows, creep from below the trees and look at us with evident wonder and some suspicion, but offer no active hostility; or we suddenly come upon them as they are shooting their arrows into a passing fish. Our padre here astonished the natives by throwing in a charge of dynamite, the result of*

which was five or six dozen fine fish on the surface within a minute. This diabolical and unsportsmanlike mode of fishing is, I am sorry to say, daily practised by these Convent fathers. There was a tremendous scrimmage in the water after the dead fish, and by the time it was over the sun was sinking behind the trees.

Gregorio was joined by his father-in-law, Elías Meza Pedro. Born in 1935, Elías worked for twenty-five years on the coffee plantation. He described himself as a 'slave' of the Peruvian Corporation. He had been coerced and beaten by the 'corporals'. Cattle had been turned loose to destroy village gardens. Elías was the senior living witness to these horrors. He had authentic memories and experiences of the last days of the Colony. Weathered under an Alianza cap, Elías shut his eyes and looked at the ground. His son-in-law sat at his side, offering encouragement. The memories were owned and given without shame. Elías smiled, but his gaze was far away, beyond the hut and across the river. Beyond cameras and microphones and moleskin notebooks.

The old man had his own version of the Apinka story: native resistance, cave of gold, secret burial at Mariscal Cáceres. He associated Juan Santos Atahualpa with fellow men living at Yurinaki, the place where Arthur stayed at the court of King Chokery. Apinka was going to cull tribesmen from downriver by beheading them. But he was ambushed and pierced by an arrow. 'So it ends.'

Bajo Marankiari was an abandoned plague camp, nothing stirred among the huts and stalls seen by visitors, or out in the scattered houses and shacks on the hill above. A good crowd had coagulated around the TV screen in one of the shops. Most of the villagers were in their performance cushmas. They rested on chairs after the latest round of dances. Some of the younger ones wore branded T-shirts from local music festivals. And the more acceptable versions gifted by visitors. The official drummer was ready. The principal cheerleader had silver-grey hair, like a ducking in sheep dip, and a flauntingly white shellsuit. At first, there were outbursts of sporadic enthusiasm, men jumping to their feet, women wailing, assaults on the drum, but soon the mood changed to inattentive resignation. Fifteen minutes and it was all over. Everton scored for Brazil with a neat volley, after a cross from the right. The Peruvians reverted to their designated role: plucky losers. In an adjacent tourist booth, the vendor, head cradled on her arms, slept on a table dressed with bead necklaces and brightly painted wooden parrots.

Excitement flared to a crescendo with a Peruvian penalty, scored by Paolo Guerrero, just before half-time, after the ball brushed the hand of Thiago Silva. One minute later, Brazil were ahead. The drummer was not required again until the seventieth minute when Gabriel Jesus received a red card. His departure was acclaimed. But the day was already lost and the village settled back into a state of vegetative suspension. This story would take its place among so many others in a litany of betrayals, gold medals buried where they would never be found. *Ad-vín-cula! Gallese! Guerrero! Carrrrr-illo!*

So much talk of fathers and grandfathers, the misdeeds of ancestral hunters posting karmic punishments towards unborn generations, made me conscious of my paternal failings. I know that is the primary role of the male, after those first delightful years, to be the one who gets it all wrong. We disregard unspoken requests. And selfishly pursue our own indulgences, work, books, instead of anticipating and responding to the slings and arrows of troubled adolescence. But Farne needed to eat *something*. While the others were resting and sorting out their digital downloads, I made a short recce along the river and up to the highway. I found a café that promised to serve dishes that did not include yucca. Collecting my daughter, I led her back to this place on the promise of burger or pizza or chicken. Earlier, when I sniffed around, the bar was rammed with football supporters. Now they had vanished, slunk away into the night.

I had a beer and Farne ordered steak – *with no yucca*. We had plenty of time to chat and to consider where we were now placed with the whole project. Farne had achieved the major interviews on her list and confirmed much that she had plotted before leaving London. I was happy to have picked up solid tracings of Arthur, but I still had no idea how our disparate narratives would fold together.

The steak arrived. And it was good. Farne didn't touch the compulsory yucca. This nourishment should carry her for the next few days, the climax of our expedition. Tomorrow it would be her birthday. I remembered that first one, the day of her birth, so well. The ambulance breaking down. *Ambulance?* Like a taxi service from Hackney? And the way we walked the last few streets to the old Charing Cross Hospital, before picking our way over the fallen drink and drug casualties of the corridor. The friendly urban cockroaches. To be born here! Assaulted by light at the heart of a great pulsing metropolis! Looking out, if there was an out, on the bogus Eleanor Cross from which all past and future journeys were measured. Being so fortunately centred – by the accident of our having attended early Natural Childbirth classes in this hospital – Farne Sinclair was obviously going to spend her life thinking of travel to distant lands.

Back in the village, at Lucho's insistence, Velisa had prepared a jug of creamy piña colada, coconut milk and rum, to wash down the weight of the evening repast. Farne made her excuses and retired. Dogs howled. Children played around the table. I dozed in a hammock, listening to the river and brooding on the wilder Arthur, poet *maudit* and colonialist. Rimbaud, the years of vision now deleted from the record, was in the living hell of Aden. Could he have coincided with his namesake, Arthur Sinclair, the traveller who was yet to become an author? In my ghost play from the days of Empire, Arthur would sail to Australia, enjoying months in which he could yarn with Conrad. He would fashion humorous anecdotes around the French trader whose career as a poet was aborted and forgotten.

> *At the end of five days we arrived in Aden, the Gibraltar of the East, and quite as essential to Britain, as a strongly-fortified coaling station, important in its position at the entrance into the Red Sea… Aden is, moreover, a very ancient and still populous town, containing some 40,000 inhabitants. But of all the miserable, rugged, sterile-looking places we have seen, none can compare with Aden. Originally volcanic in its nature, there is not a particle of soil, much less vegetation, to be seen on its grim, naked rocks,*

> *not a drop of fresh water to be had for love, and precious little for money...*
> *I saw a number of camels, each loaded with fifteen dozen Guinness's stout,*
> *toiling away into the interior.*
>
> *'What do you think of Aden?' I said to a Yankee tourist whom I had*
> *observed stalking over the place for half a day without opening his mouth.*
>
> *'What do I think of Aden? Why, I guess Satan must have somewhere*
> *to throw out his cinders!'*

Rimbaud, having escaped from the ignominy of France and the hot shame of the hormonal poems, was beginning to dig in as a man of business. On 22 September 1880, he wrote to his family. 'I am very much *au fait* with the coffee trade at present. The boss has complete confidence in me. Only, I'm badly paid...'

Coffee, the awful grading and sorting, was his punishment. But a good topic for bantering conversation with the phantom Arthur, en route to the plantations of Ceylon. The same ruin lay ahead for both of them. 'Epizootic has destroyed everything here, the coffee crop is zero,' wrote Rimbaud. 'The peasants are crushed by the requisitions of every kind by the horde of starving men... I don't fancy that they can collect more than 20,000 thalers, by dint of extortion – and these extortions are already being practised on ourselves!'

Rimbaud wrote only of debts and distances, facts, wrecked expectations, and the utter impossibility of returning to Europe. My great-grandfather laboured, too hard perhaps, for human interest, tall stories to keep the prose frisky, to lift mere journalism from the page. Describing the former poet at this point in his career, Edmund White said that 'perhaps the only sense of accomplishment he derived from his gunrunning trip was an article published in a French-language newspaper coming out of Alexandria, the *Bosphore Egyptien*. The article – in the form of a letter... – commented on the recent situation in Abyssinia and Harar.'

Arthur Sinclair had no difficulty in having his letters finessed into articles for newspapers in Aberdeen and Colombo. Rimbaud met with indifference and refusal. When, after parting from a tearful manservant, he made his final grim voyage back to Marseille, amputation and death, the ship was called the *Amazone*.

MULES

'Lord, make me as faithful in my sphere as Samson is in his.'
  – The Adventist missionary, Fernando Stahl, on his favourite mule

It was breaking up nicely now, just the way it should in a story, and just the way that has to be misrepresented, or subtly disguised, in an upstanding record of Victorian travel. There was unspoken and unacknowledged history. Arthur's branch of the Sinclair clan were confirmed Jacobites. The Ross tribe were established placemen of the German king. The twin leaders of the Perené expedition, having begun to trespass in Eden, were at each other's throats. The forest took its leisurely revenge, gifting the intruders with blistered tongues, arms swollen by insect bites, rotten food, nightsweats, paths that circled back on themselves before vanishing; untrustworthy guides, sodden bedrolls – and tragic mules scored and drained overnight by vampire bats. The animals suffered at their tethers, no longer able to bear the necessary burdens of civilised travel. Holy beasts! Driven on by unholy men. Falling by the wayside, tumbling from vine-rope bridges, loaded with impossible sacks and boxes, the mules never repined. They remained faithful to their grim contract and a trail with no ending.

The commissioned surveyors, jealous for credit, hardly dared to sit against a tree. They had to stay on watch, watching each other, like the crazed prospectors in *The Treasure of the Sierra Madre*. They squinted and sniffed. With bloodshot eyes, they waited for their rival to falter and show weakness. They gouged poisonous observations into secret notebooks, so that they would be the one, the solitary survivor bringing back the final version. There was nothing around them but claustrophobic vegetation. Shrieks of unseen birds. Rustlings of monkeys. There was nobody visible to register their tortuous advance, but they knew, like B. Traven's gold hunters, that savage eyes were always watching. 'Long before he has seen them, the Indians have left the tracks and crept into the bush... From water channels, from behind hillocks and rocks and bushes the eyes see every movement and every step the stranger makes.'

This is the madness that comes before the last planks of sanity part. The trigger for Sinclair and Ross, as is traditional on desert islands or in prison camps, was food. They had laboured over the Salt Mountain, hacked and slithered to the point of vantage on the ledge of the hill, with the promised land opened before them, before plunging once again into reeking fetid darkness, down towards the river. The characters of the two surveyors were revealed in their subsequent reports. The third man, P.D.G. Clark of the Royal Botanic Gardens, Peradeniya, remains a mystery. His handwritten report to the Peruvian Corporation has never been published. He is the silent one watching the watchers. We must appoint him agent of a higher authority, a government spy.

The crisis arrives with the approach to the settlement of King Chokery. Men and mules are separated.

'Having again committed the fatal mistake of getting too far ahead of our luggage, we had to repeat our experience of the preceding night, and go wet and hungry to our beds, which were made of a few freshly-cut palm leaves spread on the ground,' Ross reported. 'The following morning, as neither food nor anything else had arrived, I set out, accompanied by Mr Clark, up that fearful mountain in search of our mules, and to get some quinine.'

They have fallen out of step with the stately mule dance. Ross enlists Clark and makes no mention of the older, senior Scot: Arthur Sinclair. Hairline cracks in the strategic alliance are becoming fissures. My great-grandfather lies where he is, gagging on yucca, and polishing his picaresque anecdotes.

> *To scramble through such a confused mass in daylight tries the best of tempers. You can imagine what it was for tired men in the dark.*
>
> *Ashamed to think how we had again been befooled by the dissembling priest, we plodded on, shouting till we were all hoarse, and listening only*

> *to the echo from the opposite ridge… But our strength and patience were getting sadly exhausted, and every five minutes we had to sit down to breathe; the perspiration pouring from us in little streams.*

It is my impression that it was Arthur who called these halts. And far too frequently to satisfy the more thrusting, fact-chasing Ross. While my great-grandfather made notes on orchids, speculated on the utility of coca, and fantasised about a good brew of highland coffee, the younger men, after a night's fitful sleep, dragged themselves back uphill in quest of the mules.

Ross is as driven, as hard for verifiable information, as Rimbaud in Yemen, Djibouti and Ethiopia. In Africa, the former poet stripped language to the skeleton, ruthlessly suppressing metaphor and vision. He requires technical manuals, shipped out by his obliging mother. He sends a 'commercial and geographic report' to his Aden employer, Alfred Bardey, now returned to France. It is published in the papers of the Société de Géographie in Paris. And read at a meeting of the society on 1 February 1884. Charles Nicholl in *Somebody Else (Arthur Rimbaud in Africa, 1880–91)* describes the report as 'brusque, lucid and accurate'. And dry as a ship's biscuit pressed from volcanic ash. As with Ross, the motivation is practical not literary: a primer for future exploitation.

'We wandered that day in the forest,' Ross continued, 'got two doses of quinine from the road engineers; and meeting a man going with supplies to the encampment, we purchased all he could give us, namely, a tin of lobsters, one pound of cheese, and a bottle of Pisco. On this Mr Clark and I supped; we lit a fire and lay on a heap of grass, being disturbed at 2 a.m. by a heavy thunder-shower. Having my waterproof, however, I lay there, and at 6 a.m. we set out, scarcely able to move, in quest of our mules. At 9 a.m. we met them, opened a box, swallowed each a tin of Brand's chicken essence, cut a piece off some ham, and set out for the Perené again, taking with us something to eat for that night.'

To eat, certainly, but not to share. Arthur went hungry, husbanding resentment and waxing lyrical about the potential of this fertile and unexploited garden – once those inconvenient natives had been schooled to harvest some staple other than the eternal yucca.

> *Tantalised by thorny creepers, tripped up by gnarled roots, rising again only*
> *to have our hats knocked off by an overhanging branch – elegant fern trees*
> *and beautiful palms may be there, but we are in no mood to admire. We*
> *now come to a newly-burned clearing, intended for yucca, as we afterwards*
> *learned. It is not by any means the first clearing we have scrambled through,*
> *but this had been so badly lopped that the fire had only succeeded in burning*
> *the leaves and blackening the branches.*

He is out of temper, with this place, the task, his companions. With
life. Is this the bad journey that will finish it, the one that all the writers
are looking for and hoping to provoke: please god make it worse, make
it more difficult, but do not let it end? Not yet. Not now. Rimbaud
the trader, respected but forgotten in his elective exile, his staging post
to nowhere, learned languages, the customs and beliefs of natives and
occupiers. In letters sent back to his family on their farm, listing the
latest setbacks, he would stress: 'In the end as the Muslims say: It is
written! That's life: It's no laughing matter.'

Written, yes. But written *where*? And by whose finger? For Rimbaud,
with his back-to-front career and double life, with a deleted future,
the mortal shiver was registered in four years of intense and furious
activity. And movement. *He* was written. It wrote him. And wrote
him out. Then, painfully, with courage, he lived it all again. With no
requirement to be happy about it. There are no enigmatic smiles in his
three photographic self-portraits.

I began to suspect that it was written for me, mistakes, reflex habits,
inspirations, in Arthur Sinclair's 1895 book. I mentioned to Michael
Moorcock the neat alignment of *In Tropical Lands* being published in
the same year as Conrad's first novel, *Almayer's Folly*. When I contacted
him, the prodigious London author was lodged in an exile of his own:
Bastrop, Texas. With his library, his toys and mementoes of Notting
Hill. Moorcock said that 1895 was a propitious date. He understood –
and even inhabited by way of his multiverse – the period more thoroughly than anybody I knew. 'I sometimes think of building up an
1895 collection,' he told me. 'I already have a lot. It was the end of the
three-volume novel and the start of the six-shilling novel and authors

no longer had to compose that padded "middle volume" George Eliot complained about. So it's bye-bye Mudie, hello Modern Novel.'

He goes on to list *The Time Machine* by H.G. Wells, George Meredith's *The Amazing Marriage* (one of his personal favourites), three books in feverish output from George Gissing, *Terminations* by Henry James, *The Red Badge of Courage* by Stephen Crane, the first performance of *The Importance of Being Earnest* by Oscar Wilde, and *Jude the Obscure* by Thomas Hardy. It was a good year for obscurity, for complicated, clotted and digressive narratives.

It is always written. Moorcock lifts his head from the laptop to look out of his Texas window. 'Storms are raging while a programme on tornadoes runs on the telly. I still have two novels to complete, *Stalking Balzac* and *London, My Life*. My Kindle has broken down and it appears that Amazon have run out (no imports from China).' In his separation from the city of his heart, Moorcock still shredded the *Guardian* for usable quotes, but now he took it online. Like Grant Gee, slipstreaming our folly, in the Peruvian rainforest.

Infuriated by the inadequacies of the road being laid over the salt trail, to open up territory for commercial activity, Arthur strikes the construction gang encountered by Ross and Clark out of the story. If they are not in the book, they do not exist. He must have noted evidence of their activity, as the straggling expedition followed Padre Sala down towards the Perené. But it suits his narrative to move directly from the ruined shack of Juan Santos Atahualpa to the camp of King Chokery. When we picked our own way, uphill to Mariscal Cáceres, the road was still in progress. That was its essential nature: perpetual construction, with or without resident road crews. The crews established a camp, they sold luxury foods to travellers. They moved on or they moved back. Slowly, the road developed its own microclimate, its fruit peddlers and patient predators. Its holdout guerrillas and its chemical entrepreneurs.

We hit the brakes, just in time, to avoid obliterating a band of locals excavating a broad ditch, an uncivil scar, right across the provisional highway. Shoeless energy pirates were running a cable, from further uphill, down to their huts. Foraged shelters had been built as nests around disconnected television sets. Every time a vehicle approached, two or three of the men would scoop dirt back into the trench. After the car had passed over the temporary hump, they would start the process again. And wave.

But Arthur's distemper goes beyond the confirmation of political incompetence and the corruption of priests. He is getting old. The road is harder. The mules are lost. There will be no more grand expeditions. And you can only return to Scotland once: to die.

Learning the steps of the mule dance was an initiation into the Peruvian interior; over the spine of the Andes, across the arid lands, and down to the tropical forest. Arthur had travelled many miles, on horseback, between scattered coffee plantations in Ceylon. But this humble pack animal, the highland mule, was the engine of frontier colonisation. Fernando Stahl, the hardy Adventist who baptised legions of indigenous converts in the waters of the Perené, regarded his own faithful mule, Samson, as a helpmeet and disciple; a being of equal status, let's say, with the native missionaries who assisted him in the great task of capturing and disciplining unredeemed souls. It was no easy thing transporting Stahl through the wilderness. Fernando Santos-Granero, quoting a man called Lepecki, said that the Adventist's face 'bore no traces of spiritual inclination and that his somewhat obese shape reminded him of those of a good old beer drinker who likes to eat well and tell not-so-proper jokes'.

The missionary's followers were attracted by the confident announcement of the Second Coming of Christ and the imminent destruction of the colonists, their haciendas and plantations. 'Stahl was a master of calculated conceptual integration.' Riding lonesome on a buckled mule, the solid Yankee figure in the big hat was a prophet from the future crossing a lunar desert. His beast, picking his delicate way over rocks and swamps, was a detail from an Old Testament frieze. Stahl honoured the mule as a relative of the animal carrying Christ to Jerusalem and crucifixion. Knowing all, suffering all, the mule obeyed what had already been written. And what must now occur.

'I prayed that God would keep me on the right way, then I let one of my mules go ahead,' Stahl wrote in his travel journal, *In the Land of the Incas*. 'Many a time that day, this leading mule would take a course that I felt was wrong. I would try to stop him, to turn him back, but could not catch up with him, so had to follow on after him. At times, deer would spring into view. It was an altogether wild country.'

The inherited wisdom of the mule leads Stahl to a place that seeks to hold him and absorb him. But he is too American, too restless. An old man is waiting. He offers the Adventist a gold mine, if he will return. But he cannot do it. It is written. And he is not there.

Mules facilitate the dance of trade and exploration, in a fashion that Stahl approves. He does not approve the communal and inebriated dances of the indigenous people.

> I thought of old Brother Salas and his wife, who were leaders in the
> dances for many years. His head was marked with a hundred scars from
> the many battles he had taken part in; and when we first met him, he
> was almost insane from the use of cocaine. At the very first meeting we
> held among the Indians, he threw away his coca leaves.

Stahl promotes the integrity of the lowly interspecies mule (Adventist convert) over the neurotic pride, the high breeding and nobility of the (Catholic) horse introduced by the Spanish conquistadors. The mule, fathered by a male donkey, a jack, on a female horse, a mare, seems like the fortunate result of eugenicist experimentation: a creature bred to slavery.

William Faulkner is the unchallenged poet of mules. He acknowledged that they were 'obsolete before they were born'. Their hybrid vigour made them suited, their exploiters reckoned, for servitude as military porters hauling cannons, or as cheap (and disposable) transport across difficult terrain. Scots and Protestant English had to overcome a residual prejudice. They associated mules with papist iconography. Mules were favoured in Latin America and all Catholic countries. Only Jews, hawkers and gypsies kept the animals in England.

The two Peruvian Corporation surveyors, repeatedly and competitively, make reference to their mules. It is Ross who notices, after a night when the animals have been released to graze, 'that several of them were bleeding freely from wounds inflicted by vampire bats'. Later, the same day, they cross the Chanchamayo River. The bridge is managed without accident. But when they come to the Tulumayo River, as Ross records, his mule tumbles into the torrent, with the loss of papers, books, camera and dry photographic plates. Evidence has been destroyed. And lectures diminished.

At the conclusion of their adventure, my great-grandfather will have to be as stubborn and as stoic as a mule to make it back to Lima. When he sets out to cross the Andes for the second time, his identification with the suffering of the burdened animal is complete.

> *It was a weary zig-zag; my mule and I got sadly out of breath, but it had to be done… By and by the heart's action seemed to fail, and I suddenly collapsed, slipped off the saddle and lay down on my back, my mule gasping for breath beside me.*

———

More than ever an adept of silence, Rimbaud approved the conceit of mule as metaphor. In pitiless conditions, in the furnace of Aden, in train for trade, or trapped in the frustration and ennui of Harar, the man of business writes home: 'I'm still working in the same old dump, and toiling away like a donkey… If I don't write any more it's because I am very tired.' This perceived sanctity of the mule comes from our perception of its limitless endurance. The eyes start from the head in a glaze of terminal exhaustion. But the light does not die. Man and beast continue together. They hold to the trail.

On his prodigious caravan journeys, with guns, trinkets, coffee, always *against* the land, and visited with biblical torments, the muzzled poet kept a mule, but elected to walk beside it; sharing hot breath, whinnying when required. The Italian explorer Ugo Ferrandi said that 'although he had a mule, Rimbaud never made use of it on his expeditions, and always went on foot, with his hunting rifle, at the head of the caravan.'

Sunken-cheeked, shadow-moustached, with adapted tarboosh sweat-glued to shaven skull, this ultimate poet-pedestrian marched himself, almost literally, into the ground. Always in flight, from the ferocious tramping of adolescence, running from nowhere to anywhere and back, to Alp-conquering European epics, touched on in letters but never demeaned into travel literature, Rimbaud punished his body with demands he refused to inflict on his mule.

Two years from the last breath, the trader sent an urgent message to Alfred Ilg, Swiss fixer at the court of King Menelik II in Entoto: 'I earnestly confirm my request for a very good mule and two boy slaves.' The urgency was authentic. But the request was an hallucination, a telegram from another life.

While Sinclair and Ross are fretting over the spoils of the Peruvian expedition, Rimbaud is writing himself out of history in a deathbed dictation. His right leg is useless, knee swollen like a sick melon; the agonised limb, hip to ankle, a blatant invitation to the surgical hacksaw. In his terrible retreat, he had to be portered by a team of natives, whose wages he docked when they set him too violently on the ground. The poet is no longer himself, barely human: he cannot walk. Walking was more necessary than writing. 'I try riding on a mule, with my bad leg tied to its neck, but after a few minutes I have to dismount and get back onto the litter, which has already fallen a kilometre behind.' At night, rolling off his perch, he scratches a hole with broken nails, in which to defecate.

Propped up in a paying bed at the Hôpital de la Conception in Marseille, the delirious trader confuses a deathwatch companion, his dutiful sister Isabelle, with his servant boy, Djami. (Charles Nicholl described Djami as 'the illiterate scribe... who weeps as he writes.') Now, in his fever, Rimbaud is always leaving for Aden, arranging the caravan and issuing orders. Waking from a few seconds of feverish sleep, he confirms, over and over, his request for a very good mule and two boy slaves. Now he can walk again, as far as he needs to go, on the missing leg. He can follow every step of the dance of the mules through virgin deserts towards a shining city of gold.

Post arrives at the hospital from friends, associates and trading partners in Africa. There is a final letter from Constantin Sotiro. 'Brémond has unloaded 2,000 fraslehs of coffee at Aden. Savouré has gone up to Harar with his money and his wife, a white woman… Be sure to come back soon, and ready to learn to dance.'

Having achieved the camp of King Chokery – who is neither a king, nor called Chokery – it must be time for Arthur and Ross to be separated from their mules? Surely the animals cannot be taken on the fast-flowing Perené, with its treacherous currents and its rapids? There will be no standing room on flimsy balsa rafts – even if the 'King' can be persuaded to order their construction. This drama plays out a short distance downstream, and across the river from where I halt on a sandbar at Bajo Marankiari at the conclusion of my morning walk. However hard I stare I can conjure no images of the lost past.

The mules and the river cannot coexist. Mules belong to the road. When no road is available, they anticipate it. They smell the river and retreat. Ross and Clark, moving out ahead of their luggage, are disorientated. They have turned back, searching for pack animals and quinine. Arthur gives himself up to contemplation of the 'great interminable forest'. First the mules will disappear. Then the priests. And, finally, the King and all his companions. My great-grandfather will be alone with his foolishness. It is written. But he is no longer the author of his own story.

> *The night was calm, and a death-like silence reigned all around, not even a jaguar growled, not a monkey chattered, but we could now hear the distant murmur of the water… Nearer and nearer we drew to the spot, and at length, through an opening in the jungle, saw the swinging of a fire stick… The gentleman turned out to be the King's medical adviser… The King was prostrate with fever.*

The healer gives suck from a bladder of rum. The invaders have to wait while the King recovers his health.

> *We made daily excursions into the forest, with increasing interest and admiration… After a weary wait of eight days the royal patient began to show signs of recovery, his subjects coming in crowds to call upon him,*

> *bringing presents, generally large white maggots, about three inches long,*
> *which the King greedily ate.*

Just as we were held for a few days at Marankiari, acclimatising to the dissolution of our received methods of measuring time, so Arthur passed his temporal quarantine, lost to the comforting presence of mules, those familiars of the road. He was a plantsman, not an anthropologist, although he remained as open as ever to strange customs, behaviour that might energise his commissioned task: the duty of portraying the Ashaninka as primitive, forest-dwelling innocents.

My great-grandfather's late-Victorian satire, almost as eccentric as *Alice's Adventures in Wonderland*, Perené not Thames, demanded a comic 'King' and a pantomime court – as if the only valid account of the riverside settlement was a heavy-handed parody of the Saxe-Coburg-Gothas at Windsor. Ross treats human encounters of the forest with cooler precision, but a similar set of engrained prejudices. These bearded outsiders, with their maps and cameras, have been adequately rewarded, and issued with a gold card for the botanical larceny otherwise known as 'progress'.

'During our stay we were visited frequently by Campas Indians of the lower Pangoa districts, who, leaving their balsas at this place, cross the hills to, and return from, the Cerro de la Sal with their supplies of salt,' Ross said. 'Nearly all of them, on noticing us, came to shake hands, exchanging with us the salutation, "Añyee", signifying "friend". These Indians are dark, copper-coloured, of middle stature, muscular, and wiry; many, too, are not unpleasant-looking, though the features of some plainly indicate that one should beware of them. They are greedy, inquisitive, and laugh continually at everything or nothing. Raimondi says, "They are very hostile, and no friendly relations can be entered into with them." Mr Clements Markham describes them as "a barbarously cruel tribe of untameable savages."

'Thanks to the introduction of Padre Sala to Kinchoquiri, one of their chiefs, who had numerous friends along the banks of the river, we suffered no molestation, and I found, from my experience of them, though at times morose, sullen, suspicious, and shy, they are not without intelligence and humour, nor would it, in my opinion, be difficult, with tact, to civilise and make them useful. Kinchoquiri had resided near La Merced, and was, therefore, not altogether ignorant of the outer world.'

'Kinchoquiri', the punt Ross takes at the name of the chief of the Perené settlement, is a more useful approximation than Arthur's comic appropriation of royalty. There were no kings in this territory, before the coffee enclosures. There was an established Ashaninka chief called Kinchori who was photographed when he visited Lima in 1914. Arthur's Kodak portrait *might* be the same person as a young man. But the biography of their host remains obscure and unrecorded. He is outside written sources. 'Kinchori' is a name associated with places further downriver.

An Ashaninka woman called Elena Nestor de Capurro talked to Farne's contact, Elena Mihas, about the 'Masters of the Hills'. And about a mysterious being known to hang from trees, disguised among vines, having the general appearance of a crop of wavering threads. This entity overturns river craft and seizes the passengers.

When the canoe returns to its upright position, the passengers will walk along the river called the Salt River. When the *kiatsi* hears us, he will seize us… The Macaw Hill is over there. The one who is watching will make us disappear. So it was in the past, when the masters of this place were created. This is a story of my deceased husband, and my father-in-law, called Manuel Mayor Kinchori, from this pueblo, who was Chieftain Kinchori. He is dead already. Here my story ends.

Arthur's camera portraits of plants have the ambition of becoming paintings. There is a teasingly sexual orchid from the banks of the Perené, almost ready to be transported to Paddington by Lucian Freud. Trumpet-mouthed orchids are more confrontational than the modest capture of the bearded surveyor himself, gun at the ready, perched on his balsa raft. The portraits of King Chokery and his young Queen still burn through time: native people who are not yet prisoners of gifts. Not yet inducted into the labyrinth of debt peonage. It is an obligation, when it comes to the moment of our own departure from the village, and exchange of tributes, to show these photographs to the men and women of Marankiari. And to gloss over our connection with the expedition that enclosed this land.

MARISCAL CÁCERES

'All those who enter the green hell looking for black gold are ultimately damned. The jungle seduces them, the jungle retains them, and if they try to escape, the jungle brings them back.'

– José Eustasio Rivera, *The Vortex*

So much to remember and more to forget. Things left undone and things that can never be undone. Families. Histories. His story. My story. Mystery. In the improvised kitchen zone under the trees beside the river, the women chattered as they prepared breakfast on the morning of our departure, Farne's birthday: 7 July 2019. Velisa, her mother and her daughter, would be travelling with us, back to Santa Ana, on the other side of the Perené, and up the tortuous road on which Arthur spent his scorn, to the Adventist settlement at Mariscal Cáceres. And to the conclusion, we hoped, of one part of our quest. The shrine or cave of Juan Santos Atahualpa. Apinka of the forest.

Our departure is something to be marked, where our arrival had been an infliction to be endured: the sudden appearance of strangers carried an afterglow of residual melancholy. The empty watchtower was a symbol, an architectural feature fit for photographs. And a coign of vantage from which it was possible to get a good shot of the river on which no invaders could be expected.

There was a white cloth on the breakfast table. When I came back from my walk, Farne was already in her place. She was dressed, hair tied back, shining, before Lucho arrived. This was her day, to be enjoyed in the certain knowledge that she had made the fiction of a Peruvian journey real. The essential recordings had been achieved and now we were easing into the final stages, heading for river and rapids, and traces of the coffee plantations: she could afford to think of home and family.

I handed over the package entrusted to me, before we left London, by Toby. There was a necklace and a pair of self-made and decorated cards from the kids. It was too much, this abrupt visitation from elsewhere. The requirement to be present in two places at one time: preordained duty against the pull of the heart. She ran from the table, back to her hut, in tears.

But Lucho was in excellent spirits. Today was the apotheosis of 'come-on-let's-go-vamos': there would be a feast at Mariscal Cáceres, a challenge we had to fulfil, and then, if all went well, an excursion to find the cave of Juan Santos Atahualpa, local champion of the indigenous and dispossessed.

While we waited at the pristine table, Lucho took his accustomed seat with no reference to what the women were doing or the collective excitement that seemed to be building. Our guide laid out his private collection of cups and potions.

'I tell you, there is a cure for cancer. I could *market* a cure.'

Lucho indulged my interest in these morning concoctions. The bowls and spoons and packages. He lifted a forefinger for emphasis.

'I get up, middle of the night, drink baking soda and squeezed lemon. Always. To scour the guts. No mercy. *Every* night. Wherever I am sleeping. Baking soda and lemon. Burn out the dirty tubes.'

While he talked, eyes blazing, of this radical Trumpist alchemy, our guide stirred a thick glue of mushroom powder, with some additions of his own, to set him up for the day ahead. He had little screws of paper in every pocket of his fisherman's waistcoat. Silver wrappings and a big knife. He looks around, claps his hands. And I register, with some surprise, that our guide has taken onboard the date of Farne's birthday. He has ordered a presentation suitable to the occasion. He is waiting, impatiently, for my daughter's return.

As she approaches, repaired and recovered, with a bundle of neatly wrapped packages, the gifts we will make to our hosts, the village women emerge with flower-pattern plates held high, deep dishes of golden promise. It is like some Indiana Jones jungle sequence from

Spielberg, enacted and made extraordinary by laughing humans. Some of them wear long orange cushmas, overalls for the roofless kitchen, and some wear the deep-blue scrubs of a surgical team. The four plates, set down and meticulously positioned, are heaped with geometric arrangements of sliced fruit: colour co-ordinated and glistening in a syrupy lacquer. A freshness you can anticipate before ruining the display with a spoon. An outer ring has been balanced against the steep lip, halved orange slices, thicker than split thumbs. Then chunks of mango and melon and banana, graded and set off with shining buttons of black grapes and red grapes.

Food that Farne can and will eat! The women have met the challenge. And they press around as she signals her delight – as much at their courtesy as at the avoidance of more yucca and plantain. Velisa's mother, draped in a dark brown cushma, sits with us at the table, lifting her bowl close to her lips and sucking every choice segment from a spoon that darts into the fruit and is then held, while she sniffs and swallows. Working the spoon with extreme rapidity, like chopsticks, the wise old lady looks Chinese. With that kind of fatalistic, world-knowing humour. But that's not the end of our shocks, because Lucho has also arranged for cups of coffee to be brought out: bitter, black and steaming, the spurned concoction of the Perené Colony overseers was never touched by the people of Marankiari. The women press forward to watch Farne as she tastes and rinses and offers heartfelt thanks for this, the very best of gifts. In the madness of London, her shared-desk labours, her home, her husband, her children, boxes of interesting coffee selections, arriving every month, keep her fired. And afloat.

Gathered around to witness their triumph, my daughter eating and drinking with only a little more measured consideration than the rest, the women applaud, before breaking, spontaneously, into a breathtaking act of cultural appropriation: a dignified and tuneful performance of 'Happy Birthday to You' in Ashaninka. Farne has the presence of mind to record it on her iPhone. There will never be a birthday to match it. The laughter! The light! The colours! Vlaminck blue of the aprons. Burnt orange cushmas. The glowing brown of the old lady's complexion. She belongs as much to the sediment of the river as to the gardens and the forest.

But was it an appropriation by the Ashaninka or by the Adventists who inflicted the song on them? And what about copyright for unauthorised public performance? Warner Chappell Music thought they had secured the rights to song and lyrics attributed to two American sisters for twenty-five million dollars. The jingle became the highest earner in history. There are a lot of birthdays: think Marilyn Monroe serenading Jack Kennedy. With her specially tailored lyrics. And a figure barely contained in a dress stitched from bright lights and the defiance of gravity. In 2015, a federal judge ruled the copyright claim illegal. The Ashaninka were clear.

Farne is such a favourite with the women. They like the way she stands her ground and keeps control of the cash. And the way she shows the portraits she has taken to the subject children. One young girl, about nine or ten years old, never smiles. When the women clap the birthday song, she remains quite still, dignified and alert, with unblinking eyes. Then she moves back to her place beside Shima-Shima: dutiful, sad. He lifts an arm, as if to envelop her in an invisible cloak. She has been taken into his household, as property, servant or student of secrets. It is not clear. She is a watcher. If I lie in the hammock, she will come close and wait, but she will not rush to engage like the others. There is a tradition, we were told, of the authorised *jalador de niños*, the plucker (and supplier) of children.

Fernando Santos-Granero said that 'white people had for years stolen Ashaninka children either directly or through the mediation of their indigenous partners.' Children were regarded as a renewable resource. 'The capture and removal of children and young women, plus the killing of the adults that resisted or could not escape in time, was a constant drain of Ashaninka vitality.'

Confronted by a camera, Shima-Shima's adopted daughter, in red football T-shirt, with ink-black hair and long eyelashes, has an inward expression; the reluctant acceptance of the fact that her portrait has been committed to a machine. Taken from her. And carried away. The young girl has, as Farne points out, in producing the print we have brought with us, precisely the look of King Chokery's Queen when she was photographed by my great-grandfather. Hair falls over the forehead. The lips are pursed. The women of Marankiari are excited to confirm the resemblance, holding up Arthur's capture and pointing at Shima-Shima's new jungle-acquired daughter. Shima-Shima himself is vastly amused. It is agreed that the people of Chokery's village are indeed their fellow men, brothers and sisters, cousins across the river of time.

The village chief, Osbaldo Rosas, now appears: a man with a duty to perform before he returns to his office and more urgent business. Osbaldo arrives at the moment when we are producing our gifts. Someone has alerted him. The chief takes his position at the head of the table, to give us a formal blessing and to let us know how we can help to publicise available facilities. How we can contribute funds required for a tourist centre.

The first gift, a choice selection of English jams and marmalades, chosen by Farne at Heathrow, with the notion that she was reprising

Arthur's experience on the river with King Chokery, was accepted with no great show of enthusiasm. The pots were distributed among the women. Lucho said that he could see how fruits of the jungle, imaginatively processed and promoted, with commissioned designs, could be a winner: Atahualpa's Golden Shred. Farne quoted a couple of lines from Arthur's book.

My own gift, not taking account of Adventist sensibilities, fared no better: a bottle of malt whisky from the Scottish Highlands. There were no convenient priests to snatch it away. It began to feel as if we must make an unregretted departure. But the chief was delighted by the final gift, one I was embarrassed to produce: a plus size black T-shirt, embellished with LON/DON in upper case lettering, red and blue, inset with schematic versions of Big Ben and Tower Bridge. Osbaldo laughed, holding the cellophane-smelling garment against his chest. He called for a round of applause. The T-shirt was then folded, returned to its packet and removed by an attendant.

Then we came to the tricky part: the revelation of Farne's photocopied documents. The confession of our ancestor's devastating intervention in their tribal history.

There had already been some animated discussion among the women over the portrait of King Chokery's wife. It could have been a mugshot for a Twitter account. A promotion for the Ashaninka brand. They recognised the markings on the face and the status of the necklace and bodily adornments. But it was the copy of the original contract between the Lima government and the Peruvian Corporation on which Osbaldo swooped. He had no idea that such a thing existed. Along with Arthur's Perené photographs, this legal document was received as a valuable contribution to the archives of the village. Osbaldo removed all the papers, at once, to be scanned in his well-equipped hut (and business office). Every page would be put on record as evidence for the prosecution.

We depart on the best of terms. Beyond the dangling key ring of coffee beans and gold-veined orange stones, the object from the trinket table originally chosen as a suitable exchange, Osbaldo brought me a woven shoulder bag. It was very strong and I have used it constantly, on walks around London and elsewhere. We also received a crate of bananas, a jar of some fermented liquor and the salutes and embraces of all the villagers. Waving and calling, we bumped off on the road to Mariscal Cáceres and the golden cave.

———

It is a twisting and dusty progress and the only incident of note is when Velisa calls a sudden halt, darting away into an unfenced plantation and straight up a tree with no convenient lower branches. Perched comfortably, as if born in a nest, she strips the greenish balls of fruit. I don't know what they are called. There is no sense of private property, the fruits of the earth are available to all who recognise their virtues. Velisa fills the pockets of her waistcoat and packs the rest into a lifted skirt. Lucho says these things are good for dyeing the hair and for dissolving the bones of infamous fish that violate unwary swimmers through anus or penis. The fruit also breaks up kidney stones. Velisa, happy with her bounty, harvests everything that has fallen to the ground.

Arthur's catalogue, 'Flora of Peru', is comprehensive. It is the most useful dividend of his Peruvian journey. He speaks of 'undescribed varieties' of walnuts growing on the Perené. Of grapes from the same location that were 'a pretty deception'. He notices 'bitterwood' and *Xanthoxylon*, 'sometimes called the toothache-tree'. He admires the *Tabernaemontana*: 'A very remarkable tree growing about 40 feet high, yielding good fibre, also good milk.' He investigates parasites 'unique in Peruvian vegetation'. He enquires, he observes. But does he ask the right questions of the right people? And will they tell him? I wish I could bring my great-grandfather back, to travel alongside us, so that he could tap the botanical and herbal knowledge of Lucho and Velisa. And Shima-Shima.

'The wildest savages I ever saw appreciated their plantains,' Arthur wrote. He could not step around the rebarbative preconceptions of his period and his culture. The bearded Scottish colonist has been admitted to the Garden of Origin: he is 'alive with excitement' and lost in wonder at its immoral fecundity. 'The question here naturally arises, Why has this rich country been allowed to remain, from the creation to the present day, in a wild and desolate condition?'

But there is an obvious conclusion: because there are older gods than your gods. Other beings inhabited this Paradise where plants, stones and animals shared a common language, common knowledge, before the expulsion, before that cursed primal couple sampled the fruits of the magic vine. My great-grandfather listed, photographed and sketched multitudes of flora and fauna in ways I could not begin to attempt, but he would not break the accepted commandments of Empire, or the contract with his own harsh upbringing, the task imposed on him by his London employers. Arthur Sinclair had come to this place with ruin in his train.

Sensing that Velisa's spontaneous harvesting of the fruit was a more accessible secret than anything we would find at Mariscal Cáceres, I turned to Farne rather than to Arthur. We had reached the point in our travels, and in my personal pilgrimage, where I began to understand that I should listen to the living before the dead. Go to my clever daughter and not to the words in a forgotten book. Those who came after me contained within them seeds of the wisdom of the ancestors as well as intimations from the future. There was no time for this until we were in London. Then Farne made it very simple. She tapped the oracle and interrogated Lucho by way of his digital account. Our guide was, as I had suspected, the ultimate shaman of adventure tourism. But the questions had to be put in the right way, through a Facebook group, and at a safe distance.

Velisa, it seems, had harvested a medicine plant called *huito*. It was used, as Lucho had already mentioned, to dye hair in the favoured blue-black colour. It was also used to dye the skin. When it is drunk as an extract – and I'm sure our guide had samples in his pocket – it will dissolve the stones in your stomach. Or take care of Candirù, or Canero, the tricky opportunists swimming up the anus and infiltrating open wounds.

On their return to the farm, Velisa planted some of her plunder. The trees were growing well. Lucho attached a short film for Farne to view. Here indeed was knowledge that remained just out of Arthur's reach: *the use of huito was a ritual*. The potency of the plant had to be approached through rhythms and waves of sound: heartbeat drumming, accompanied by the pounding of a staff dangling with shells. A young boy sliced the fruit with his machete, then grated the segments to achieve a fine grey powder. Juice was squeezed into a bowl. It was painted by the women over the body of a baby, a girl. The naked infant, barely able to stand, accepted these attentions with equanimity. She seemed to know, before birth, that this was her initiation. She tasted the sharp juice. Another child was painted and daubed with white feathers. There was more drumming on a tortoise shell. Before the group, women and painted children, began the dance. All this – sound, time, ritual, respect – were part of the power of the plant. There are no shortcuts.

Metraro/Mariscal Cáceres, the twinned Adventist settlements, shimmered in a mid-morning heat haze. The village was drifting about its business, a day of competitive sport for males and females, in such a sleepy and distracted fashion that I was more than ever convinced that the location was protective of a great secret. Arthur's party had blundered through here, too tired to make an adequate survey. They were tricked down false paths by the dissembling priests. Fed an outrageous fiction about the Inca Atahualpa, the Scottish surveyors were diverted from further investigation of Apinka, the Ashaninka divinity. And the golden cave or shrine of his avatar, Juan Santos Atahualpa. A compensatory myth was offered to trespassers to keep them away from more substantial revelations.

Unlike Bajo Marankiari, where we were always watched, even when the village seemed to be at siesta or totally abandoned, it felt as if, although fully visible as we wandered from netball court to football pitch, unable to find a spot on which to settle, we were never really there. We were without consequence. Existing, if we registered at all, in a discrete time frame. We had not yet departed, but our relevance, if any, would only be weighed after we were gone.

There was a low perimeter wall beside the area where the fiercely committed netball competition was taking place. I knew how long it took to prepare a meal, two or three hours at least, and I had already investigated the village, the schoolhouse, church and medical centre, the tidy gardens with their rows of beans and their bushes of coffee: I wanted to find shade and rest. The animal energy on the court was exhausting. Young women in the uniforms of their various schools, in shorts or kilts, moved swiftly and athletically, without pause, without screams and obscenities, but with furious grace. It would be impolite to pause for more than a couple of moments. I ambled, more comfortably, around the painted rectangle of the much less intense male football match.

Lunch is a trial for participating visitors, with advice coming from all sides, from donors and diners and unoccupied witnesses. A collection of root vegetables and varieties of hairy yucca are being ruthlessly hacked into chunks on the mud floor of an outhouse, which is set conveniently close to the tilted sentry box with the hole for relieving urgent bodily functions brought on by the feast. Between deft surgical strikes, the machete is plunged back into the ground.

Lucho intended to bring pork as his offering, but he remembered, just in time, that this would not sit well with Seventh-day Adventists, strict followers of Fernando Stahl. He went early to market and chose an adventurous range of prehistoric mud creatures, all bone and spine, along with a dressing of open-mouthed piranhas showing off a rictus of needle teeth. The fish simmered on a rusty grille. They made good smoke, keeping villagers, still occupied at a distance, informed about the progress of the meal.

Entitled diners, emerging from nowhere, took their places at a table set up in the shack. They received, with nods of appreciation, deep bowls of thin salty broth in which floated the skeletons of the ancient fish, revived by a potent brew of herbs and vegetables, and on the point of returning to life. After the soup had been gargled and gulped, with companionable lip-licking relish, social dialogue can begin. A spilling platter of guinea pig in peanut sauce was reserved for Lucho's driver, a man from another place. With a status, through his role in our guide's entourage, closer to that of a town person. The broiled guinea pig winks in collusion on his couch of sticky rice.

Beyond the cooks, respected elders of the village, and younger ones who fetch and carry, all the figures we had already met and interviewed at Marankiari manifested to take chairs reserved for them at the table. Bertha Rodríguez de Caleb and Elías Meza Pedro told different stories by daylight. Their versions of the depredations of the Perené Colony held firm, but we were now on plantation land. The Adventists paid mouth service to their medical and social benefactors. But their relationship to Juan Santos Atahualpa and the cave was completely different; those Marankiari hints and memories belonged to night and smoke. In different places, as we knew all too well, we are different people.

We had arrived, by force of circumstance, at the pivotal point of our journey. We had to deliver what we understood of Arthur's 1891 expedition and its consequences. And to confess ourselves, as we sat among them, as being his inheritors, now practising a revised, but no more reputable form of cultural colonisation. We were eager to carry away not physical trophies and surveys intended to ease the path towards enclosure and exploitation, but stories. Appropriations. We wanted to steal, as the old people recognised, their most sacred legends and symbols. The hidden gold that was a condition of light.

What can we offer in thanks for the food? The old ladies of the village, joined by Bertha and the mother of Velisa, sing their songs. Elías chants an Adventist grace in Spanish. The chief of the village, Benjamin Medina, in blue Homeric T-shirt, joins us; a parrot perched on his finger. From the files, we take out the portrait of our ancestor, Arthur Sinclair, and Arthur's photographs of King Chokery and his young wife. They are passed around with little comment or interest. Lucho is dismissive. These faded ghosts are downriver people, not fellow men. Not true believers.

But when Farne, generously, donates her own copy of the government contract with the Peruvian Corporation of London, and the documents revealing the exchanges between Fernando Stahl and the company, the chief is mesmerised. Here is hard evidence that Stahl was allowed into enclosed colony land on the understanding that he converted the indigenous people and made them amenable to the laws and conditions of labour. The thick wad of paper, to be carried away and evaluated by Benjamin Medina, rewrote history. The parrot shrieked, picking up on a rising zephyr of excitement.

It had been hinted, in our original negotiations, that if all went well at the meal we would be guided directly to the shrine of Juan Santos, a short walk from where we were now sitting. But, in the aftermath of our gift, exposing the duplicity of Stahl, everything changed. Benjamin now offered to lead us through the jungle to the golden cave. We must return immediately to our car and follow the two men of the village on their motorbike.

The biker was a slight, stringy character, sallow, with nice residue of bandit beard. And a red cannabis cap improved by a bright green leaf and an italicised boast: *dope*. Surely we had been here before? This moment was part of the dream related to me by the Advocate on our walk across London. My contact was locked down in Brussels, no longer able to sleep. His dreams were getting away. He predicted a long circuitous drive past plantations of blackened bananas, over mud tracks fast reverting to streams. He knew where we were going, but not how the story concluded. He told me that he was able to turn the pages of a future book, but whenever he reached this point, the jungle penetration, all the letters fell from the paper.

There was a resting space to which we kept coming back, on the forest path, a steep descent. We were stalled, gripping vines, while the chief in his flip-flops, wielding his machete, rushed ahead, out of sight and, finally, out of our hearing. The clot of the blue T-shirt, a stolen segment of sky, was absorbed in a curtain of liquid greenery. The cracking of branches became the warnings of unseen birds. We were so alert here, engaged in our senses, sensually replete: we knew we would never move again. The cave was no longer accessible. That neat resolution of the quest was beyond the range of our permissions. And it felt right. We were contributing, for the first time, in a small way, to the depth of the silence.

I understood and appreciated failure. Benjamin Medina had made his gesture and shepherded us to the only position where we could hear, but not approach, a thundering waterfall. The cave remained a mystery and better so. It had taken me fifty years to find my way inside the Goat's Hole Cave at Paviland on the Gower Peninsula in South Wales. The site associated with the misnamed 'Red Lady of Gower' held secrets much nearer to the myths on which I had been nurtured as a child. Better to have come close, as Arthur did, and to have staggered on, in the dark, towards the river.

Back in the car, we seemed to be travelling in another direction entirely, perhaps bridges were down, sections of the track lost to landslips. I felt that, as penance or exorcism, we were being conducted by the motorbike tricksters around the entire perimeter of this section, the outermost limit of the Perené Colony.

The chief slows, parks his bike. He presents us, offering no explanation, with an ugly concrete building associated with the former coffee plantation. Huge mats have been laid out for the drying and raking of the cherries. Further up the track from this sinister relic, which recalled Tasmanian houses of correction inspected by Arthur, are domesticated gardens with well-tended sections reserved for coffee bushes. They look like Bethnal Green allotments and are worked by smiling women, happy to pass the time of day.

You have witnessed what we had to endure, the chief implied. And how well we live now. But he said nothing. He walked straight ahead, flanked by Lucho and the bike jockey in the *dope* cap. He moved through a green tunnel, alive with scarlet blooms, in a golden afterglow of revelation. Benjamin ran his bare arm against the coffee bushes. And then, out of nowhere, with no preamble, we were confronted by an imposing pyramid. An obstacle it was impossible to steer around. Judging from the way the chief froze, hands forming an arch across his chest, he anticipated and indeed required the photographic recording of this moment. The Mediterranean blue of his T-shirt set him apart from the deeper, flaking blue of the paint splashed across the base of the structure.

Here, the chief implied, is the Spike of Truth. We did not know what we were looking for but I think we found it. This road-hogging, overstated symbol reminded me of the Masonic pyramid tomb in the grounds of St Anne, Nicholas Hawksmoor's encoded Limehouse church. The Metraro pyramid was taller, closer to heaven, cruder in surface and proportion: more like a maquette for another notorious 'spike', Renzo Piano's river-dominating Shard. This unexpected and unavoidable concrete boast marked a significant territorial frontier, but it lacked the ambiguity of our Limehouse pyramid, speckled with the subtle shadowplay of established London plane trees. And dressed with erased inscriptions and symbols. The impression on the coffee plantation road was of a construction more akin to the apparent openness and the buried finances of the Shard. The more visible, the more mendacious. When you are forced to see a thing from every street in a city, you know that it is not really there.

The strangeness of the day tips the biker. He has to lean against the unyielding support of the pyramid, in the belief that it will not slide away or topple over and crush him. The pyramid does have a purpose: it is a tribute to Fernando and Ana Stahl, and to their mission, spreading the love of god through the highlands of Bolivia and Peru. Whether the natives signed up willingly or not.

A new plaque was unveiled by Lael Caesar, an editor of the *Adventist Review*, in 2014. Caesar spoke to the assembled leaders of the church about the solemn privilege of standing on the ground where 'God's pioneer' had once stood. Stahl could bask in the evidence of his achievements, the schools and medical centres and plantations. The monument was erected in 1999. Stahl's manifest sword of truth, Caesar concluded, had 'disrupted Satan's organised hostility'. The pyramid distributed a long shadow across a forbidding and resistant geography. It carried revelation to more than 430,000 newly baptised Adventist believers.

'This is a monument to conspiracy,' Lucho said. 'Stahl must have been a Mason, like all the Jesuits, senators, drug barons and presidents in Peru. But it was a good ride today. We will do much more tomorrow. Come on, vamos, let's go.'

PICHANAKI

'Some dead seem more dangerous than others.'
 – Michael Taussig, *Shamanism, Colonialism, and the Wild Man*

Pichanaki was the abrupt end of a long hot road. It was the final fold in the 'zone of interest' map Lucho colour-copied for our enlightenment. Beyond Pichanaki we were free to make it up as we went along. The Perené, flowing east, would all too soon be absorbed into two other rivers, the Rio Ene and the Rio Tambo: two distinct and frequently opposed cultures. The Tambo joined the Ucayali and eventually became the Amazon. The received wisdom from published sources, and from casual conversations overheard at roadside halts, was clear and simple: 'Don't go there.'

We disappointed our guide, when we announced, after bedding down with due appreciation in the jungle and staying in huts beside the river, that we fancied a couple of nights, at very modest expense, in this new border town hotel. The notion being that if we were approaching the crisis in Arthur's narrative, and about to be carried downriver on a 'sea of bones', we would prefer to do it decently scourged under a hot shower and in clean shirts.

Local history made great play of remaining Maoist guerrillas striking informal and insecure treaties with shadowy drug traffickers. Politicised city boys, mountain folk and disgruntled rural schoolteachers banded together to wander through a riverside terrain to which they did not belong. They were a threat because they had lost the war without being formally defeated. Their oppressors, better armed and financed, swept around them, to leave them in situ but redundant. There were no exchanges of unfriendly fire. No dialogue in a common language. The violent idealists were marooned in the wrong television channel, a subtitled Amazon Prime series that was never going to be renewed. The Gran Pajonál was a wilderness aspiring to the status of eco-park or game reserve. It was an Adventist protectorate, supplied with the migrant processing plants of a worldwide drug economy, fattened on rumour. Rumours were the engine of protection. And they were serviced by dangerous airstrips not always to be found on the map.

Michael F. Brown and Eduardo Fernández, in *War of Shadows (The Struggle for Utopia in the Peruvian Amazon)*, write about the sudden appearance of fifty guardian angels, 'all with Winchester rifles'. The angels tell the indigenous people to board canoes that are waiting on the Perené. 'God wants to be seen at a stream found further downriver.' The Ashaninka embark as instructed. They are taken to Ucayali. And are converted into plantation slaves.

It did not improve matters when the government took back land in the Perené Valley from the Peruvian Corporation. The farmers had already been pushed onto the steepest and least accessible hillsides. 'Special Project' economic status, funded by the World Bank, led to the squeezing of production from thinning soil. Hillsides were stripped. Brown and Fernández reported that 'the sharp red of the lateritic soil was clearly visible in land slips and deep erosion cuts.'

A shaman called Pichári made a prophecy: 'Just the other day, a dead man came back to life… That's when I began to understand that the time is near. As my grandfather told me, there will come a day of darkness, without daylight, without sun. When you see these strange things, it's because the end approaches. We will be changed into something else… But I tell you that it will be this way. Because that's the way my grandfather told it… Here it ends, the story of my grandfather. It takes him to tell stories.'

In order for the name of Pichanaki to come into existence as a viable destination, the shaman revealed, certain people had first to be annihilated. 'They had killed that enormous snake, they had shot arrows at it. When the snake died, the river began growing bigger and bigger, sweeping away all our fellow men living in Pucharini and Pichanaki. Everything was annihilated.'

———

When we had dragged our bags and camera boxes up the stone stairs of what felt like an unfinished office block, but what turned out to be a smart and efficient hotel, there was a bulky package waiting for me. Our arrival, it seems, had been predicted, even though it was a complete surprise to the lady at the desk.

'You have made a booking? You want three *separate* rooms?'

A comfortable bed secured, books for the night chosen, and the most-needy shirts nominated for laundry service, I ran my fingers over the elegantly inscribed package left by a mysterious stranger, passing through on his way to Jauja and the airport. It was the Advocate. I would save this treat for our return from town.

'Don't go anywhere beyond the main square,' Lucho advised. 'This is not a good place.' He declined to join us for our evening saunter and the quest to find a perfect pizza for Farne's birthday supper. Pizza and ice cream. And coffee. And pisco sour for Grant. Lucho took care of his own comestibles. He used his hotel room as a bivouac. He also planned ahead and made arrangements to secure a boat for our voyage to the rapids. In such a place, where mules and traffickers meet, and where investors from the city fly in and out, or are deposited and collected in large black cars, it is important, our guide stressed, to be professional. And circumspectly paranoid. A few moves ahead of the game. But never to the point of standing out from the essential flow of sellers and buyers. Lucho remembered, all too clearly, the way that his sedimentary sample, that vial of potential gold, vanished from a bedside just like this one. And how, as victim of the outrage, he was the one who ended up in custody.

There was a certain edge, it's true, to this town. A cruising motor-cyclist swerved towards us to shout some derogatory challenge. But we strolled on, easy in the authentic disguise of not belonging. Farne and Grant thumbed digital devices for restaurant recommendations. That was as risky as it got. The hustling bikers kept their distance. An Italian ice-cream parlour was located only a couple of streets beyond the safety zone of the main square. The most sinister evidence I could collect in Pichanaki was shop signage that reminded me of horrors waiting

for us at home in England: NEGOCIACIONES BORIS. One of the
breeze-block, fly-by-night dealers was advertised by a pair of open
hands stacked with unripe coffee beans. Negotiate away, Boris! We have
coca, cocoa and achiote for tribal identification. A global free-market
for rainforest products.

After the pizza, we circled the square, looking for the least unpromis-
ing option for pisco sours. Farne was wearing the scarf Anna had given
her for her birthday, the one from Columbia Road. My wife said that
it would smell fresh, smell of London. Which sounded like a contradiction. But the scarf was stylish and right for the occasion, this celebratory
lacuna, before the final adventure.

The drinks took time to assemble. We chatted, enjoying the passing
scene. Grant was a man who played his cards so close to his chest, where
the film was concerned, that they might as well have been tattooed
between his nipples. Footage was being shot, certainly, but did that
amount to 'product', until many hours of material had been evaluated
and made new through the process of editing? The director's monkish
resolve was seductive. It could be that the third person on our venture
was gathering evidence against us for use by a higher power, unknown
commissioners and approvers. Judges of an acceptable degree of cultural
appropriation. Grant might, that was the beauty of our coffee-fired fantasy, be the P.D.G. Clark of this expedition. Man of secrets. Composer
of unpublished revelations.

Getting her hands around a good cup of the real stuff, the rip-
ened brew of the hills, while being, simultaneously, both chilled and
aroused by the aroma, Farne, with racing heart, and neurotransmitters
blinking in sympathy with the neon lights of the bar, the red and blue
bulbs strung around the gardens at the centre of the square, called up a
moment of existential panic, back in our Miraflores hotel, at the start
of all this.

'I woke up in Lima after dreaming that I could fly. I hadn't had
that particular dream since I was a child. Maybe because I had just
flown thousands of miles? Or because I was about to jump off a cliff?
Or maybe I had already jumped and was still falling? I was scared and
I didn't know why. This should have been just another day in a city in

the world. And I knew that I was meeting you for breakfast. Everything was happening as we'd predicted, but it felt like it was happening too fast and in the wrong order.'

Even before Farne had finished talking, I found myself making one of those unforeseen lurches straight to my childhood in Wales: a vivid dream of flying. My parents had left me to make what felt, back then, like an enormous journey to another country far away to the north, a place called Aberdeen. There had been a death and now there was to be a funeral and the settling of affairs. It couldn't have been my paternal grandfather, Arthur's son: he died when I was a baby and my only memory of him is through 16mm film and unlabelled photographs. It might have been the youngest of Arthur's three daughters, a spinster my father must have known in his days as a medical student, specialising in tropical medicine. The young doctor had the firm intention of leaving Wales, leaving Scotland, following the family tradition. Shipping out to West Africa. It didn't happen. My grandfather sickened, my father came home to help. He never left. He married a Welsh girl, dispenser to the medical practice. But he was haunted, as I was, by his ancestor's global peregrinations. With his 16mm camera and a marked copy of *In Tropical Lands*, he took customised package holidays to Sri Lanka and Peru. The retirement voyage booked through the South Seas had to be cancelled when his own health gave away, after a lifetime of avoiding treatment from fellow doctors. I inherited several copies of Arthur's book. I gave one to Farne when she arranged her own pre-university trip, a century after Arthur's arrival in Lima.

I was left, quite happily, at home with my mother's Welsh speaking parents. And I dreamt, as Farne had, of flying: not as a migrating bird but on a bed. It sailed out over the narrow hillside terraces, over the mountains, beyond my knowledge, under the stars and through the night, to this bleak northern land. To high basalt cliffs. And a pounding sea. Years later, I would travel to Aberdeen, for another death, another forgotten relative.

With my parents off the scene, I was invited into my grandparents' borrowed bed, with its different heats and smells. And to the stories my mother's father liked to tell.

'What's that?' I said, pointing to the faded bruise-blue tattoo on the chapel deacon's white arm.

'From France, a long time ago.'

My grandfather, William Jones, as a young man, had been a purser employed by the Elder Dempster Shipping Company of Liverpool. He made short voyages between the Welsh coal ports and western France. And sometimes as far as West Africa. Both my grandfathers had their time at sea. Henry Sinclair, the young medical man, now buried in Aberdeen, had been a ship's doctor. There was even a myth that he had been born during a voyage to Australia. 'Elder Dempster' had a different resonance now. The Liverpool company gave the sixteen-year-old Roger Casement, sent over from Ireland after the death of his father, employment as a clerk. They dominated transport to the Congo in the darkest days of Leopold II's colonial kleptocracy. Much later, they had a monopoly in the dubious trade of repatriating 'lunatics', as a certified cargo, to Nigeria. Where, it was deemed, unfortunate psychiatric conditions might be calmed and healed by a return to the point of origin; familiar scents and sounds and culture.

After finishing our second round of drinks, we made a slow circuit of the public gardens. I wanted to take a closer look at a surreal sculpture set among palm trees lit from below. Here was a giant ceramic coffee cup painted with a grinning bean-man, crowned with an Ashaninka headdress, but acting as a café waiter, obliged to deliver an order of the hated beverage. And with good grace. This ill-considered cartoon was the symbol of the '20th National Coffee Festival'. Supporting posters touted, quite shamelessly, for the tourist trade. A handsome Hispano-Peruvian lady, with the sophistication of the city, touched cups with a leering indigenous man who carried a red parrot on his shoulder. The visitor had been dressed in a designer orange cushma and draped in coffee-bead necklace. The shaman had a pouch of feathers and a loop of jaguar teeth. Beyond the conspiratorial couple, sealing their compact with a shared beverage, was a section of the Perené, down which a canoe, overcrowded to the point of recklessness, was being launched on some demented Herzogian voyage. A bunch of wild native saints clustered around a Christ figure.

The redeemer's arms were spread like Peter Schmeichel facing a Bergkamp penalty for Manchester United: the miracle of the Blessing of the Beans. But the most significant imagery was found on the back of the hoardings, with iconic representations of the personage most associated with resistance against the colonists in this area: Juan Santos Atahualpa. The Apinka was in an uneasy partnership with the decapitated Jesus. Juan Santos gripped a spear in his left hand. He had been modelled on the late Muammar Gaddafi. He had the proud but ready-for-business expression of the warrior stepping out of his desert tent, in costume, to greet Tony Blair. Let's do it. Let's make the deal with the devil.

> I am struck by the radiant appearance of the object itself, as a piled up sequence of repeated prayers. A stack of broken crockery, forming a pyramidical tower in a restaurant kitchen. Or a 'stupa' as the Buddhists have it.

So began the latest letter.

> A monument desperate to recall a sacred place on the earth, such as the tree under which Gautama sat to receive enlightenment. *That all is emptiness*. But Stahl's pyramid is a much cruder marker. Here, for the first time in your journey, you have father, daughter and great-grandfather, all together on the same road. The Salt Road to Metraro. And it is not even a dis-placement, but an abundance of 'other' in the hollowed place of 'same'. Like the innumerable versions of a myth that is only a myth by virtue of not being one.
>
> Forgive me, Iain. It is my work in Brussels. I am exhausted to the point of death from interminable months of preparation, before meetings like a papal audience with a revolving door. Then weeks of debriefings to frame the terms for further briefings, before indefinitely postponed decisions. We are unpicking a culture that has long since decamped.

It was the Advocate. Who else? How did he know that we had been led to Fernando Stahl's pyramid on the border of the old coffee estate?

The village chiefs communicated through the internet, when connections were available. The Advocate's office would have ways of tracking and tapping. But I don't think it was that. The desire to be with us was so powerful: my translator was determined that we should be prepared for every eventuality or change of plan. This man with his double life, the hours in trains and planes and cars with darkened windows, had devoured all the books of the river. He was always a step ahead. He teased out the play in the image vine.

The business of the sudden confrontation by the Adventist pyramid struck the Advocate as having special significance *because it was never part of Arthur's story*. It was a diversion from the trajectory my great-grandfather laid down and that we were now following. The Advocate was hungry for a new mapping, a grand theory of everything. He quoted Hans Magnus Enzensberger on Bruce Chatwin, how the author of *The Songlines* had freed himself 'from the very rigorous ideas of literature in England'. It was a question of dissolving the perceived distinction between fiction and documentation, memoir and confession. 'In psychological terms, Chatwin suffers from *Beziehungswahn* – a delirium of establishing connections.'

The Stahl pyramid, as an actively transmitting radio beam, feeding on the acoustic footprints of missionary journeys across mountain and desert, formed a triangulation with other pyramids, other lands. Erected as memorials, the surviving structures were memorials to forgetting. 'To subsist in bones, and be but pyramidally extant, is a fallacy in duration,' Sir Thomas Browne wrote.

Guided by the Advocate through a twilight Brussels, and ducking out of the rain into an enclosed market, which now operated as a packed pre-Covid bar, we were confronted by a pyramid, a pyramid elevated on a plinth. None of the drinkers paid it, or us, any attention. Like Stahl's Metraro monument, the pyramid had the ambition of becoming an obelisk. Or some other mystical form detached from its ecclesiastical host. This was an architectural distinction we would surely debate.

I opened a bottle of water, lay on the bed, shut my eyes and listened to the dogs. Before going back to the Advocate's letter.

The Saint-Géry pyramid, in its little island in that covered market, is a fundamental piece of fabricated evidence; an attempt to legitimise the Brabant ducal dynasty, and to link the dynasty to an otherwise obscure outpost in the swamp that was Brussels. There was no glorious past. The market was established on an emptied plot around 1801. This obelisk/pyramid was placed on the precise spot where a statue of Saint Géry once stood. When the river went underground and the ugly Huysmanian boulevards were laid out, the open market was enclosed.

Today the pyramid presents itself, both openly and covertly, as the omphalos of Brussels. A marker of origin. But it does not belong in Brussels. It was expropriated from a monastery fifteen kilometres outside the city. There is speculation about the meaning of the golden star on the tip of the obelisk. It represents the symbol and the motor of Abbot Sophia: SUPER ASTRA SOPHIA. A pun. Wisdom over the stars.

My son, who is an apprentice architect, says that the location of the obelisk was determined by a group of Masons – like so much else in Brussels. It is a clear, deliberate act, aiming to re-signify the mythic foundation of the city. A pagan symbol erected where a Catholic saint once stood in his transcendent glory.

——

I couldn't formulate an adequate response to the Advocate's lengthy and impassioned missive, this notion of the linked and interchangeable pyramids, space-time portals, until I returned to London. I would walk to the familiar monument in Limehouse Church, the conclusion of a previous day's tramp with the Advocate, and look at it once again, in the light of its projected relationship with the structures in Brussels and Metraro.

Everything happened at once. A plague hit the city. I began at the obelisk, which was an obelisk, dedicated to Daniel Defoe in Bunhill Fields. I stumbled across Michael Ayrton's *Minotaur* on its most recent plinth, in the constantly revised centre of the broken London labyrinth.

But the Limehouse vicar had not only sealed his Hawksmoor church, keeping the malignancy within, he had also padlocked the gates and secured the grounds. No forensic inspection of the pyramid was possible.

Retracing my steps, I tapped around the surviving vertebrae of the Roman wall, noting excavated hospices, deleted Bedlams. Terry Farrell, the visionary of that great Mayan jukebox, the MI6 building in Lambeth, all pyramids and swooping cameras, had also delivered a set of quite distinct obelisks for a new development close to the Barbican. A temple of worship for a set of beliefs as yet to be defined.

A rough-sleeper, nested in his bivouac alongside the Barber's Physic Garden, and primed to keep the undeserving away from the healing plants, sprung up to curse and spit. A discharged squaddie.

'*Fuck* off!'

I finished where I started, in Bunhill Fields. A raven was sitting on the pointed feet of the sleeping effigy of Bunyan. Blake's ancient slab, a scholar's slate shared for so long with his wife, had been downgraded in favour of a 'more accurate' burial site, where her services were no longer required. No record is available of the other paupers who went into the communal pit to keep the poet company. Beyond these all too frequently visited prompts, I discovered for the first time a modest freestanding memorial. Its text, when I leaned forward to peer at it, was deeply incised in honour of A MOST LABORIOUS AND PERSISTENT ADVOCATE.

The shirts, ironed and restored, hidden away in the drawer of my hotel room should have been welcome. But they belonged to Farne. She was still awake and making notes ahead of the next day's river trip. It turned out to be a fair trade: she had some of my shirts, among others, origin unknown. I carried them back to my room, to fold away at the bottom of my black bag. Now I would have something decent for Lima and London. The shirtfronts, when the moment came, were immaculate. But the backs had been printed, like the walls of a 30,000-year-old Palaeolithic cave, with stencils of large human hands in ineradicable engine oil.

PUERTO YURINAKI

'Do you want me to vanish? To dive into the deep to fetch the Ring? What do you want? I'll make gold... Trust me.'
   – Charles Nicholl, *Somebody Else (Arthur Rimbaud in Africa 1880–91)*

Coming back to the river road, before crossing the bridge on our way to Pichanaki, after our challenging confrontation with Fernando Stahl's pyramid, we requested a brief twilight halt at Yurinaki, the reputed place where Arthur made contact with King Chokery, and took to the water. This was important, even vital, for Farne and myself. Lucho, wanting to get to the hotel in time to confirm arrangements for our voyage to the rapids, or the 'cascades' as he called them, was irritated. But he recognised the combined weight of our demand. He instructed his driver to make the short detour.

Our guide stayed with the car. Grant slid into the shadows, in pursuit of his own unspecified Conradian ambiguities. He never complained; wherever we took him he waited until we were out of the way before identifying the perfect position from which to decide not to make the shot. He was that barely registered but significant le Carré character sent on a betrayed suicide mission, limping back across the border, hamstrung, nerves in tatters, and condemned to an exiled afterlife in preparatory school or film school. The one who will be confirmed as the silent keeper of the secret all the other spooks have missed.

It is just after six o'clock. We have arrived in the benediction of *la mala hora*, the evil hour, when light is glamorous in its treachery. Spectral buildings ripple in the water. Red and blue bulbs from bars, yellow and green bulbs from the distributors of coca leaves and home-brewed beer: they flicker and fuse in the damp evening air. A single streak of dying light spills across the river to drown. It is said that the ultimate breakdown of the primal force that was Rimbaud came from 'gold dysentery', the consequence of marching so many stony miles with a belt of hoarded coins strapped across his stomach.

PUERTO YURINAKI: the white letters stood out in the darkness. As we rambled along the dirt track beside the Perené, in this most fitful dusk, through puddles of illuminated reflections, we both confessed to the conviction that another person was walking beside us. A presence not exactly approving of our nuisance, but admitting that he felt, on his 1891 expedition, communications from a remote and unknowable future. Pulled up on the beach were long canoes and river craft: this was certainly the place where Arthur Sinclair, after many days waiting on the chief's fever, took to the river. Tied up to an improvised pier made from small stones was a balsa raft, touting for desperate excursionists.

King Chokery at length gave orders for balsas to be made, and trees were at once cut down and fixed together by pins of palm wood. The balsa, or raft, consisted of seven logs, about 24 inches in circumference, rather roughly pegged together, but sufficiently buoyant to support three of our party on each. Seven of these rafts carried our company of twenty; the King accompanied us, and as he himself had never been forty miles down the river, it was an interesting voyage of discovery to all concerned.

We started in single file, I electing to sit in the prow of the foremost balsa. It was a glorious morning, and as we glided onward at the rate of four miles an hour, through ever changing, but always enchanting, scenery, the effect was indescribably exhilarating. Every nerve seemed stretched to the highest pitch of enjoyment; the eyes, glancing from scene to scene, took in more impressions than the mental powers could take note of. Such a wealth of vegetation seems to mock at the idea of a few poor puny planters ever making any impression upon it… Beautiful as these creepers are as they hang in festoons from the lofty trees, they almost bid defiance to the progress of explorers, and a path cut, which in other countries would remain open for years, would here close up in a few weeks. Such seems the inexhaustible fertility of the soil, and such the forcing nature of the climate, that there is a

mixture of awe in our admiration… But, as an old planter, I do not despair
of its fertility being yet turned to good account.

We know what happens: mules abandoned, derangement of the river, squatting on damp logs, swept downstream, weapons nestled comfortably across tensed knees. Watchful. Suspicious. Reverie of consistently ripening and thickening impressions. Alexander Ross is determined to stick to his task, to measure, survey, list, count. And report. Arthur is beginning to give himself up to sensations of faunal luxuriance. To fantasy and drift. The division between the twin commanders is emphasised by the distance between their separated rafts. Arthur has the virgin river before him. Ross turns his gaze to the hills. The King's court is afloat and scattered. And soon to pass beyond their permissions. But we know what is ordained for rivers of no return. The undeniable impulse to keep going. The next bend. The first faint intimations of Atlantic salt. The golden madness of Aguirre and Raleigh. Carlos Fermín Fitzcarrald, the rubber baron, face down in the shallows. And Fernando Stahl conducting a mass baptism of indigenous people at the cascades on the Perené

River. As if he wanted to drown them all, the duped savages. He would gather their unmortgaged souls into his own safekeeping. The voyagers have one impulse in common, they risk everything for the chance to reach places god has forsaken. And where, as Rodrigo Hasbún says in his book *Affections*, 'God finds solace away from our ingratitude, and our depravity.' Solace and solitude. A god without disciples. Faceless.

Within hours, the hallucinations begin.

> *Turning a bend in the river we are struck by what seems the ivy-clad ruins of an ancient castle; but it turns out to be only an aged tree clad from top to bottom with verdant creepers, its huge horizontal arms supporting a perfect screen of living trellis-work below, while ferns, lycopods, and rare orchids, beautiful in hue as they are grotesque in form, grow upright from the damp decaying bark. The original tree itself is so hidden that it is barely recognisable, but from its curious buttresses we suppose it to be a ficus.*

His lenses are cloudy cataracts, but Arthur's internal vision is purified, enhanced with the dawning realisation that natural features can inhabit several states of being, and any number of disguises, at any one time. This hypnagogic state recalls not only the fever dreams of Herzog's *Aguirre*, ships in the trees, but also the Perené legend of a Stone Ship. On the far side of the rapids, it was rumoured that an old brown rock, midstream, somewhere near the place where the river branched for Satipo, took the shape of a seventeenth-century slave ship. We recognise the way that rivers discount similes in favour of metaphors. The rock was not *like* a slave ship, it was a slave ship. And a rock. And a tree. Branches dripped with a treacle of blood.

Venturing craft were a money plague: fetid, reeking with shit and sweat and greed. Captured Ashaninka were reckoned a valuable cargo, and pliant enough when taken aboard and secured in chains. They would be traded in the slave markets of Lima and Huancayo.

White mist condoned the low hills to which natives withdrew when their watchers warned of invading ships. Spies, hidden in the trees, reported that this black boat had been transformed in the night and was now a great brown rock, crawling with red ants. But when the

Ashaninka returned to their village, there was no boat, no rock. The ants had worked their demented architecture. They sculpted an anchored obstacle in wood. With time, it would become rock again.

When unholy darkness is absolute and noises from the forest change their pitch, the rafters come ashore. They make camp. One day fades into the next. Supplies dwindle, the river is remorseless. It is now the whole world. The priests are thirsty and are paid in diminishing supplies of rum. It will be Clark's duty to guard the medicinal brandy. One night there is meat. Charred and stringy, lifeless. Probably animal or bird. Arthur, spitting a mouthful into the dirt, is possessed of a horrible thought: he is devouring one of the mules that carried him so far, over the mountains, down to the river.

> *We followed the Chunchos into the jungle by tortuous paths for about a mile ere we came to a hut; but before being permitted to enter, we were first led to witness their prowess as marksmen, the target being a banana tree at about 40 yards distant, which was soon bristling with arrows. Sufficiently impressed with this, we were allowed to enter a hut, about 10 by 20 feet, into which we all (about 30 in number) were huddled for the night, and, after drinking a little Liebig's Extract, tried to sleep, but without success… The Chunchos drank their abominable masato, and soon became uproarious, evidently cracking their favourite jokes, judging from the screaming laughter. This was varied by an idiotic war dance, and in other respects their deportment was even more objectionable. We are apt to imagine that man in a perfectly natural state must be a very delightful and interesting creature. On the contrary, my experience is that no other animal is less lovable or more repulsive in its habits than a thoroughly untamed man or woman. These Chunchos, or 'Campas', are evidently the remnant of a very barbarous and low caste race of untameable savages, recognising no laws, and killing each other with as little compunction as we kill our rodents.*
>
> *On the night before we passed down the river, a woman and two children were tumbled off a raft and drowned. It seemed the standing joke of the day, and no one more enjoyed it than the woman's husband, who danced with fiendish glee the whole night through, encouraged by the screaming*

> *laughter of the native ladies… I was not sorry to see the sun rise next morning, and did not linger long over our early breakfast, which consisted of tea and yucca, the latter like badly-boiled potatoes.*
>
> *Once more on the river we were all alive with excitement. Several tributaries fall in; one, the Ipuki, equal to the Don in volume, adds palpably to the depth and force of Perené, upon which we are now carried at the rate of about 5 miles an hour. Denser and denser became the forest, now no longer relieved by patches of grassy land. Such perfect lands for coffee and cocoa cheered the hearts of old planters, while such unheard-of varieties of orchids, ferns, gloxinias, begonias, and caladiums, were enough to drive a botanist frantic.*

Arthur's perversity, in refusing to engage with the habits and ritual practices of the Ashaninka, forest dwellers whose knowledge of plants, and whose respect for the realities of place, should have provided so many fresh insights for the planter, was extreme. My great-grandfather's patience was exhausted. He was undone by a mortal weariness in the bones. There was too much land to secure in his memory. He suffered under the duty laid on him by his patrons: to record, evaluate, and justify investment. The river stripped away illusions. The last reflexes of declared scientific progressivism.

For Farne, schooled to be alert to the charge sheet of *isms* for which elderly white males are properly held accountable, and guided by the tactful anthropology of Elena Mihas, Arthur's genially patronising overview was especially awkward. I had come through post-war schools where token liberalism did little to ameliorate long-established military discipline, as useful training for the exploitation of colonies that were no longer there. Watery John Piper heritage prints, or Stanley Spencer's bread-and-butter Cookham landscapes, were hung on the wall outside the headmaster's study, where nine-year-old children lined up for a character-forming thrashing. Only the British middle-class system of privilege could deliver six of the *best*. There must have been something useful in the regime of this institution, to breed the resistant genius of Patrick White, quarrelling with history in Australia. And Lindsay Anderson, who blagged his crew back to the old place, to film the subversive *If...* But what Arthur did not recognise, and what, up to this point, I had not myself recognised through reading him, was that the tribal people were *celebrating* the good fortune of the drowned woman and her two children, because this living river, their god, had chosen them. They were specially blessed. And remembered in song. They had been swallowed by, and were now a part of, the great snake.

Long processional days on the river, sometimes being overturned and drenched among minor rapids, sometimes racing onwards, reminded the surveyors that the moment was approaching when favourable reports would have to be filed. The professional botanist, Clark, unnoticed by the others, was scribbling in a sodden notebook. The dynamite priest, Padre Sala, and his young associate, had fulfilled their necessary role in Arthur's narrative: colourful villains. They dropped depth charges into the river. They filched the last of the brandy. And they prospected new territory from which to harvest a bounty of orphan children. But the further King Chokery travelled from Yurinaki, the uneasier he felt. The ministrations of his shaman, blowing powder into the nostrils, lost potency with every nautical mile from the home village. Regal misgivings were communicated to the courtiers and boatmen obliged to venture on a foolish enterprise that promised neither goods, animals to hunt, nor the wisdom of the whirlpool of ancestors: an oracle only to be accessed by those who come safely through the rapids.

Ross, swept along now at ever greater velocity, notes how 'a more steep, transverse range of mountains delivers a considerable volume of water shortly before the cascades are reached.' He has invigilated the land through which they have passed and he looks to a brighter future.

> Here is an obstacle to navigation; but from what we saw of them we should say there was nothing that engineering skill cannot overcome; and, if further down the difficulties are not immeasurably greater, there exists no reason why, almost at once, or at least simultaneously with the opening of the Chanchamayo-Tarma road, a way could not be found of connecting the railway system of the western coast with the waters of the Amazon.

Before the balsas commit themselves, without reservation, to the turbulence of the rapids and the siren songs of the hungry dead, the border from which there is no coming back, Arthur delivers himself of his vision for the inevitable prosperity of the land.

> ... *a country capable of supplying many millions of inhabitants with not only the necessities of life, but also all the luxuries the most fastidious appetites could desire. When we see so many less favoured countries crowded and cultivated to the utmost, it does seem strange to see this magnificent land left to a few Chunchos, who are really little better than the monkeys that grin on the branches above them. Practically, it is no man's land, for it has never been taken possession of, the present nomadic tribes recognising no laws, no government, no God.*
>
> *In every other country we know men have succeeded in subjecting the productive powers of nature to his sway; and is there no hope that such will yet be the case with the valleys of the Amazon? Are men always to despair of utilising this marvellous vegetation, and to be for ever overwhelmed by the excessive bounties of nature? Surely the time has come, or will soon come, when this, the richest portion of the globe, will no longer be entirely left to nature and the few wandering tribes who are so utterly incapable of making any proper use of it.*

That twinkle in Arthur's weathered face, the enigmatic smile. The years of his travels and voyages have played the vine out to breaking point: blindness to the intricate contract between people and place. He is in thrall to the doctrine of material progress, as delivered by Victorians with a single stern, but obligingly English-speaking, god. A god of hygiene and warships. And silence. Like something masked and hidden under the heavy layers of a queen's black skirts. She is an unmoving monolith around which the world revolves. Wilderness vegetation, so brilliant in display, must be brought to use. Now, as the material and moral beneficiary of Arthur's youngest son, his education and good works, and his son's son, continuing in the same Welsh mining valley, I have come back to the rapids for a witness that cannot be exorcised. Even in drowning.

No doubt about it: if Arthur had become an Aberdeen statue, he would now be sprayed a lurid red like a warring tribesman, torn from his plaque, and flung in the river. My ancestor presented himself as a bearded Prospero heading for the rocks, electively shipwrecked with his box of books and his Kodak camera, scorning an island of misunderstood Calibans, trapped between river and salt mountain.

And to what purpose? There are only two photocopies of Arthur's portrait left. Tomorrow, if Lucho's projected arrangements hold, we will take to the same river and head for the rapids. If there is recompense for the manifesto my great-grandfather preached, this is surely the last chance to identify and deliver it.

CASCADES

'We warned him; but he went out there, and stood on the rock, and shouted, "Boatman! Boatman!" – and the Boatman came.'
  – Bruce Chatwin, *Patagonia Revisited*

It is obvious now that the murder of the totemic snake was the defining incident of the long journey through Peru. After that ill-considered action, on the darkest of nights, everything that could go wrong went wrong for Arthur's party. Or perhaps the reflex act of lifting and sighting the rifle was, in itself, confirmation that the colonial incursion had been malfated from the start.

History can be rewritten but not revised. 'From here on out,' Mark Zuckerberg boasted in spoken defence of global digital domination, 'it's a frictionless experience.' Everything said is recorded, everything done is seen. There is no longer shame or consequence, no action that cannot be re-edited and denied.

'Fake news! Faux history! Fixed witness!'

We breakfasted, silently and obediently, in our dealers' boutique hotel at Pichanaki, with the ocular friction of *live* television rubbing against us: the same motorcycle shoot-outs, the same inconvenient body spillage, the same triumphant mercenaries shouting at the lens, the same melancholy politician making the same walk to face the same judge, who will himself, on one of these mornings, be the accused, cuffed and shipped out to the same customised prison in the jungle, from which he will escape or disappear. They have the news so well managed here. It is shot and cut with verve, like an abbreviated feature film. The actors know how to perform themselves without winks and nudges and hair revisions. History sucks, the TV implies, but we are happy to be making it on your behalf, so just concentrate on your coffee, your cakes.

On the other wall, the blatant fake, put up to hide surveillance cameras, is a nicely composed animation framed to look like a still life: planks of purple knotted wood with excessively blue flowers and an overhead shot into a cup of swirling coffee with a ruff of septic bubbles. The coffee has been left to cool for the approved duration; at least half a minute before boiled water is poured over the grains. Then four minutes to settle in the warmed cafetière. It makes the pulse race: nothing is happening very slowly. The perfect morning fix. Your classic antidote to the deranged news channel.

Now, with the climax of our expedition approaching, Lucho is the supercharged embodiment of friction. Every surface he rubs against gives off sparks. 'Vamos, let's go.' The day's downriver itinerary is so complicated that he can't begin to lay out a working schedule for us. It's a headlong charge into transport systems on a road yet to be mapped. 'Come on, come on, let's go.'

Climb aboard while the vehicle is still in motion, that bright red tuk-tuk; elbow to rib to shoulder to thigh, an insecure heap, the four of us, camera kit, bulging rucksack of essentials Farne never leaves behind, the money belt, squeeze up and hang on, half in and half out. Breathe those fumes! We must *will* the shuddering heap up the ramp and into the weaving, honking maelstrom of the main highway. If we travel fast enough, Lucho implies, the difficulties, miscalculations and aboriginal curses won't catch up. And we will arrive right back, in the same pool of shadows, on the same street, outside the same hotel, unscathed, unblooded, fed and watered, our quest completed: THE CASCADES! It will be as if we had never decided to come down those stone stairs. And we had spent the allotted hours of an ordinary day meditating on our curved miniature portraits in the bright bubbles of the coffee mug.

The tuk-tuk jockey, glad to be shot of our impatience and simmering revolt, drops us in a soon-to-be-completed, body-surgery and respray garage that doubles as a collection point for the communal minibus service to Satipo. It should have been run by Bryan Cranston, moonlighting from Nicolas Winding Refn's film of *Drive*, a pacey novel by

James Sallis. But that was my fantasy, in truth the operatives were calm and without friction. They found slots on the bus for all of us. And we splashed away through the mirage puddles of the river road.

When the gimp mechanic played by Cranston sorts out a suitable car for the criminal enterprise plotted by Ryan Gosling's stunt driver, he tells him that he looks like a zombie. And offers: 'Benzedrine, Dexedrine, caffeine, nicotine.' Beyond the secular vision of the coffee animation on the wall of the hotel, we haven't enjoyed any of these boosts, but we seem to have reaped the after-effects: shivers, twitches and cold-turkey migraine. We are the undead, pale faces pressed against the glass, in a happy bus of chattering travellers. They are happy to see us disembark, on the melting road, in the middle of nowhere.

Our painfully assembled fiction of ourselves as a functioning familial group was fractured by the loss of Velisa, our conduit to the Ashaninka. She had returned home, and now in her absence we appreciated what she brought to the expedition. I'm sure Lucho, confident as always, felt this too. He had talked with the boatmen and the drivers, but that did not help. Yesterday was yesterday. Each new morning was a new world. 'These people,' our guide said, punching at a phone that was out of range of all his contacts, 'they will not adapt to the basic requirements of tourism. Tourism is a culture.'

Deposited beside a novel stretch of the Perené, with a stilted hospitality shack guarded by an impressively alert wolf-dog scuffling around a dusty circle of his own drool, and leaving us intact only because, being suddenly woken up, he was unable to decide where to take the first bite, it was hard not to conclude that the attractive longboat on the deserted strip of sand wasn't going anywhere. Lucho, silver mane tossed back, fighter's chest thrust forward, one fist in waistcoat pocket, the other squeezing the last drop of life from his phone, swept the shoreline, in unblinking challenge, horizon to horizon.

'What is the point of this country, if you can see for miles but you can't *hear* a thing? Nobody will answer. It doesn't matter to them. They don't want our money. They don't have money. So they don't want money. They go fishing. And there aren't any fish.'

While we waited, not knowing what we were missing, but grasping all too clearly that the river trip to the rapids, the only way out of the story I was trying to tell, and the only place – *moving water* – where I could become part of Arthur's voyage, was off. The boatman had better places to be and it was of no account how long we stood on the rock and called. Lucho seethed. He ran up the slope to the stilted bar to discuss the other major aspect of the day, lunch. Hopeless. He sprinted into the road, waving his phone like a grenade from which the pin had been removed, until he reached Velisa just long enough to persuade her to find a car and a driver, and to come back here, with the necessary ingredients, to cook a proper meal. We would push on, but we would surely return.

Grant, wasting no time, had stripped to his black undershorts, and was laundering his camera beneath the fast-flowing river. When he re-emerged, admitting to an opaque vision of sediment, he said that he would trust everything to his instrument. This was about dowsing for correspondences. Then and now. Here and not here.

I arranged the penultimate photocopied portrait of Arthur in a dugout canoe made from a single tree. When Grant was ready, I let the portrait float away, curl back on itself and sink. Ripples in the water made the portrait look like a fossilised reproduction of the Turin shroud. Drowned paper became cloth. Arthur's enigmatic smile was permanently calcified. The print sunk and would travel no further, until the river accepted possession and dragged it away downstream.

We wait. We sit. We talk. We separate. We walk off, sniffing after aspects to exploit. We hustle back to the rocks when the dog emerges from the trees. Grant has a book. Rather than reveal its author and title, when I approach, he reads aloud, a passage that, by implication, performs a critique of my present situation; how I am losing friction against the constantly changing structure of our stalled quest.

'What appears instead is a breakdown in narrative continuity reflecting the dissociation of that causal logic on which conventional stories are built. Since there is no place to go, why not intensify where one is? The road followed is no longer "on the road"; it symbolizes our thinking process.'

_____

First finger raised, now more than ever the Padre Sala of our fading excursion in the traces of another expedition, Lucho shouldered resist-ant air, forging ahead down the molten highway.

'First lesson: think with your feet. Stay still and you burn.'

The boatman had let him down. The food in the shack on stilts was inadequate and would take all day to prepare.

'We find another way.'

Wilting under our various burdens, threatened by remorseless traffic and divorced from the river, we trail behind our ranting guide. Spotting a satellite dish bolted to a thatched and windowless hut, Lucho darts across an orange metal bridge over the Perené. There is no sign of life. And no signal for the phone. Better to shout down a sliced coconut and some taut string.

A truck is jolting at pace along the dirt road towards the silvertop highway. Lucho steps out to wave it down. There follows a confron-tation that is less a negotiation than a capture. By force of personality, our guide commandeers the vehicle. For an agreed fee, the trucker, with his cargo of empty fruit crates, will allow us to climb aboard, while he tries to track the river to the cascades.

'Ten minutes, no more? Good, very good. Perfecto. Let's go.'

The truck sails under the logo of FUNDO LA VICTORIA. There is a rail to grip for our bone-shuddering safari among the fragrant banana, avocado and pineapple crates. Squelching among the wet mush of oranges, we duck under low branches and wonder about the route Lucho is taking when he orders the driver to detour away from the established river road.

'Are we still heading for the rapids?'

'Of course. Yes. The cascades. Ten minutes.'

Like Arthur, when his balsa picks up speed from the tumbling rush of tributary water arguing for equal status with the Perené, there is exhilaration in submission: hanging on, white-knuckled, swaying and bending, slipstreaming through buffeted air. Grass shudders at our pass-ing, trees shiver and bow.

Lucho bangs on the driver's cab, to signal a halt. He prods his dead phone and invents a mountain village where he can access current data on our vanished and migrating cascades. The vision, from our achieved elevation, back along the thickly forested valley of the Perené, with the snaking river and its sandbars, is one of those opportunities for summoning Arthur's flood of landscape lyricism.

The river is mirror smooth, with no rocks or rapids or streaks of white. Lush and unbroken vegetation pushes to the edge of the water. The world and its past must have pressed in on the rafts of the 1891 expedition. There was no way for Arthur but on.

The truck parks beside a village school. A polite dialogue is attempted with a young teacher, surprised and alarmed by the sudden arrival of strangers, asking for the best path to the cascades. The children, their routine shattered, stare in wonderment.

'She says: "Ten minutes". Through the village. Follow me. Let's go. They know nothing, these people.'

It is Lucho's task to get us, as we have repeatedly asked him to do, to the cascades. But, as we hack once again into the steamy microclimate of the rainforest, and we hear at a distance the rumble of a torrent, we know that language has undone us. Our guide, scorning the flapping angel of history, is leading us towards another adventure tour photo op: a virgin waterfall.

Farne stalls and sits. She isn't going into the silence of the forest for a second time. Grant cannot wrestle his heavy boxes down the treacherous and tangled gradient. The triumphant Lucho surges ahead. I push hard to catch him. And to tell him that the others are flagging and they want to know how far it is to the falls.

'Ten minutes. No more.'

I sweated back up the winding track to pass on the news. Now our small party was clenched in private contemplation at various stages of the trail. We had been here before, in quest of Juan Santos Atahualpa's cave. But then we were a group, united in the sudden and profound stasis. The busy silence. The gradual acceptance of the way of the forest. We felt the lascivious run of sap, the sugar droplets forming and dripping from broad leaves. The splintering wheel of dying sunlight. We were in the wrong place, on an unnecessary detour. If we lost the river and the rapids the story was done. We would turn back on ourselves and come home without making contact with our ghosts.

Arthur felt the same irritation, with his own circumstances, with those around him, with their imbricated and futile expectations and desires. With an enraptured and increasingly sensual abandonment to the seductions of the river.

Our guides, who were fast becoming insufferable nuisances, urged us onwards, stating that the cascades were still a long day's journey off and that we ought to push on for a few hours more, so as to reach them before next night. So again we started, but had scarcely moved 300 yards when I, still in the prow of the first balsa, began to feel we were gliding along rather faster than was pleasant, and distinctly heard a not very distant roar like muffled thunder. All at once it dawned upon us that we were uncomfortably near the rapids, and the greatest possible exertion was required to beach our rafts.

I never jumped on the banks of a river with a greater feeling of relief. We had now time to take a leisurely view of the rapids. Though not more than four or five feet of a fall in any one place, a succession of these was sufficient to obstruct further navigation, though lasting only for a few miles, probably under ten. Our aneroids told us we were now 1,050 feet above sea level, and as the water has quite 3,000 miles yet to run before reaching the Atlantic, the average fall is not great. We would now have naturally wished to work our way down to the Atlantic, by far the easiest and most natural outlet, but we were under orders to visit other tributaries of the Amazon 200 miles to the north, so we had reluctantly to wend our way back.

What hurt most was the dawning conviction that the Scottish planter would not live to see the promised land. Neither would he arrive at the place where the natives spoke of holding converse with unborn generations, the ones who were still in their dreamtime.

I heard the cascades long before I saw them. I lost the sound of Grant shouting up to Farne, who had settled on a rock, keeping watch on the truck, waiting for Lucho. Then, for some time, I was out of sight and sound of all of them. I confused glimpses of our guide's red Manchester United strip with brilliant birds among the greenery. Lucho was not a supporter. He had picked the shirt up, so he told us, in a charity shop in New Zealand. Panting and mopping salt sweat from my eyes, I drudged on. I found the man. He flung out his arm: 'Cascades!' A whitewater stream plunging over the rocks. Our guide had captured a new waterfall for his website. We stood together for a brief instant of triumph. Lucho made an entry in his reporter's notebook. I suggested a brisk resumption of our quest, before the driver took off with the fruit truck.

Rejoining the highway, and wind-surfing on the back of the truck as the road declined to flattened dirt, we pass through a number of shack settlements. We try to assess the state of the river. The first signs of turbulence, narrower bore, faster water, long white streaks, coincide with the termination of the navigable road. There is a cola-dispensing hut with a limited range of stale biscuits, offered with the usual complimentary bunches of small green bananas.

Lucho translates a warning from the hospitable vendor.

'She says, "Turn around. Turn back." She says, "There is no more road for you." The footpath that follows the Perené through these cascades is impassable without guides and machetes. There is great difficulty and danger.'

But it is not clear if the woman means that the bad thing comes from the river itself, or the jungle, or miscreants we might encounter. Or ancestors trapped in whirlpools. Plantations of the restless dead.

Our finish is not an acceptable conclusion. Alexander Ross was also convinced that he had reached the outer limit of his permissions. The territory rejected the invading party.

'We had intended to explore these rapids throughout,' he wrote, 'but Padre Sala intimated to us that neither he nor the Campas Indians would proceed any further with us, and that we must return forthwith. The reason assigned was that some festival was due at which Padre Sala's presence was imperatively required at the Convent; but no doubt there were other causes of which we knew nothing. A great change had come over our guides, who were now morose and sullen. Eventually the Padres, though I had the repeated assurances of Padre Sala that they would not leave us, after gradually drawing ahead of us on the river, left us, taking our food with them.'

The film is beginning to run backwards. If we have now reached the ultimate point to which Victorian confessions and justifications can carry us, then we must submit, willingly, to the gravity of home. It is over. Velisa has arrived, as instructed, at the shack on stilts, and is hard at work preparing and cooking a haul of market fish for lunch.

The feral dog snaps and snarls. Lucho arranges himself at the table and settles to his beer. When I point out that there is now a man tinkering with an outboard motor in the launch that should have carried us to the rapids, he says, dismissively: 'He is a man in a boat. But he is not a boatman.' Then our weary guide, his day's work done, sets his back to the window and opens another chilled bottle.

The temporal investment in the long afternoon meal has become intolerable. Policed by the circling wolf, we drift down to the river, to have a fit of pique confirmed in the right setting. On a narrow spit of sand, on the far bank, a woman is stepping ashore from a dugout canoe. The ferryman, an indigenous boy in a football shirt, paddles back towards us. Could he be the one who has been summoned from the past? I remembered the legend of the river spoken by Carmen Pachiri Quinchori and recorded by Elena Mihas. After an earthquake, the Masters of the Hills left this place and the river was choked with small rocks and boulders. Pichanaki came into existence when the people shot and killed a snake with their arrows.

The shamans were angry. The snake was the essence of the living river. The people had sacrificed their god and they would be annihilated. Young girls who went to the river to wash and swim would become pregnant. 'That demonic snake would impregnate them.' That was the reason why the men shot their arrows. But the snake was the owner of the river. The snake was the only map.

> We always hear about our fellow men and Andean settlers getting drowned, this is troubling... So it was in the past. Now, no, it does not happen; we live well, we go to the river and come back, and nothing happens.

We talk to the boy and he agrees, for two soles, to take us on the river in his canoe. Farne is carried across and brought back in a wide sweep favouring the pull of the current. Grant, in his turn, dangles a Go-Pro camera from a length of fisherman's twine. The lure snares cloudy sediment and strips of weed. Ectoplasmic ripples in a scryer's mirror that will never achieve resolution.

The fading afternoon inscribes its timeless particulars on forested hills from which the old masters have departed. There is not another craft to be seen, not a single human habitation. Trees and bushes press to the edge of the river. When we can't make a place come alive through our powers of description, we are not really there. There is no way into the reality Arthur's story without risking the rapids. When it comes to my turn to climb aboard, I point downstream, towards the blind bend where the force of a tributary has brought water to the boil. As if some great submerged beast were about to break through the placid surface.

The boy does some rapid bailing with a tin can. He brushes the narrow plank on which his passenger must perch. And we are away. In the prow, I have my back to the paddler, but he requires no instruction. He takes us right across, almost to the other shore, before heading back, in a delirious sweep, towards the reach where layers of opposed currents catch us and the boatman no longer needs to work his long paddle. He laughs now but he does not speak.

> *We slept that night rather comfortably under a tree, but before going to rest I shot a large snake which hung from a branch above us, and the only one we saw during our sojourn.*
>
> *Next morning we arose more refreshed than usual, explored the country a little… took some photos of the rapids, and then prepared to start on our return voyage. We found, however, that something like a mutiny was brewing in the camp. The priests declared that the rum was done, and that it was ridiculous to think that men could live in this country without drink. The King grumbled because the jam was finished, while the Chunchos struck work for no earthly reason at all. For a time we moved away slowly and sullenly, chiefly by walking along the margin of the river, for about two miles, when matters came to a deadlock. The chief priest disappeared, and we never saw him more, the reverend brother slyly followed, stealing the few bottles of spirits we had carefully laid aside in case of sickness. Our own servants also vanished, we knew not why nor where; and just as the shades of evening were closing in we could see by the lurid light of a log fire, suspicious movements in the surrounding jungle. The natives, in short, were gathering in force, each armed with a bow and a bundle of arrows. They peered at us from behind trees, and apparently awaited a signal. It was a trying moment, and the probabilities were against our escape. Still, the uppermost feelings in our minds seemed to be that the actions of even those creatures are under the control of a greater Power than a Chuncho chief or a pseudo priest, and that practically we were in no more danger than we might be comfortably sleeping at home.*

―――

The boatman dips and stirs once more, nominating a preordained line, as if there were only one possible thread to be followed, in order to carry us through the treacherous teeth of visible and submerged rocks. The hollowed log is still enough of a tree to resist the drag of the river: it puts out phantom branches and clumps of root to slow our downstream foolishness. Two soles is not nearly enough to pay the ferryman for the risks he is taking. The sharpened fins of the obstacles among which we twist and sway, letting in water, are warnings on a liquid flightpath into the past. It is when the paddle is shipped that the dugout picks up momentum. The boy calls a warning, to let me know that we are approaching the point where his skills will be redundant. Eight miles of white water lie ahead and this is the last moment at which we can turn or beach, by our own choice.

Every minor readjustment, every tilt of the canoe, is a memory prompt. What did the Advocate tell me? 'Killing a snake is perilous.' He recalled how the art historian Aby Warburg travelled, like Ed Dorn's *Gunslinger* (always a point of reference), to the Hopi pueblo at Mesa Verde, where he witnessed, and even photographed, the Hemis Kachina dance. The scholar did not attend the Snake Dance that was the inspiration for his famous and much-disputed 1923 lecture. The Hopi Indians, who had already been betrayed by collectors of tribal artefacts and ritual masks, men like the Mennonite missionary the Reverend Voth, were suspicious of intrusion.

In the year of publication of *In Tropical Lands*, Warburg left Florence for New York, to attend the wedding of his brother Paul. And then to follow his blind hunch to a conceptual Wild West, tracing certain aspects of the Italian Renaissance to a remote and ancient pueblo, held to be the oldest continuously inhabited settlement in the United States. The demigods of Greece and Rome, archetypes of a tottering civilisation, must get down and dirty with the Python: the universal source of a dark kundalini energy.

The pattern was hidden within the dance. Which was formal, cosmologically aligned and divorced from the serpent-swallowing, sexualised frenzy that the invading European intellectual wrestled to impose. The Snake was Warburg's salvation.

'He was placed in an asylum,' the Advocate said. 'He asked for permission to address a conference on the topic of the snake ritual. The chief psychiatrist agreed.'

Warburg was released from Ludwig Binswanger's sanatorium in Kreuzlingen. David Freedberg, in his essay 'Warburg's Mask: A Study in Idolatry', described this plunge into this intellectual whirlpool as a 'failed navigation toward the light of reason'.

I see the smiling face of the Brussels Advocate emerge, close-shaven, from the floating photocopy of the bearded Arthur. He is showing me a figure that he calls 'the Spirit of the Vortex of the Rapids'. It is a direct capture from Warburg's journey: a man with matted hair and painted face gripping a living snake firmly in his teeth. 'I am drowning in the stupidity of these last days,' the Advocate says. 'When will I sleep again, even for one night?'

After that oracular visitation, I was overwhelmed, as we drifted on in silence, surging then stalling, by identification with Arthur, in the prow of the balsa. I think he was beginning to admit the futility of making a report that would lead to enclosure and exploitation. The land belongs with the songs and memories of the people. Describing is destroying. What I also have to acknowledge, in using Arthur's account as a prompt for our own journey, is that I have been guilty, on my own small London patch, of the same crimes. Cultural appropriation with greedy hands. My great-grandfather, over many decades of hard travelling, taught himself how to write. How to combine his researches, the stories he heard, the characters he met, into a genial narrative with forward momentum. I only struck out on an expedition in the hope that it would lead me forward to the next project, the next book. And therefore keep me alive.

At the end of Arthur's career comes the fictionalised figure of the young and untutored Scot who returns home broken from his colonial failures, to fade away in some freshly established asylum.

We hugged our rifles and revolvers, collected our cartridges, and continued rubbing our weapons. It was at this moment that one of our party burst forth with 'O, gin I were whar Gaudie rins' which he rendered with much pathos. Shortly afterwards we observed our Chuncho visitors being served with drink by an old crone whose vocation was evidently to prepare the stimulating beverage. The drink was followed by a dance, and again the old crone appeared with the big pumpkin bottle, and drink and dance alternated till the hilarious company seemed to forget and ignore our very existence. This went on 'till daylight did appear'. We had, of course, never shut an eye, and did not feel very brilliant, but considered ourselves fortunate in being alive enough to coax a few of the soberest of the gang to help us up the river with our rafts. By dint of great exertions we succeeded in getting about six miles onwards before breakfast, overtaking the truant padre, No. 2, who, having drunk a whole bottle of brandy, fell asleep over it. It would be tedious to tell of our struggles for the next few days and nights; suffice it to say we once again reached the King's hut in safety, which, after such roughing as we had gone through, seemed a palace indeed.

It is over. The opportunity to pass through the Homeric barrier of the rapids, Arthur's Scylla and Charybdis, to the reservation of the dead and the whirlpool of unforgiving ancestors, is spurned. The traumatised 1891 expedition came back to reality: inconvenient natives hanging around, drunk, dancing, disobedient, on land that must be chartered, in order to pass into the control of benevolent exploiters waiting behind their desks in the City of London. Commission fulfilled. Snake slain. Justifications published.

We parted from the royal family in the most amicable of terms, presenting them with souvenirs of our visit in the shape of beads, mirrors, hatchets, and a gun. King Chokery – or, as the Peruvians prefer to call him – 'Kinchoquiri', is by no means a very powerful potentate; his followers are not numerous, nor very energetic. A nomadic tribe, the Campas, or Chunchos, are here to-day and fifty miles off to-morrow… They are usually found in groups of two or three families, living under the shelter of palm leaves. They chiefly feed on fish, at the catching of which – with rude wooden hooks – they are very expert. They also appreciate the yucca when obtainable, while white grub, ants, and even lice are great delicacies. When travelling, the coca is an absolute necessity. Their language is an extraordinary jargon, intelligible only to a few, a totally different language cropping up every forty or fifty miles... We were told they had already massacred and eaten several European planters – and though we are bound to say that their reception of us was not particularly gracious, yet they showed no active hostility, and we shall ever take a kindly interest in watching their future fate.

The world was probably very young when you first found your way into this warm valley, but you have failed to 'dress it and keep it', and the fiat has gone forth. You must make way for others. Albeit, this is not a case of dispossessing. In no sense can those vagrant tribes be called possessors of the soil... Still, it is devoutly to be hoped that the rough and ready way British pioneers too often take to civilise such aborigines will be avoided in this case; and who knows but even the Chunchos may in the course of time learn the arts of civilised life?

The conclusion, as we know, and as our journey has confirmed, and as I must repeat, is bleak.

In short, this beautiful valley of the Perené has now become the property of a British Corporation, the concession having been duly ratified by the Peruvian Government, and arrangements are in progress for establishing a planting colony upon a scale never before attempted in Peru.

PAMPA WHALEY

'The promise of an unknown landscape… the perfect destination… it was a
way of completing the trip my great-grandfather had wanted to make.'
   – Paul Theroux, *Patagonia Revisited*

Confronted by a raked carpet of coffee cherries, under the merciless sun
of Pampa Whaley, the once dominant plantation, now removed from
the control of the Peruvian Corporation and worked by a co-operative
stacked with former engineers and overseers, we understood that this
renewable harvest was the true currency of the hills, a rich and blood-
bright form of gold. Beads to be dried and husked and transported,
made ready for the baristas of Hackney.

'But was this gold as we knew it?' Bruce Chatwin asked in his Prague
novel, *Utz*, when he considered the manufacture of porcelain. Gold,
according to the Chinese alchemist, was the 'body of the gods'. The
residue of solar fire. And this red sea of coffee cherries, on the drying
court above the Perené, echoed that great work: 'crystals reddened
into rubies, silver into gold'. The condition of redness telegraphed the
moment of transformation. Paraphrasing Chatwin, the search for the
ideal ground for the cultivation of coffee and the search for gold were
identical quests: 'to find the substance of immortality'. This unadmitted
task of Pampa Whaley, the transmutation of coffee into currency, was
the vision that Arthur carried back from the river. The story he told in
his book and the substance of the lectures he delivered to Australian colonists and the investors of Aberdeen and London. The pitch for labour.

A series of rectangular strips of polished coffee beads were laid out
behind buildings that still had the aspect of a political prison or a military camp on the edge of insecure and densely forested hills. A beach,

like the gleaming wet shingle of Hastings, was being raked and swept, by two boys of the locality. They are synchronised, up and back: one of them in a woollen helmet and the other with his shirt tied around his head like a pirate. Both are wired to their private playlists, and watched from a high window by an Andean overseer who has a share in the enterprise, and who takes his orders from the man on the telephone in Lima. The rakers, chosen for their slender physique and grudging obedience, spread the seeds into furrows, tilling up and back, up and back, without relief, to expose the secret essence of the future coffee to Peruvian sun and air.

'Here, as elsewhere,' according to Roland Barthes, 'the enclosure permits the system, i.e., the imagination.' The eastern raker, shot close by Grant, has the tragic expression, with those timeless astigmatic eyes, of a special imagination, gravid with particulars of place. The young man is tolerant of what must be endured, unprotected and modestly rewarded, under the hammer of sun, on this wide-open parade-ground square.

A veteran videographer of the scene, having worked with Radiohead and Blur, having tracked Bowie through Berlin, and covered Joy Division in Manchester, Grant couldn't resist putting a fist through the membrane of moviemaker cool. He abdicated his detached status by asking the inevitable and obvious question.

'*What* are you listening to?'

He leaned right in, to clarify the one-word answer.

'Electro.'

Boom boom! An Eighties retro binge, Grant surmised. Electro-funk. Pounding mechanical drumming, no vocals. Transporting the raker into the best possible state for the robotic routine of combing his windfall cherries, hour after hour. Under the sun. Skull ringing.

Who are these rakers? Families? Loves? Ambitions? Unknown. And therefore inadequately described anywhere beyond the lines traced by their immediate actions. No before and no after.

'Once you have a given name,' the Advocate told me, when we sat over our drinks in the bar of the station hotel, 'you can be sold. You can be waged and fined. You are lodged in the company archive.'

I don't know how the management and workers of a functioning coffee estate, with so much history invested in architecture and location, regard our intrusion. What do we offer them? There is a camera, of course, and the vague promise of some future report; news carried back to Europe, to potential clients.

Climbing out of the car and into the heat of the morning, taking stock of the white colonial buildings, this frontier fort captured by a new regime suspended between superstitious respect for the old ways and the requirement to make new, was an immediate shift into the labyrinth of memory; those archive photographs of armed Ashaninka warriors posed against these walls, primed to strike against other plantations, to kill invading overseers and incompetent managers. God, they were persuaded, had returned to earth at Metraro. The dead had climbed from the ground to join the uprising. 'The Indians,' according to Michael F. Brown and Eduardo Fernández in *War of Shadows*, 'were happy to suggest a target: the coffee hacienda.'

The break with the monolithic dominance of the Peruvian Corporation began around 1946 when the Colony transferred parcels of land to approved smallholders, with the intention of preventing settlers from cultivating coffee. Eventually the Corporation split into two independent companies. Under pressure from militants and an uncertain world market, they turned the last estate over to a co-operative of farm families and former employees. Pampa Whaley was once more a viable concern.

A solitary dog chased shadows down the dusty track alongside the still occupied living quarters. White walls, blind windows, palm fronds and a tight mesh fence protected the company offices. Across the track, looking down on the river, unexplained grey brick columns were in the process of being overwhelmed by vegetation. Naked ruins the co-operative didn't have the funds or the inclination to demolish or to preserve as the archaeological record of some forgotten atrocity.

The plantation manager, introduced as 'Felix', greets us. He is an obvious graduate of physical labour, now entitled to wear spectacles with blue temples on a cord around his neck. His hair is close-cropped and black. His T-shirt is also black and carries the imprint of a much-laundered or suppressed logo. Felix delivers the official company line, emphasised by chopping motions of his powerful arms, before handing us over to the care of the operational chief. Don Armando, a shorter indigenous figure in a baseball cap, was an accredited 'soil fungus specialist' in the last days of the Colony. His football shirt has the legend PERENE stitched in white capitals around a deep collar, the colour of cherry yogurt. Felix offers a careful pitch, as if he thinks a company snoop might be listening behind that grey mountain of coffee sacks. He does not want to be found guilty of omitting any important fact. Armando defers to his boss, a guillotined nod for every well-made point. But our guide comes into his own, gaining natural authority with the first step away from the office. He walks us through the stages of coffee production, from bushes on the hills to Lima trucks.

As we clamber over a series of concrete troughs, it feels as if we are being given a tour of a recently decommissioned gladiatorial arena. Pens for crocodiles. Stone bleachers for an audience that cannot afford to pay for shade. Gurgling tunnels from which lions or Christians might emerge. Armando points out the gates where the trucks, loaded with freshly picked berries, arrive. The best coffee, Arabica, he tells us, is processed from bushes planted on the steepest slopes. There has been a long cultural migration from the cradle of mankind in East Africa, from Rimbaud's Ethiopia, to Yemen, Arabia, Turkey and Europe. To coffee houses in the City of London. Lloyd's moved into marine insurance, underwriting the darkest voyages, after starting as a modest establishment serving coffee and gossip to gamblers and profit takers. The stain is still there in Leadenhall Street, along with the former offices of the Peruvian Corporation.

Surely one of the most prophetic and disturbing images of the late nineteenth century is Rimbaud's self-portrait 'in a coffee plantation' at Harar, in 1883? I place this wilted survivor alongside *Les Illuminations* and Conrad's *Heart of Darkness*. The poet/venturer, words spent but never squandered, is skeletal. As he should be. Exposed in dirty-white Conradian beachcomber pyjamas: tenured lunatic. Fugue walker hospitalised. Trustee of the asylum after many years of incarceration without trial. A premature spectre of the looming century of progress, barefoot on inhospitable rocks. The frosty burn of the pyjamas separates the victim, making his own portrait, no strings or wires, from the unruly backdrop of the native coffee thicket. The poet is outside race now, neither European nor African. No hat, no uniform, no weapon. He is outside class and status. *But in the only place.* Where it all started, the coffee fantasy. The Advocate, when I made the pitch for the potency of this image, quoted his favourite contemporary poet. He said that Rimbaud was *listening*: 'and in the distance he could hear / a vast rheumatism'.

The French poet's other magnificent photographic capture, its authenticity confirmed by a slight shiver in focus, is a portrait of a Harar trader, also from 1883. A graduate in the business of ruin. A squatting man legless under his sack of terminal rags. A few broken pots. An empty bowl. Crumbling pillars of 'civilisation' becoming the trunks of stone trees. A padlocked door. Some unclassified leaves on cured animal skin. The reality of everything that is found and lost.

Don Armando is on message, but sad. He takes a forgiving view of the declining days of the Company, his apprenticeship. There is no talk, as was reflex among the Ashaninka, of 'slavery'. Instead, he mentions excellent healthcare, provision for meals and entertainment. The benefits of belonging to a great global enterprise.

He did not speak of it, but I knew from my reading, and from what we had been told at Bajo Marankiari, that the original coffee economy depended on quasi-theological definitions of slavery. On the big estates, a slave would be responsible for 4,000–7,000 plants. It was not until 1871 that the 'Law of the Free Womb' declared that the children of slaves in Brazil would be free from birth. In 1888 slavery was abolished entirely. This was known as the 'Golden Law'. Coffee and gold boomed and dipped in close alliance. The first coffee-roasting company in San Francisco was floated during the 1850s Gold Rush. More fuel for speculators. More songs for the campfire. And more of those twilight, day-for-night sequences, cowboys yarning, smoothing their bedrolls, without which the cattle-drive film, the pioneer epic, would lose its soul. Bitter dregs thrown in the embers. Strange bird calls in the darkness. 'Night, ma'am.'

We can see the classic *terroir*, the slopes on which coffee cherries are picked and fed into long tubes for their steep descent to the ground where they will be bagged and loaded on waiting trucks. The simple mechanics of this operation have replaced the devastating grind of the slave days, the impossible loads. The mules with broken backs. Now there is a death rattle in the forest as they test the chutes with small stones. No obstructions, no intruders sheltering in the tube. Then the red flood, the promise of a golden harvest.

When the trucks arrive at the rear gates of the Coffee Colony, the berries are fed into stone troughs, some now puddled with a green slime. They will be thoroughly washed, passed through the water channels. They have been inducted, stage by stage, down the concrete levels where don Armando, balancing on a narrow ledge, leads us. There follows a priestly ritual of selection, sniffing, fingering and grading: painstaking repetitions required to achieve the spiritual transformation of this green alchemy.

On the exposed parade ground below us, carpets of cherries have been laid out, side by side, like a series of carefully prepared cricket strips. The red-brown of the coffee harvest complements the corrugated tin roofs of the rusting work sheds. Unexplained ladders lean at crazy angles against unexplained chutes. The monkish raking of the two synchronised young men continues, in energy-sapping temperatures, with Zen fatalism. Up and back. Up and back. To an unheard Electro beat. The enclosed plantation 'garden' has become as much an art manifestation as a grid of future profit. Don Armando's explanation is hushed and reverent. He is verger to the dedicated cathedral of progress in which he has a very small share.

Coming back inside the cool of the sheds, we are shown treatments reserved for the elite beans. Their quality revealed only when the husks have been split and discarded. Ordinary cherries are left outside, to be combed and smoothed by the twin rakers. In the trays of the shrouded interior, behind flapping white sheets, the speciality coffee, Geisha, the richest of the rich, is pampered. Here is the innermost chapel of the cult. Geisha is a natural Ethiopian variety introduced into Central America in the 1950s. While most of the native plants valued (and stolen) by P.D.G. Clark's employers, the Royal Botanic Gardens, were spirited to Europe, and then some suitable colony, coffee was a tolerated but highly profitable immigrant. Arthur said of Coffee Arabica: 'Though not indigenous, it grows and bears, as it was never known to bear in the old world... It bears enormously with judicious culture. The Pampa Hermosa is specially adapted for its culture.' Pale complexioned Geisha is a prized and acknowledged rarity. The discriminating sippers of Shoreditch and Hackney actively want to pay more, in order to display their hipster credentials. Jonathan Morris, in *Coffee, A Global History*, reports that 'in 2007 one lot sold for over one hundred times the price of commodity coffee.'

Milling and roasting and grinding: beneath the main warehouse floor, machines clattered and roared. An amorous dust ameliorated the thundering rapacity of the furnaces. Forests have been hacked into chunks suitable for the fire. Grey sacks are mounded like the charitable aftermath of a catastrophe. They are driven away by a fleet of panting trucks.

The final revelation came in a chamber with long tables, bubbling retorts and polished vessels. Even an appreciative whisper is too loud. This chapel/laboratory is reserved for a silent order of coffee initiates. And the presiding priestess is a swift and certain woman called Maria. She performs her duty with none of the showmanship of the urban barista. She lays out five glasses, spoons and thermometer. She sniffs. She skims. She waits. She dips a spoon, rinses and spits. She awards her secret score after a blind testing in which the contestants are identified only by number. Only the best are judged as fit for purpose. Maria is a person to be respected. Stern but fair. She is impervious to outside influences.

The warehouse floor was heavy with the furniture of absence, the ejected managerial overlords had left some of their toys behind when the peasants broke down the gates. Much of the evidence of former crimes has been bagged and stacked, ready for disposal. Too embedded to shift, a grandfather desk with satellite belts of cigar burns summons a vanished supervisor with time on his hands. And months, staring out of the window, between letters of instruction from home. Felix, with his blue-armed spectacles on a string, is camped in a smaller, more functional office, from which he can watch the Electro boys mark out their eternal coffee pitches, while staying within reach of a telephone, should the call come from Lima.

The cherry-raking ritual reminded me of my days painting white lines on the 120 football pitches of pre-Olympic Hackney Marshes. A good week's labour, eyes-down miles walked under a big sky, only to have this elegant geometry, as mysterious as Nazca lines, wiped out over the weekend by howling savages. On Monday morning, bicycle parked, I started again. Mixing the paste.

The end wall was blank but seductive. When I made a closer inspection of a painted framework of snakes and dragons, I took the decorative inspiration for some forgotten Chinese enterprise, or wistfully imported Parisian decadence. The wall had a double nature: it kept the jungle out, by reducing it to a noose of elegant calligraphic squiggles – and it worked, pretty well, as a screen for the projection of mute Mexican movies, shoot-'em-up romances with musical interludes that should have carried sound, if the plantation had the budget to invest in the technology. But many of the film cans muled up the dirt road from the last outpost of civilisation were silent; cinema in its purest form, with a blink of intertitles, meaningless to most of the audience.

I was imposing a Chinese element on the yellowing wall because I tried to stay alert to clues flattering Arthur's prejudices – and because of a memory flash of the 'exotic revivalism' of Grauman's Chinese Theatre on Hollywood Boulevard. A theatre which was not Chinese but Jewish; although the facility's 'naming rights' were purchased, like everything else, by a Chinese electronics manufacturer, TCL Corporation, in 2013. It goes without saying that Howard Hughes, the eccentric aviator, producer, sexual predator, recluse and world-class freak, was involved in the deal somewhere. Cultural appropriation in wide-screen action. Like the movie stars, their dogs and horses, leaving their prints on the pavement in Hollywood, the audience for the plantation show had to get down on their hands and knees in the dust to view the latest screening.

This coffee warehouse cinema, now reduced to an archaeological stain on the post-functional west wall, was evidence. It was the fossil survivor of the presentation made by Felix and don Armando, when they asserted that the Perené Colony had been a benevolent employer, laying on schooling, medical care, Adventist baptism, and entertainments to be shared, not quite equally, by the entire workforce. Those leaking armchairs, they were for the bosses. With hard swivel chairs for office staff. The field labourers, cooks, drivers, woodchoppers of the flaming furnace, cherry rakers: they had their unreserved places. On the floor, the lower floor. The raised area with the offices now has a suspended TV screen, inactive, but available for football, when appropriate.

Imagine the blessing of the cone of dusty light, from the grinding teeth and cogs of the 16mm projector on the upper deck, throwing moving pictures on that reserved wall. Romance. Comedy. Revolution. Some strange and wonderful films came from Mexico.

I was captivated. The coffee plantation screen could be the answer to my problem: how to make restitution for my failure to pass through the Perené cascades on a raft, and therefore to go that one short step further than my great-grandfather. And, in so doing, exorcise the killing of the snake. And lesser 'crimes' highlighted by our meddlesome time-travelled judgements. Disparate narratives, separated by more than a hundred years, might yet fuse. What if… somebody as foolish as myself, a collaborator like Andrew Kötting, could be persuaded to engage with the Ashaninka of Yurinaki, to cut down the right trees, to lash together a balsa raft, and to head off downriver. To the whirlpool of dead ancestors and beyond. The enterprise, in all its stages, would be filmed. The cans of film carried on mules to Pampa Whaley and projected here, to an audience of participants, on this wall.

THE CAGE OF PAPER

'Pilar provided me with the transcription of an important document on the slaving activities of the Upper Ucayali… that no longer exists because the papers of the Archivo de la Prefectura de Loreto were burned in 1998.'
— Fernando Santos-Granero, *Slavery & Utopia*

At the lunch table, always a significant hiatus in the day, it was time to offer proof of our credentials, through the gift of paper; photocopied documents and fading images from the archives of the Peruvian Corporation of London. Our cover, as disinterested outsiders and potential promoters of the coffee enterprise, would not survive the gentlest of interrogations: we were here as messengers from an unresolved past. Two of us, father and daughter, were in a direct line from one of the men who scouted the territory and delivered the favourable report that led to land enclosure and its bloody consequences. Blood ties are everything; children, grandchildren and great-grandchildren must act in accordance with the remembered deeds of those who came before them.

It was Lucho's métier, bringing in a cook. As honoured guests, we were receiving special treatment. The women preparing the meal had worked all morning. In the early days of the plantation, females were not employed, or were grudgingly paid with a few coins when there was a labour crisis. They might, eventually, be trusted to undertake tasks of grading and inspection, for which men were deemed to be too impatient, too easily tempted to wave through flawed product. Now Maria was highly respected, her qualifications and gifts given due deference. But she was not invited to join us at the dinner table. Perhaps she was too busy. There was a chequered tablecloth and a set of large white plates. Felix sat, on a white plastic chair, at one end, and Farne, with her rucksack of papers, at the other. We were served with steak and tomatoes, on a mound of white rice, accompanied by beakers of diluted orange juice. With the arrival of the coffee essence, we opened our discussion.

Felix enthroned, with don Armando standing at his shoulder, listened intently to the recitation of the evidence my daughter had uncovered in the files. The manager lifted his spectacles to find loopholes in the fatal contract. A portrait of Arthur lay on the tartan cloth, held down by emptied platters. My ancestor's smile seemed to relish our discomfort and his re-engagement in the conversation, the society of an active plantation. He was right. In the end the ground had yielded up its benefits. And the workers were industrious and god-fearing. *But where were the Chinese?*

I read aloud a brief extract from Arthur's book, showing how his acknowledgement of the potential of this valley anticipated a 'progressive' resolution.

> *It is impossible to avoid asking the question what is to become of this great region, these thousand and one products of nature? The wealth of an empire is yearly lost in these boundless forests. These rich resources, lying almost at our very doors, must soon appeal to that restless spirit of enterprise which, not content with its past triumphs, longs for new conquests and a wider field of exercise. One looks forward to the dazzling future.*

It is clear that, as far as Arthur was concerned, this country was a vision of paradise, before the fall. Further travels among the mining towns were a barely tolerated grind, before the collapse, fainting and tumbling from his mule, as he crossed the Andes. And a gradual recovery, as with his much more serious crisis in Ceylon, when he got back to sea level in Lima. Time to visit the botanical gardens. Time to read and reflect, to dip again into Humboldt, one of the inspirations of his Aberdeenshire youth. The excursions he now chose to make were echoes of Humboldt's passage through the same territory in 1802.

My great-grandfather finds himself inspecting Inca ruins that he has discovered among 'clusters of thriving fruit trees'. And in this strange suspended interval, like a person emerging from quarantine or stepping ashore after a long sea voyage, Arthur loses himself and his habitual confidence of address. He composes a fable, drawn from his mentor, about the implications of stealing knowledge from an enchanted garden. A resource can only remain a resource if it is untapped. In adopting the voice of another writer, he begins, at the very last, to know himself.

The young son of a local chief, who guided Humboldt over the surviving traces of the palace of his forefathers, 'filled his imagination with images of buried splendour and golden treasures hidden beneath the masses of rubbish upon which we trod'. An ancestor, the boy said, had blindfolded his wife and led her through a labyrinth carved from the rock and into the fabled 'subterranean garden of the Incas'. There she found artificial trees 'formed of the purest gold', with leaves and fruit and birds on the branches. 'There, too, was the much-sought-for golden travelling chair of Atahualpa.' This vision, 'in glory of changeless metal', is like a preview of the poem 'Byzantium' by W.B. Yeats: 'Planted on the star-lit golden bough'. Arthur, stepping aside from his commissioned task, uses allegory to reconfigure the conclusion he submitted to the Peruvian Corporation.

The indigenous boy, the conduit of ancient tales, is challenged. 'Since you and your parents believe so firmly in the existence of this garden, are not you sometimes tempted in your necessities to dig in search of treasures so close at hand?'

The answer is shaped as a coded version of what my great-grandfather now knew. 'If we had the golden branches with all their golden fruits our white neighbours would hate and injure us. We have a small field and good wheat.' Subsistence is more than enough.

Rummaging through her papers, Farne retrieved a clear demonstration of the foolishness of the colonial project, as Arthur was obliged to pitch it, when he spoke about finding 'elbow-room of the most lucrative and interesting description' for restive country youths and younger sons of the landed gentry. There were letters, and Farne passed them around, from hopeless plantation managers, shipped out in the 1920s and '30s, now begging for instruction in the assembly and operation of machines.

How should they control men who spoke impossible languages? They were so many Crusoes, cast adrift, and oppressed by the hills and forests that surrounded them.

The lecture Alexander Ross delivered to the Royal Geographical Society in March 1892 was a promotion for the Peruvian Corporation, a teaser for investors, and a recruiting speech for patriotic sons squandering their inheritance between wars. It was a nicely balanced recitation of pertinent facts. The lecture was attended by the senior patron of Ross and Sinclair, Sir Arthur Dent. Dent was a man of the City, responsible for major land transformation in distant places. But he vanished from the pages of history – until his name was satirically retooled by Douglas Adams in *The Hitch-Hiker's Guide to the Galaxy*. And a spurious celebrity, with no backstory, was achieved. The old gods do have a sense of humour.

As some of the familiar characters we had tracked faded from the official record – and Ross disposed of his fellow travellers, Sinclair and Clark, in a couple of sentences – so the established power brokers, the diplomats, bankers, committee men (and they were all men), stepped out from the shadows. The 'questions' that followed the well-received Ross presentation were like pronouncements from Mount Olympus, approving judgements delivered by those for whom the savage world was a virgin text, waiting to be re-edited according to the rules of civilisation.

Señor F.A. Pezet, the Peruvian Consul-General in London, acknowledged how much his own government had done to explore the unmapped interior. What modern transport systems they intended to build. 'You have just seen from the photographs that these roads are mere bridle tracks, but we hope in time to come to have good roads and railroads to join the navigable rivers... This road opens up a great amount of country... It is understood that with steam navigation on this river, and with railroads running as far as this navigable point, it will be possible to journey from Lima, on the Pacific coast, to Pará, on the Amazon, in about eight days. Thence to Liverpool would be a ten days' trip, thus bringing Lima within twenty days of London.'

How the teasing mirage of futurity shimmers on the horizon! Señor Pezet is carried away. Great highways, penetrating the sullen interior, will inevitably pass through districts rich with gold, silver and quicksilver.

> What would commerce be without geography? This island has been explored and studied so thoroughly that you do not want geography for England, but for other countries it is all important. When these roads are opened, you will have cheaper sugar, cheaper coffee… In a very short time, Peru will be able to present to the scientific world a very good account of itself.

Mr Clements R. Markham responded: 'There can be no doubt that coffee can be grown in any quantity there… but it should always be remembered that in Peru quality goes above quantity. The coffee grown there is the best that was ever tasted; and it is the same with the other natural products… Although the small quantity produced is due partly to the enormous quantity of trees that have been cut down… still the quality is superior… This valley of the Chanchamayu is only one out of a great many extending up to the Bolivian frontier, all of great richness, and some of them will, I trust, when the railroads are finished, be almost equally accessible. One of them, that of Caravaya, also yields an enormous quantity of gold.'

Who is this Markham, a 'handsome fellow', who speaks with such authority of these distant lands? Joe Jackson, writing *The Thief at the End of the World*, pictures him as having 'a broad forehead, muttonchops, and pale, distant eyes'. A man 'irritatingly destined for high office'. And high office is duly achieved. Markham is made President of the Royal Geographical Society. He publishes forty-four books. He is knighted by Queen Victoria. Jackson gives him credit for 'painting Latin America as a land of unlimited resource ripe for the taking… It was "gold and diamond country" awaiting the cultivation of coffee.'

It was the same Clements R. Markham who brokered the marriage of convenience between the India Office and Kew. Cinchona from the Andes would be monitored by gardeners who had been trained by Kew to collect and cultivate, while hiding their true intentions from the 'narrow-minded' jealousy of Peruvian officials. In March 1860, Markham headed an expedition into the interior, to collect seeds and seedlings. Two months later, as Jackson reports, 'he watched his precious seeds stowed away onto a steamer for London.' And then Ceylon. Where the convalescent plantsman, Arthur Sinclair, witnessed their arrival at the Royal Botanic Gardens in Peradeniya. Gardens from where his fellow traveller P.D.G. Clark would be seconded for the survey of the Upper Amazon.

Markham contextualises the account delivered by Ross. He makes it clear that the point of any wilderness journey is economic geography, but he has not been immune, during his own adventures, to the essential myths of place. He detours, without drawing breath, towards 'the interesting history of that chief calling himself Atahualpa, whose tomb has been mentioned by Mr Ross... His real name was Juan Santos. He raised up the Campas Indians, and drove the Spaniards out of the montaña in 1740... Nobody knows what became of him... The Spaniards did not again appear in these forests for forty to fifty years, and it was due to the missionaries of Ocopa that the country was again opened up. Father Sobreviela, one of the Ocopa fraternity, explored the montaña towards the end of the last century, and wrote an elaborate report... I have a copy of it, but it has never been printed.'

So much wasted paper! So many lost or burnt reports. So many redacted files in vandalised safes. So many golden legends told and mistold, recorded in the dust, in the footprints of the snaking, circular dances of the dispossessed. What have we added to the mountain of powdery landfill? Farne has her stash of podcast recordings, from trains and huts beside rivers, and frontier hotels where we could sit, morning or evening, with our coffee. Grant has his oblique and tactfully harvested images, but this evidence will be manipulated in the cutting, until it is almost as unreliable as my prose.

Geography endured and conquered gives Markham prescience, the confidence of a shrewd gambler on a roll. He guesses that coca will be hipper and more profitable than coffee: before the world speeds towards self-destruction, and the comfortable classes solicit and require gestures of condescending ecology. The great bureaucrat is gripped by visions of the future. The time will surely come when the wealthiest of landowners, even unto princes of the blood, assassins of birds, fish and stags, will wail over climate change. In the seizure of his own oratory, Markham seems to predict the way that solar power, for example, has greatly increased the capacity of Afghan poppy farmers in the perpetual war zones on the borders of Empire. 'Coca requires more care in its cultivation than tea... But efforts should be made to learn from the Incas their art of maintaining the quality of their products. I am sure that all geographers will welcome the work now being done by the Peruvian Corporation in this interesting country.'

Reading Markham's improvised rhapsody, delivered without notes, but with the authority of a knighthood, I wondered what we had missed by not getting our hands on P.D.G. Clark's handwritten report to the Peruvian Corporation. Clark was the suspected plant, the agent of Empire on permitted sabbatical. Arthur makes reference to the 'illustrious traveller', Clements Markham, on page 11 of his published account, but says little or nothing about Clark, beyond a token gesture of thanks for his companion's 'keen enthusiasm for economic botany'. Ross, as fellow planter and rival, hovers over my great-grandfather's narrative, admonished for his impatience, but Clark? The third man is treated somewhere between a minor functionary, keeper of notes, and a nuisance to be endured. A potential quisling imposed on the expedition by the paymasters.

We are not yet writing about it, making claims for one version over another, but we are enjoying this guided tour of the abandoned offices, the cupboards and secret storage spaces of the Pampa Whaley Coffee Colony. We are being led through all the decommissioned parts of a resurrected plantation that Arthur Sinclair could only imagine, as he kept his eyes fixed on the river ahead of him. The tour is our reward for the gift of paper.

In the former payroll office there is an ancient safe, stuffed with bundles of useless documentation, but yawning open, as if untouched since the day Butch Cassidy blew the hinges and made his escape to Patagonia. This, we are told, is where the plantation wages were kept. Every payment, however small, was entered in a ledger. Many of the entitlements, in the early days, were in the form of food. The heart of the operation was the small kitchen. It was a nice calculation, to give the workers just enough energy to keep them going, but not enough to make them dream of escape. If their bellies were too well filled, they would not return. Horticulture, outside the daylight hours of labour, was not to be tolerated. Their humble plantings of beans and avocados should be cleared at once or trampled by cattle.

The 'communications room' was a shelf with a plug-in phone system, now a tangle of trailing leads and a crank. It took eight stiff turns to contact Metraro. Nothing has been preserved as mere heritage. The detritus of history is still around because there is no obvious profit in clearing it away. So we trail behind don Armando, interrupting his day's work, from forgotten office to dormitory. Out of the upper-floor windows of a dusty warehouse with the optimistic ambition of becoming an interesting stopover for adventure tourists, we enjoy spectacular prospects of the Perené. It would have been easy to picture the thing that never happened, the steady transit of coffee sacks to river, river to ocean.

'What are those ruins?' I asked.

'They are other times,' Armando said, moving us swiftly on.

He did not mean the lethal squabbles between plantation bosses, or the attacks carried out by indigenous people inspired by Juan Santos Atahualpa or manipulated by competitive missionaries. He meant recent history, if history can be assigned a linear progression. If it does not happen everywhere at once. Over and over.

'Sendero Luminoso.'

In the later stages of the armed struggle, disaffected Maoists followed the money into illicit coca cultivation and processing. According to Michael F. Brown and Eduardo Fernández, a climate of lawlessness was created in the cloud jungle, in which the insurgents thrived, by aligning themselves with the peasant farmers and against Peruvian paramilitaries and police. They associated uniformed militias with protection offered to the large coffee estates. These grey columns, set among skeletal ruins, were the residue of a resisted Shining Path assault on Pampa Whaley.

But the guerrillas did not reach the heart of the operation, the cave of paper. Out of nowhere, at the end of our tour, we were treated to the ultimate revelation, the surviving archive of the Pampa Whaley plantation. Correspondence with the Peruvian Corporation of London: *all of it*. Don Armando was slightly reluctant, ushering us into the chamber, stepping quickly aside from an aura of non-specific shame. Like a man with a collection of stolen paintings in his garage; masterpieces that could neither be restored nor sold off.

I saw Grant move swiftly and silently to catch the frame: don Armando trapped, imprisoned. The post-historic inner room with the mounds of archive – sacks, ledgers, maps, cashbooks, labelled files and ring binders – was divided from an outer office by an oxidised set of security bars. A cage. A jailhouse unable to shake off its stench. Like the ones Arthur inspected in Tasmania. Like somewhere to hold Billy the Kid. But I'm sure that our Conradian filmmaker was referencing another, more Amazonian image: Klaus Kinski in *Fitzcarraldo*, in his fouled white suit, driven beyond endurance, shaking the bars of the Iquitos prison where he has been lodged after raging at fate. And at the rubber barons' complacent dictatorship of unreason.

The Lima records have been burnt or shredded, so that official accounts do not contradict the version of progress, exploration and road building, promoted by Peruvian diplomats like Señor F.A. Pezet. This insane lumber room of pre-bonfire documentation is everything there now is. It is, in essence, the whole world of the plantation; a mausoleum of fiscal fingerprints and triple-entry bookkeeping. Tangible evidence for any future prosecution. The tattered confessions of pioneer planters. Here was a pitiful fence of numbers erected against the evil fecundity of the forest. It was easier to keep everything, and to ignore it, hide it away, than to make cosmetic changes to a system of coercive slavery and exploitation.

Swollen safes had burst, heavy metal rotted by tropical rains and the lustful heat of languid and drunken afternoons. Coffee sacks could not contain the papers with which they had been stuffed. Bugs feasted on ink and cardboard. Rats gnawed new trails across fabulous hand-drawn treasure maps. Every coin paid out was recorded. Every complaint registered. This was the Peruvian version of a Stasi surveillance bunker unpillaged and unexamined.

I noted a straining shelf loaded with box files marked LIQUIDA-CIONES. I photographed charts of the Perené, the reaches beyond the rapids. You could lie down, sleep on mattresses of unpaid bills and buried invoices, and never wake into the same reality. There were even bundles of books, paperback and antiquarian, novels and manuals of instruction glued into blocks by the liquors of entropy. Forensic teams could disappear into this cage and emerge, decades later, with a comprehensive record covering every last aspect of the rise, fall and resurrection of the Pampa Whaley plantation.

Such a wealth of facts, a cave of paper heavier than the legendary gold of Juan Santos Atahualpa, was open to interpretation from all parts of the cultural spectrum. Marxist–Leninists, with a profound distrust of coffee politics, could identify the misuse of the thermodynamic energy of labour. Leopold II of Belgium, the ultimate Third World predator, could write home, as he did from Seville: 'I am very busy here going through the Indies archives and calculating the profits which Spain made then and makes now out of her colonies.'

It would take a witness with the rigour of Conrad, right back at the start in 1895, the year of the publication of Arthur's book, to do justice to the way a discontinued space registers the futility of progress, the beautiful collapse of objects left to their own devices.

> He went towards the office door and with some difficulty managed to open it. He entered in a cloud of dust that rose under his feet.
>
> Books open with torn pages bestrewed the floor; other books lay about grimy and black, looking as if they had never been opened. Account books. In those books he had intended to keep day by day a record of his rising fortunes. Long time ago. A very long time... The very dust and bones of a dead and gone business. He looked at all these things, all that was left after so many years of work, of strife, of weariness, of discouragement, conquered so many times. And all for what?

I was dizzy, choked on sentient dust. In this barred cell was the explosion of my project; all the words, false starts, digressions, dictated runs and rushes; all the libraries I had asset-stripped; all the books and maps and photographs stacked so menacingly around my desk. Here was a conceptual exhibition spearing my vanities. I saw my proposed book gutted and spilled and broken down into its constituent parts. But while I indulged the unexpected gift of this archival metaphor, while I jumped about, gleaning for the most potent images to carry away, Farne was reading. She was assessing and evaluating. She found one bunch of papers, among so many, to be photocopied when we returned to the company office.

Grant never disclosed his scenario or offered any commentary on what he had captured, but now, in this library of madness, I caught a glint of satisfaction in his steady gaze. It was the filmmaker's solemn belief that he preserved all the imagery he needed in his head and that the decisions of a documentarian were never more than fitful moments of recognition, confirming a belief that the exterior world could not begin to match an already resolved vision of it.

There was no going on, no going back. My correspondent and moral conscience, the Spanish lawyer battling in Brussels with plagues and endlessly revised treaties, said that my photographs from the Pampa Whaley archive, although terrifying in their call for action, were nothing on the computer files with which he was assaulted, day after day. And that is why he made it his business to emphasise by messenger, letter, fax and telepathy that when there is no other place to go, and no way of getting there, the writer must intensify, to the ultimate degree, the place he or she is fortunate enough to occupy. Start with a few yards of ground, the length of your own shadow. My friend referred me to the split vision of the poet Ed Dorn in the closing book of his definitive quest narrative of the American West, *Gunslinger*. A journey to nowhere that arrives, many times over. 'I had one eye out / for the prosecutors of Individuality / and the other eye out for the advocates.'

That evening, in the foodless cocktail hour of the frontier hotel, under the muted frenzy of the suspended TV screen, I discharged the task laid on me by a walking companion from England. Before he settled in Deptford, and launched a life of high-octane fatherhood and film-making, Andrew Kötting spent a golden year with his partner, Leila McMillan, venturing around the fiction of Latin America. It proved to be the 'time of their time': bed bugs, buses and visions. A whirling delirium of subsistence travel and intertwined loving elation. Andrew came back with a collection of tin charms known as *milagros*. They functioned as ex-votos, offerings made in the wake of miraculous recovery. Kötting wanted me to return two of these to the territory from which they had originally emerged. And to gift them to anybody who would appreciate their special qualities.

It was time for me to make some small restitution to Lucho. Without his contacts, his experience, his stories, his single-minded investment in a shamanic brand of tourism, Arthur's journey could never have been tracked in the time available to us. Lucho understood, immediately, what I was giving him: a gilded mask for the eyes. Eyes like winged insects. The *milagro* represented the divided vision of the true pilgrim as described by Dorn: the ability to scan the far horizon, while remaining fully conscious of the next huckster lawyer tapping on your shoulder. Our Andean guide was moved by the gesture. He tucked the *milagro*

away, safely, in one of his many pockets, along with the blades, oint-
ments and scavenged pills. And he made me a reciprocal gift, a bag of
coffee grown on his own land. This proved to be a challenging drink,
but excellent compost for tomatoes.

The other *milagro*, a golden arm and hand, was for Farne. It would
return with her to London, she said. There was still much work to be
done. But the device was also a symbol of release, the bent arm of the
wildwater swimmer. And it might, one way or another, carry her back
to Peru. Swimming or flying. Alone or with her own children. Without
her diligent digging in other archives, there was no spine to our expedition. No check to my romance.

And Farne had an interesting package too. From those impossible
stacks of paper she had extracted a telling fragment, an obituary from
the Aberdeen press that I had to strain to interpret with my most powerful magnifying glass. *'Planter in Ceylon. Mr Patrick Clark's Death. Had
Retired to Murtle.'* Mr Patrick D.G. Clark, 'Government official and
planter', is recorded as being 'a prominent figure in the development
of the tea and rubber industries in Ceylon.' He was trained at Kew
Gardens before being shipped out to the colonies. 'He was lent by
the Colonial Office to visit Peru with the commissioners appointed
to report on land held by the Peruvian bondholders.' In later life, he
became the representative of 'various big tea and rubber companies'.
He was also a keen sportsman with rod and gun. In politics, where
Arthur Sinclair declared himself a Liberal, Clark was a convinced and
active Unionist.

And there was more. Farne had photocopied a new map, to set
against the versions published by Sinclair and Ross. Here already were
the faint outlines of the coffee estates that would emerge like phantoms
from the virgin forest. The map was drawn by a government agent, a
certain Mr Clark. We also had in our possession the full one-hundred-
page text of a covert report on 'The Central Territory of Peru' by the
Curator, Royal Botanic Gardens, Peradeniya, Ceylon, as delivered on
19 December 1891.

My fitful story, already persuaded into many bifurcating channels,
was once more in question. Clark's report to the plant pirates at Kew,

while never receiving the exposure of those delivered by his better-known companions, was the one that finally settled the fate of the fertile valley of the Perené. And the one proving that however many times I revised my own version, however many documents Farne supplied, I would never understand or retrace the epic journey undertaken by my courageous and undeniable great-grandfather.

MELBOURNE

It was the name of the vessel carrying my great-grandfather back to Australia, so soon after his return from Peru, that caught my eye: RMSS *Oroya*. The ill-omened smelting town on the railway over the mountains. I wondered if, like me, Arthur was superstitious about the implications of misguided naming. Leaving his homeland for the first time on the *Albemarle*, a clipper tainted by its association with a military commander charged with subjugating the Scottish highlands, and now, crossing the world to promote land seizure in the valley of the Perené, onboard a ship boasting of industrial blight.

A few weeks of adjustment passed in a dream, a self-imposed quarantine, before I started to work through the photographs I had made of certain maps, contracts, invoices and preserved newspaper cuttings, in the 'Cage of Paper' at the coffee plantation of Pampa Whaley. When the impulse to hack on through this tangle of images and friable information was beginning to wane, I found the smudged but still decipherable news report from the *Melbourne Argus*, Monday 3 April 1893.

BRITISH SETTLEMENT IN PERU.
A COLONIAL ENTERPRISE.

"Yes, I went out to select 10,000,000 acres of the best land I could find in Peru. I have already marked out about 2,000,000 acres and have my eye on the rest. Before long I expect to have 25,000 men working there for the Peruvian Corporation, a company consisting of British holders of Peruvian bonds, to whom the Government of Peru has made over certain assets in the country, including this amount of land, in default of meeting the bonds. We shall grow coffee principally, and as both soil and climate are admirably adapted for cultivation, we have every prospect of getting a magnificent return for our labour. As for the Chunchas or Indians who are now spread over the portion of the country which I have selected, they will simply retire further back to the limitless unexplored forests and pampas eastwards of the Cordilleras."

Mr Arthur Sinclair, a native of Aberdeen, an ex-coffee-planter of Ceylon and a mighty traveller, was the speaker. He arrived in Melbourne by the RMSS Oroya, and is paying a flying visit to Australasia in order to prime himself on the spot with the least information as to the suitability of coloured labour for plantation work in a tropical climate. For an enterprise of such magnitude it is necessary to examine witnesses and take the evidence of men of experience. When 25,000 men have to be conducted over the double range of the Andes and down into a hitherto unknown region in the valley of the Amazon, a journey which occupies several months, and has to be made through the territory of Indians armed with rude but effective weapons, and presumably as ready to fight as their forefathers were for their prairie homes, it is necessary that some care should be taken in selecting the colonists, or to put it more plainly, the invaders.

Mr Sinclair's own feeling is in favour of Chinese labour, although the opinion in London leans rather to the white man. The ex-coffee-planter's own experience has been that white men are not suited for field work in the tropics, and though the temperature in the selected region is not unduly oppressive, rarely rising above 80deg. Fahr. in the shade, its persistence is decidedly trying for the normal European constitution… Already 50 families of Italians and Frenchmen have been sent out to the chosen spot, which lies between the parallels of 5deg. and 10deg. south latitude, and between longitude 80deg. west and longitude 75deg. west. A few of the Frenchmen, scared by the solitudes that stretch away for millions of square miles towards the undulating plains of Brazil, bolted back to Paris immediately; but the remaining pioneers, under the control of a Scotch overseer, are devoting themselves to the cultivation of coffee, cinchona, rice, and manioc. The overseer, who is the only representative of Great Britain in the place, hails, as might be expected, from Aberdeen.

The directors of the Peruvian Corporation in London, whose chairman is Sir Alfred Dent, picked out Mr Sinclair as the best man that they could find to be entrusted with the duty of selecting the 10,000,000 acres handed over by the Peruvian Government, and Mr Sinclair, accompanied by Mr Ross, a coffee planter, and Mr Clark, the director of the botanical gardens in Ceylon, started on the long journey in the spring of 1891...When they left the train at Chicla the troubles of the travellers began in earnest. Friends in London had said good-bye to them without disguising their apprehensions that the explorers would never return alive, and they are now going forward into country where no native Spanish Peruvian even had ever shown his face. The three men were well armed and well equipped, and they started in good heart... with a cavalcade of 20 pack mules and two Spanish priests, who undertook to act as guides...

Making their way down towards the river Perene, a tributary of the Amazon, the travellers came upon the monarch of the Chunchas, King Chokery, an affable potentate... When King Chokery had shaken off his indisposition and been photographed with his wife and family, he caused rafts to be built and accompanied the explorers with a bodyguard of troops for 50 miles down the river, where the camp was pitched. Presently the troops became restless, and Mr Sinclair and his companions had an anxious and sleepless night, waiting, revolver in hand, for the expected rush. The warlike designs of the Chunchas were, however, peacefully dissolved in potations of native spirit, and the explorers lived to select the site of the new settlement. The first block chosen had a frontage of 60 miles on either bank of the Amazon, with a depth of 50 miles back, and here the experiment is to be begun by planting nurseries of the coffee shrub as well as cocoa and cinchona. The Chunchas, stupefied with drink, look on in blissful unconsciousness at this second invasion of their country. Not many miles from the new settlement the travellers were shown a crumbling tomb, said to contain the remains of the unfortunate King Atahualpa... Pizarro went through the country with a Bible in one hand and a sword in the other. The bondholders in London are taking a ledger instead of a Bible, and a ploughshare instead of a sword, for the enterprise is made in the name of commerce, and not in the name of religion... That is why the invasion has been planned, and as far as can be seen at present either Tamil Indians or Chinamen will form the bulk of the mercenaries.

And so I recognised, as a warning, with only the first part of the job achieved, the easy part, the journey, how swiftly myths can be cooked, and how casually 'facts' are suborned. The Australian journalist dutifully reported my great-grandfather's pitch, while listening to the first rehearsal for a fiction of the 1891 expedition still to be written. In this Arthur was a true modernist, he fulfilled his contracted PR requirements *before* the book was published. He got his retaliation in first and he left the clues by which his descendants would be seduced into rounding out the history and accepting the consequences.

PROXIMA CENTAURI

SOLLY MANDER

'When you travel you step back from your own days, from the fragmented imperfect linearity of your time. As when reading a novel, the events and people become allegorical and eternal. The boy whistles on a wall in Mexico. Tess leans her head against a cow. They will keep doing that forever.'

– Lucia Berlin, *Evening in Paradise*

You can always return, but you don't come back. Sleeping dogs around the domestic hearth know your shape and smell, but they will not lift their heads to growl a welcome. You are indeed fortunate if your abandoned wife is not planning to murder you in the bath. A questionable fiction of distant adventure, explored and exploited, has become the pale shadow of a larger truth. Our remembered London, on the wrong side of the Peruvian expedition, was a sonar echo of that remark by the Theodor Koch-Grünberg character in *Embrace of the Serpent*. 'When I came back, I had become another man.'

The implication being, although the foolish traveller has not yet begun to grasp it: *he never did come back*. Another entity has taken his place. The old self is extinguished: a shade, a replicant. One of those affectless spectres wandering jungle trails that disappear immediately behind them. The historic Koch-Grünberg, romanticised through a film impersonation, is obliged to reoccupy the hollow shell waiting for him in his old country: in his house, the marital bed.

We have inspected the cave of evidence, the story of the Perené Colony reduced to its constituent parts, bagged and left to rot on the floor. Because of our failure to reach the territory beyond the rapids, there would be no resolution to my great-grandfather's unspoken challenge. And no confrontational encounter with his querulous spirit.

Without an achieved destination for the balsa raft, there was no fixed point from which we could depart. I would have to re-learn, yard by yard, how to haunt myself on home ground where my footsteps no longer registered the faintest imprint.

My account now completed, I had to admit that my great-grand-father, author and performer in the drama of Peruvian coffee coloni-sation, was finally unknowable. Out of reach. Retracing his footsteps brought me no nearer to an understanding of my own impulses, flaws and obsessions. Soaking in a warm Hackney bath, I dipped into a recov-ered first draft of W.B. Yeats' *Journal*. A couple of sentences took my eye: 'Today, for the first time, I lost my temper with an actor. Sinclair refused to play the part he was assigned.' And so he did. I had pre-scripted a narrative, based on a book published in 1895, but the main character stubbornly declined his 'assigned' role in a revised afterlife. Yeats was out of humour too, with the provincial politics of the Abbey Theatre, with endless squabbles over Irish nationalism. And with con-jured spirits and projections with a mind of their own. But, worst of all, were the long hours these tedious affairs stole from the real business of doing nothing creatively; listening and waiting. The poet's life task, as he acknowledged (and as I have quoted, time and again), was to 'assist the imagination of the dead'. The ones who are always nudging and whispering at the window.

I couldn't resist investigating this other Sinclair, the Abbey Theatre regular. He was billed as 'Arthur Sinclair': that was a good start. Arthur took the character parts, the comic roles, especially in O'Casey and Shaw. He married Maire O'Neill, sister of the celebrated performer/director Sara Allgood. Hitchcock wanted him for Captain Boyle in his film of *Juno and the Paycock*. Wanted his bluster. Arthur had to pass on that one, he was already under contract to tour the play. But he made an impression, supporting Margaret Lockwood and Dennis Price, in Brian Desmond Hurst's film of Daphne du Maurier's *Hungry Hill*. Much more pertinent was the role of 'Patsy' O'Brien in the 1937 film of Rider Haggard's *King Solomon's Mines*. Sinclair plays an Irish 'dream chaser' who fails to strike it rich with a South African mine. He persuades Allan Quartermain (Cedric Hardwicke) to give him a ride to the coast in his wagon. Along the way they pick up a dying man with a map of the route to the fabled treasure of King Solomon. Sinclair/O'Brien steals the map and vanishes into the night. It doesn't turn out well. 'Unfriendly natives' are waiting on the other side of the mountains. There are rituals for 'smelling out evildoers'.

'Arthur Sinclair, Stage Star, Dead – Seen in Many Movies,' reported the *New York Times* in December 1951. But 'Arthur Sinclair' was not really Arthur Sinclair. He was born in Dublin as Arthur McDonnell. The aspiring actor thought the Scottish adoption would look better on playbills. The Dubliner was ten years old when *In Tropical Lands* was published. I like to think he might have read it. He was the right age for stories of imperialist adventure, treasure maps, and magical ceremonies. But, on just one occasion, he wouldn't take the role assigned to him by the great W.B. Yeats. And, thereby, earned his solitary reference in the *Journal*.

Something happened. The news from Bajo Marankiari was not good, Grant reported. Forbidden to return in order to complete his film without interference from his fellow travellers, the director was prospecting on Skype. Ashaninka internet, he said, was 'patchy'. It was the rainy season. Shima-Shima, the weather shaman, would dive into Lucho's taxi while they headed off in search of a signal. Roads were flooded. But shaman and guide were 'in good form'. The village was isolated now, cut off by roadblocks. One old man had died. The chief's mother, mistress of the smoke, had lost her mind and been taken to another place, where, it was hoped, she might in time recover it. Shima-Shima was brewing anti-Covid potions for the local police, the ones enforcing the enclosures. Denied all access to tourist income, the Ashaninka had reverted to planting and self-sufficiency. Velisa and her mother found a secret place in which to see out the time of the virus, while they dosed on ayahuasca.

Warnings from the spoiled past soured the light over Stratford. Something held the court of crows to worn grass still recovering from a lost summer's parties. Immersed for winter months in the privileged darkness of research and recovery, I woke one fine spring morning, when those weeks of 'female' rain finally relented, to news of the latest and most resistant plague. A gift from the animal markets. An interspecies message from the last wild places. And a gift that keeps giving. I hoped it was not part of the luggage of guilt I carried home with me from the cloud forest. I was one of the fortunate few whose lives were easily accommodated to forms of elective lockdown, randomly imposed (and instantly revised) from above. I walked out early and then stayed at my desk. The cancellation of public events, talks, promotions, university classes, was even an advantage. But we couldn't visit our children and grandchildren on the other side of the park, or entertain them in our house. It was a particular pleasure, therefore, to listen to Farne's first edited podcasts from the trip we had made together, just in time. In the last days of freedom.

One of the recordings brought home to me how lacking in emotional intelligence my father's side of the family had always been. Self-sufficiency, against all odds, as a highland boast. And how I had, in my own turn, inherited aspects of that. Farne opened one episode with a lovely insert. On the night before she departed for the airport, while she was still trying to force everything into her zipped carrying bag, she 'interviewed' her two children, asking them how they felt about the adventure on which she was launched. Her nine-year-old son said that he didn't want her to go, he would miss her. But then he rallied with the order that she must promise to come home safely. Her twelve-year-old daughter, in a very measured and sensible response, said that she understood why the journey was necessary at this point in her mother's life. And she supported it. It had taken Farne a long time, back with London, her job, her family and the dictatorship of the virus, to listen to those hours and hours of conversation from Peru, but in editing and introducing this material, she proved that she really had returned, undamaged.

Arthur Sinclair's pilgrimages in tropical lands, his colourful experiences, dramas and comic encounters, are reported without reference to wife and family. His published autobiographical sketch positions him as emerging from a certain landscape, to which he makes continual reference. And to which he pays allegiance. He acknowledges, reluctantly, that he had a father. His mother, siblings and intimate connections are nowhere to be found.

Having mapped out the story of our trip in my great-grandfather's footprints, instinct told me that I needed to make a week's excursion, in company with Farne, to Aberdeen, Banff, Cults, and the other addresses where Arthur lived in his ten-year retirement. And Orkney too. Especially Orkney. Those unvisited islands held some teasing secret of origin. Scottish retrievals would, I felt, close off the book. I was especially taken with Arthur's epiphany, in the teeth of Tasmanian horrors, when he remembered 'rambling on Holburn Head, near Thurso' and lying down 'full length on the grass' to listen to laverocks keening against the violent suck and pull of the sea. My great-grandfather experiences 'something' that cannot be named. But which must, surely, be still there, in that place, open to access. Such was my tentative plan. Dates were found. Census forms scoured. Graves located and inscriptions recorded. The solution was far too tidy. It was rapidly shredded by news reports and impossible government instructions.

Footballers in an Aberdeen pub closed off the city to outsiders. Trawlermen exported the virus to Orkney. There was even a train derailment to chime with the railway disaster on the Great North of Scotland line opened up by Sir James Elphinstone, Arthur's patron.

My Scottish forebears told so many stories, described and evaluated so many lands, shaped so many anecdotes of human absurdity and savage accident, as a smokescreen. Readers must never notice that the closest things are left unspoken. And perhaps unfelt. Unconfessed. One time, when I was due to be collected from school in Gloucestershire by both parents, nobody appeared. And then, very late, when I was about to walk to the station, humping my bags, my father came alone. We drove back to Wales, not a word was said about my mother. I looked around the house for her. She wasn't there. 'Oh yes,' my father admitted. 'She's in hospital for a little operation. She'll be back in a few days.' I did think, even then, that this was a little odd.

Farne, active on her laptop, sent me a photograph of Arthur Sinclair's grave at Springbank Cemetery, Aberdeen. A sombre granite tongue for a man whose life, with dates, is summarised as: 'Late of Ceylon'. His wife, Margaret MacGregor, who lived on until 1914, is interred with him. Along with their daughter Margaret Mary Rowlands, who died in 1927. The one who stayed in Scotland.

There was more. Farne discovered that Arthur rented Banff Castle from the Earl of Seafield for £55 per annum. She also turned up his Last Will and Testament. When 'Debts on Heritage' (and Funeral Expenses) had been subtracted from 'Value of Heritage', £751. 2s. 2½d was left. The youngest son, Henry Sinclair, a medical practitioner in Glamorganshire, is named as one of the executors.

Uncomfortable stories are suppressed. Gravestones advertise them. I found an album with the usual mix of known and unknown relatives and curious strangers. There was another Aberdeen memorial. I thought, at first, it was for my grandfather, the doctor. There was a tremendous spread of flowers, cards and messages. But then I looked more closely: Henry Sinclair, M.D., C.M., had designed and erected the gravestone for his daughter, Sheila Margaret Mary, who died at the age of seventeen. An aunt about whose existence I knew nothing. This loss was never mentioned. Her life was an unspoken mystery. There was a second photograph, without the flowers, taken some years later of the same memorial. Now the name of my grandmother, Jeannie Stratton Grassick, has been added. And my father's younger brother, Leslie, is standing there, dressed in mourning black: 1938.

Going through the album, Sheila can now be identified, with her two younger brothers, among the dogs, horses, cats and Maesteg maids in starched pinafores. She poses by studio seascapes. She acts out, with her brothers, costumed scenes from Shakespeare. Then she is gone and removed entirely from the family legend, such as it is.

I heard about my own older sister, another Sheila, who died as a baby. Hardly in the world. But she was part of the Welsh story and always present, shadowing the drama of my own birth. Again it was Farne's persistence that recovered my erased aunt. She died, in the house where I grew up, from an epileptic seizure. Painful as that must have been, the diagnosis carried a residue of shame. It was folded away in a sealed drawer. Like her father and mother, Sheila was buried in a far country. In a city we would not now be visiting.

———

The pirate had a ridiculous *Treasure Island* tricorne hat with skull and crossbones. And a jungle green T-shirt emblazoned with a yellow aya-huasca-nightmare iguana creature. A psychedelic lizard infected with floating green spots. The wheeled and wheezing skateboarder was old, around my age, black, wasted and lean, but fit enough to punt along the pedestrian strip of the Green Way at pace, using ski poles to propel himself like an Ashaninka riding the currents of the river. He came on us from nowhere, mid-monologue, and he carried right on, adjusting his speed with subtle courtesy to flatter our gentle ramble. A solid phantom left over from a voodoo carnival, the pirate manifested from some parallel dimension, to appear right alongside the octagonal concrete bunker that I had always identified as the shelter of the local oracle. If that oracle was not the building itself, occupied or unoccupied: a source of embedded 'stone tape' whispers. Anna dropped back, hoping the whole thing would go away, but I knew immediately that *this was it*. The conjured messenger. The word. Revelation. Resolution. Release.

I had been roaming through those first months back in London without getting any confirmation that the ground was alive, open to my unjustified intrusion. The sites I knew no longer knew me. Local gardens had never received such close attention. The rainy season gave way, as soon as citizens were confined to their houses, flats, doorways and hedges, to a miraculous spring of wilderness profusion. Streets blossomed. Parakeets swooped and screamed, bullying from tower blocks. Magnolia trees flourished. Early roses. Blue eruptions of ceanothus. It was a Sunday morning. Anna decided that we would walk by the river. I hadn't been on any form of public transport since February, but getting down to the Thames, then over to Rotherhithe and back, was pushing it for my wife's first spontaneous post-Covid outing.

The Overground wasn't operative. Weekend engineering work. Anna surprised me by nominating instead a hike down the Northern Sewage Outfall towards the Olympic site. I finessed the route, to take the edge off obvious blight. We came at the obtrusively curated blacktop cycle path by making a gentle trajectory across Victoria Park, before weaving down a moderately frenetic stretch of the Hertford Union Canal and the reinvigorated Lea Navigation border of the post-Olympic recreation and entertainment zone. Crossing back at Old Ford Lock, we climbed the steep stone steps to the Green Way.

COFFEE? Tea, Juice, Frap? THE ETHICAL BEAN Co.

Ethical beans and swaggering fuck-you builds with picture windows and boasted surveillance: we were right on track.

SMASH NAZI HIPPIES!!!

An orthodox urban comedy of signage and counter-signage was licked and pasted to a set of poles, traffic-calming obstacles and leftover tank traps. Access to the Green Way invoked a Covid-19 testing station without the tired military presence. We took the hint and walked down the permitted airstrip to a masked and hand-squirted refreshment cabin where you could phone for a cup of cinnamon tea and a sticky bun. While contemplating the criminal absurdity of the ArcelorMittal Orbit, a sculptural intervention that looked like an X-ray of the anaconda Arthur shot, left to bleed out in an abandoned Soviet funfair.

On our return to the bridge over the Lea, turning our backs on carcinogenic dust heaps grown overnight on the former warm-up tracks, we sat for a moment on an accidentally aesthetic concrete barrier. I tried to tell Anna something about the Oracle bunker: the weirdness of it being located on this spot, right across the water from the spoiled nest of the Death Star Stadium. And how my run here, in the rain, so many years ago, was the confirmation of an impulse to try to write something about the place where we had chosen to settle and make our lives. And how, not so many weeks ago, but in another life, I returned with the Advocate. And heard the gasping breath of whoever or whatever had taken up residence in the stinking militarised fridge of memory.

My wife did not respond. She already knew those things that didn't need to be spoken and were much better left unsaid. She lived with it, but preferred not to have the madness laid out for her benefit. The stretch of the Lea on the far side of the lock was undergoing a visionary transformation that required no comment: sludgy brown streaks of misinformation, slinking down from Hertford, a prisoner waterway, were mutating as we watched, to a lovely tinge of coppery green; chlorophyll country ripeness activated by bands of gleaming city gold. From the elevation of the ramp on which we were sitting, arboreal abundance swallowed the Stadium like a Mayan pyramid lost in the jungle. A prodigious weight of willows and creepers, sycamore and buddleia, smothering the banks of the river, brought back the mornings when we infiltrated the enclosed Olympic Park by exploring tributary streams in an inflatable kayak. Kingfishers darted and flashed. 'The flowers in the field happen,' the poet said. And he was right. Without our notice or nuisance, they always return. They do their thing. They remember. They remember the time before our time.

If the business of the oracle run in 1974 opened a psychogeographic force field without a whisper from the octagonal bunker, the sudden manifestation of the skateboard pirate seemed to close it again. Obligations fulfilled. Permissions rescinded. Story told.

The Green Way path is divided into two strips segregated by colour. The old black man, whipping along with ski poles and customised skateboard, takes the blacktop reserved for pedestrians. To stay alongside him and to follow the rap, which is not addressed *at* me, but projected straight ahead, I have to invade the white strip down which entitled cyclists bomb. Anna drops behind.

The pirate knuckles his chest like a drum, spiked pole waving and threatening. He says that he was once famous. He was known everywhere as 'Solly Mander'. The steady, low-pitched, rhythmic drone is an incantation. Solly Mander: The Man with the Wisdom of the Sun. He dropped his hand. If his eyes glittered, I couldn't tell. They were hidden behind round bottle-green spectacles. I couldn't choose but hear. And willingly. So willingly! There was no promotional pitch, no call for a contribution. No attempt to batter down my prejudices or offer me a gold card to heaven.

'We listened and looked sideways up!'

The carnival mariner, the black pirate, had us firmly in his socially-distanced hoop.

From time to time, once in a decade, over the last thirty years, a figure has emerged from the universal maelstrom to embody some aspect of the soul of the city. I took this man, constantly moving, rabbiting, never drawing breath, never addressing anyone in particular, to be the direct contrary of the vanished Vegetative Buddha of Haggerston

Park. The Buddha, as I named him, took up residence on a bench. He was mute, slumped, invertebrate. In pain? He spent the hours of day-light pillowed among bags. He absorbed light, but gave nothing out. He was an anchor to the old ways. The pirate carried nothing apart from his ski poles. He talked and talked.

'Fifteen years! They know me, Solly Mander. Prince of the Ramp. Soon to be king. To America, man! To California. A *child*!'

This was the legend: a local skateboard hero, South Bank to Tottenham to Croydon, respected by his peers, serene in anticipation of golden times, flies to the USA for a title shot: Los Angeles. Venice Beach. Pacific Ocean Park. The Cove. Dogtown. The Z-Boys? Tony Alva? Remember Peggy Oki? Injury follows. Resurrection is already too late, the circus has moved on. Sand swallows the ramps. Empty swimming pools are cratered. He serves his time. He is pressed. He submerges. He plays mad and is discharged. He comes home cargo class. And he recites his story.

'Free! You free when you *know* you free. Understand? White ones pay dollars for ounce jar. I done walking on country roads.'

Now Solly preaches the limits of the city he should never have left. He bears witness, but nobody attends. We have, he says, betrayed our essential humanity. Now is a prodigious tryst with destiny. There have been whispers from the stars. A splinter of the sun has lodged in the whorl of his ear. Proxima Centauri has spoken to him across the ocean of space-time. The Skateboard Oracle filters the narrowband radio signals from dead stars. He says the sound is something like mirthless laughter. These are the days of signs and marvels. Those ripples you see on the river are flowering into holy flame. In the Church of St John there is a man of stone with no left hand. He walks on water. There is a boy who stole bright gold coins from his grandfather's desk. We *know* what we must do.

Solly Mander. He slaps his T-shirt, the scrofulous lizard. The resi-due, the ash of his fame as skateboard hero: Salamander.

'Better be Solly Mander, man. And *live* in that fire.'

Neotropical lizards. Intermittently aquatic. Survivors. After plague comes fire. The fire lizard. Dreams of drowning in a Babylonian furnace.

The resinous stench of molten gum. Patterns of stained glass shattering on stone. False prophets in high places. Who cares what the cave says? The empty bunker.

'Him you threaten, brother, and he shit you out.'

We come to the end of the straight path and out on a sliproad to the real, climbing towards the rush of the A102, the never quelled Blackwall Tunnel Northern Approach. There is a single chimney like La Oroya, now advertising a self-storage facility. Anna catches my sleeve and tugs me back. But the pirate does not pause, he bounces the skateboard off one kerb and up another, and away, still talking, down Wick Lane.

Standing firm, Anna holds me back. She says this man might be the messenger of the virus. The slope gives him fresh momentum. Strong arms drive him up towards the St Mark's Gate of Victoria Park. I can just about hear him still, but he hasn't attached himself to his next disciple. I'd like to follow in his wake, to see if he travels as the spirit moves him or if he marks out previously established channels.

My wife is having none of it. Coming under the motorway, we can't speak for the surf of constant traffic. The panels of the tunnel shine like polished catacomb marble. One spray-painted black graffito stands out: COURAGE.

The land was relieved. I had drawn my length all this way
and had covered this place too

    – Charles Olson, *The Maximus Poems*

I'm almost tired of travelling – but it's quite possible I may meet you
there once more… The *boom* being *on* all the time I was there last, and
I always said the danger was of the people getting *sane* again before
one had time to realise!

    – Arthur Sinclair (letter from 'Meadowbank', Cults, Aberdeen, 15
December 1892)

SELECT BIBLIOGRAPHY

ADAMS W.H. Davenport. *The City of Gold; or The Wonderful Story of Hernando Cortes and the Conquest of Mexico*. London: J. M. Dent & Co, n.d. (c. 1891).

ALLEN Stewart Lee. *The Devil's Cup (Coffee, The Driving Force in History)*. Edinburgh: Canongate Books, 2000.

[AMAZON STEAMSHIP NAVIGATION COMPANY.] *The Great River (Notes on the Amazon and its Tributaries and the Steamer Services. With Maps and Numerous Illustrations)*. London: Simpkin, Marshall, Hamilton, Kent, 1904.

BÁRCENA Juan Gómez. *The Sky Over Lima*. London: Oneworld Publications, 2016.

BERLIN Lucia. *Evening in Paradise (More Stories)*. London: Picador, 2018.

BOOTH Charles. *Charles Booth's London Poverty Maps*. London: Thames & Hudson, 2019.

BRAKHAGE Stan. *A Moving Picture Giving and Taking Book*. West Newbury, Massachusetts: Frontier Press, 1971.

BROWN Michael F. and FERNÁNDEZ Eduardo. *War of Shadows (The Struggle for Utopia in the Peruvian Amazon)*. Berkeley and Los Angeles: University of California Press, 1991.

BURROUGHS William. *Blade Runner: A Movie*. London: The Tangerine Press, 2019.

BURROUGHS William and GINSBERG Allen. *The Yage Letters*. San Francisco: City Lights Books, 1963.

CARTER Angela. *Expletives Deleted (Selected Writings)*. London: Chatto & Windus, 1992.

CHATWIN Bruce. *In Patagonia*. London: Jonathan Cape, 1977.

CHATWIN Bruce and THEROUX Paul. *Patagonia Revisited*. Salisbury, Wiltshire: Michael Russell, 1985.

CHATWIN Bruce. *Utz*. London: Jonathan Cape, 1988.

CLARK P.D.G. 'Report on the Central Territory of Peru'. 19 December 1891. Unpublished holograph report to the Peruvian Corporation of London.

CLARK Tom. *Charles Olson: The Allegory of a Poet's Life*. New York: W.W. Norton, 1991.

CONRAD Joseph. *Almayer's Folly*. London: T. Fisher Unwin, 1895.

CONRAD Joseph. *An Outcast of the Islands*. London: T. Fisher Unwin, 1896.

CONRAD Joseph. 'Heart of Darkness'. *Youth: A Narrative, and Two Other Stories*. Edinburgh and London: William Blackwood & Sons, 1902.

CONRAD Joseph. *Nostromo, A Tale of the Seaboard*. London and New York: Harper & Brothers, 1904.

CONRAD Joseph. *Victory, An Island Tale*. London: Methuen & Co., 1915.

DeLILLO Don. *Americana*. Boston, Massachusetts: Houghton Mifflin, 1971.

DEVINE T.M. *The Scottish Clearances (A History of the Dispossessed, 1600–1900)*. London: Allen Lane, 2018.

DORN Edward. *Abilene! Abilene!: Variorum Edition with Appendices & Commentary* (two volumes). Edt. Kyle Waugh. New York: City University of New York, 2013.

DORN Edward. *Gunslinger*. 50th Anniversary Edition. Durham, North Carolina: Duke University Press, 2018.

DOYLE Arthur Conan. *The Lost World*. London: Hodder & Stoughton, 1912.

FAULKNER William. *Absalom, Absalom!* New York: Random House, 1936.

FERGUSON John. *Ceylon in 1883: The Leading Crown Colony of the British Empire*. London: Sampson Low, Marston, Searle, & Rivington, 1883.

FOSTER Harry L. *The Adventures of a Tropical Tramp*. New York: Dodd, Mead & Co., 1922.

FREEDBERG David. 'Warburg's Mask: A Study in Idolatry'. *Anthropologies of Art*. Edt. Mariët Westermann. Williamstown, Massachusetts: Sterling and Francine Clark Art Institute, 2005.

GINSBERG Allen. *South American Journals (January–July 1960)*. Edt. Michael Schumacher. Minneapolis: University of Minnesota Press, 2019.

GRANDIN Greg. *Fordlandia (The Rise and Fall of Henry Ford's Forgotten Jungle City)*. New York: Picador, 2010.

GRANN David. *The Lost City of Z*. New York: Doubleday, 2009.

HASBÚN Rodrigo. *Affections*. London: Pushkin Press, 2015.

HERZOG Werner. *Conquest of the Useless (Reflections from the Making of Fitzcarraldo)*. New York: Ecco, 2009.

HERZOG Werner. *A Guide for the Perplexed (Conversations with Paul Cronin)*. London: Faber and Faber, 2014.

HILL Geoffrey. *The Book of Baruch by the Gnostic Justin*. Edt. Kenneth Haynes. Oxford: Oxford University Press, 2019.

HOCHSCHILD Adam. *King Leopold's Ghost (A Story of Greed, Terror, and Heroism in Colonial Africa)*. Boston, Massachusetts: Houghton Mifflin, 1999.

HOLLIS Leo. *Inheritance: The Lost History of Mary Davies (A Story of Property, Marriage and Madness)*. London: Oneworld Publications, 2021.

JACKSON Joe. *The Thief at the End of the World (Rubber, Power, and the Seeds of Empire)*. New York: Viking, 2008.

JAY Mike. *Mescaline (A Global History of the First Psychedelic)*. New Haven, Connecticut, and London: Yale University Press, 2019.

LEES A.J. *Mentored by a Madman (The William Burroughs Experiment)*. Widworthy, Devon: Notting Hill Editions, 2016.

LEES A.J. *Brazil that Never Was*. Widworthy, Devon: Notting Hill Editions, 2020.

MACFARLANE Robert. *Underland (A Deep Time Journey)*. London: Hamish Hamilton, 2019.

MacINNES Martin. *Infinite Ground*. London: Atlantic Books, 2016.

MIHAS, Elena. *Upper Perené Arawak Narratives of History, Landscape, & Ritual*. Lincoln, Nebraska, and London: University of Nebraska Press, 2014.

MINTA Stephen. *Aguirre (The Re-Creation of a Sixteenth-Century Journey Across South America)*. London: Jonathan Cape, 1993.

MORRIS Jonathan. *Coffee, A Global History*. London: Reaktion Books, 2019.

MORRISON Arthur. *Tales of Mean Streets*. London: Methuen & Co., 1894.

NICHOLL Charles. *The Creature in the Map (A Journey to El Dorado)*. London: Jonathan Cape, 1995.

NICHOLL Charles. *Somebody Else (Arthur Rimbaud in Africa 1880–91)*. London: Jonathan Cape, 1997.

NICHOLL Charles. *Traces Remain (Essays and Explorations)*. London: Allen Lane, 2011.

OLSON Charles. *The Maximus Poems*. Edt. George F. Butterick. Berkeley and Los Angeles: University of California Press, 1983.

OLSON Charles and PRYNNE J.H. *The Collected Letters of Charles Olson and J.H. Prynne*. Edt. Ryan Dobran. Albuquerque: University of New Mexico Press, 2017.

PARKER Matthew. *Willoughbyland (England's Lost Colony)*. New York: Thomas Dunne Books, 2017.

POPESCU Petru. *The Encounter, Amazon Beaming*. London: Pushkin Press, 2016.

RICHARDS Jim. *Gold Rush (How I Found, Lost and Made a Fortune)*. Tewkesbury, Gloucestershire: September Publishing, 2016.

RIMBAUD Arthur. *Selected Poems and Letters*. London: Penguin Classics, 2004.

RIVERA José Eustasio. *The Vortex: A Novel*. Durham, North Carolina: Duke University Press, 2018.

ROSS Alexander. 'A Recent Journey to the Head Waters of the Ucayali, Central Peru'. A talk 'read at the Evening Meeting, March 28th, 1892'. *Proceedings of the Royal Geographical Society and Monthly Record of Geography*, vol. 14, pp. 382–98.

ROSS Alexander. 'Exploration of the Amazonian Provinces of Central Peru'. Off-print of an account 'read before the Society, 5th April, 1893'. *Proceedings of the Royal Philosophical Society of Glasgow*, vol. 24, pp. 148–69.

SANTOS-GRANERO Fernando. *Slavery & Utopia (The Wars & Dreams of an Amazonian World Transformer)*. Austin: University of Texas Press, 2018.

SEDGEWICK Augustine. *Coffeeland, A History*. London: Allen Lane, 2020.

SHAKESPEARE Nicholas. *The Vision of Elena Silves*. London: Collins Harvill, 1989.

SHAKESPEARE Nicholas. *Bruce Chatwin*. London: Vintage, 2000.

SINCLAIR Arthur (as 'Auld Scotchman'). *How I Lost my Wattie. Or, Life in Ceylon and the Coffee-Planting Experience of an Auld Scotchman.* Colombo: A.M. & J. Ferguson, 1878.

SINCLAIR Arthur (as 'Old Colonist'). 'In Search of a Home in Australia'. 'A Trip into the Interior: Mining Prospects'. And other reports from Tasmania and Australia. Uncollected. Aberdeen Free Press, 1886.

SINCLAIR Arthur. *In Tropical Lands: Recent Travels to the Sources of the Amazon, the West Indian Islands, and Ceylon*. Aberdeen: D. Wyllie & Son; Edinburgh: John Menzies & Co.; London: Simpkin, Marshall, & Co.; Ceylon: A.M. & J. Ferguson, 1895.

SINCLAIR Arthur (as 'Old Colonist'). *Pioneers of the Planting Enterprise in Ceylon (Third Series): The Late Sir James D.H. Elphinstone, Bart. and Sir Graeme H.D. Elphinstone, Bart*. Colombo: A.M. & J. Ferguson, 1900.

SINCLAIR Arthur. *Planter and Visiting Agent in Ceylon (The Story of his Life and Times as told by Himself)*. Colombo: A.M. & J. Ferguson, 1900.

SINCLAIR Iain. *Dining on Stones (or, The Middle Ground)*. London: Hamish Hamilton, 2004.

SINCLAIR Iain. *Calor de Lud*. Translation of *Lud Heat* by Adolfo Barberá del Rosa. With afterword essay: 'Calor de Lud: Una Approximación al Oráculo'. Valencia: Fire Drill Ediciones, 2016.

SOLNIT Rebecca. *A Book of Migrations. (Some Passages in Ireland)*. London: Verso Books, 1997.

STAHL F.A. *In the Land of the Incas*. Mountain View, California: Pacific Press Publishing Association, 1920.

TAUSSIG Michael. *Shamanism, Colonialism, and the Wild Man (A Study in Terror and Healing)*. Chicago: University of Chicago Press, 1987.

THOM Martin. *CLOUD, a coffee cantata*. Cambridge, UK: Equipage, 2020.

THOMSON Hugh. *Cochineal Red (Travels Through Ancient Peru)*. London: Weidenfeld & Nicolson, 2006.

TRAVEN B. *The Treasure of the Sierra Madre*. London: Chatto & Windus, 1934.

VARGAS LLOSA Mario. *Conversation in the Cathedral*. New York: Harper & Row, 1975.

VARGAS LLOSA Mario. *The Dream of the Celt*. London: Faber and Faber, 2012.

WEISS Gerald. *Campa Cosmology: The World of a Forest Tribe in South America*. Anthropological Papers of the American Museum of Natural History, vol. 52, pt. 5. New York: American Museum of Natural History, 1975.

WELLS H.G. *The War of the Worlds*. London: William Heinemann, 1898.

WHITE Edmund. *Rimbaud, The Double Life of a Rebel*. New York: Atlas & Co., 2008.

WOOLCOCK Helen R. *Rights of Passage (Emigration to Australia in the Nineteenth Century)*. London: Tavistock Publications, 1986.

ACKNOWLEDGEMENTS

The journey reported here came into being as a long-distance conversation between my great-grandfather Arthur Sinclair, who laid out the original narrative of exploration, and my daughter Farne, who felt herself obliged to respond to challenges the confident Victorian story provoked. Farne needed to listen to the Ashaninka people of the Upper Perené region, the ones who lived with the consequences of Arthur's survey for the Peruvian Corporation of London. She understood that the settlements along the river had their own ways of demonstrating respect for ancestors. And what was due to those troubling presences in the contemporary world.

Arthur Sinclair's 1895 publication, *In Tropical Lands*, a book from my childhood that has continued to haunt my work, was the inspiration for our 2019 attempt to track his movements in Peru. Reading everything I could find by my great-grandfather, I came to know him a little; to admire his energy, his fortitude, his humour, while arguing with aspects of character and rhetoric that belonged too resolutely to the period when his books were written. The old planter's voice stayed at my shoulder through all of this. Now it is a part of me.

Farne was responsible for smoothing the logistics of travel. She made contact with Lucho Hurtado, our guide and translator. Without Lucho, a goad, an instructor, a storyteller, the expedition could never have been accomplished in the limited time available. He helped us define and sometimes kick against the concept of 'adventure tourism'.

Grant Gee, with tact and unyielding witness, kept his own visual record of the entire enterprise. He also, involuntarily, played the important role of the mysterious 'third man', to keep our travels in alignment with the 1891 survey.

I am grateful to Adolfo Barberá del Rosal for information, contacts, and, above all, for sustaining an active and engaging correspondence, before, during and after the Peruvian trip. Like William Faulkner's ghosts, he travelled half an hour ahead of us. And he always put his finger on the telling quotation.

For advice, suggestions, gifts, encouragement, company on conversational rambles, I'd like to thank: Renchi Bicknell, Toby Brown, Keggie Carew, Brian Catling (whose sequence of *Vorrh* novels fired and refined my notion of an animist forest sheltering or ejecting the expelled of Eden), Gareth Evans (always alert to every shard of potential inspiration), Greg Gibson, Hugh Hawes (for hospitality in Seville), Andrew Kötting, Ian W. Lee, Rachel Lichtenstein, Janine Marmot, Michael Moorcock, Anthony O'Donnell, Chris Petit, Kevin Ring, Duncan Wu. And my Australian cousins, Susan and Catherine Voutier. My editor at Oneworld, Sam Carter. Jonathan Bentley-Smith, also at Oneworld, who scrupulously policed my infelicities, repetitions and errors of fact. My agent Laura Longrigg was an early and encouraging reader. And, as always, everywhere, and beyond, Anna Sinclair.

My account of the encounter with the Ashaninka at Pampa Michi was first published, in a very different and much abbreviated form, as a 'Diary' in the *London Review of Books* (10 October 2019). My thanks to the editor and commissioner, Jean McNicol.

Farne's contacts with Elena Mihas were invaluable to her evolving conception of the project. I am grateful for permission to quote from *Upper Perené Arawak Narratives of History, Landscape, & Ritual*. Farne would also like to acknowledge Gregorio Santos Pérez, a collaborator with Mihas, for his services as consultant. And we are especially grateful to Bertha Rodríguez de Caleb for her interviews. Bertha died a few months after our return to England, while the Ashaninka community was cut off from the wider world. As did Elías Meza Pedro, the last man with memories of working at the Coffee Colony under the direction of the Peruvian Corporation of London.

Fernando Santos-Granero was generous in sharing information, passed on to me, with Adolfo Barberá del Rosal. I am grateful for permission to quote from *Slavery & Utopia: The Wars & Dreams of an Amazonian World Transformer*.

With thanks to Joe Jackson for permission to quote from *The Thief at the End of the World*. Barry Miles put me in touch with Peter Hale, who granted permission to quote from that rich source, Allen Ginsberg's *South American Journals*. Thanks also to the other authors who have inspired and informed this project.

In Tropical Lands is now an eight-part podcast, written and produced by Farne Sinclair, and edited by Anonymous Bosch. The podcasts cover in-the-moment conversations between father and daughter along road, rail and river in Peru. They are available on Apple Podcasts.

Grant Gee's essay-feature *The Gold Machine* was produced by Janine Marmot and co-produced by Katja Draaijer, with support from the BFI Doc Society Fund and the Netherlands Film Fund and development support from In Between Art Film. Grant was very much part of the 2019 expedition, but his use of material derived from our journey is entirely independent of the book and grounded in a more complex mythology of a literary past and its relationship to colonialism. This film is the third panel of a triptych that already includes *Patience (After Sebald)* (2011) and *Innocence of Memories* (2015), inspired by Orhan Pamuk.

Iain Sinclair is the award-winning writer of numerous critically acclaimed books on London, including *The Last London, Lights Out for the Territory, London Orbital* and *London Overground*. He won the Encore Award and the James Tait Black Memorial Prize for his novel *Downriver*. He lives in Hackney, East London.